THE MANSHIP SCHOOL

THE MANSHIP SCHOOL

A History of Journalism Education at LSU

RONALD GARAY

With a Foreword by JOHN MAXWELL HAMILTON

Louisiana State University Press
Baton Rouge

Published by Louisiana State University Press
Copyright © 2009 by Louisiana State University Press
All rights reserved
Manufactured in the United States of America
First printing

Designer: Michelle A. Neustrom
Typefaces: Arno Pro, Myriad Pro
Printer and binder: Thompson-Shore, Inc.

Library of Congress Cataloging-in-Publication Data

Garay, Ronald.
　The Manship School : a history of journalism education at LSU / Ronald Garay ; with a foreword by John Maxwell Hamilton.
　　p. cm.
　Includes bibliographical references and index.
　ISBN 978-0-8071-3382-8 (cloth : alk. paper) 1. Manship School of Mass Communication—History. I. Title.
　PN4791.M35G37 2008
　302.23071'176318—dc22
　　　　　　　　　　2008019361

The paper in this book meets the guidelines for permanence and durability of the Committee on Production Guidelines for Book Longevity of the Council on Library Resources. ∞

To my good friend, Billy Ross

CONTENTS

Foreword
ix

Acknowledgments
xiii

Introduction: A History of Journalism Education at Louisiana State University
xvii

1 Virginia Connections and the Seeds of Journalism Education
1

2 Post–Civil War Conditions and LSU Journalism Education
6

3 Journalism Education versus Professional Journalism
13

4 Thomas Boyd, the *Reveille*, and the Seeds of LSU Journalism Education
19

5 Hugh Mercer Blain and the Birth of the LSU Journalism Department
27

6 LSU Journalism Program at a Crossroad
45

7 Raising LSU Journalism Education to the Next Level
60

8   The J-School Settles In
    81

9   World War II, Accreditation, and
    a Permanent Home
    105

10 Changing Times
    130

11 Uncertain Times
    162

12 Return to Prominence
    191

    Postscript: A Storm Like None Other
    221

    Notes
    227

    Index
    267

    Illustrations follow page 104

FOREWORD

Professional journalism is younger than professional baseball and psychoanalysis. Younger still are advertising and public relations. Louisiana State University was one of the first universities to offer journalism instruction, and that was less than one hundred years ago—in the 1912–1913 academic year, to be exact. We did not change our name to *mass communication* until 1992.

The Manship School, thus, has one of the longest histories in the short history of the study of media. That is both a point of pride and a reason for caution.

Training in and the study of media are still in the formative stages. Much is being written today about the demise of newspapers. But newspapers have not yet come to an end, and challenges to the print tradition are a sign of the robust nature of the professions we serve. While ink-on-paper publications accounted for all media at the beginning of the twentieth century, they are now just one of many forms of information delivery. While only a few individuals owned printing presses in 1900, ordinary citizens today use the cell phones tucked in their pockets to view video, take pictures, read snippets of news, check email, watch short shows, surf the net, and, if time is left over, call home to say they'll be late for dinner. Just a few years from now, that equipment will seem as antique as carrier pigeons and the clunky black telephone of the not-so-distant past.

When journalism schools emerged during the Industrial Revolution, academics as well as professionals fiercely debated the nature and purpose of such education. We are now in an era that is named just for us, the Information Age. Once considered trade schools at the margin of universities, schools of mass communication now are at the very center of the purpose of universities. And yet, the debate continues.

In the beginning, some critics said journalism schools should not exist at all. The newsroom was the place to learn news. Others thought we should concentrate on skills only. A. J. Liebling, the provocative and amusing *New Yorker* press critic, argued for a "School for Publishers, failing which, no School of Journalism can have meaning."[1] In 1903, *The Nation*, which has made a habit of press criticism for well over a century, suggested "it is the newspaper-reader who needs to go to school, and not the newspaper-maker. Let the reader but learn to discriminate between honest and upright newspapers and those that sell their opinions as they do their advertising space, and the uplifting of the profession will come quickly enough."[2]

We have come a long way since then, occasionally addressing some suggestions from the past that once seemed offbeat. More than ever our schools pay attention to the business side of media, not exactly what Liebling had in mind, but close—and certainly addressing his observation in 1961 that newspapers were disappearing. The Manship School recently secured funding for an endowed chair in media literacy, just as *The Nation* suggested. Our Reilly Center for Media and Public Affairs has held national conferences on new approaches to funding original newsgathering as well as on the future course of mass communication education.

As much as the Information Age is our age, our School and others like us do face major, ongoing challenges, the greatest of which at the moment is keeping up with new media without allowing it to elbow out instruction in good writing and responsible social behavior. How we maintain the high-minded verities of the past while incorporating new technologies goes to the heart of political and economic democracy—and our mission.

Ronald Garay, a longtime LSU faculty member and associate dean, has traced a history that illuminates not only the story of the Manship School but the evolution of media education in general. In his book we see the tentative first steps of offering journalism courses; the subsequent building of full-fledged academic units in liberal arts colleges, which happened in our School in 1926; the addition of new fields such as broadcasting, advertising, public relations, and (a specialty at our school) political communication; the creation of doctoral programs; and the emergence of serious research about the impact of media on society.

Each school, of course, has its own traditions. Some of the Manship School's are obvious to anyone who visits our building, the oldest on campus. On a second floor wall are listed alumni, friends, and faculty who have been voted into the Hall of Fame. Outside the building on a terrace plaques bear the names of our Ph.D. recipients, along with the names of their main professors. Our Holliday Forum, in the center of the building, was designed as a place for students to study and converse, and to serve as a forum for speakers. It is a vivid symbol of the School's belief that students should be exposed to the issues of the day.

Bricks and mortar, however, cannot sum up a school's history or its virtues. Three intangible lessons, which are central to our current success, are worth keeping in mind as one reads this book and thinks about the School's future.

The first is the establishment of the School in 1994 as a college-level unit. Programs like ours are hybrids, a blend of the professional and the scholarly. We were hampered in our development when the University did not take advantage around the time of World War II to separate the School from the College of Arts and Sciences. For all their merits, liberal arts colleges do not have the perspective to evaluate professional schools on matters such as promotion and tenure. The director of the School in the 1980s, John Merrill, was a through and through scholar, but he understood the dangers of combining our School with the Speech Department. We would lose our professional center of gravity. Merrill won that argument, but it was a decade before we became a college-level unit reporting directly to the provost. Because of the relative small size of schools like ours, there is always the temptation for university administrators to move them into larger units that are, as Merrill noted, "incompatible." Maintaining this independence will remain one of the School's major challenges and imperatives in the bright future.

The second lesson—related to the first—is the need to respect and embrace diversity. Our program has become healthier in each passing year thanks to the range of faculty who have been recruited. These are men and women with varied professional experience and degrees in political science, law, history, and sociology as well as in print and broadcast journalism, public relations, and advertising. This range of expertise is unusual in a single mass communication school. Equally remarkable is the level of mutual respect among these professors. Schools falter when individual faculty members think his or her discipline or way of studying problems deserves more credit than any other. Goodwill and tolerance elevate the learning experience for our students generally and enhance the quality of intellectual collaboration, which is essential for studying the all-embracing aspects of the Information Age.

The third lesson of our history is the need for ambition and focus. This is particularly important for a unit of relatively small size, as ours is. Our greatest contribution to the university will never come in the quantity of students we educate. It must come in quality. Today our agenda is driven by a dual purpose, producing well-rounded undergraduates prepared for the challenge of the Information Age and striving to be at the top in the field of media and politics, especially in graduate education. Media and politics is a nascent field in which we have secured a leadership position.

These lessons have produced conditions for success: the recruitment of excellent students; the support of top administrators on campus, for which we are grateful; the formation of an outstanding national board of visitors, that has been both counselor and advocate, as well as an equally committed local alumni association; and the long list of distinguished donors who have invested in our ambitions.

As a result, the School has continued to make strides beyond the time frame of this book, which ends with the two great Louisiana hurricanes of 2005. Since then, Lou Day and Ralph Izard, members of our faculty, have won prestigious national teaching awards. The School's responsibilities have grown to include oversight of Student Media, with the *Reveille*, KLSU radio, Tiger Television, and *Legacy* magazine. Our research productivity is recognized nationally. Our Reilly Center for Media and Public Affairs continues to build programs for studying and thinking about democratic discourse.

There is more to come. And with this book we have a history to show us the way.

John Maxwell Hamilton, Dean

ACKNOWLEDGMENTS

Books, especially books of this kind, do not just happen by themselves. Like things produced on an assembly line, many people have had a hand in creating the finished product. I am grateful to all who helped along the way.

The two persons to whom I owe my highest debt of gratitude are Whitney Mundt and Bill Ross. Whitney, who passed away several years ago, was a Manship School colleague. He loved LSU, and he loved this School. Anyone who ever visited Whitney's office realized immediately that he was a collector. And what he collected most were stories about the Manship School (actually, the Journalism School for most of the time Whitney was here), its students and its alumni. Whitney was the Manship School's archivist and historian. His curiosity and foresight led Whitney to save bits and pieces of the School's history that otherwise might have been lost forever. And it is from such sources—the boxes of documents, newspaper clippings, and assorted ephemera—that much of what resides in this book originated. Had Whitney been around a while longer he would have written this book.

Bill Ross and I share much in common but our attachment to West Texas probably has been the major cement in our friendship. Bill came to the Manship School after retiring from many successful years as chair of the Texas Tech Department of Mass Communications. Texas Tech is in Lubbock, just a short distance north of Lamesa where my family moved when I entered high school. Bill probably never thought that his time at LSU would stretch far beyond the year or so he intended when he came here as a visiting professor. Nor would he have realized how important his knowledge of journalism education would be in transitioning the Manship School to college status in the 1990s. Along the way, Bill realized that there was an important story to tell about the School's origins, growth, and contributions to our discipline. He was persistent in pushing the need for a School history, and I am grateful that he saw me as the person who could write that history.

Thanks also to Jack Hamilton, dean of the Manship School, who acted upon Bill Ross's insistence that someone write the School history. Jack is a gifted historian himself, so it was only a short hop from Bill Ross pushing the idea to Jack's finally deciding that it should be done. I appreciate his entrusting me with the job and providing sabbatical time to get it done.

Absolutely none of the research for the Manship School's history would have been possible had it not been for the incredible resources available at LSU Library's Special Collections. I came to know these resources well. And my time spent culling through the documents, papers, letters, pictures, and books housed there was absolute pleasure—I felt like a kid in a candy store. So much of what I came to love and respect about this storehouse of history, of course, was due to the expert assistance available to all researchers. For helping me find my way when I seemed completely bewildered, I will be forever indebted to Faye Phillips, Elaine Smyth, Judy Bolton, Tara Laver, Germain Bienvenu, Jennifer Abraham, Gina Costello, Mark Martin, and Barry Cowan.

My thanks also to members of the Manship School faculty and staff who contributed comments and suggestions for the School's history. Most especially, my thanks to Assistant Dean Linda Rewerts. Linda quietly but efficiently works miracles. In both small and big ways Linda was a major contributor to this book. She helped locate obscure documents and important reports. She helped immensely in finding photographs for the book. Linda also helped indirectly by writing, editing, and producing the Manship School's annual report. These reports (award-winning reports, it should be added) proved an invaluable resource in compiling the School's most recent history.

I thank my wife, Mary Sue, who gave up our summer vacation in order to allow time for completing this book. Mary Sue has always been supportive of my writing projects, even when that support required giving up our dining room table for nearly a year in order that I might "spread out" with my writing paraphernalia and my teetering stacks of books and files.

I also extend my appreciation to MaryKatherine Callaway, Alisa Plant, and the LSU Press staff for encouragement and assistance in completing this book. I shall be eternally grateful and proud that this great press chose to publish the Manship School history.

Finally, my thanks to all the students, faculty, administrators, staff, media professionals, friends, and others who have played a role in building the Manship School through the years. I had little idea when beginning this book of just how rich and colorful the School's history had been, and little did I realize about the School's significant contribution to the development of journalism education in this country. So, to all who have been part of the Manship School legacy from its earliest days to the present, my heartfelt thanks.

INTRODUCTION
A HISTORY OF JOURNALISM EDUCATION AT LOUISIANA STATE UNIVERSITY

Newspapers freshly delivered and stacked neatly atop one of the tables in the Journalism Building's Holliday Forum usually do not arouse much attention. After all, newspapers are as commonplace in the Journalism Building as test tubes in a chemistry lab. But these newspapers were different; they were special. These newspapers, in fact, were the New Orleans *Times-Picayune,* and their delivery came only days after Hurricane Katrina had laid waste to so much of the Crescent City, including the *Times-Picayune*'s news operation. Reporters, editors, staff personnel—practically everyone associated with the paper—had fled New Orleans as part of the mandatory evacuation, and no doubt each person thought that he or she would be heading back to the city once the storm had passed. That was not to be. They were, in every sense of the word, refugees.

Unbeknown to the *Times-Picayune* staff and to thousands of other New Orleanians who had fled the city, Katrina-induced flooding had so inundated major portions of New Orleans that it would be weeks before anyone could once more set foot onto dry pavement there. What's more, it would be even longer before anything resembling a newspaper might once more roll from a New Orleans press. But the *Times-Picayune* family had a paper to publish. And they lost little time in heading to LSU's Manship School of Mass Communication where they were welcomed and where they immediately set up shop in the School's Journalism Building computer labs. Within hours, the *Times-Picayune* website began filling with Katrina-related stories. Within days, plans were underway once more to begin publishing. So, when that stack of newspapers appeared on the Holliday Forum table, it represented a triumph of will and determination that transcended the pain and frustration and absolute weariness that fashioned each letter of each word of each sentence on every page of the New Orleans *Times-Picayune* of September 2005.

The Manship School also played host in the same emergency fashion to a crew from New Orleans's WWL-TV. On-air reporters set up shop in the School's Hodges Hall television facility and within a few hours of their arrival, they were on the air, telling Katrina's story.

There had been no hesitation from Manship School dean Jack Hamilton about how to handle the situation that confronted him. When colleagues from the *Times-Picayune* and WWL-TV asked for the Manship School's assistance, the School was not only willing but able to provide it—at a moment's notice. The School's facilities were meant for teaching, but for one incredible week in September 2005—a week that forever would be etched in the memories of persons in South Louisiana—they became home to a rag-tag bunch doing the real work of real journalists.

What happened at the Manship School during that September week affirmed the ascendancy of an academic program rooted in journalism and later to include advertising, public relations, and political communication. From a single journalism course offered during the 1912–1913 session, the LSU Manship School of Mass Communication, known affectionately by so many alumni as the "J-School," had traveled a road of many twists and turns, starts and stops, but always moving toward excellence.

What follows is the story of that journey.

THE MANSHIP SCHOOL

1

Virginia Connections and the Seeds of Journalism Education

Journalism education was born in the South. Tradition places the birthplace at Lexington, in Virginia's Washington College (now Washington and Lee University), where its post–Civil War president Robert E. Lee saw fit to approve a journalism program in 1869. Other colleges soon followed Washington College's lead, although debate within the professional journalism community raised questions as to the need or benefits of such academic pursuits.

The idea to create a journalism program at Louisiana State University did not blossom for more than forty years after its initial attempt at Washington College. Why it took so long is uncertain. One reason might have been that LSU's earlier incarnation, Louisiana State Seminary, was governed very early in its history by leaders whose views on college education were shaped by the institution's strict military traditions. These traditions mired LSU in a conservative curriculum quite typical of the period. And while efforts were underway late in the nineteenth century to broaden that curriculum somewhat, conditions (political, social, and economic) outside the university were such that change came much too slowly. There seemed to be little interest in adding a course in journalism to the curriculum. But more about this later.

The story of how Washington College set the stage for journalism education in the United States is an important starting point for what later would happen at LSU. This chapter's abbreviated version of that story begins by making an important connection between the Virginia birthplace of journalism education and Louisiana—one of several such connections between the two states that will surface along the way. Robert E. Lee indeed may be credited with being the force behind the first academic journalism program in this country, but Lee's biographer Douglas Southall Freeman cited one of Washington College's young professors, William Preston Johnston, as the program's actual architect.[1]

When General Lee arrived at Washington College the existing curriculum followed a traditional structure whereby all students took courses in the same six subjects: political economy, philosophy, Latin, Greek, mathematics, and "natural philosophy" (i.e., chemistry and physics). Lee, according to biographer Freeman, "did not think that these of themselves sufficed to meet the needs of the impoverished South, whose first problems were those of economic recovery and enlarged trade."[2] Rather, Lee "saw that the struggling South required men trained for the vocations as well as for the professions." His aim was to provide students what later would be termed a "practical education."[3]

Into this progressive educational environment came the idea to create a course of study in journalism. The idea was included at first in a faculty committee report prepared at General Lee's behest for presentation to the Washington College Board of Trustees on March 30, 1869. The report carried several major curriculum revision recommendations and was approved with few changes in June 1869. Central to the curriculum changes that now could be implemented was a philosophical premise by which students could learn practical vocational skills but within "the cultural atmosphere of a university rather than in separate technical schools."[4]

To that end, the March 1869 report recommended that fifty "press scholarships" be established for "young men intending to make practical printing and journalism their business in life."[5] The scholarships would pay for tuition and fees and require that recipients work at least one hour per week in a local printing office (or perhaps one maintained at Washington College) where they would receive instruction in what then was called "typographical art." Washington College subsequently solicited the help of typographical unions in the region both to publicize the scholarships and to nominate persons for scholarship consideration.

The idea to award "press scholarships" and to engage in what must be considered a very rudimentary form of journalism education (what today would be akin to an internship at a print shop) was itself newsworthy enough to merit the attention of the *New York Sun*. When a reporter from the *Sun* arrived at Washington College to write a story about the venture, General Lee sent him to William Preston Johnston. Johnston at the time was a professor of English, known to be interested in public affairs, and a member of the faculty committee that had submitted the March 1869 curriculum revision report to General Lee.[6] Little more than a decade later, Johnston would assume a new position—that of LSU's second postwar president.[7]

What Johnston told the *New York Sun* reporter was the essence of what journalism education eventually would become and why such education was so important. "Printing is one of the arts which diffuse education," said Johnston, "and we should therefore seek to qualify printers for the task of educating as far as possible." Ultimately, it was Washington College's intention, according to Johnston, to give its press scholarship recipients "as thorough a training as possible in the ways of their profession and to give them as good an education as possible that they may make better and more cultivated *editors*."[8]

Within William Preston Johnston's remarks to the *New York Sun* reporter were embedded two important observations. The first was a worldview of just what role journalism and its practitioners had come to occupy in this country— a role of power, prestige, influence, and persuasion with the potential of adding to each of these in time to come. The second was a narrower, more pragmatic view of how journalism actually was practiced by newspaper editors in small towns across America, particularly—and most important to Washington College—in the South.

The state of American journalism familiar to William Preston Johnston in the late 1860s was far different than it had been less than half a century before. "The typical American newspaper in the early years of the nineteenth century was a journal of opinion, a cheerleader for politicians, and a vehicle for cultural discourse and cultural pretension. It was not, however, much of a *news* paper."[9] Technology was to change that by midcentury, though. By then, "the telegraph had wired much of the continent; the steam-powered rotary press allowed the larger metropolitan newspapers to turn out thousands of copies per hour; the railroad linked major cities with travel times not much different from those of today and provided timely distribution of the product."[10] Along with these technological advances came honest-to-goodness journalists—men like James Gordon Bennett, Horace Greeley, and Henry J. Raymond, whose *New York Herald, New York Tribune,* and *New York Times,* respectively, were newspapers the likes of which no one ever before had seen or read[11] and the seed pods from which all newspapers of the future would spring.

The number of newspapers grew markedly during the early nineteenth century as America expanded westward. There were 650 newspapers, of which 65 were dailies, in 1830.[12] In 1860, the number of American newspapers had ballooned to nearly 2,500. Only about a quarter of these were Southern newspapers. And of the roughly 375 dailies published then, only about 80 were published in the South. New York City alone could boast of supporting 17 daily newspapers; Richmond, Virginia, on the other hand, supported only 4 dailies.[13]

The gap between the North and South was even more pronounced with regard to newspaper circulation. It has been said that "the great majority of Southern newspapers numbered their readers by the hundreds rather than thousands."[14] In 1860, combined circulation of all 66 daily newspapers published in states that soon were to join the Confederacy numbered approximately 150,000—or about twice the circulation of the *New York Herald* alone. "In the south, where cities were fewer, population less dense, and illiteracy rates higher, editors had to be satisfied with substantially fewer subscribers."[15]

Southern newspapers were diminished further during the Civil War. By 1864, they numbered only about thirty-five. Some were closed by Northern troops, while others were forced to reduce operations or to close altogether when so many subscribers joined the military.

Ironically, even though printers themselves may have felt moved by patriotism to join ranks with their Southern brethren, several Confederate states cited the importance of newspapers during the war as reason enough to exempt printers from conscription that otherwise applied to most Southern males. Virginia, for instance, exempted newspaper editors and any employee deemed by the editor as indispensable as long as the paper appeared at least once every week.[16]

How better to illustrate the value of the Southern newspaper than to single out editors, as Virginia had done, and to treat them as a special class by exempting them from military duty. The act, as well, underscored how the job of publishing a newspaper at the time often fell to one person who gathered the news, wrote the stories and editorials, set the type, and printed the newspaper. City newspapers after about 1830 had become enough of a business to require a staff of employees including persons hired especially as writers or reporters.[17] But such was seldom the case in small towns. Scattered throughout the countryside were newspapers whose publishers in so many instances were the editors as well. And it was to these "editor-publishers" that Washington College opened its doors in 1869 in the hope that through education they would become better, more intellectually prepared editors.[18]

The offer was made. But no one took advantage of the Washington College press scholarship. After nine years with not a single applicant, the scholarship program ended. Blame for its demise was placed at the feet of "skeptical newsmen"[19] who were at odds with General Lee's and William Preston Johnston's fledgling grassroots effort to create America's first cadre of college-trained journalists. Not until 1926 would the institution known today as Washington and Lee University return to the idea of 1869 and once more honor the name of its past president by establishing the Lee Memorial School of Journalism.[20]

2

Post–Civil War Conditions and LSU Journalism Education

Successfully or not, Washington College had taken the first step to move journalism education into the college mainstream. LSU in time would carry General Lee's and Professor Johnston's vision forward by offering the first journalism course at a major southern university in 1912–1913. Several other colleges and universities in the East and Midwest predated LSU's efforts. Still, LSU was very much a pioneer in the field and was destined eventually to become one of its leaders. Why journalism did not enter the LSU curriculum any sooner is a matter of conjecture. The nature of LSU's military traditions and the university's overall educational mission, as noted in chapter 1, certainly played a major role. Most important, though, might have been prevailing economic, social, and political attitudes and conditions arising from post–Civil War Reconstruction. All of these are examined below.

THE MILITARY NATURE OF LSU

There is good reason for calling LSU the "Ole War Skule." For all intents and purposes the Louisiana State Seminary of Learning and Military Academy, as LSU was called at its founding, was the military academy that its name implied. Even so, state legislators refused to formally designate the new college at Pineville as Louisiana's version of West Point. Rather, the Louisiana State Seminary was meant to be a "literary and scientific institution under a military system of government" that would provide military instruction, whose president (called "superintendent" for many years) would be designated a "colonel," whose faculty would be given a military rank, and whose students would be called "cadets."[1] Traditions are slow to die: not until June 1969 did the LSU Board of Supervisors finally vote to end compulsory ROTC.[2]

The Seminary, whose doors opened on January 2, 1860, modeled its "program and plan" after that of the Virginia Military Institute (VMI) with "departments of instruction" designated in "English and Ancient Languages; Modern Languages; Chemistry, Geology and Mineralogy; Engineering, Architecture and Drawing; Mathematics and Natural Philosophy."[3] William Tecumseh Sherman was chosen to head the school because of his impressive military credentials. Sherman was soon to depart, however, when he and many of his faculty and students left campus for military service during the Civil War.

When the Louisiana State Seminary resumed operation in 1865 it did so under its new superintendent (hereinafter, president) David French Boyd. Boyd was a returning member of the faculty, hired originally by his predecessor as professor of ancient languages and English, who now brought to his position the military experience of having served as a Confederate cavalry officer. Boyd would lead the Seminary through many significant changes, one of which was the institution's move from Pineville to Baton Rouge. One year after the move the state legislature officially changed the Seminary's name to Louisiana State University or LSU. One additional physical change owing to President Boyd's persistence came in 1886 when land belonging to the U.S. military where the new Louisiana State Capitol now stands was donated to Louisiana in order to provide a "permanent" home for a new LSU campus.[4]

President Boyd maintained strict military discipline at LSU throughout his presidency from 1865 to 1880 and then briefly from 1884 to 1886. He also maintained the University's rigid curriculum. Nonetheless, historian Walter Fleming characterized Boyd as a "constant student of school and college problems, of state and national educational systems."[5] If so, then it is likely that he was aware of the plans Robert E. Lee had for journalism education at Washington College. In fact, General Lee was said to have been a great inspiration to fellow Virginian David Boyd.[6] Journalism education at Washington College, whose curriculum was founded on a civilian and not a military tradition, emerged naturally and was not transplanted at LSU.

There is another possible reason for David Boyd not replicating Washington College's journalism experiment: the negative attitude toward journalists shared at the time by many military veterans. It was an attitude that grew from relationships begun during the Civil War when reporters or correspondents were dispatched by metropolitan newspapers to cover war-related battlefield news. Many of these correspondents traveled with the soldiers and officers and were said to have shared the "dangers and hardships" of those about whom they wrote.[7]

But the competitive nature of the news business meant that correspondents might report news that could endanger the lives of their military companions. Some generals, in fact, believed the endangerment was on purpose. "It was reasonable to suppose, after all," as historian George Douglas has noted, "that anyone reporting troop movements, battlefield formations, or methods of supply was a spy for the other side, and sometimes this supposition was correct."[8] Bad feelings toward reporters sometimes went to the extreme, as in the case of General Sherman, who had a "lifelong bitterness toward the newspapering profession, which he made no attempt to soften or conceal."[9] Calling reporters "the most contemptible race of men that exist[ed], cowardly, cringing, hanging round, gathering their material out of the most polluted sources," Sherman made the lives of reporters he encountered during the Civil War as uncomfortable as he could—even threatening at one point to hang one.[10]

General Sherman's problems with reporters may have been the exception rather than the rule—certainly, General Lee seemed not to share Sherman's extreme views. Nonetheless, evidence suggests that the relationship between the press and military, particularly at the officer level, was frequently less than cordial. So, it is not unreasonable to assume that Civil War veterans returning to the LSU faculty and classrooms were aware of or had firsthand knowledge of reporters who behaved in an unacceptable manner. These same faculty and students also might have taken a dim view of journalists in general and journalism education in particular.

THE RIGID LSU CURRICULUM

College education to David Boyd was heavy in the traditional and very, very light in the practical. "If education is to consist in the so-called practical, if the knowledge alone is desirable which enables one to make a dollar, then away with all colleges," Boyd once said. And he added, "No commercial school is equal to the counting-house, no agricultural college like the plow, and no mechanical institute so good as the factory and the workshop."[11] He just as easily might have asserted that a journalism school never could equal the education journalists would receive in the newsroom. Such sentiment would have placed Boyd squarely among the many newspaper editors of the day who, as shown below, were saying the same.

In fairness, President Boyd does deserve credit for loosening to a small degree the LSU curriculum in place when he arrived. The old curriculum was fixed, meaning that everyone who entered LSU was required to take the same classes until graduation. There were no electives and no alternative degree programs or tracks. All LSU cadets took the same classes, period. David Boyd revised the curriculum during his 1865–1880 tenure to eventually introduce five new fixed courses or tracks of study: the Literacy (Classical) Course, the Scientific Course, the Civil Engineering Course, the Pre-Medical Course, the Commercial Course, and something called the Optional Course. Only the Optional Course allowed for anything similar to what would be called elective classes today. All others required a narrow regime of class work with heavy doses of science and languages.

While the LSU curriculum remained little changed as the 1870s came to an end, LSU fell in step with other colleges by creating separate departments to house appropriate disciplines.[12] The organizational change was noteworthy, but nowhere to be found as LSU entered the 1880s was any hint that journalism education was on anyone's mind.

The absence of even a single class in journalism was even more remarkable given the resignation of David Boyd in 1880 and the appointment of William Preston Johnston as LSU's new president.[13] In view of his efforts to create the country's first journalism program at Washington College, was there not some possibility that Johnston at least would attempt to duplicate a similar program at LSU? The answer, of course, was "no!" For most of his brief time as LSU's president, William Preston Johnston had his hands full dealing with political powerbrokers. Curriculum revision was not on his agenda.[14] And when Paul Tulane offered Johnston the presidency of what later became Tulane University in January 1883, Johnston took little time in accepting.[15]

Following William Preston Johnston's departure, the LSU presidency changed hands several times until 1896. J. W. Nicholson followed Johnston but resigned the presidency within one year in deference to the reappointment of David Boyd. Boyd left after two years and was replaced by his brother Thomas Boyd. Thomas Boyd remained for less than a year in what would be his first term as LSU president and the position was filled once more by J. W. Nicholson. Nicholson's second term extended for eight years to 1896. At that point

Thomas Boyd returned to the presidency and, as discussed below, changes aplenty at the Ole War Skule would follow.

The LSU curriculum gradually incorporated more class work in science, engineering, and agriculture as the 1800s wore on. Agriculture actually entered the picture only after LSU merged with Louisiana's Agricultural and Mechanical (A and M) College in 1877. The merger, in fact, brought the A and M College to Baton Rouge from its original location in New Orleans.[16]

SMALL AND SLOW TO GROW ENROLLMENT

LSU was slow to attract students once it reopened in 1865. Even in the 1880s, after LSU's move to Baton Rouge, enrollment never exceeded 200 during any one session (what now is called an academic year) of the decade. Not until the 1894–1895 session did enrollment top 200. And not until the 1899–1900 session did enrollment top 300. The enrollment of 371 during that session set the stage for progressively higher enrollments year after year into the new century. A milestone was achieved in the 1911–1912 session when LSU undergraduate enrollment stood at 1,331. These numbers are all unofficial, but their appearance in documents originating from the LSU President's (now Chancellor's) office would suggest their near accuracy.[17]

The reason for emphasizing LSU's small enrollment for the remainder of the nineteenth century and for most of the twentieth century's first decade is to suggest that had a journalism class been offered at the University during this period, it is highly unlikely that many students would have enrolled. Not until total enrollment at LSU reached a critical mass in the early 1900s were there enough students beginning to exhibit an interest in studying journalism to make it worthwhile to make journalism classes available.

POOR SECONDARY SCHOOL EDUCATION

One guess as to why LSU's enrollment in the late 1800s was so small was the university's military discipline. Probably a much better reason was the poor quality of Louisiana high school or secondary school education. Historian Joe Gray Taylor spoke of "the attitude of white Louisianians toward public education" at the time as "hostile overall,"[18] and Minns Sledge Robertson remarked that the period should be "considered a dreary waste in Louisiana's educational history."[19]

The Louisiana Constitution of 1898 created for the first time a state system of education, making "it possible for a community to vote taxes to build good school buildings and to provide money to pay salaries and other operating expenses."[20] But language in the constitution that provided for a system of state-supported education did not immediately make that system operational. That would take several years. In the meantime Louisiana had a distance to go before education at any level gained sufficient respect.

Several parishes did build high schools, primarily in the parish seats before the 1900s, but there were no accrediting standards by which to judge their quality. Nor were there uniform standards for certifying the few persons who chose to make teaching a career. Until matters began improving in the first decade of the 1900s, only 10 percent of Louisiana graduates chose to enter college.[21] And, of course, only a fraction of that 10 percent chose to attend LSU.

POLITICAL, SOCIAL, AND ECONOMIC UNCERTAINTIES AND DISRUPTIONS

Low numbers of students attending LSU and Louisiana high schools as well as inattention to building and maintaining schools resulted to a great extent from the state's Reconstruction-era constitution, ratified in 1864. The constitution supported public schools, provided they were integrated.[22] To what extent enforcement of this provision might have improved race relations will never be known because integration was supported neither by the Louisiana governor nor by white citizens. It was said that "white parents preferred to send their children to private schools, or to no school at all, rather than to let them share a classroom with black children."[23] As a result, school-age children in so many of Louisiana's rural parishes simply had no school to attend. Or, if the children lived in more populated parishes, they might attend a segregated school that by law was operating illegally.[24]

The same indifference that led to little if any support for Louisiana public schools, with the resulting low number of ill-prepared high school graduates, affected LSU as well. But here the problem was even more insidious. State officials were not above meddling in University affairs to fulfill their own political ambitions. Refusal of LSU administrators to heed to requests or demands from these officials often resulted in slashed budgets or withheld funds altogether.[25] David Boyd often found himself having to battle legislators or governors who were intent on having their way with LSU. As a result, the University's budget suffered and debts mounted.[26] President Boyd somehow had to keep LSU open and operating while he dealt with these political forces. On top of that he also had to placate faculty who grumbled over their lack of pay and how Boyd handled his job.[27]

Placating LSU faculty members was important because there were so few of them. LSU had reached a post–Civil War high of eighteen faculty (including President Boyd) in 1871, but that number declined in the next few years until there were only four in 1877. Numbers began to rise gradually, but not until 1891 would the twenty LSU faculty members top 1871's previous high. The number of faculty from that point remained fairly constant through the rest of the decade and then began a steady growth in the early 1900s.[28]

The dearth of faculty throughout LSU was most obvious at the departmental level. Take, for example, the English Department, where the first journalism course most likely would have been taught, had journalism education any chance at all of taking hold at LSU in the late nineteenth century. Until 1899, when a second instructor arrived, only one faculty member was assigned to teach every course offered in the department.[29]

No doubt, the forces arrayed against LSU and journalism education in particular in post–Civil War Louisiana had done their damage. The military nature of the university, LSU's limited and stodgy curriculum, the small enrollment, and the state's dismal secondary school system all played their part in delaying any chance for journalism education to be taught on the LSU campus. But the single force that hurt LSU the most was Reconstruction. Given the conditions associated with that period, could anyone—administrators, faculty, or students—really give thought to LSU's academic program when the very survival of the university was uncertain?

Reconstruction officially ended in Louisiana when all remaining Union forces finally were withdrawn from the state in April 1877.[30] Within a short time, according to Fleming, "the legislature became more friendly" toward LSU, and the way cleared significantly for the University to begin improving its finances, bringing more faculty to campus, increasing its student enrollment, and expanding its curriculum.[31] Most important, and perhaps most providential, was the arrival of leadership that could take advantage of these changing conditions to move LSU into the twentieth century.

3

Journalism Education versus Professional Journalism

The forces and conditions that slowed LSU's physical and academic development effectively pushed aside any consideration of journalism education. But even when serious attention began turning toward the subject, LSU, like its sister institutions where fledgling journalism programs already were underway, had to contend with additional restraints—the philosophical kind—to bringing journalism into the classroom. The philosophical restraints included the opinion shared by many, if not most, practicing journalists (and a few educators like David Boyd) that while theory well might be taught in the classroom, learning the crafts and skills of journalism was best done either at the elbow of a veteran editor or, in the case of a reporter, from peers in the field.

Advocates of journalism education tangled with the skeptics from the very beginning. After all, as journalism historian Richard Terrill Baker claims, "Journalism in the United States came from postmasters, printers, and pamphleteers. One could scarcely say of those early days that the qualifications for a journalistic career were educational ones."[1] But the Civil War brought changes to journalism, as General Robert E. Lee so astutely observed. Skills and intellect that perhaps were not quite as necessary before the war were essential afterward. What's more, continues Baker, "Newspapers were beginning to take a bit more seriously their role as responsible civic institutions. Journalism was coming of age professionally. And part of that maturing process was a professionalization by way of education."[2]

Many leading journalists advocated a liberal intellectual preparation for the newsroom but stopped short of supporting purely "journalism education." Soon after the short-lived Washington College experiment and perhaps anticipating efforts already underway at other colleges to duplicate or even to improve upon General Lee's efforts, New York newspaperman Charles F. Wingate published a collection of interviews with major newspaper and magazine editors and publishers who responded to questions posed about the journalism business. In particular, Wingate asked several questions that specifically gauged attitudes toward journalism education. Frederic Hudson, former managing editor of the *New York Herald,* and Horace Greeley, founder of the *New York Tribune,* were most adamant in their responses. "The only place where one can learn to be a journalist is in a great newspaper office," said Hudson.[3] Greeley agreed, adding wryly that the best way to make an editor was "to feed him on printers' ink."[4]

Henry Watterson, editor of the *Louisville Courier-Journal;* J. C. Goldsmith, former editor of *Frank Leslie's Illustrated Newspaper;* and E. L. Godkin, editor of the *Nation,* all commented that journalism education was best acquired through on-the-job training. Each agreed as well that a successful journalist had to be well read in the classics, history, and economic matters and well practiced in writing.[5] R. R. Bowker, editor of the *New York Evening Mail,* was the only one of Wingate's interviewees who gave an accepting nod to the journalist's need for a broad college education, although he too held back an endorsement for journalism education in particular. Bowker did suggest that a college newspaper could provide an excellent training tool for aspiring journalists.[6]

Eugene M. Camp, a member of the *Philadelphia Times* editorial staff, undertook a survey similar to Charles Wingate's in the late 1880s. To his very distinguished group of journalist interviewees, some of whom Wingate also had interviewed, Camp addressed the following question: "Granting ability and aptitude, can oral and written instruction accomplish as much for the future journalist, as for the future lawyer, doctor, or divine?"[7] The time period that separated the Wingate from the Camp survey saw several colleges in the East and Midwest introduce journalism instruction into their curricula. Perhaps for that reason, views on such instruction were beginning to change. Charles Dana of the *New York Sun* and E. L. Godkin of the *Nation* remained opposed to it, but others such as George William Curtis of *Harper's Weekly,* George Jones of the *New York Times,* and Murat Halstead of the *Cincinnati Commercial Gazette* gave their qualified support to college-level journalism courses.

There was more enthusiasm for general college training than for journalism training in particular. If colleges did teach courses in journalism, the consensus favored that they should be taught by practicing journalists. The strongest and most unqualified statement in support of journalism education came from

Joseph Pulitzer of the *New York World*. "I see no reason why a chair of journalism, filled by a man of real talent and character, could not be beneficial," said Pulitzer. "I have thought seriously upon this subject," he continued, "and think well of the idea, though I know it is the habit of newspaper men to ridicule it. The value of the idea would depend upon its execution."[8]

The tone of the debate over journalism education in nineteenth-century America was not rancorous; rather, it helped ensure that serious and deliberate attention would be given to budding journalism programs.

Colleges, therefore, moved carefully, but move they did. Kansas State College, in 1873, was the first to follow Washington College's lead by offering a course in "practical printing."[9] Five years later, in 1878, University of Missouri Professor David Russell McAnally offered a course in the History of Journalism. The fact that Professor McAnally was head of the English Department[10] represented a trend that would last for years to come in which journalism courses would grow from English Department curricula and be taught by faculty members—usually those most proficient in composition—from that department.[11]

By the end of the nineteenth century, several more colleges would be added to the list of those offering journalism programs of some kind: Denver University (1882), Temple University (1889), Iowa State University (1892), Indiana University (1893), University of Kansas (1894), Ohio State University (1895), University of Michigan (1895), University of Nebraska (1898), and the University of Chicago (1899).[12] The University of Pennsylvania's Wharton School of Business inaugurated a journalism education program in 1893 that has been recognized as constituting "the first comprehensive journalism curriculum offered in the United States."[13] A look at the courses that were part of the curriculum shows a breadth of study that was unique for the time and that established a model for other programs. One course entitled "Art and History of Newspaper Making" appeared to be a general survey of the newspaper business; another combined instruction in libel law and business management; a third called "Newspaper Practice" included instruction in reporting and editing; and a fourth examined domestic and foreign issues. The curriculum also included guest lectures by practicing journalists.[14]

In what appeared to be a kind of capitulation (perhaps less by design and more by circumstance) to criticism from professional journalists about teaching editing and publishing, the emerging journalism curricula reflected a growing emphasis on news gathering. Many of the so-called editor-publishers who had been in the newspaper business for many years had risen through the ranks at a time when news reporting was not considered that important.[15] Matters changed during the Civil War, however, as 350 reporters representing newspapers of the North and about 150 representing newspapers of the South[16] began covering every facet of the conflict. The often slanted, opinionated nature of their reporting[17] was proof enough that proper (and ethical) techniques of news gathering and writing would be superb subjects on which to build a journalism curriculum.

It was practical training like this that formed the nucleus around which the University of Missouri organized America's first actual school of journalism in 1908.[18] The Missouri journalism program had gained momentum from its initial course offering in 1878. Along the way the program not only continued to build a curriculum, but it also gathered support from the state press association, prominent state legislators, university officials, and alumni.[19] The University of Missouri School of Journalism's 1908 curriculum was comprehensive. Its focus on pragmatics was supplemented by the *University Missourian,* a laboratory newspaper published daily by the School of Journalism.[20] What was perhaps even more important to the bonding that occurred among early journalism students at Missouri was the university's provision for a building that would be occupied exclusively by the School of Journalism.[21]

Another journalism school—this one endowed by editor-publisher Joseph Pulitzer—already was in the planning stage when the University of Missouri School of Journalism first opened its doors.[22] As his responses to Camp's questionnaire suggest, Pulitzer's attitudes toward the benefits of journalism education were growing apart from those of many of his fellow journalists. His thinking on the subject clarified a bit when he learned that one of his rival publishers, James Gordon Bennett of the *New York Herald,* intended to create a trust to be used to found a journalism school. Pulitzer immediately (in August 1902) dictated a memo outlining his own idea on the subject. His intentions were to go Bennett one better by funding creation of a journalism school at New York City's Columbia University. He intended that the school, similar to Missouri's, teach practical skills of "news gathering, news editing, news writing, style, composition, accuracy, everything, even to the makeup of a newspaper."[23]

One year after writing his memo, Pulitzer announced his gift of two million dollars to Columbia University to found the very school that he envisioned. Pulitzer's gift, its purpose in particular, sparked much commentary by leading journalists of the day. Most, but not all, were supportive.[24] *Chicago Tribune* editor Horace White's contribution to a persistent, albeit shrinking, pool of criticism appeared in the *North American Review* and said little that had not been said already. "Every experienced journalist will agree that a nose for news cannot be cultivated at college,"[25] wrote White. Joseph Pulitzer answered White and his other critics in the next *North American Review* issue and in doing so, laid a foundation for what he felt was an idea whose time had come.[26]

Pulitzer did not live to witness the opening semester of the Columbia University School of Journalism in 1912.[27] The school was the first to open at an eastern university, and according to historian Willard Grosvenor Bleyer, Joseph Pulitzer's "detailed exposition of the possibilities of such a school" that appeared in the *North American Review* helped push more colleges in that direction.[28] Certainly, Pulitzer's prestige and influence lent considerable momentum to the idea.

Encouraged by Joseph Pulitzer's enthusiasm and the University of Missouri's example, other colleges launched their own journalism programs as the twentieth century began. Newspaper editors and publishers, press associations, students, and college faculty were among those responsible for developing programs between 1902 and 1912 at the University of Illinois (1902), University of Kansas (1903), Iowa State College and University of Wisconsin (both 1905), University of Oklahoma (1908), University of Colorado and University of Washington (both 1909), Stanford University, University of Minnesota and Marquette University (all three in 1910), New York University (1911), and Columbia University, University of Oregon, Emory University, University of Notre Dame, Grinnell College, and Trinity University (all in 1912).

There were few models for the academicians who inaugurated these programs. There also were no textbooks to use in what generally were basic newswriting courses. Moreover, there was no professional organization through which neophyte journalism faculty might exchange useful teaching ideas, until the formation of the American Association of Teachers of Journalism (AATJ) in 1912.[29]

Journalism education grew regionally. With only a few exceptions the "movement," as James Melvin Lee called it, "spread more rapidly in the West than in the East, which clung to more conservative policies about new subjects in the curriculum." Schools in the West and Midwest especially, said Lee, "were more willing to make the experiment."[30] Excluded entirely from Lee's observation was the South, where journalism education was exceedingly slow to take hold. Save for the short-lived effort at Washington College, the only colleges in the deep South where journalism education had been attempted were at Emory University in Georgia and Trinity University in Texas.

At roughly the same time that these two programs were getting underway, LSU was moving on a parallel path. A news-writing course in the making in 1912 would become part of the LSU English Department curriculum by fall of that year. The course was step one in developing a curriculum around which a department and then a school would evolve. The push to make all this happen would come from an LSU president whose unassuming demeanor concealed his passion and determination to make the University's journalism program the best in the South.

4

Thomas Boyd, the *Reveille*, and the Seeds of LSU Journalism Education

Thomas Duckett Boyd returned to the university's presidency in 1896. He brought enormous integrity to the position. He was conscientious, deliberative, and determined in what he planned to achieve. Thomas Boyd already had proven himself capable of dealing in the rough-and-tumble world of Louisiana politics. He was up to the challenge of moving LSU forward, and he was devoted to the university in a way that only an alumnus might understand. All in all, Thomas Boyd possessed the needed qualities it would take to transform LSU into a modern university.

Most important to the history of the Manship School was the new president's interest in journalism, his assistance in starting the LSU student newspaper *The Reveille*, and his encouragement to move ahead with creating a journalism program at LSU once the right person was in place and the time seemed ripe for making that happen. In 1906 Thomas Boyd personally recruited the "right person" when he brought Hugh Mercer Blain to campus as an assistant professor in the English Department. Unbeknown to Boyd at the time, that hire would prove remarkably important to journalism education both at LSU and at colleges and universities across America.

Thomas Boyd, like his brother David, was born in Wytheville, Virginia. When David assumed the presidency (or superintendency) of the Louisiana Seminary, Thomas, twenty years his brother's junior, moved from Wytheville to Louisiana in 1868 to enroll in the Seminary.[1] Thomas graduated with a master of arts degree in 1872. (At the time, LSU awarded M.A. degrees to cadets who completed a standard set of courses beyond what was typically required to receive a bachelor's degree.)[2]

Two years after graduation, Thomas Boyd returned to LSU as adjunct professor of mathematics. He held that position until invited by his brother David to join the LSU faculty fulltime during the university's 1878–1879 session as commandant of cadets and professor of drawing. By the 1882–1883 session, when William Preston Johnston had replaced David Boyd as LSU's president, Thomas Boyd had taken a new title: Professor of History, English Language and Literature, and Acting Professor of Mental and Moral Philosophy.[3]

Thomas Boyd's move from faculty to short-term LSU president in 1887 has been noted already. When he left LSU in 1888 to assume the presidency of the Louisiana State Normal School (now Northwestern State University), Thomas Boyd had served LSU for fifteen years.[4] During that time, Boyd probably had taken on a greater variety of responsibilities at the university than any LSU faculty member before or since. He was well prepared for a return to his alma mater and its presidency in 1896.

President Boyd, known as "Colonel" in a bow to tradition, immediately went to work expanding LSU's courses (or curricula). Among the new additions were courses in civil engineering (separated from mechanical engineering), electrical engineering, philosophy, and education.[5] A major nonacademic, extracurricular addition occurred on January 14, 1897, when LSU's first student newspaper, *The Reveille*, appeared.

The Reveille was curiously introduced to its readers with two four-columned pages devoted entirely to a eulogy in honor of Professor of Philosophy and Civics Wilmot H. Goodale, who had served on the LSU faculty for nearly twenty years before his recent death. Not until *The Reveille's* page two was the reader introduced to the weekly newspaper's annual $1.00 subscription rate (with its plea that "the success of a paper depends on only two things—brains and money") and the newspaper's staff: editor-in-chief Robert Roberts; associate editor Robert H. Plaisance; editorial committee members Roger P. Swire, Dudley L. Guilbeau, and W. D. Smith; and business manager J. H. Arrighi. This staff eventually would be responsible for producing twenty-two *Reveille* issues before turning over responsibilities to a new management team.[6]

The next item to appear on page two, column one of *The Reveille's* first issue was a brief poetic excerpt from Sir Walter Scott's *Lady of the Lake*: "Dream not with the rising sun, bugles here shall sound Reveille." And then a little further down column one came an explanation for the newspaper's name: "The word Reveille means to awake to watch. Let the founding of this publication be indeed an intellectual awakening at our university."

At no point was there acknowledgment that *The Reveille* of 1897 actually was the second incarnation of another LSU publication of that name. The first *Reveille* was published in 1872, during David Boyd's presidency. The publication, however, was not conceived as a newspaper but rather as a literary journal.[7] *The Reveille's* earlier version had been published under rigid faculty oversight, but there was little supervision of any sort in 1897. *The Reveille* staff reportedly "studied local and college papers and patterned their [paper's] makeup accordingly."[8] But only after the paper was in print did Professor C. Alphonso Smith from the English Department critique its content for grammar and style.

Regardless of sparse faculty oversight, President Boyd had more than just a passing interest in *The Reveille's* success. After all, it was Boyd who had persuaded Robert Plaisance, a student acquaintance of his from the State Normal School, to come to LSU in order to launch *The Reveille*. Boyd was also responsible for appointing the paper's entire staff.[9]

Several Louisiana newspapers—*Lafayette Gazette*, *Natchitoches Enterprise*, and *Assumption Pioneer* to name a few—received copies of *The Reveille*, and their acknowledgment of receipt and congratulatory messages appeared in *The Reveille's* third issue. The Baton Rouge *Daily Advocate* in particular welcomed "its young contemporary into the ranks of newspaperdom" and predicted that *The Reveille* would "grow in interest until it becomes a power in Southern college journalism, and a factor for good at the Louisiana State University."[10]

Editorial positions taken by *The Reveille* during the newspaper's first years were varied, ranging from pleas for greater alumni support and increased state appropriations, to a defense of military discipline. *Reveille* editors also devoted their editorial support to campaigning for a yearbook to serve as *The Reveille's* sister publication. The campaign proved a success in 1900 with the appearance of the first *Gumbo*.[11]

The *Gumbo's* foundation was laid in 1899 with selection of a board of editors consisting of representatives from all LSU literary societies and fraternities, and one from each class. When the board met, its first order of business was choosing Robert Plaisance and H. L. Lazarus as editor and business manager, respectively. Next came selecting the yearbook name. *The Pentagon*, *The Creole*, *L'Ecrevisse*, and *The Gumbo* were names receiving the most support. *The Gumbo* emerged as the favorite. Its choice was a natural, as explained in a *Reveille* editorial: "Gumbo is wholly typical of Louisiana, in as much as it is a Creole dish, and very little known outside the state. Further the name is suggestive of the contents of an annual for Gumbo is more or less a mixture. Also, the name has the added attraction and charm of being both catchy and original."[12] From then until now, *The Gumbo* has existed "to depict college life and serve as a reminder of college days to those who have graduated from [LSU]."[13]

The Reveille immediately began supplementing its subscription income with advertising. The newspaper's third issue of January 30, 1897, devoted the entire fourth column of page two to ads for a clothing store, a tobacco shop, and a dry goods company, among others. The newspaper's first full page of display advertising space was split on page three of the November 29, 1905, issue between the Grouchy Hotel and the Farrnbacher Dry Goods Company. Nothing about *The Reveille's* advertising rates for that period seems to have survived.

Still, advertising income combined with subscription income proved insufficient to support *The Reveille*. "Students were not required to subscribe to [*The Reveille*], nor did the University provide it with very much more than an office containing a table that had been used by the school's first superintendent, William Tecumseh Sherman." As a result, each new *Reveille* editor for many years traditionally would "beg students to support the paper financially, to patronize its advertisers and to contribute to its columns."[14]

Money was in such short supply at times that both Thomas and David Boyd actually personally paid to print *The Reveille*. Charles E. Bauer, whose company printed the paper in its early years, once related how *Reveille* "editors would pass the hat for funds to finance the paper. Once when payment was overdue, I sent one of my devils over to the campus to collect. The boy had trouble locating any of The Reveille staff, but met Col. David F. Boyd. . . . Colonel Boyd paid the bill himself."[15] Bauer's story is confirmed by a bill from his company, dated April 23, 1898, found among Thomas Boyd's papers at LSU. The bill was for two *Reveille* printing runs of 500 copies each. Total cost was $28. A penciled notation from Thomas Boyd at the bottom of the bill directed the LSU Treasurer to "pay this bill and charge to account of my salary."[16]

Sports very soon began to dominate *The Reveille*. Nearly two columns appeared in the newspaper's first issue with commentary on the LSU football team's past season and future prospects. The two columns, incidentally, accounted for a hefty portion of the entire issue. In years to come the percentage of *The Reveille* space devoted to sports would continue to grow. One of the more unique sports stories appeared in the January 10, 1908, issue. The story gave a vivid account of the LSU football team—now called the "Tigers"—playing its final game of the 1907 season in Cuba against the University of Havana. The Christmas day game, a 56-to-0 rout won by LSU, was presumably the first international collegiate football game. "The game was a brilliant one from start to finish, and remarkably clean," reported *The Reveille*.[17]

One major first for the newspaper occurred during LSU's 1906–1907 academic year when *Reveille* editor R. J. Mouton was joined by two female associate editors, Nellie Wright Spyker and Caroline Kaufman.[18] Spyker and Kaufman's staff positions were indicative of the greater role that women were beginning to play at LSU. President Boyd had taken the initiative only two years before to allow a woman, Olivia Davis, to attend an LSU calculus class. The next year, 1905, when a second woman was admitted to graduate study, Boyd announced that LSU's doors would swing wide during the 1906–1907 session to begin admitting women to the University both at the undergraduate and graduate levels. Misses Spyker and Kaufman were among some thirty-one women (including President Boyd's own daughter, Annie) who registered for fall classes in 1906.[19]

The Reveille should be credited not only with immediately opening its own doors to women, but also for an advocacy campaign for permanently admitting women to LSU that began during the newspaper's first year of publication. Just how supportive *The Reveille* was is reflected in this excerpt from a 1902 editorial in which the paper's editor asked, "Why are the fairer portions of our race barred from our State University. Are not the fair belles of Louisiana as worthy of a University education as those from any State on the face of the globe?"[20]

More attention was given to female LSU students when *Reveille* editor Herman Moyse placed the paper's April 2, 1910, edition entirely in the hands of a female editorial staff led by Elizabeth L. Pirie and assisted by Carrie Dougherty, Ella Bow, Ena Paulsen, Fannie Burgess, Mary Pirie, Nell Lemon, Jessamine Ellsworth, and Louise Thonssen. Editor Pirie and her staff made full use of this *Reveille* "Co-Ed Edition" to state the female position on a number of campus issues. Surprisingly, they seemed quite pleased with how well females had been received on the formerly all-male, military-oriented campus. A little bit of condescension from among the cadets was noted, but the major complaint seemed to be the faculty's failure to apply the same strict discipline to female students as was applied to the males.

The Reveille increased its size, eventually moving to eight pages in 1910. The paper also published occasional special editions, turning over editorial responsibility for such issues to persons representing particular groups or activities. Examples included summer school editions, law school editions,

YMCA editions, and commencement editions. For a while *The Reveille* published a monthly alumni edition in 1905.[21] Ironically, David Boyd, who had been brought back to campus by his brother, was stricken by apoplexy while preparing one such special *Reveille* edition in May 1905. He passed away only a short time later.[22]

The Reveille remained a weekly until 1934, when the newspaper expanded to a semi-weekly. February 3, 1938, marked the first appearance of *The Daily Reveille*.[23] Publication returned to semi-weekly status at the outbreak of World War II and throughout the war's duration. The newspaper returned as a daily in 1946[24] and once more became known by its *Daily Reveille* title.

Below *The Reveille's* masthead in its early years was the slogan "The South's Greatest College Weekly." That sobriquet, however, was not considered fitting by the newspaper's editors as it moved into its second decade. In fact, Herman Moyse, *Reveille* editor during LSU's 1909–1910 session, assumed control of a publication that he and his staff felt needed a major overhaul. Attention went to athletics but not much else when it came to campus news. *The Reveille* staff had not even begun "systematic gathering of news." So, Moyse laid plans to transform the newspaper's operation, appearance, and content. When Edward White Robertson succeeded Moyse as editor for the 1910–1911 session, the two worked together to further refine and implement the Moyse plan. *The Reveille* was expanded from four to eight pages, and beats were assigned to staff writers who for the first time were given specific reporting assignments to cover.

The newspaper's makeover continued under D. J. Ewing, who followed Edward White Robertson as *Reveille* editor for the 1911–1912 session. Ewing succeeded in putting the final pieces of the Moyse plan into place by organizing the newspaper around special departments and by adopting "a strict newspaper make-up."[25]

The Reveille as well as *The Gumbo* had achieved a degree of permanency among LSU student publications by the 1911–1912 academic session. And both, as the following promotional piece from an August 1911 *Reveille* describes, were serving not just as LSU information media, but also as laboratories for aspiring writers looking for places to hone their journalistic skills.

> During the regular session of the University the publication of college papers and annuals is encouraged as an aid to the student in acquiring the ability to express his ideas in clear, concise and convincing language. Several such are published by the students alone without aid from the faculty,

although a supervision is retained by the President and the Department of English. All who desire to write for these publications are encouraged to do so, and if the matter submitted is available it is printed; otherwise, it is not.[26]

The English Department in a short time would begin building a journalism education program at LSU. The three most recent *Reveille* editors (Moyse, Robertson, and Ewing) had taken the newspaper in a significant direction, creating a first-rate laboratory for would-be journalists while at the same time setting in motion a perfect reason for LSU to justify teaching students the art and craft of journalism.

Journalism education at LSU began in the English Department as a natural academic nest from which such a fledgling program might take flight. Many journalism programs at other universities in the East and Midwest also traced their origins to English departments. What was unique about this at LSU was the message it carried about conditions at the university in general: and the message was growth.

Since Thomas Boyd had assumed control at LSU, the campus had steadily grown. Student enrollment of 220 during Boyd's first year as LSU's president doubled within seven years (1903–1904 session) and tripled within twelve (1908–1909 session). The faculty had grown accordingly from the twenty who were at LSU during President Boyd's first year to more than sixty during the 1909–1910 session.[27]

LSU's physical plant was growing as well. No new structures had been built on the LSU campus for forty-seven years prior to President Boyd's arrival. Perhaps taking advantage of the honeymoon period for new university heads, Boyd appealed to the state legislature for building funds. He got the money for a new classroom/laboratory building. Next came an unsolicited $10,000 gift—the first of its kind at LSU—from William Garig, wealthy vice president of the LSU Board of Supervisors, for a new building. Other monetary gifts soon followed, and more buildings began to appear. The legislature appropriated yet more money for construction projects, and more buildings began rising on the LSU campus. One of the most important buildings to appear during this growth spurt was Alumni Hall, a memorial to David Boyd paid for partially by alumni donations. Alumni Hall would house administrative offices following its completion in 1910.[28] The building, as discussed below, had an interesting future in store, and in time it would become home to the well-traveled School of Journalism.

As the first decade of the new century came to a close, LSU had witnessed the most explosive ten-year building growth spurt in its history. Twenty-two of the forty-eight buildings that stood on the campus were constructed between 1900 and 1910. President Thomas Boyd had overseen "the greatest building program for an educational institution that Louisiana had ever witnessed." And, according to his biographer, Marcus M. Wilkerson, "[Boyd's] boldness in asking for larger and larger building funds while at the same time seeking additional sums for maintenance purposes was only equaled by the success of his efforts. The University at last was in a position to grow and expand beyond the expectations of its most optimistic supporters."[29]

Expansion of the curriculum under Thomas Boyd has been noted already. Within that context the growth of the LSU English Department during the 1900–1910 decade was particularly significant to initiating journalism education at the University. In 1896 when Thomas Boyd became LSU's president, Professor C. Alphonso Smith did not just head the LSU English Department, he *was* the department. Professor Smith was responsible for teaching every English course offered at LSU—from composition and Old English to literature, philology, and everything in between. By the 1897–1898 session the English curriculum had expanded both in number of courses and course content and even included a postgraduate course. But Professor Smith remained the sole English Department faculty member. Finally, during the 1900–1901 session, Julian Huguenin joined C. Alphonso Smith to form a two-person English Department faculty. The next year the department expanded to a three-person faculty, and in 1907–1908, the English Department faculty grew to four with the addition of Professor Hugh Mercer Blain.[30]

Hugh Blain was a special person with extraordinary talents. Almost from his arrival on campus, Blain began working with students to transform *The Reveille* and to lay the foundation from which would spring LSU's first journalism course, then its first journalism curriculum, and in time, the LSU School of Journalism.

5

Hugh Mercer Blain and the Birth of the LSU Journalism Department

President Thomas Boyd personally recruited High Mercer Blain to join the LSU English Department faculty. Fortunately for the future of journalism education at LSU, Blain responded favorably to Boyd's overture.[1] It was, in academic jargon, a good hire!

Hugh Blain brought yet another Virginia connection to more closely link LSU with that state. He was a native of Christiansburg, a small town about forty miles to the east of Thomas and David Boyd's Wytheville, Virginia, birthplace. Blain's B.A. (1894) and M.A. (1895) degrees from Washington and Lee University also connected LSU in a scholarly sense with the birthplace of journalism education.

As Hugh Blain set to work at LSU, he was joining a full-time university faculty numbering only about thirty. Among these were persons who in years to come would be memorialized by campus structures and nearby streets that would bear their names. Professors Nicholson, Coates, Dodson, Atkinson, Dalrymple, Prescott, Himes, Herget, and others would become familiar names to LSU alumni in years to come. For Hugh Blain, they were his first LSU colleagues.

Hugh Blain's range of expertise within the English Department was impressive, and his teaching talents obviously were well-utilized. Blain had a particular interest in southern humor. In fact, he developed quite a reputation during his years at LSU for presentations on the subject.[2] His expertise even found its way into The Reveille when the newspaper launched a short-lived monthly magazine supplement in 1911. Under the heading, "Cullings from Southern Humor," Hugh Blain announced to readers in the newspaper's November 1911 Magazine

27

Section that there "will appear, from time to time, brief, pithy sayings of our Southern humorists who deserve to be better known."[3]

Hugh Blain's association with *The Reveille* actually stretched far beyond that of a sometimes contributing literary essayist. At some point—and there is uncertainty as to exactly when—Blain became the paper's "faculty critic."[4] Whether he took on this advisory task voluntarily or perhaps was appointed by President Boyd also is unknown. Blain was well-prepared for his new role. His father once had edited a country newspaper,[5] and Blain himself, during his pre-teaching days, had spent time as a "correspondent for the Charlottesville *Progress* and the Richmond *Times-Dispatch*."[6] He obviously knew his way around a newsroom. What's more, Blain had more than a mere passing interest in the newspaper profession.

Working with *The Reveille*, however that came to be, was a natural for Hugh Blain. Once established as the newspaper's advisor, his influence there would be substantial. There is reason to suspect that Blain's handiwork at the newspaper began early enough to show up in the changes that occurred under the editorships of Moyse, Robertson, and Ewing, as noted above.

It is unclear just exactly how, when, or why the decision was made to expand Blain's duties from *Reveille* advisor to actual teacher of journalism. The evolution from one to the other seems to have happened while Blain informally instructed *The Reveille* staff. As he later would tell the story: "I began teaching the staff news writing, studying a correspondence course in the subject, and keeping just a lesson or two ahead of them. The work proved more interesting to my class and myself than composition work, so we added more and more subjects in the journalism field."[7]

Informal instruction advanced to the next level when a course entitled "Advanced Composition: The Newspaper" was first announced in LSU's *General Catalog* for the 1911–1912 session. The course would be introduced during the 1912 first (fall) term and would extend into the 1913 second (spring) term. It would be worth three hours credit, and Hugh Blain would be the course instructor. The *Catalog* described "Advanced Composition: The Newspaper" this way:

> This is a course in practical composition, with special application to newspaper writing. The outline of the work is somewhat as follows: materials and methods; the human interest story; the feature; the editorial; the lead; the heading; the organization of the office and functions of the officers, reporters, etc.; press associations; special correspondent; law of libel and copyright, etc.; gathering campus news and handling the above forms.[8]

The actual number of students enrolling in Hugh Blain's Advanced Composition course, like so much else from this period, is not absolutely certain. However, there is indirect anecdotal evidence to put the number at twelve. That same evidence also suggests that the following students—all male—were part or all of the entire enrollment in LSU's first journalism course: Y. Boatner, J. H. Brown, A. Smith, H. M. Moseley, H. C. Boyd, L. Gottlieb, H. L. Hughes, E. R. Stoker, J. L. Dale, Geo. Baillio, and S. E. Dunn.[9]

The practical rather than theoretical emphasis of LSU's first journalism course was obvious. Announcement of the course in *The Reveille* even stated that the "Advanced Composition" course was "intended primarily to facilitate the work of the student publications" and that students who completed the course would receive "a thorough training to fit them for work on the University publication or for outside newspaper work."[10] Hugh Blain augmented the formal classroom instruction in his new course with occasional special talks to *The Reveille* staff on such matters as the duties and traits of a good reporter and the role of college newspapers.[11]

Blain's success with his inaugural journalism course was such that a second reporting course was added for the 1912–1913 session. Without providing specific numbers, Blain did say that enrollment in the basic journalism course "has increased fully one hundred percent over that of last year."[12] In order more thoroughly to integrate instruction in both courses with *The Reveille*, the newspaper staff periodically turned over all reporting and editorial responsibilities to class members.[13] By allowing *The Reveille* to be used in this way—essentially, as a writing laboratory—its editors left little doubt as to how closely connected the newspaper was with LSU journalism education during the latter's formative years.

Enthusiasm for journalism education at LSU was moving at a fast pace by the 1913–1914 session. Compared to the speed with which courses are approved and added to LSU's curriculum today, the tempo of curricular development during that session was near phenomenal. Maybe it was Hugh Blain's persuasiveness or perhaps it had to do with the growing popularity of journalism courses. Whatever the stimulus, the fact is that an honest-to-goodness journalism curriculum was beginning to take shape.

The *LSU General Catalog* for the 1913–1914 session provides an interesting look at just how far journalism education at the University had progressed in two years. One noticeable change from the previous catalogs was the separation of journalism courses from English courses into a section all their own. Then there were the five new or revised journalism courses: "The Newspaper" (a general introduction to the newspaper business with instruction in basic reporting techniques), "Newspaper Reporting and Correspondence," "Magazine Writing," "Reporting and Editorial Work" (open only to *Reveille* editors and reporters with emphasis on preparing and editing stories for the newspaper), and "Industrial Journalism" (open only to editors and staff of *The Demeter* with emphasis on preparing and editing stories for this agricultural periodical). Hugh Blain continued to be the only faculty member assigned to teach all the journalism courses, although *Reveille* editor T. M. McLamore joined him as an assistant.

The *Catalog* text that introduced these courses also told quite a story about the physical progress of LSU's journalism program, noting that "laboratory equipment should be fairly complete by the opening of the session. Several more typewriters will be installed; a number of the leading newspapers and magazines will be on file; and a reference file of typical newspaper and magazine articles will be completed as models for the use of the classes."[14]

Within a short time *Reveille* stories about journalism education at LSU began referring to the "journalism department" and to Hugh Blain as the department's "director." However, neither departmental status nor the director's title actually would become official for several years. Nonetheless, their unofficial use became routine.

Also becoming routine was the acknowledged quality of *Reveille* writing that Blain continued to maintain. The quality resulted from his careful oversight of the newspaper's content in addition to the training that *Reveille* writers received in Blain's journalism courses. A 1915 *Reveille* article remarked on just how important the relationship that existed between newspaper and classroom had become:

> The salient features of good journalism were from time to time impressed upon the staff members, and with the journalism classes under Prof. Blain's direction reading copy and making it conform to proper newspaper style, The Reveille in point of make-up, content and general all-around newsiness has become so nearly perfect this session that it is used in at least one University class-room as a model of newspaper English.[15]

The journalism program's period of rapid growth slowed and stabilized as LSU's 1914–1915 session opened. Thirty-five students now made up the cadre of those regularly enrolled in Hugh Blain's journalism courses.[16] Course offerings narrowed somewhat from the previous year and began to form into content areas that would serve as a solid foundation for years to come. The curriculum comprised five new or revised courses: "Newspaper Reporting and Correspondence" (a basic introduction to newspaper theory, business practices, and writing styles and techniques), "Newspaper Reporting and Editing" (more writing with a heavy dose of editing), "Newspaper Practice" (meant for advanced students who wrote and edited copy for *The Reveille* and Baton Rouge newspapers), "Newspaper Problems and Policies" (business, legal, and ethical issues with particular application to small or "country" newspapers), and "Special Feature and Magazine Writing" (preparation of articles primarily destined for special interest agriculture and engineering publications).

Once again, the entire 1914–1915 session journalism course load fell to Hugh Blain and his assistant T. M. McLamore. And once again, Blain apparently continued to teach English Department courses as well.[17]

During the next three sessions, 1915–1918, neither the journalism curriculum nor Hugh Blain's teaching assignments changed appreciably. He did have teaching assistance from *Reveille* editors E. Stanley Ott during the 1916–1917 session and T. G. Lawrence during the 1917–1918 session.[18] Work load did not bother Hugh Blain. More than anything, he seemed a man on a mission, and he was intent on building a journalism curriculum that would be recognized for excellence.

Hugh Blain was not happy just to teach journalism or to assist *The Reveille*; part of his own personal mission was to introduce students to the kind of journalism that exists beyond the boundaries of the college campus. To do that, Blain brought local journalists inside the classroom to meet with students and to discuss issues affecting journalism and with which journalists had to cope.[19]

Next, Blain assigned his seniors to certain LSU campus beats and required that they write publishable stories related to their beats. They also were assigned to write human-interest stories about LSU students and to submit their stories to Baton Rouge newspapers and to the students' hometown newspapers. Most newspapers were pleased to receive these news items, since they hardly were able to cover LSU news themselves. Student journalists thus received real-world experience in preparing the news and a sense of pride when their stories actually appeared in print.[20]

Requests for LSU news items coming from weekly newspaper editors from around Louisiana began flooding Hugh Blain's mailbox. By the end of October 1913, he had gathered a cadre of senior students who were enrolled in his advanced news-writing course and put them to work preparing a *Weekly News Letter* containing bits and pieces of LSU news. The *News Letter*, edited by *Rev-*

eille editor Joseph Hubert Brown, was distributed to more than one hundred newspapers statewide every Monday.[21] The *News Letter* was something more than just a student activity. Its appearance represented the seeds of a service orientation that would gather momentum through the years and help cement the all-important relationship between the LSU academic community and the media professionals in Louisiana.

Bringing professional journalists to LSU and arranging for student journalists to assist newspaper editors at a distance was fine, but Hugh Blain was determined to put LSU students right at the doorstep of the working press. His idea was to arrange field trips for students to observe the actual operation of a metropolitan newspaper. The first of many such field trips occurred in 1913. Taking advantage of an invitation from New Orleans *Item* publisher James M. Thomson, eleven students accompanied Blain to New Orleans in April to spend an entire day touring the *Item* facilities and receiving a thorough grounding in the newspaper's operation.[22] Blain repeated the New Orleans visit the next spring with a tour of the *Times-Picayune* facility.[23]

Hugh Blain's outreach to the journalism community drew closer to home when he persuaded Baton Rouge newspaper publishers to put qualified journalism students to work at their papers. Placement of one student each at the *Weekly Chronicle* and *Southern Farmer* was important in creating an internship program that would continue well into the future. Without a doubt, though, the most important arrangement was made with the Baton Rouge *State-Times* where publisher Charles Manship put four interns to work. These "cub reporters" were assigned stories to cover by city editor Yandell Boatner, himself a recent *Reveille* editor during LSU's 1912–1913 session, and performed their reporting tasks just like any other *State-Times* reporter. Their reward for a job well done was not a paycheck but rather college credit and a bundle of invaluable professional experience.[24]

The quality of student journalists sent by Hugh Blain to the *State-Times* and later to the Baton Rouge *Morning Advocate* coupled with the interest shown by publisher Charles Manship in supporting LSU's journalism program would help create an important bond between LSU and Manship (and future generations of the Manship family) that would prove invaluable in years to come. LSU also had much to gain through the positive impression that such well-trained, competent interns were making on their professional newspaper colleagues and, more important, on Charles Manship—by far one of Louisiana's most influential publishers.

Academicians at several other colleges and universities around the country were busy developing their own journalism programs by this time. As these programs developed, so did the need arise to form associations among both journalism students and faculty that would facilitate sharing of interests and ideas. The Sigma Delta Chi journalism fraternity was one such association at the student level. Sigma Delta Chi, or SDX for short, began at DePauw University in 1909 and was "composed entirely of men who expect to enter the profession of journalism."[25] Seventeen SDX chapters existed nationally when several students from Hugh Blain's journalism classes petitioned to establish a chapter at LSU. The petition was approved, and in March 1915, the Louisiana-Chi chapter of SDX was formally installed. Louisiana-Chi became the first SDX chapter in the Southeast. Eleven men were inducted into the fraternity during an initiation ceremony conducted in the faculty club rooms of Alumni Hall on the old LSU campus. The chapter's inaugural inductees included honorary member Hugh Mercer Blain, T. J. Magee, T. M. McLamore, G. K. Favrot, E. R. Jones, C. R. Fridge, O. J. Mestayer, D. D. Morgan, W. M. Phillips, T. R. Mobley, and Otto Claitor.[26]

A few years after SDX appeared, another organization called the American Association of Teachers of Journalism (AATJ) formed in Chicago in 1912. The AATJ proposed to create a cooperative means by which college journalism instructors could meet periodically to share ideas about teaching methods and to discuss journalism education issues they all had in common. Representatives from twenty-two colleges attended the Chicago meeting. Willard G. Bleyer of the University of Wisconsin was chosen as AATJ's first president, James Melvin Lee of New York University was elected as vice president, and H. T. Harrington of Ohio State University became the AATJ secretary-treasurer.[27]

Hugh Blain was not among the AATJ organizers, but Willard Bleyer did invite Blain to attend the AATJ's second annual conference scheduled to meet at the University of Wisconsin in Madison. Blain also was invited to present a paper to the gathering.[28] It was an invitation for him to join with what was then still a relatively small group of like-minded journalism education pioneers coming together to form the nucleus of academicians who in years to come would perfect a new discipline of study.

So off to Wisconsin Blair went to present his paper entitled "The Relation of Instruction in Journalism to Courses in English."[29] There were fewer university representatives—only about fifteen—attending this conference than attended the organizing conference the year before. Still, Hugh Blain came away from

Madison with some valuable insight. He found, for instance, that journalism education at LSU was following a similar trajectory to that at other universities. Most journalism programs began in English departments and many, like LSU, continued to be housed there. And most programs, so Blain observed, were heavily oriented toward the vocational side of journalism.[30] Blain also gained immensely just by his association with colleagues from around the country. He apparently had a talent for what today would be called "networking," and he used that talent to its utmost.

The AATJ's third annual conference met in New York City and was attended by representatives from thirty-nine colleges and universities, including Hugh Blain from LSU. Mingling and speaking with the academicians were editors from all the major New York newspapers and magazines. Blain later remarked that "the conference . . . was the most profitable gathering of any kind I ever attended." It was profitable in another way as well. Hugh Blain, attending only his second AATJ annual conference, was elected the group's secretary-treasurer. The position would require that Blain keep in "the closest touch with prominent journalists and publishers, as well as with the widely scattered members of the Association." What's more, remarked a *Reveille* reporter, "the publicity [resulting from Blain's position of national prominence] will benefit the University no little."[31]

Indeed, to be elevated to the AATJ position by his peers was a personal honor for Hugh Blain. It was also an honor to LSU, showing as it did a recognition for the position that the University's journalism program now held among peer institutions nationwide. And it opened doors that Blain was willing and able to work to his and LSU's advantage.

While at the New York conference, Hugh Blain devised a plan for an AATJ *Monthly News-Letter* that he would edit and that LSU would publish. The *News Letter* would be sent to AATJ members, major publishers, and major newspapers and magazines.[32] The *Monthly News-Letter* was up and running less than two months after Blain's return to LSU from his New York trip. The first issue, dated February 15, 1915, was on its way to readers in what had to have been record time, especially considering the information from across the country that Blain had to compile and edit. The *News-Letter's* first four-page issue was understandably short on news items. Its primary purpose was to ask fellow AATJ members whether such a monthly publication was desirable. Answers came quickly, and practically all were in the affirmative.[33]

The *News-Letter* was here to stay. By the third issue, Blain had settled on a format that combined short essays of a pedagogical nature, news of happenings in journalism education elsewhere, reviews of the many new journalism textbooks that were beginning to appear, and advertisements from textbook publishers. The April *News-Letter* had grown to six pages.[34] By May, the page count was up to eight.[35]

The *News-Letter* was quickly developing into a tremendously helpful information-clearing source. Better yet, for LSU, Hugh Blain was taking full advantage of the *News-Letter* to publicize the University's journalism program. Hardly a month passed without some mention of LSU. Appearing in the very first issue was an item describing the internship program that Blain had arranged with the three Baton Rouge newspapers.[36] News about the installation of the SDX chapter at LSU appeared in the second issue.[37] And so it went, month after month (excepting the summer months), news about the LSU journalism program was delivered to journalism department heads and directors and newspaper editors around the country.

The *Reveille* editorial page took note of Blain's *News-Letter*, calling it "a masterpiece of editorial management" that was "full of meat for the journalistic world." These words were followed by words of praise for the quality attained by the LSU journalism program. And then came deserving accolades for Hugh Blain himself.

> Due credit should be given to the man who has directed this great work at L.S.U.; to the man who has brought our institution to the front in the training of men for the greatest profession of all ages. The Department of Journalism at Louisiana is yet in its infancy, but it is a lusty infant destined to develop into gigantic proportions. Dr. Blain is fostering this infant, and it is being well cared for.[38]

Hugh Blain continued editing the AATJ *Monthly News-Letter* through its April-May 1916 issue when his term as AATJ secretary-treasurer ended. In 1924 the *News-Letter* evolved into the more elaborate *Journalism Bulletin*. Within one year the *Bulletin* itself had evolved into *Journalism Quarterly*. Today, the publication whose idea was the brainchild of LSU journalism professor Hugh Blain is better known as *Journalism and Mass Communication Quarterly*.

Hugh Blain's stature in the journalism education arena climbed one more notch when he was invited to join the 1916 summer session staff of New York

University in New York City. He was scheduled to lecture on newspaper writing and newspaper practice and to share additional teaching responsibility with Dr. James M. Lee, director of New York University's Department of Journalism.[39] Upon receiving word of Blain's appointment, *The Reveille* once more gave praise in the editorial page. "Dr. Blain has been the life of university journalism, university student publications, and the inspiration to students of journalism, and they rejoice that his worth is so recognized."[40]

Blain used his growing prominence among his academic peers in 1916 to help leverage some needed improvements in his LSU teaching facilities. For a program whose reputation was growing by the day, teaching tools and space were meager at best. No earlier requests to LSU administrators for assistance in running and equipping the journalism department have been found. But in 1916, Blain made such a request, couched within the context of his annual report. Here is how he described the "Quarters and Equipment":

> The class room and laboratory are in what is known as the 'Reveille Building,' the laboratory being also used as the Reveille office. There is practically no equipment. With the laboratory fees a newspaper file has been purchased, and two typewriters are owned in conjunction with the Reveille. A few metropolitan newspapers are received complimentary. These are used constantly by the students as models. A number of the State papers also come complimentary.[41]

The *LSU General Catalog* description of journalism facilities, as noted earlier, certainly was less dire than Blain's. Nonetheless, a close reading of the above suggests that the entire LSU Department of Journalism in 1916 was operating in one classroom and one laboratory room shared with *The Reveille*. Close quarters, to say the least! But, according to a *Reveille* article, some space relief apparently occurred in September 1916, when *The Reveille* and journalism department were moved to Irion Hall (or the chemistry building on the old LSU campus). The article said that the "new Reveille room will be more spacious and will be conveniently situated with regard to the work of the department of journalism, as Professor Blain will conduct his classes in the adjacent rooms."[42] The reference to the plural *rooms* must have meant that Blain finally would have more space.

Hugh Blain also requested in his 1916 report the purchase of a minimum of eight new typewriters and "a complete new printing plant" at an estimated cost of nearly $8,000.[43] The need for an entire printing plant might seem excessive by today's standards. It might even have been outdated in 1916, since Blain appeared headed in a similar direction as Robert E. Lee some fifty years before in training college students as printers. Whatever arguments existed to the contrary, Blain appeared convinced of the printing plant's worth. His reasons for buying what amounted to a Linotype machine, flat bed press, cutter, folder, binder, supply of type, rules, and assorted other odds and ends, were these:

> For the full training of men and women who could go out in the state and become successful editors of country papers, a complete printing plant is absolutely essential. Moreover, according to statistics in my possession from other institutions, such a plant would be a paying investment for the University. Under an experienced printer as superintendent, most of the mechanical work can be done by students earning their way through college. At the same time these students will get the training they must have in order to become successful editors and job printers. I take it that the greatest need in Louisiana in the field of Journalism is the intelligent, educated man or woman, with a sound knowledge of the printing business and the management and editing of a weekly paper. A glance at the majority of the country papers of the State is sufficient evidence of that fact. With the proper equipment I believe the Department of Journalism of the State University can in a few years supply this great need and thus give to the State an intelligent press, the greatest power for progress in modern times.[44]

LSU administrators did not respond favorably to Blain's request, if they responded at all.

Hugh Blain's persuasive efforts proved more successful when he joined with President Boyd and LSU's SDX chapter president Otto Claitor in bringing the 1916 convention of the Louisiana Press Association (LPA) to Baton Rouge and LSU. The LPA actually had organized in Baton Rouge in 1880, following the decline of Reconstruction-era turmoil throughout the state. Since then the LPA had met in Baton Rouge three more times prior to the 1916 convention.[45]

By inviting the LPA to meet on the LSU campus, Hugh Blain hoped to draw attention to LSU's journalism program. Better still, Blain hoped to expose his students to the editors and publishers from throughout the state who would bring a wealth of experience to LSU. He explained in the LPA invitation just how the organization's members and LSU students alike stood to benefit from one another.

> The Journalism Department, youngest and most vigorous of L.S.U.'s offspring, feels that it would be to its advantage to receive suggestions and hear of the experiences of the men who are out in the field doing the real work of gathering news and putting it before the public. We should like the students in the journalism classes to hear you tell just how you do it, and to get first-hand information concerning all the practical phases of newspaper work. Then, too, we are doing some things that should be of interest and value to the editors of the parish papers. The Journalism Department has developed to the point where it can serve you in many ways, and we wish to confer with you and formulate plans as to how this may best be done.[46]

The LPA accepted LSU's invitation. Members arrived in Baton Rouge to begin their convention on May 1, 1916. The LPA was headquartered in Alumni Hall during its three-day meeting.[47] *The Reveille* published a special edition both to commemorate the event and to highlight the journalism activity then underway at LSU.[48] One of the articles renewed the plea made earlier by Hugh Blain for a new printing plant. The plea's artful language as it now appeared in *The Reveille* seemed squarely aimed at any LPA members who might be willing to underwrite the printing plant's cost. To wit:

> If the journalism department should receive an endowment of an appropriation of $10,000, it would be sufficient to erect a building and buy a printing outfit that would put it on such a basis that it would soon rival any other college here in fame and importance. Journalism is one of the coming professions and the excellent work that has already been accomplished with the meager equipment the department now has is indicative of the great strides that would be taken if the equipment were satisfactory.[49]

Also appearing in this special *Reveille* issue were the results of a survey conducted by senior journalism students on the health of Louisiana country newspapers with follow-up recommendations on what the editors of these newspapers might do to improve local coverage.[50] The survey results carried a value of their own but not to be overlooked was the survey's much broader symbolic value. It proved that the LSU Journalism Department was capable of undertaking such research and that the effort's end product yielded practical benefits to the entire professional journalism community.

Hugh Blain suggested that one other practical way the LSU Journalism Department might assist the professional community would be through implementation of an "editors' short course." Other universities were using short courses with great effect, bringing together editors from around the state in a two- or three-day period to discuss solutions to problems of all sorts that each shared in common.[51] The editors' short course idea was a good one, but not until two decades later, in 1937, would the first short course become a reality at LSU.[52]

Meanwhile, as LPA members met in Alumni Hall, something was happening nearby that indirectly would have far-ranging implications both for the newspaper industry and for journalism education in general. The LSU Physics Department was operating a wireless (radio) station that Professors D. V. Guthrie and Thomas Atkinson had constructed and put on the air earlier in the year. The station was intended to be used as an instructional tool for teaching electrical engineering students the rudiments of wireless technology. Thus far, the kind of point-to-point communication undertaken by the LSU station's wireless telegraphy students with oceangoing vessels and faraway wireless stations[53] was quite remote from the kind of radio broadcasting into which wireless shortly would evolve. Even the term *radio* and the concept of *broadcasting* were things of the future, certainly not to be considered in 1916 as important players in an approaching mass media revolution. But it is likely that practically every newspaper editor and publisher in attendance at the 1916 LPA Convention would be competing with a radio station operating in their community in the not too distant future. Moreover, the radio station that naturally grew from the LSU wireless operation begun in 1916[54] eventually would become a major component of journalism education at the University.

The seeds for cooperation between the Louisiana professional journalism community and the academy were sown during the 1916 LPA Convention. Relationships would grow in years to come that would benefit the LSU Journalism Department (and later, School) in practically every facet of its academic program. And the department's service outreach in turn would prove equally beneficial to journalists statewide.

Changes in the Department of Journalism's academic program during the next few years came in bits and pieces. Two such changes of major significance occurred during the 1918–1919 session. The first was formal recognition of journalism as a department of instruction within the LSU College of Arts and Sciences.[55] What had been nominally acknowledged for several years now was official! Even so, Hugh Blain's teaching duties in the English Department continued unchanged.[56] He would be the first but certainly not the last member of the LSU Journalism Department whose interdisciplinary teaching expertise would spread across curriculum boundaries.

The second change came with the addition to the journalism curriculum of a course in basic advertising. The course was taught by the advertising manager (possibly, Herbert Benjamin) of the Baton Rouge *State-Times*.[57] The Journalism Department for the first time was embracing an area of study that moved the unit beyond a narrow emphasis on news reporting alone. The advertising course, with its content directed toward "instruction and practice in soliciting, writing and laying out advertising," was joined by an equally pragmatic course in "publicity" during the 1919–1920 session. The publicity course combined "instruction in planning and executing all kinds of publicity campaigns" with "practice in handling the publicity work of the University and that of business firms in the city and state."[58] As the advertising course expanded the Department of Journalism in one new direction, so did the publicity course expand it in another, helping to lay the foundation for the future public relations area of concentration.

Other important changes occurred during this period that would significantly affect journalism education programs throughout the country. During the AATJ's seventh annual convention of April 1917 in Chicago, a new organization was formed called the American Association of Schools and Departments of Journalism (AASDJ). AASDJ membership was institutional, not individual, and it was restricted to journalism programs "offering at least twenty-four hours of journalism, including certain courses, such as reporting and editing and leading to a degree."[59] LSU's Journalism Department failed to meet both the credit hours requirements and the degree requirement and, thus, was unable immediately to join with AASDJ's charter members: Missouri, Wisconsin, Columbia, Kansas, Ohio State, Oregon, Texas, Montana State, Washington, and Indiana universities.[60]

The AASDJ, now better known as the Association for Education in Journalism and Mass Communication, was quickly recognized as an organization of the elite journalism education programs in the country. In years to come the AASDJ would develop standards and a system of accreditation that would add even greater prestige to its members. The LSU Department of Journalism finally would make the grade for membership in 1928. Even then, the AASDJ membership list had grown only to twenty. What's more, LSU was the only southeastern college or university admitted to the organization's roster.[61]

LSU assumed a wartime posture in April 1917, when the United States entered World War I. By the end of the 1916–1917 session some two hundred LSU students had left the University either to enlist in the armed forces or to assist the war effort in some other fashion. Faculty members, including President Boyd, also were active in organizations devoted to some phase of wartime preparedness. *The Reveille* did its part to stimulate patriotism, passing along President Boyd's suggestions to students that they enlist in a regiment designated as "The Louisiana Cadets."[62] Throughout the duration of World War I, "nearly twelve hundred L.S.U. alumni or students served in the armies and navies of the United States and of the Entente allies. About half of them were commissioned officers ranging from second lieutenant to Major General."[63]

Former LSU journalism students and *Reveille* editors and staff contributed their fair share during the war. A November 28, 1918, *Reveille* article collectively described the kinds of things these persons were doing at the time. For example, Lt. Stanley Ott was "somewhere in France," Mary Bird was "en route to France to do canteen work," George Favrot was "in the service at the front," T. M. McLamore was "in the army," Lois and Hilda Simmons were "en route to France with the American Red Cross," J. C. Rogers was serving in France with the Army Signal Corps, and D. J. Ewing, *Reveille* editor during the 1911–1912 session, gave the ultimate for his country, losing his life "on the firing line in France."[64]

Lt. Herman Moyse, *Reveille* editor during the 1909–1910 session, not only served his country well, he returned home from Europe a hero. He had been wounded while leading an attack on German machine gunners near Paris but had continued "until the object of his attack had been accomplished."[65] For his bravery, Lt. Moyse was awarded the Distinguished Service Cross by U.S. General John J. Pershing and the Croix de Guerre with Palm by Marshal Petain, Commander-in-Chief of the French Army. The Croix de Guerre with Palm was the highest award that members of the French military could receive and was "only awarded for personal courage in face of the enemy." At war's end, Lt. Herman Moyse had "received more distinctions than any other Louisiana soldier with the American expeditionary force."[66]

Journalism students played roles both large and small during the war, and women students contributed to the cause right alongside their male counterparts. In fact, female journalists at LSU were moving into a male-dominated profession in greater and greater numbers. Hugh Blain noted in March 1917 that women constituted 35 percent of all students taking journalism courses at LSU. That figure was five percentage points ahead of the national average and more than double the percentage of women journalism students at the University of Missouri.[67] The 35 percent figure presumably was based on enrollment statistics gathered prior to the departure of so many students occasioned by World War I.

Given that LSU's overall enrollment dropped from 802 during the 1916–1917 session to 713 during the 1917–1918 session,[68] it is probable that an enrollment drop proportionate to these numbers also occurred specifically among journalism students. But what also might be assumed is that far more men than women departed LSU, leaving women to play more prominent roles both in the journalism program and at *The Reveille*.

Women journalists and editors at newspapers around the country obviously were fewer and less well-known than men who performed the same roles. Certainly, such women as Elizabeth Cochrane, writing under the pseudonym "Nellie Bly," and Ida Tarbell had made names for themselves as reporters in the late nineteenth and early twentieth century. Beyond these, however, women were not viewed as traditional leaders in the news business of the period. However, journalism in Louisiana—a state not known for nurturing progressive trends of any kind—seemed more inclusive of women reporters and editors than was the case in other states.

There is good evidence that Hugh Blain played a major role as both advocate and facilitator in opening doors for women interested in pursuing a career in journalism. He was the father of two daughters,[69] so perhaps motivation came from home. Blain's effort to involve women in the LSU journalism program is documented in a photograph captioned "Louisiana's Embryo Journalists" that appeared in a 1913 issue of *The Reveille*. Students in the photograph were enrolled in Hugh Blain's introductory journalism class. Nearly one-third of those pictured were women.[70]

A *Reveille* announcement in March 1913, that students who wished to write for the newspaper henceforth would be required to submit copies of news stories they had written to Hugh Blain, stated emphatically that such competition by examination was "open to *all students* of the University."[71] And in 1915, when the Department of Journalism extended its invitation to the LPA to hold its 1916 convention in Baton Rouge and LSU, Blain noted that one reason for bringing the LPA to campus was to help promote the department that was "training *men and women* for the editorships of the newspapers of the state."[72] It was during the 1916 LPA convention, coincidentally, that Mrs. J. Vol Brock, editor of the Franklinton *Era-Leader*, became the first female president of the organization.[73]

In March 1917, Hugh Blain's thoughts about women in journalism came together in a speech delivered to the LSU women students during Vocational Guidance Week. The speech, entitled "Woman's Opportunities in Journalism," was published in its entirety in *The Reveille*,[74] a newspaper heretofore not known for publishing verbatim speeches, regardless of subject or speaker. But the newspaper had editorially championed the admission of women to LSU, and more and more women writers and editorial staff members were playing bigger roles in its production, so it was not altogether surprising that Blain's speech would appear in *The Reveille*.

Hugh Blain's words were not impassioned; Blain simply reminded his listeners that women had come a long way as journalists in a short time. "Twenty-five years ago her sphere was limited to the society column," he said. "Now in every state of the Union women are progressive and successful editors of papers."[75] Then Blain gave his listeners a history lesson to remind them of the legacy that women journalists in Louisiana had left them. He cited women journalists and editors at metropolitan and country newspapers throughout the state. Among them was Dorothy Dix, described by Hugh Blain as "the highest salaried newspaper woman in the world, a New Orleans woman who started with voluntary news notes for the *Picayune*."[76]

LSU women already had decided on ways to showcase their writing talents in the pages of a humor magazine called *The Giggler*. Begun in 1914, *The Giggler* was the work of the Scribblers Club, said to be "composed of some of the most talented co-eds in the University." Their intended purpose seemed to be in composing poems, short stories, and "witty articles and squibs" destined for the pages of *The Giggler*. Mary Bird was the publication's editor, and Martha Stumberg was its managing editor.[77]

Within two years, during the 1919–1920 session, Hugh Blain had invited a woman, Helene Robbins, to become a teaching assistant in the Journalism Department.[78] Miss Robbins would be the first of many outstanding women to hold a faculty position in journalism at LSU. And it might be assumed, given Hugh Blain's influence with decision makers at *The Reveille*, that he played at least a passing part in helping to name Elmore Lawrence as *Reveille* editor for the 1920–1921 session. Miss Lawrence was the first woman ever to hold that position.[79]

Hugh Blain had made an indelible imprint on LSU's Department of Journalism since his arrival at the University. He had given his best to create a program whose quality was nationally recognized, and he had placed LSU in a leadership position among its peer institutions. Much remained to be done to continue building the journalism program, but for Hugh Blain, the 1920 spring term was his last at LSU. He announced in August 1920 that he had accepted a position as manager of Associated Rice Millers of America (ARMA), headquartered in New Orleans. Left to teach Blain's freshman journalism class was S. J. Gottlieb, Elmore Lawrence's predecessor as *Reveille* editor.[80] Why Blain departed LSU remains unknown. Salary may have been the deciding factor. LSU likely was hard-pressed to match any salary offer coming from private industry. It could have been, too, that money was not the major issue and that Blain simply was ready for a new challenge.

Gratitude for Hugh Blain's work during his time at LSU was expressed by many with whom he had come into contact in the classroom or at *The Reveille*. Such appreciation already had been expressed in a more tangible form in 1917 when a portion of funds donated to LSU by alumnus and former *Reveille* assistant editor Henry Vincent Moseley was dedicated to establishing the Blain Foundation Library of Journalism.[81]

The gift Hugh Blain received upon his departure in 1920 came not in money but in the words of a *Reveille* editorial:

> Dr. H. M. Blain's resignation is a paralyzing loss to the Department of Journalism. He was its founder, almost ten years ago, and has been the most consistent worker for its furtherance since then. He had, in fact, become so much a part of his work that to the average journalism student he was the department.
>
> He was first a personal friend and then a professor to those students who were fortunate enough to come in direct contact with him, and he worked with and not over his pupils. His reward, if such it may be called, is to know that he leaves behind him a circle of friends who have for him a warm, sincere liking and admiration instead of the usual stilted respect for those in authority.[82]

Hugh Blain's first order of business in his new position was to hire two former LSU journalism students, Eldon F. Roark Jr., and Sam B. Dunbar, to assist him.[83] His job as ARMA manager was essentially that of public relations. Campaigns that he developed "to promote the sale and consumption of rice" proved enormously successful. One observer credited Blain's campaign with "tripling of the volume of rice consumption and a corresponding increase in the general prosperity of the rice industry."[84] All of this happened in less than a year after his departure from LSU.[85] His first love, though, was teaching. In 1923, Hugh Blain returned to the classroom, joining the faculty of Tulane University where, for the second time, he went to work to create a department of journalism.[86]

6

LSU Journalism Program at a Crossroad

The LSU Department of Journalism was still in its infancy but already it had reached a critical crossroad. Hugh Blain, the department's founder, leader, and lone full-time faculty member, now was gone. His replacement would have to be capable of sustaining what Blain had begun, and if the new person could make the kind of impact that Blain had made outside the department, so much the better. Finding someone who would be so energized and so devoted to journalism education as Blain would not be easy—or so it seemed.

Before commencing a search for Blain's successor, though, a key decision would have to be made. Was there value in continuing the journalism program? At this point, in 1920, the LSU Dean of Arts and Sciences (assuming he was the decision maker) could hire a new faculty member with orders to continue and strengthen the Department of Journalism, or the dean could dissolve the department and either drop the existing journalism courses or absorb them back into the regular English Department curriculum as they were before. The former would require both financial and personnel commitments if the journalism program was to continue developing, but the latter probably would require no commitments of any kind.

Much of the dean's decision rested on answers to two questions: First, were students sufficiently interested in journalism as a career to continue taking journalism courses and maybe in time even to major in journalism if LSU were to offer a degree in the discipline? Second, was the journalism profession in Louisiana sufficiently developed to where college graduates—perhaps those with journalism degrees—might find gainful employment?

PURSUING A JOURNALISM CAREER

Evidence that LSU, via Hugh Blain, vigorously built its journalism program is indisputable. Evidence that students were persuaded to study journalism as a career goal or that their intention to become journalists compelled them to enroll in journalism courses in the first few years those courses were offered at LSU is a little less certain. Student intent and postgraduate work activity are two matters about which little information seems to exist, at least for students during the first two decades of the 1900s. What is known of student interest in preparing for a journalism career at the time consists largely of pieced-together anecdotal commentary.

Of some interest is a list that appeared in the *LSU General Catalog* showing the occupations of LSU graduates from 1869 through 1910. The list suggested rather clearly that at least up to the period (1910 and beyond) when journalism education began to take shape at LSU, journalism had not proved a particularly attractive career choice for LSU graduates. Only one of the roughly six hundred graduates noted in the list indicated any interest in pursuing a journalism career. G. D. Bently, a 1904 graduate, listed his occupation as "editor." Three others listed dual occupations: H. A. Mangham and J. B. Martin, both 1902 graduates, listed "editor/legislator" and "teacher/editor," respectively, and F. J. Whitehead, a 1908 LSU Law School graduate, listed "lawyer/editor" as his occupation.[1] Other than these, LSU graduates during the period made no mention of a career in journalism.

Neither were many of the early *Reveille* editors inspired enough by their work on the college newspaper to choose journalism as a career. G. D. Bently, the 1904 graduate mentioned above, had served briefly as *The Reveille* editor in fall 1903. C. S. Miller, *The Reveille's* 1908–1909 editor, gave his occupation as lawyer and editor. Not until D. J. Ewing, who served as *The Reveille* editor during the 1911–1912 academic year, was there someone who actually identified himself as a newspaper reporter. Ewing reported for the New Orleans *Times-Picayune*, but even he was studying to become a lawyer.

Law, in fact, was the career choice of a number of pre-1920 *Reveille* editors. According to retrospective articles appearing in the newspaper, Robert Roberts, C. M. Roberts, Herman Moyse, John Y. Fauntleroy, N. H. Feitel, L. L. Perrault, and E. W. Robertson practiced law. Roberts eventually became a floor leader in the Louisiana House of Representatives before taking a seat as a U.S. district judge in Shreveport. Herman Moyse also served in the Louisiana legislature, and E. W. Robertson moved from law into banking. Other careers included medicine (Lestre J. Williams), the sugar industry (Thomas D. Boyd Jr., and J. A. Verret), the military (C. S. Miller and E. Stanley Ott), the ministry (H. LeRoy Johns), publishing (Otto Claitor), and academe (James F. Broussard and H. A. Major). From what information is available, only two of the thirty LSU students who served as *Reveille* editor during all or a portion of an academic year from 1896 through 1920 chose to remain in journalism following graduation. T. G. Lawrence became a lecturer in journalism at New York University,[2] and as noted in a previous chapter, Yandell Boatner became city editor of the Baton Rouge *State-Times*.

No information is available on the careers of about one-third of *The Reveille* editors who served during the period under review. Perhaps some and maybe all of them continued in journalism. And, of course, there are the many *Reveille* staff members and reporters about whom no career information is available. Maybe many of them also chose to remain in journalism.

Career choices of students associated with *The Reveille* is of particular interest because of the close connection between the newspaper and the LSU Department of Journalism. Indeed, the University's entire journalism education effort during the early Hugh Blain years seemed directed almost exclusively to training *Reveille* personnel. What's more, courses that appeared in the journalism curriculum as Blain developed it were electives and not meant to be building blocks in a foundation of courses necessary to prepare someone for a journalism career. The courses were not required of anyone nor did they particularly advance anyone toward a degree. Completing one or more or all of the courses certainly would have helped prepare a student for future work in journalism, but in the eyes of LSU the courses simply augmented that preparation. Courses in journalism during the first few years they were offered were viewed as subordinate to a wider array of courses meant to educate a student in the most liberal sense. That plan of education appeared in successive volumes of the *LSU General Catalog* at the time. Here is an excerpt from the 1914–1915 version explaining the role of the College of Arts and Sciences:

> The work in the College of Arts and Sciences is planned so as to give a broader training than that of the strictly classical courses of earlier days, and at the same time to avoid the narrowness that has sometimes resulted from the excessive specialization of later times. With this end in view, certain courses in the fundamental branches of knowledge, which are regarded

as essential to a liberal and efficient education, are required of all candidates for a degree.³

These "courses in the fundamental branches of knowledge" were supposed to be completed during the student's first two years. After that, he or she then could choose elective work which, as the *Catalog* suggested, "may be arranged with a view either of securing a general cultural training without regard to any particular vocation, or of pursuing intensive study in some special field. . . . A proper selection of studies," noted the *Catalog*, "will enable the student to pursue a course that will afford excellent training for the teaching profession, commercial pursuits, journalism, or for the study of law or medicine."⁴

Including journalism among the other occupational pursuits in the preceding passage was tacit acknowledgment that journalism was a career goal worth pursuing. In addition, it suggested that LSU officials at the time were in possession of enough information to prove to them at least that many students who were taking journalism courses had their sights firmly set on becoming professional journalists. The *LSU General Catalog* went so far as to suggest that journalism courses should appeal to a wider range of students than just those preparing to work for newspapers and magazines. The courses were "recommended to all students who have an aptitude for writing and wish to improve their powers of expression. . . . Prospective teachers of English [were] especially advised to take up one or more of them."⁵

Listing journalism courses within a mix of other liberal arts courses was important as well. Journalists of the period and of earlier times, as noted above, felt that persons wishing to enter the journalism profession would do well to learn as much as they could about as many subjects as possible. The growth of journalism education at LSU and at most other colleges and universities within English departments that were part of a liberal arts college was in keeping with that idea. As it happened, the mark of a quality journalism program from this time forward (and in later years as a requirement for accreditation) rested on how well that program integrated a broad liberal arts curriculum with the more narrowly defined journalism curriculum.

Without knowing how many LSU students completed journalism courses and then moved into a journalism career during the Blain years, it might be surmised that the number was high enough to encourage his continuing to build the LSU program. Statistics have been cited above showing enrollment growth year after year in journalism courses. The internship program at Baton Rouge newspapers, also noted above, proves the seriousness with which students pursued a journalism career. And it might be assumed that the statement appearing in the May 15, 1915, issue of *The Reveille* asserting that the LSU Journalism Department "is training men and women for the editorships of the newspapers of the state"[6] had some basis in fact, though how many editors at how many newspapers remains unknown.

Enrollment in LSU journalism courses and positions at newspapers claimed by (or for) LSU graduates were two very good reasons for continuing to build the University's journalism program. But competition from other universities provided equally good reasons. Statistics compiled by Hugh Blain for the AATJ *Monthly News-Letter* showed that, as well as LSU's journalism program was doing, similar programs at other colleges and universities were doing better. Responses from 40 institutions to survey questions regarding enrollment during the 1915–1916 academic year showed that 21 of them had more students enrolled in journalism courses during the year than LSU with its enrollment of 59. For example, New York University had 316, the University of Missouri had 275, Iowa State College had 220, and the University of Oregon had 175. In addition, all of these colleges had more faculty members—many more in some cases—teaching their journalism courses than LSU with its one full-time faculty member and his teaching assistant. New York University had 13, the University of Missouri had 11, Iowa State College had 3, and the University of Oregon had 9.[7]

The high enrollment numbers accounted for the lion's share of journalism graduates across the country who were entering the job market. One observer placed the number of graduates during journalism education's first decade (1908–1918) at about one thousand. That number jumped fivefold during the second decade from 1918 to 1928.[8] The number of students leaving colleges and universities who were well-trained and well-equipped to move immediately into the journalism profession was growing exponentially, and LSU certainly was adding to that total. But as the second decade of journalism education began, the LSU journalism program—regardless of the strides it had made and the prominence it had attained under Hugh Blain—lacked the one thing that so many programs elsewhere could offer: a degree in journalism.

Hugh Blain had said in 1913, "The professional press is keenly interested in the schools of journalism. The student of journalism, after being graduated, stands a better chance of employment than he would stand if he had not prepared himself by collegiate training for the occupation."[9] Since the LSU journalism program had barely begun in 1913, Blain presumably was peering into the future and already making plans for the school of journalism that he assumed would be created eventually. A little more might be read into what Blain said by assuming that he saw the school as a degree-granting unit where the diploma would represent completion of a unified, rigorous body of journalism courses and the attainment of a certain level of journalistic skills, knowledge, and competence. Hugh Blain gathered all the pieces and set in motion all the forces that would achieve these goals. But his departure in 1920 left him short of that achievement. Turning the existing Department of Journalism into a degree-granting school was a job left to Blain's successor, if and when that successor might be named.

LOUISIANA NEWSPAPERS

If the number of LSU students who aspired to become journalists did materialize in the early decades of the twentieth century as expected, then what kind of newspaper industry might they have been preparing to enter? Were jobs available? Were Louisiana newspapers plentiful enough to provide employment for the numbers of journalism graduates likely to be entering the job market? Was the newspaper industry financially sound enough to provide a decent living for journalists fresh from the college classroom? How had the industry survived the social and cultural upheavals of Reconstruction and post-Reconstruction Louisiana? And what was the outlook for the Louisiana newspaper industry in general, in both the short term and long term?

These questions about the newspaper industry are pertinent because for all intents and purposes that is where journalism graduates were headed. The advertising industry had been around for centuries, and the public relations industry was beginning to establish itself, but neither had developed to the point where students had begun looking at them as career possibilities.[10] So newspapers—and more often than not, Louisiana newspapers—would be the workplace of choice for most LSU journalism students.

The Louisiana newspaper business, at least from the publisher's and editor's perspectives, had always comprised independent thinkers and doers. LSU journalism graduate student Frank James ("Jim") Price, in his thesis "The Country Press of Louisiana, 1911–1940," had observed that "there were no typical or average country papers in the state" and that editors adapted newspapers to follow closely the needs and wants of their respective readers, addressing themselves, as Price put it, "to the publics that they have found."[11]

Price's study concentrated on what he called "country newspapers" or those newspapers, from what can be determined of his definition, that were published outside of New Orleans. Thus, all but a very small percentage of Louisiana newspapers fell into the "country newspaper" category.[12]

Changes in the Louisiana newspaper industry that began occurring in the early twentieth century reflected changes that were occurring nationwide. For one thing, newspapers in ever increasing numbers were becoming big business, like so many other American industries of the period, and were yielding to a more unified appearance and content. The period from 1900 to 1910 brought changes to the newspaper industry that were nothing short of revolutionary. "Within the decade," read one history of the period, "new machines multiplied the mechanical capacity of newspapers. New circulation techniques were developing. New features were attracting to newspapers people who, apparently, had done no reading in their earlier years. Most important, a new species of advertiser had emerged since the century opened."[13]

The "new species of advertising" referred to "prestige advertisers" like the emerging automobile companies and companies manufacturing "packaged and branded food, [and] drug and cosmetic products" that heretofore had confined their advertising to magazines with a national distribution. Local newspapers that had depended largely on retail outlet and patent medicine advertisers for much of their income now were beginning to solicit business from these prestige advertisers.[14]

New trade organizations such as the Southern Newspaper Publishers Association (SNPA), founded in 1903, also helped add uniformity and strength to the newspaper industry. In particular the SNPA assisted newspapers in the twelve southern states (including Louisiana) composing its membership area with a means to discuss matters of mutual interest. It so happened that in 1921, SNPA members took on a special project when they approved a proposal to raise funds to help rehabilitate the long dormant journalism program at Washington and Lee University. A $50,000 pledge dedicated to honoring journalism education's pioneer program was met during the SNPA's 1923 annual meeting.[15]

Much of the story of a changing newspaper business in the United States but more precisely in Louisiana comes from production and circulation statistical data sources of the period, particularly from the U.S. Bureau of the Census and the Jim Price thesis noted above. One other period data source frequently cited by researchers, N. W. Ayer and Son's *American Newspaper Annual and Directory*, is not cited here since, according to newspaper historian Alfred McClung Lee, Ayer's data corresponds very closely to the census data.[16] An important point to understand about census data cited here is that such data for the 1920 census actually came from 1919, and data for the 1910 census came from 1909.

With that in mind, sources show that 17 daily newspapers (5 morning and 12 evening) were published in Louisiana in 1919. This compared to 23 daily (6 morning and 17 evening) newspapers published in the state in 1909. The decade-long decline in the number of dailies reflected a similar decline nationwide.[17] Census data for the number of weekly Louisiana newspapers and periodicals published in 1909 (141) and 1919 (117) shows a decline also reflective of a national trend.[18] The numbers are not absolutely reliable, however, since they combine both newspapers and periodicals.

Newspaper circulation figures, measured for comparative purposes between 1914 (not 1909 as above) and 1919, show a very different picture. Census data show that circulation per issue of daily newspapers in Louisiana rose from 139,686 in 1914 to 233,160 in 1919. This was nearly a 67 percent increase. Circulation figures for both morning and evening dailies increased, but the increase was most pronounced for evening newspapers where the number went from 69,399 in 1914 to 141,432 in 1919. Once more, these numbers reflected national trends in newspaper circulation, although the interest in evening editions of daily newspapers was stronger in Louisiana than nationally.[19] Average circulation for weekly newspapers (in combination with periodicals) in Louisiana stood at 125,262 in 1919 and represented a nearly 16 percent decline from circulation figures from 1914 and, even more dramatic, a nearly 29 percent decline from circulation figures for 1909. These data are not a reflection of national trends, which showed a roughly 27 percent increase in circulation of weekly newspapers and periodicals from 1909 to 1919.[20] One thing the reader should keep in mind is the likelihood that the magazines included in the periodical category would have had a higher readership nationally than in Louisiana during the period under review.

All of these statistics are important in the broad picture they paint of the Louisiana newspaper industry at a time critical to the status and development of the LSU Department of Journalism. A closer analysis of that picture follows shortly, but before that a different perspective from the Jim Price thesis sheds a somewhat different light on the numbers and locations of Louisiana newspapers. Price was not as exact with pinpointing how many newspapers were published during a given year; rather, he described the newspapers' entire publication history as accurately as possible. A little detective work has pulled from the Price thesis some publication information that varies slightly from what the 1920 census showed. As far as can be determined, some ninety newspapers (combining daily, weekly, and semi-weekly) were published in Louisiana in 1920. And these ninety papers were spread among seventy-nine communities, representing every geographical region of the state. In fact, six communities (Abbeville, Houma, Natchitoches, New Iberia, St. Martinville, and Thibodaux) were home to at least two newspapers, one (Shreveport) was home to three, and New Orleans was home to four. Roughly 85 percent of the newspapers were either weeklies or semi-weeklies. Once more, discerning what can be gathered from the Price thesis, the only daily newspapers published in Louisiana in 1920 were the Alexandria *Town Talk*; Baton Rouge *State-Times*; Crowley *Signal*; Jennings *Times-Record*; Lafayette *Press and Advertiser*; Lake Charles *American-Press*; Monroe *News-Star*; New Orleans *Times-Picayune, Item, Tribune,* and *States*; and the *Shreveport Times* and *Journal*.[21]

Although Jim Price disagreed slightly with census figures for the number of weekly and semiweekly newspapers published in Louisiana, he did agree with data that showed such newspapers on the decline during the first two decades of the twentieth century. Reasons for the decline, said Price, were the "miserly" growth in population between 1910 and 1920, "the exploitation of natural resources," and "the reduced acceleration of business adventurousness [that] drove out the shoe-string editors."[22]

Departure of editors and their newspapers from communities where advertising dollars were too few to support the papers was not altogether bad. Operating on the financial edge often meant that newspaper content suffered. Better to see a newspaper fold than to have a community poorly served by that paper. Weekly and semiweekly newspapers that did survive, however, often were well-run and more robust.

Circulation figures tell the most intriguing story of what direction the Louisiana newspaper industry was taking in 1920. There were fewer newspapers published, but newspaper readership, judging from circulation data, had climbed at a remarkable rate during the years preceding 1920. Two factors that probably accounted most directly for the rise in circulation were increases in urban population and increases in the state's literacy rates.

Jim Price observed above that Louisiana's population grew at a "miserly" rate between 1910 and 1920. That certainly is true if the state's 8 percent growth from 1910's 1,656,388 to 1920's 1,798,509 is taken into account. And while Louisiana's rural population (measured as inhabitants living in communities of less than 2,500) rose slightly during the same period, the *percentage* of the state's population living in rural areas actually declined. Obviously, a population shift from rural to urban areas was underway. In fact, Louisiana's major metropolitan area of New Orleans grew by over 14 percent between 1910 and 1920. The state's smaller cities of Alexandria, Baton Rouge, Lafayette, Lake Charles, Monroe, and Shreveport grew as well. Most growth came in the three-city corridor running diagonally from Shreveport through Alexandria to Baton Rouge. Shreveport grew by nearly 57 percent, Alexandria by almost the same, and Baton Rouge by over 46 percent.[23]

Urban growth was paralleled by an equally positive growth in Louisiana's literacy rate. The rate for persons 10 years old or older stood at 71 percent in 1910 and had risen to 78 percent by 1920. No doubt, the rise in school attendance for persons aged 5 to 20 from 1910's roughly 41 percent to 1920's 53 percent[24] accounted for much of Louisiana's improved literacy rate.

A higher literacy rate favored newspaper growth, but urbanization was even more important. Alfred Lee stated the point emphatically: "The spread of urban characteristics in this country more than any other factor correlates closely with the marked increases in daily [newspaper] circulation."[25] More interest in access to news by greater numbers of readers resulted from urban settings with their clusters of readers. More businesses needing to reach consumers with their advertising messages also was good for growing the newspaper business.

The decline in weeklies and semi-weeklies, most of which made up Louisiana's country newspapers, by no means meant their disappearance. It did mean, however, that editors in country newspaper communities where readers now were finding easier access to newspapers from a nearby urban location were having to change their own papers' content. Country newspapers that previously had carried a heavy helping of state and national news began carrying more and more local news. In Jim Price's words, the country newspaper editor now would be "obliged to plow a deeper furrow in the immediate home area."[26]

All of these changes—growth of the urban press and the altered content emphasis of the country press—opened the avenue wider and wider for dedicated, highly skilled, and well-educated journalists. These were just the kind that LSU's Department of Journalism had shown itself capable of producing. But as important as were dedication, ability, and intellect, neophyte journalists were not totally prepared to practice their craft in Louisiana until they had gained some appreciation for the unique brand of journalism found in the state.

That unique brand of journalism is a legacy of conditions prominent in the South in general and in Louisiana in particular. Regarding regional conditions, Hodding Carter, himself a Pulitzer Prize–winning journalist and onetime publisher and editor of the *Daily Courier* in his hometown of Hammond, Louisiana,[27] made the following observation in 1969:

> Whatever else may be said of the Southern press, the newspapers of the South have certainly demonstrated closer identification with the aspirations and turmoil and tragedy of their region than have those of any other part of the United States.
>
> The Southern editors for 150 years have been spokesmen, defenders, and firebrands in their regions to an extent not in evidence anywhere except perhaps in the old West.[28]

Characteristics uniquely associated with Louisiana journalism include toughness, tenacity, and resourcefulness—surviving and sometimes thriving in the most difficult of times—and existence within a political environment that occasionally has been volatile and in which newspapers at times have been forced to advocate unpopular positions.

Just how tough, tenacious, and resourceful Louisiana newspaper publishers have been was put to the maximum test during the Civil War. When the war began there were about eight dailies and seventy weekly English language newspapers published in the state. Once the war's full effects filtered down to the Deep South, the Louisiana press was especially hard hit. The problems with which publishers and editors had to contend mounted almost daily and included loss of staff to military service; uncertain communication and transportation; heavy newspaper tax imposed by the Confederate Congress; rising costs of commodities that led to higher newspaper costs and fewer customers; and scarcity of newsprint that was remedied by reducing the number of printed pages per issue, physically reducing the page size of the newspaper, printing with smaller type, and in the worst cases printing newspapers on wallpaper or wrapping paper. Newspaper publication also was suspended temporarily in those communities occupied by Northern troops, but once the troops departed the newspapers resumed printing whatever they pleased.

Occupation of New Orleans by Northern troops in April 1862 brought very tight control over what newspapers in that city were allowed to print. Anything related to the U.S. military was suppressed. In addition, the editorial positions of New Orleans newspapers were carefully monitored. Shorn of their ability to express any point of view or opinion that rankled the military authority of the occupied city, the journalistic functions of New Orleans newspapers "became that of the chronicler of facts, the mere historian of the condition of the city."[29]

The marriage between politics and the Louisiana press began earlier, in fact, with the first newspaper to appear in the Louisiana territory, *Le Moniteur de la Louisiane*. The French language newspaper, issued first on March 3, 1794, and published by Louis Duclot, a refugee to Louisiana from Santo Domingo, was almost exclusively an instrument to criticize the Spanish government which at the time controlled the territory. The newspaper was said to have flourished during its twenty-year history and "was the only paper printed in Louisiana up to the time it [Louisiana] was purchased by the United States in 1803."[30]

Other newspapers appeared in New Orleans in the early nineteenth century, before settlements like Baton Rouge and St. Francisville on the Mississippi and Alexandria and Natchitoches on the Red River began attracting their own newspapers. Most of these were English-language papers, but some were published in French or Spanish or a combination of one or the other with English.[31] These newspapers formed the vanguard of the country press. They were the only means, besides personal letters and word of mouth, by which many Louisiana villagers and plantation dwellers learned about events, political or otherwise, happening beyond their immediate locale.[32]

Prior to the Civil War many Louisiana newspapers were highly politicized and used primarily to promote partisan views of their publishers, many of whom also were political office holders. Good examples of partisan newspapers of the period were those in Baton Rouge where the *Weekly Gazette* promoted the views of the Whig Party; the *Daily and Weekly Comet* represented the views of the "Know Nothing" Party; and the *Advocate*, as its name aptly suggested, advocated the views of the Democratic Party.[33]

The politics-press connection that began before the Civil War was just a warm-up to what occurred during the post–Civil War Reconstruction era. The political caste of newspapers divided sharply between the Republican papers that were regarded as the instruments of the "radical" Reconstruction government and the Democratic papers that were the instruments of Southern conservatism and tradition. According to historian Donna L. Dickerson, "Despite having hard times reestablishing newspapers after the war, Democratic and Republican newspapers throughout the South participated in a raucous, excessive, and biased form of journalism seldom seen before or since in the United States."[34] The two also were viewed by Southerners as representing racial orientations: the Republican newspapers being seen as black, and the Democratic newspapers as white.

Republican newspapers were unwelcome in most Southern communities. Because they had so few readers and so few merchants who were willing to buy advertising space in the papers, publishers of the Republican newspapers generally relied upon government and military contracts to print official legislative and court documents, announcements, and proclamations as well as orders from local military commanders.[35] With so many impediments it is ironic that the sixty-three Republican newspapers that existed in Louisiana far surpassed the number of Republican papers in other Southern states. The reason for so many was that the Republican-dominated state legislature "had the most liberal system of awarding patronage" and, thus, provided publishers subsidy after subsidy to keep the Republican newspapers in business.[36]

Operating alongside the Republican newspapers in many Louisiana communities were the Democratic newspapers, editors of which often were outspoken against military occupation—even at the threat of arrest.[37] Under such pressure a number of Reconstruction-era newspapers closed while others struggled to remain afloat. Some, like those among the nearly fifty-four newspapers published in New Orleans during the period, merged with their competitors and prospered.[38] They prospered as well because of the kind of leaders who guided the papers' editorial policies. Many of the editors were identified as "men of legal training and keen interest and long experience in politics, and, in a surprising number of cases, they were Northern men who through long residence had become thoroughly imbued with Southern ideas and ideals."[39]

When Reconstruction ended and the Southern conservative newspapers whose publishers and editors had been denied a full voice to their views began once more to assert themselves, those dormant views more often than not gave vent to anger over many issues, not the least of which were racial issues. Too few years had passed since these same newspapers or ones like them had defended slavery. And many more years would have to pass before emancipation would begin to soften the passions of those who were troubled at seeing the former slave as equal. There were publishers and editors in Louisiana who did take a heroic stand to oppose racial injustice. But too many failed to do so until events occasioned by civil rights struggles of the 1950s and 1960s began to change attitudes.

The politics of race as it was practiced for so long in Louisiana was pervasive among all the state's institutions, especially its institutions of higher learning where segregation policies closed the doors of LSU to all blacks. As a result, the history of journalism education at LSU for much of its existence is a history that includes neither students nor faculty of African-American descent. That picture would not change until LSU officially integrated well past midcentury. Later chapters of this book document how the Manship School's more recent history includes systematic and aggressive efforts to reverse past practices by bringing more and more students and faculty of every racial and ethnic orientation into its classrooms.

The unpleasantness of racial divisions aside, the Louisiana press of 1920 had survived the difficult days of Reconstruction to emerge in excellent shape. Readership was growing, and the post–World War I economy was pushing manufacturers of consumer goods to spend lavishly on advertising.[40] The elevated stature of newspapers among a more literate and better educated population also signaled great potential for the Louisiana newspaper industry. Employment opportunities in that industry and shortly in the advertising industry as well held considerable promise for trained journalists.

At LSU in 1920 there were questions raised, as noted above, about whether the journalism program should continue, given the void created by Hugh Blain's departure. Evidence showed that the journalism profession had reached a point of maturity, growth, and stability that would sustain and indeed encourage the employment of college-trained journalists. The LSU Journalism Department's curriculum proved itself capable of supplying such journalists the necessary intellectual tools, and the link between the Department and *The Reveille* provided ample laboratory means for testing student abilities in a near real world workplace.

The question about the level of interest among students in taking journalism courses and majoring in journalism if the opportunity arose was more difficult to answer. Hugh Blain seems to have had no problem in attracting students to enroll in journalism courses. Who was to say that such interest would not continue under Blain's replacement, especially if a journalism degree were offered as an incentive both to attracting students and to improving the journalism curriculum? If earning a degree in journalism at other universities was gaining in popularity, might that also be the case at LSU?

If students were going to populate the program, the program was in need of solid, dynamic leadership. But who could fill Hugh Blain's shoes? That person would have to have some very special credentials that included more than just dynamic leadership. He or she would have to have an ability to work with LSU administrators and faculty, be respected within the professional journalism community, bring experience as a journalist to the position, have outstanding organizational skills, be conversant with LSU policy and tradition, and demonstrate an ability to represent LSU among colleagues at the national level. An individual who possessed all of these characteristics and the forcefulness to push the Department of Journalism to a higher level would have to be someone special.

Fortunately, the search to find such a person was neither lengthy nor extended beyond the LSU campus. Maybe it was providential, maybe the stars were perfectly aligned, or maybe it was just plain luck, but that person, Marvin G. Osborn, not only was already at LSU, but he had been a member of the LSU family for years. He had the qualifications, he was an LSU alumnus, he had worked closely with President Boyd, and he was excited about the job that lay before him. Hugh Blain may have created the LSU Department of Journalism, but Marvin Osborn would carry that creation to its next plateau. In the thirty-five years that he served as director of what eventually would become the LSU School of Journalism, Osborn would carry the School to a level of excellence on par with any other college journalism program in the nation and certainly unequaled by any other such program in the South.

7

Raising LSU Journalism Education to the Next Level

Marvin Osborn really needed no time to acquaint himself with the LSU Journalism Department. He had worked with Hugh Blain on one occasion to persuade the LPA to hold its 1916 annual convention in Baton Rouge.[1] The two also had co-written a newspaper supplement to promote LSU.[2] There is strong evidence to suggest, in fact, that Hugh Blain was one of the first persons to whom Marvin Osborn turned for advice upon assuming his new position. In a letter from Blain to Osborn, dated January 18, 1921, Hugh Blain congratulated his friend "on your plan for journalism."[3] A few months later, Blain wrote Marvin Osborn another note, perhaps to encourage the new chairman. "It does my heart good to know that journalism work at L.S.U. . . . is in such good hands and has permanent future in prospect," said Blain. And he added, "I hope I can do something some of these days to help it along."[4]

Marvin Osborn's connection with LSU extended in many directions and already accounted for eighteen years of service. Osborn was an LSU alumnus, class of 1906,[5] had served on both *The Reveille* and *Gumbo* staffs while a student,[6] had held a campus correspondent position for Baton Rouge newspapers, and from 1908 to 1910 had served a dual position as LSU registrar and President Thomas Boyd's secretary. In 1913, Osborn became editor of publications in the LSU Agricultural Extension Division where he happened to be when President Boyd summoned him with a request that he assume his new duties in the Journalism Department.[7]

Marvin Osborn knew LSU intimately, and he was known and respected by many at LSU, including Thomas Boyd. But Osborn brought even more to his new post. At the time of his appointment he was serving as president of the

American Association of Agricultural College Editors.[8] Respect for his abilities from among colleagues across the country had helped elevate Marvin Osborn to a nationally prominent position. That would be of immense personal importance to him in years to come, but such prominence also would prove of great importance to the LSU journalism program in just a few short years. Like Hugh Blain before him, Marvin Osborn had the right stuff to hoist LSU's name up into the elite of journalism education.

Marvin Osborn led the LSU journalism program for over a third of a century. Yet this chapter concentrates on his first decade at the helm, since many of his most significant accomplishments relative to advancing journalism education at LSU occurred during that ten-year span. Some of those accomplishments were small and short-term, but some were huge and long lasting. Consider that within five years of Osborn's arrival the Department of Journalism became a degree-granting unit.[9] Five years after that, on September 1, 1931, the Department of Journalism was officially elevated to the LSU School of Journalism, and Marvin Osborn's title was elevated as well from chairman to director.[10]

How Marvin Osborn accomplished these and other feats is left to speculation, since no record of memos or other documents seems to exist detailing the administrative machinations that always accompany structural changes of this kind. It might be assumed that Osborn, who probably maintained a close personal relationship with President Boyd through the years, had won some major concessions from Boyd in return for taking the Journalism Department job. After all, Osborn obviously was doing quite well at the Agricultural Extension Division. Perhaps Boyd agreed to help build the journalism program as a condition to secure Osborn's joining the program. Maybe, though, it was the challenge itself that attracted Osborn—in changing direction and taking on the tough job of building the journalism program. Whatever the reason, the "change agent" role that Marvin Osborn assumed fit him and LSU perfectly.

There were numerous changes in the journalism program, but all of these took a momentary back seat to a major institutional change underway at LSU during the 1920s. As with journalism education, there was much else also on the move at the University. By mid-decade the entire LSU campus, in fact, would be on the move—literally.

Changes that were beginning to happen at LSU would carry the University gradually into the highest ranks of academic respectability. One of the first was an annual increase in state appropriations that made attracting and retaining quality faculty easier. Louisiana Governor John M. Parker was credited with persuading the legislature to boost appropriations. Throughout the 1920s and into the 1930s, LSU was engaged in a kind of "quality thrust" that brought bright, energetic faculty to the campus and thus strengthened the academic programs. Quality programs subsequently built LSU's reputation and at the same time brought more students to the University. Enrollment increased steadily throughout the 1920s.

Another change of major note was the gradual decline of LSU's military tradition. A good deal of that tradition of LSU as the Ole War Skule would continue, of course, but military training and discipline would become less practiced and less a part of university life.[11]

Physical growth of the LSU campus also brought monumental change. The campus had reached the limits of expansion during the second decade of the twentieth century, hemmed in as it was by downtown Baton Rouge business and residential developments. New campus buildings in recent years had been clustered wherever they would fit. When time came to expand the College of Agriculture there simply was no more space to grow. The only option was to move LSU to a new site. President Boyd explored several possibilities before settling on a tract of land known as the Gartness Plantation, located some distance south of the existing campus. Dr. J. M. Williams, owner of the land, was willing to sell the property for $82,000. Through various means the money was raised and purchase of the Gartness Plantation was finalized on May 23, 1918.

Groundbreaking for construction of the Greater University occurred on March 29, 1922. The first shovel of earth was turned over by Governor Parker and the building that would rise on that particular site later would bear the Governor's name. Enough classroom and administration buildings, dormitories and support buildings were in place for business to commence at the new campus in September 1925, although its official dedication was scheduled for April 30 through May 2, 1926, to commemorate Louisiana's admission to the United States.[12]

The downtown LSU campus, now referred to formally as the Old University Plant, was not abandoned when the new campus opened. Many of the buildings there, including the dormitories, were converted into facilities for exclusive use by female students. Freshmen and sophomore women in particular took all their courses on the old campus. A number of administrative offices also were maintained there, and "various University gatherings and social functions" continued to be scheduled in old campus buildings.[13] Persons traveled back and forth between the old and new campuses via a special bus service and shuttle trains operated by the Y and MV (Yazoo and Mississippi Valley) Railroad.[14] Not until 1932 would all LSU academic activities, offices, and student living and classroom facilities finally move to the new campus and most of the old campus buildings be demolished.[15]

In the Journalism Department, Marvin Osborn had a budget to prepare and faculty to hire. There actually is little specific budgetary information available from 1921. Records do show, however, that Osborn's total departmental expenditure for the year was about $1,100. His 1922–1923 budget request was somewhat more specific and happens to be the only one that seems to have survived from the Journalism Department's earliest years. Osborn's request for $2,225 actually was a 100 percent increase over the previous year's budget request. Even so, equipment and supply needs and costs for such things as twelve new typewriters (totaling $840), newspapers and magazines ($300), postage ($150), and general office supplies ($50) were minimal when compared with budget requests in later years.[16]

One of Marvin Osborn's first faculty hires was Marjorie Arbour, a colleague at the Agricultural Extension Division.[17] *Reveille* editors such as Beverly Latham, Robbin Coons, Benjamin Dugas, and Marcus Wilkerson also continued assisting with news writing instruction.[18] Marcus Wilkerson, like Arbour, would move eventually to a full-time position in the Department and make a name for himself through his pioneering work as the first director of the LSU Press.[19] Other faculty members arrived and departed, but by the end of the 1920s the Journalism Department could boast of a faculty of five—three men (Osborn, Wilkerson, and Paul C. Jones) and two women (Arbour and Ida Ogden).[20]

One of the first matters addressed by the faculty was the curriculum. Hugh Blain had created courses and settled on course content that would serve as an excellent starting point for continuing to build, revise, and refine the Journalism Department curriculum during the 1920s. Unlike curricula in tradition-bound disciplines such as history, English, math, and so on, journalism education was more fluid. Changing circumstances required that the journalism curriculum be in nearly a perpetual state of evolution. That remains true even today. New and necessary courses might be added to the curriculum, while old and unnecessary courses might be deleted. Course names might stay the same even though their content is altered. A single course that worked well for a while eventually might evolve into two different courses in order to reflect a changing emphasis of the course subject matter. Many things happen to a curriculum over time, but by and by, courses begin to emerge that are so integral to an academic program that they become a kind of fulcrum around which other courses revolve. These courses would become the core of the curriculum.

Careful examination of the LSU Journalism Department's curriculum as it tracked through the 1920s on its way to becoming the Journalism *School* curriculum illustrates the application of all of the evolutionary motions described above. What cannot be seen, of course, is the careful attention given by faculty members in fashioning a journalism curriculum that by the early 1930s was strong enough and comprehensive enough to stand nearly unchanged for many years to come. Indeed, there are plenty of remnants of that early curriculum found in the Manship School's curriculum today.

The basic course that most definitely was the journalism curriculum's cornerstone was the "News Writing" course. Here is where students learned the fundamentals of reporting and writing. This course also served as a laboratory course for *The Reveille*, helping the newspaper to fill its pages with basic classroom assignments. By the 1930–1931 academic year there was an "Advanced Reporting" course that placed students into a real newsroom setting by requiring that they prepare copy for the Baton Rouge *State-Times*.

Special writing courses appeared early on in the journalism curriculum. Leading the pack was "Agricultural Journalism." Taking advantage of Marjorie Arbour's expertise in the subject, the course remained part of the basic curriculum into the 1930s. Of equal importance was the "Community Newspaper" course meant to introduce students to the fundamentals of managing and editing the weekly or small daily newspaper.

Courses in "Newspaper and Magazine Departments" and "Trade and Technical Journalism," whose content examined specialized kinds of writing, editing, and publication needs, were added to the curriculum by the 1930–1931 academic year. Also added was the "Newspaper Publishing" course that concentrated on the business side of publishing.

During the 1927–1928 academic year, the Journalism Department significantly expanded its advertising curriculum. "Principles of Advertising" and "Advertisement Writing" were joined with courses in "Advertising Plans and Procedure," "Direct Mail Advertising," and "Retail Store Advertising."

Two other very important courses added to the Journalism Department curriculum during the 1920s were "Law of the Press" and "History and Principles of Journalism." Both courses were comprehensive in nature and applied both to journalism and to advertising. The "Principles of Journalism" portion of the history course was expanded into a separate course prior to the 1928–1929 academic year and was intended to concentrate on issues of journalism ethics.

Curriculum change occurred throughout the 1920s, but curriculum revision and expansion were most robust during the decade's midpoint when the Journalism Department began granting degrees, and just prior to the 1930–1931 academic year when the Department became a School.[21]

Curriculum revision was accompanied by other programmatic changes during the mid-1920s. At the time, students (who were not admitted as majors until their sophomore year)[22] were required to complete a four-year course of study in order to receive a Bachelor of Arts in Journalism (B.A.J.) degree. Required subjects were rigidly prescribed with little room for variance. Course subjects required outside of journalism included English, history, economics, and foreign languages—generally, an assortment of social science and humanities subjects not unlike those required of today's majors. Unlike today, though, male LSU students were required to complete several hours of military science courses, and female LSU students were required to complete a similar number of hours in home economics courses. Of minor note was the LSU calendar, which at the time was based on quarters rather than semesters. The University adopted the semester calendar prior to the 1929–1930 academic year.[23]

Requirements changed even more once the Department of Journalism became a School. Majors now would be required to complete 128 semester hours in order to earn a B.A.J. degree. Female students no longer were required to complete courses in home economics, and male students (with the de-emphasis on military training noted above) now had the option of course work in military science or physical education. Most important for journalism majors was the selection of journalism electives now available to them as a result of so many more courses added to the curriculum. For example, students in their junior and senior years could choose to specialize in advertising, country journalism, and trade and technical journalism.[24] All in all, the inaugural LSU School of Journalism degree program demonstrated the journalism faculty's dedication to designing a flexible curriculum that could best serve an expanding field of career possibilities.

Marvin Osborn implemented other, perhaps more subtle changes; one of these was the immediate acquisition of sufficient typewriters to permit all news copy prepared in class and destined for *The Reveille* to be typewritten. Previously, copy written in longhand had been acceptable.[25]

Reactivation and *innovation* are the best two words to characterize Marvin Osborn's first full academic year (1921–1922) as Journalism Department chair.

Annual spring visits by LSU journalism students to New Orleans newspaper plants were reactivated. Hugh Blain had taken the first group to see a metropolitan newspaper operation in action, and in May 1922, Marvin Osborn continued what was becoming a tradition.[26]

Another tradition, this one of much greater practical and professional consequence, began in 1922. Taking advantage of the relationship that Hugh Blain had forged with Charles Manship and his Baton Rouge newspaper staff, Marvin Osborn arranged something unique—possibly unprecedented—for his advanced journalism students. On Tuesday, April 11, specially selected students would replace the regular Baton Rouge *State-Times* editorial staff and publish the entire paper themselves. The regular staff, in the colorful words of a *Reveille* writer, "will take a holiday. From the managing editor to the reporter, all will go gaily forth for a good time, with easy consciences and light hearts."[27]

Marvin Osborn was to serve as acting managing editor and appoint the editor, department heads, and reporters from among his best students. Advertising copy preparation (and, presumably, sales) would be supervised by *State-Times* advertising manager Herbert Benjamin, who was himself an adjunct member of the Department of Journalism faculty.[28]

This experiment in reality would serve as an enormously valuable teaching tool. *The Reveille* editorial staff, however, viewed it as a means of proving something to a Louisiana newspaper establishment that still seemed reluctant to fully embrace the quality of LSU's journalism students. Said *The Reveille* in its editorial page, "We hope the doubting, rusticating editors in Louisiana—sadly in evidence in some parts of the state—will be convinced that the Journalism department of the Louisiana State University does produce real newspaper material."[29]

The student-edited *State-Times* edition proved an overwhelming success. Charles Manship extended his congratulations via remarks in the paper's April 12 editorial page. He commented that some people had "paid the students the compliment of wondering why we do not let the [Department of Journalism] get out the paper all the time."[30]

In 1926, Charles Manship invited students to publish an edition of the *Morning Advocate* as well as the *State-Times*. The *Morning Advocate* was less than a year old when the paper's first "Journalism Student Edition" appeared on April 20. Two complete staffs of eighteen students were assigned to each newspaper.[31]

The opportunity to join the student edition staff at either the Baton Rouge *State-Times* or *Morning Advocate* was something that students looked forward to. And they valued the real-world work experience gained there and in many instances put it to good use after leaving LSU. Examples of student edition editors of the 1920s who would be working in some capacity as a professional journalist by 1930 included Marcus Wilkerson, who joined the Journalism Department faculty; Beverly Latham, writer for the American Radio Corporation; Robbin Coons, Hollywood syndicated columnist for the Associated Press; Alcee Alleman, who remained with the *Morning Advocate* as its managing editor; Margaret ("Maggie") Dixon, *State-Times* reporter; and Helen Gilkison, who served as capital correspondent for the New Orleans *Item-Tribune*.[32]

Perhaps as a token of the outstanding job that journalism students were doing, or perhaps merely as a means of strengthening the relationship between the LSU Department of Journalism and the Manship newspapers, Charles Manship announced in June 1922 that the news publishing facility he was building in downtown Baton Rouge would have a specially outfitted newsroom adjacent to the editorial department dedicated entirely to the use of LSU journalism students.[33] When the Journalism Department students finally settled in to their newsroom, Marvin Osborn remarked that it was the only department in the country "that has been granted the privilege of regular working room in a newspaper office."[34] What's more, the Department's *State-Times* newsroom added considerably more work space to the cramped campus lecture/laboratory classroom located in what was referred to as the "old pest house."[35]

News about all that was happening with LSU's journalism program began to spread across the country. First, a brief mention about the relationship that had developed between the Baton Rouge *State-Times* and the Department of Journalism appeared in the first issue of the AATJ's *Journalism Bulletin*.[36] The *Bulletin* was the quarterly magazine that succeeded the *News-Letter* that Hugh Blain had created. Next came a more in-depth article about the Department in the January 16, 1926, issue of *Editor and Publisher* magazine. At the core of the "*E and P*" article was a discussion of the "practical nature of the newspaper training" that LSU journalism students received.[37]

And students were responding to all the new teaching ideas and practical classroom training that were now available to them. A total of 144 students were enrolled in journalism classes during the 1921 fall term. Many of these, according to *The Reveille*, had come to LSU intent on studying journalism.[38] Enrollment jumped to 168 during the 1924 fall term.[39] By the following year, LSU had occupied buildings on its new campus and had acknowledged the increasing popularity of journalism courses by moving the Journalism Department from the "pest house" of the old campus[40] to the more spacious second floor of the Agronomy and Animal Industry Building (known as Stubbs Hall today). Four rooms were reserved for Journalism Department lecture and laboratory space (just down the hall from "three cotton and grain storage rooms") and a fifth room was reserved for *The Reveille*.[41]

Enrollment declined somewhat once the Journalism Department's degree program was activated.[42] But after the program had settled in, enrollment once more began to climb. The transition from Department to School of Journalism in 1931 coincided with a total enrollment increase to 173 students during the 1930–1931 academic year. Seventy of these were majoring in journalism. Total enrollment the next year jumped to 253 students, 121 of whom were journalism majors.[43]

Impressive as the enrollment numbers were, even better were the employment reports for journalism graduates. Marvin Osborn remarked in a 1926 article that "Louisiana editors employ every student that we have had ready for a position, and ask for more."[44] Somewhat supporting Osborn's claim were statistics noted in the *1930–1931 LSU General Catalog* showing that "some sixty graduates and former students in journalism are now engaged in newspaper and related work in Louisiana and fourteen other states."[45]

While all these statistics tell a story of sustained growth and success, they nonetheless raise an issue about which the reader should be aware. Until the late 1920s, the actual identification of LSU students as "journalism students" and the number of "journalism students" enrolled in Department of Journalism courses both were a bit vague, in some respects confusing, and not altogether reliable. Information about persons who were considered journalism students and how many such students there happened to be at any given time prior to 1926 (when the Department of Journalism was authorized to actually begin awarding degrees) is almost entirely anecdotal. That is, the information comes principally from newspaper articles (*The Reveille*, the Baton Rouge papers, etc.), photograph captions, and a scattering of other unofficial sources.

One overarching question among several others here is just what criteria qualified a student to be called a journalism student? After 1926, it was easy enough through identification in the *LSU General Catalog*, the *LSU Gumbo*, and other official and semiofficial LSU information sources to determine whether a student actually was a journalism major and thus qualified as a journalism student. But before 1926, the best that can be assumed is that any student who took at least one journalism course possibly could have been referred to as a journalism student if he or she wanted it that way. So, quite a number of students who graduated from LSU between 1912, when the journalism program began, and 1926, when it actually was possible to major in journalism, were subsequently identified in various places and at various times as journalism graduates, regardless of their actual depth of study in the journalism program or the number of journalism courses completed.

In matters of enrollment, the Journalism Department faculty, prior to 1926, was proud of the growing number of students who were enrolling in journalism courses. These enrollment numbers have been noted as kinds of markers to measure growth and popularity, and they indeed were impressive. Nonetheless, indications are that these numbers represented the total enrollment in all the journalism classes that were offered during an academic year. At no time, until after 1926, did enrollment figures apply to the number of majors. After 1926, and all the way to the present, enrollment figures for the journalism program have been divided between total enrollment (i.e., the number of students enrolled in all journalism or, more recently, mass communication courses offered per semester) and the number of journalism or mass communication majors enrolled during a particular semester.

The really inquisitive reader might ask why it is that official LSU student records could not yield precise information about journalism student identification and enrollment during those 1912 to 1926 years? The answer is that they probably do. Unfortunately, student records of that period are not easily accessible. Remember, computer records and electronic data processing, filing, and storage were not around then. So, searching student records is cumbersome, time-consuming, and frustrating, and there is a good chance that the search will yield incorrect or unhelpful data. What's more, the only complete record search would require that records of every student who attended LSU between 1912 and 1926 be examined to see if he or she enrolled in a journalism course. A search of this kind would be impractical at best.

Interestingly, at least three documents exist in the Manship School Archives that provide unofficial identification of journalism student names and enrollments during the 1912 to 1926 period. Unfortunately, very little of the data appearing on any one of these documents match the data on the others. The documents are imprecise, fail to identify their sources and, obviously, are not of much use.

So, when all is said and done, there is little choice but to say for LSU students from the 1912–1926 period who referred to themselves as journalism students and maybe even journalism graduates that neither of the two references is technically correct. If they did earn an LSU degree during the period, the nearest they could have come to a journalism degree would have been a B.A. in Arts and Sciences with perhaps a concentration in journalism. But journalism degree or not, many of these graduates, as noted in earlier chapters, went on to work in some capacity as journalists. Quite a few of them even had distinguished careers in journalism. They might not have carried the formal degree, but their identity as an LSU journalism student was and is no less valid. And their dedication to the LSU journalism program should be recognized and at the very least should earn them special status as honorary journalism graduates!

In 1926 the Department of Journalism became authorized to grant degrees. Even so, there still remained a question as to who precisely received LSU's first bona-fide B.A. in Journalism degree. Since it would have been nearly impossible for anyone to have completed all degree requirements in order to qualify for graduation in 1926—the Department of Journalism's inaugural degree-granting year—the first actual graduate would have come from the class of 1927. So, as close as can be determined, LSU's first official journalism degree was awarded in 1927 to Benjamin Dugas of Napoleonville.

By the end of the 1920s, fourteen more journalism degrees were awarded. Recipients in 1928 included Alcee Alleman of Jeanerette and Margaret Richardson of Baton Rouge. Six degrees were awarded in each of the next two years. Those graduating in 1929 included Annabel Atkinson of Shreveport; Alex Daspit, Thomas Downey, and Helen Gilkison, all of Baton Rouge; Ernest Gueymard of St. Gabriel; and Evelyn Teller of Vicksburg, Mississippi. Students graduating in 1930 included Raiford Dorsey and Georgia Wilson, both of Baton Rouge; A. S. Williamson of Lake Providence; Thomas Quillman of Benton, Illinois; Orene Simmons of Poplarville, Mississippi; and Margaret Stephenson of Plainfield, Indiana.[46]

The number climbed year after year as more names were added to the list of graduates. By the end of the century, the Manship School graduation rosters numbered into the hundreds annually. And that included students earning master's degrees and doctor of philosophy degrees in addition to bachelor's degrees. All told, thousands of students working for media organizations around the world or pursuing careers in dozens of non-media-related occupations carry the pedigree of LSU journalism students.

So much was happening with the journalism program at the local level that it is surprising to realize how active the LSU Journalism Department remained at the national level. LSU was in the thick of things during the 1920s, precisely as intended by Hugh Blain many years before. Blain's active involvement in the American Association of Teachers of Journalism (AATJ) was continued by Marvin Osborn. Osborn's involvement, however, went beyond even Blain's. He was elected vice president of the organization in 1925, and in 1926, he became the AATJ's president.[47] Osborn earlier had served in the top spot of the American Association of Agricultural College Editors, and now after having been a college professor for only five years, here he was at the pinnacle of his newest professional organization.

Recognition of another sort came to the LSU Journalism Department in December 1927. This was an institutional recognition by the American Association of Schools and Departments of Journalism (AASDJ) that awarded the Department a Class "A" rating—a distinction shared by only twenty of the nearly 250 colleges and universities then offering courses in journalism. Some of the universities whose company LSU now would share included Columbia, Syracuse, Northwestern, Illinois, Ohio State, Michigan, Wisconsin, Missouri, Texas, Kansas, Washington, and Oregon.[48]

Residing within such an exclusive group was important to LSU's prestige, but it also signaled that hard work by members of the Department of Journalism to reach a certain level of proficiency had paid off. What's more, it put LSU among a pioneering group of peer institutions that were attempting to sort out which of the 250 colleges and universities where journalism courses were taught actually were most committed to offering quality journalism education.

Journalism educators in the early 1920s had realized for some time that journalism programs were beginning to proliferate. As a result, scores of college graduates who had taken only a few courses in journalism—and courses that perhaps had not been well taught at that—were entering the job market. Newspaper editors, many of whom were just beginning to overcome their long-held skepticism about journalism education in general, were being inundated by these ill-prepared journalism graduates. Those who were hired too often made a bad impression—an impression that potentially could reflect poorly on journalism education nationwide.

The same problem had plagued medical education in the United States just past the turn of the century. Too many medical schools, or so-called medical schools, were graduating too many poorly trained doctors. In order to deal with the problem the medical profession established standards by which to judge the quality of medical training in this country and created a method for grading medical schools according to the level of preparation demonstrated by their graduates. The result was a swift decline in the number of medical schools and a corresponding drop in the number of medical school graduates. More important, though, was the improved level of training that eventually would lead to the respected medical profession that rose in this country during the early years of the twentieth century.[49]

Journalism educators decided to adapt the medical school model to their own needs and to set about creating an early form of journalism program accreditation. The initial step came in 1917 when ten universities—Missouri, Columbia, Wisconsin, Ohio State, Oregon, Texas, Indiana, Kansas, Washington, and Montana State—met to form the AASDJ. The AASDJ and the AATJ began meeting together in 1921, and in 1923 they formed the Council on Education in Journalism (CEJ), "whose purpose was to be that of formulating and maintaining standards of journalistic education and the classification of schools and departments of journalism in accordance with such standards."[50]

The CEJ, with members Willard G. Bleyer (chair) of the University of Wisconsin, Eric W. Allen of the University of Oregon, John W. Cunliffe of Columbia University, Nelson A. Crawford of Kansas State Agricultural College, and Joseph S. Myers of the Ohio State University, devised the "Principles and Standards of Education for Journalism" that were adopted during the AASDJ and AATJ annual meetings in Chicago in late December 1924. Among the General Principles were the following:

> Because of the importance of newspapers and periodicals to society and government, adequate preparation is as necessary for all persons who desire to engage in journalism as it is for those who intend to practice law or medicine.... Adequate preparation for journalism, therefore, must be sufficiently broad in scope to familiarize the future journalist with the important fields of knowledge, and sufficiently practical to show the application of the knowledge to the practice of journalism....
>
> All instruction in journalism should be based on a recognition of the function of the newspaper and other publications in society and government, and should not be concerned merely with developing proficiency in journalistic technique. The aims and methods of instruction should not be those of a trade school but should be the same standard as those of other professional schools and colleges.[51]

These principles would apply from 1924 forward as the goals to which all journalism education programs should aspire. They were broad both in scope and application. However, the "Standards of Education for Journalism" were more specific. Here were twelve key practices that members of the CEJ felt departments or schools of journalism should employ in order to be considered among the best at what they do. The AASDJ, in adopting the Council's recommendations, created a classification system of four groups—A, B, C, and D—into which journalism programs might be placed, depending on the degree to which a particular program met the "Standards of Education for Journalism." Class A programs were judged the best because they met all standards. Journalism programs across the country collectively empowered the AASDJ to act as the "only accrediting agency recognized within the field" and thus to have the authority to classify programs.[52] The CEJ would become the mechanism accountable to the AASDJ for actually conducting the accreditation. That authority in time would pass to other groups as the accrediting process itself became more formalized and more pertinent to a program's welfare.

Obviously, a journalism department or school hoped to achieve a Class A rating. And in order to do that, it was considered essential that the AASDJ's twelve standards be met. In brief, the standards required that the journalism program be housed in a "separate academic unit"; that no fewer than 120 credit hours be required for receipt of a bachelor's degree in journalism; that the course of study leading to the degree consist of a representative mix both of liberal arts and journalism courses; that journalism courses where writing was emphasized be taught by someone competent to critique the quality of writing; that students have the opportunity of preparing their work in a professional environment and of submitting that work for publication; that the journalism unit have a sufficient number of instructors for optimum instruction; that journalism instructors conduct research and contribute to the literature of their field; that sufficient journalism laboratory and library facilities be available to students; and that "standards of admission to and graduation from the department, course, or school of journalism shall be sufficiently high to prevent students lacking in knowledge, ability, and proficiency from obtaining a degree in journalism."[53]

The LSU journalism program was justly proud of achieving the AASDJ's Class A rating. It was a mark of distinction that the University touted when promoting its Department and later its new School of Journalism.[54] And it was emblematic of a point of arrival within the academic community that no doubt would persuade even more students to study journalism at LSU.

No less important was the position that LSU's Class A rating gave the Department of Journalism when compared with other southeastern colleges and universities. When awarded the Class A rating no other southeastern institution shared that distinction. Indeed, the University of Texas was the only southern university at all to have earned the Class A rating.[55] A 1927 study of the status of journalism education in the Southeast found that those universities in the region whose journalism programs were of high enough quality to put them within reach of the Class A rating included North Carolina, Kentucky, Mercer, Washington and Lee, South Carolina, Florida, Georgia, and Wesleyan College. And of that group, the University of Georgia appeared to have the best chance of achieving Class A status anytime soon.[56]

Membership in the AASDJ and AATJ, especially with Marvin Osborn's leadership role in the latter, allowed LSU the privilege of hosting the combined conventions of the two groups from December 30, 1929, through January 1, 1930. It marked the first time that the two groups had met in the South. The roughly sixty college journalism teachers and administrators from around the country who were present in Baton Rouge for the three-day meeting reportedly set an attendance record. Some of the most notable names of the day in journalism education—Frank Luther Mott, Willard G. Bleyer, and Ralph D. Casey, for example—were there. Hugh Blain, now carrying the title "public relations counselor," also attended as one of the program speakers, addressing the issue of "Public Utilities and the Press." Speaking events were spread between the old and new LSU campuses. Most events on the old campus were scheduled for Alumni Hall.[57] This quite possibly was the first time that the LSU Journalism Department met on a formal occasion in a building destined to play such an important role in the School's future.

A few months following the AASDJ/AATJ convention in April 1930, the Department of Journalism was admitted to membership in yet another organization, the Southwestern Journalism Congress (SJC). LSU joined with Tulane, the University of Arkansas, and the University of Oklahoma, as the first universities outside the state of Texas to be admitted to this important regional group.[58] One more climb up the leadership ladder for Marvin Osborn occurred in 1935 with his election to serve as SJC president.[59]

Student organizations and happenings related to extracurricular matters also were part of the journalism program during the 1920s. One of these pertained to organizing a women's journalism sorority. The Sigma Delta Chi fraternity that already existed was, for all intents and purposes, a male-dominated organization. The women student journalists in 1919 had formed their own local sorority known as Theta Sigma Sigma.[60] National sorority Theta Sigma Phi granted LSU a charter to establish the Alpha Kappa chapter on campus in May 1927.[61] Installation of the local chapter occurred the following fall with the induction of fourteen female journalism students. Officers elected for the sorority's first year at LSU were Margaret Richardson, president; Estelle Tannehill, vice-president; Helen Gilkison, secretary; Lucy Mercer, treasurer; and Mary Webb, keeper of the archives.[62]

A somewhat different kind of journalism fraternity, this one recognizing high academic achievement and open to junior and senior men and women alike, arrived at LSU in 1931. Kappa Tau Alpha, in fact, was very early in the process of organizing nationally, and the LSU School of Journalism, as it happened, was among seventeen other journalism programs nationwide that would be counted as a Kappa Tau Alpha charter member. Those at LSU who were among the first to be initiated in the new campus chapter were seniors Bessie Hackett, Evelyn Lopoo, and H. G. Spencer, and juniors Ed Kalshoven and Carol Lefkovits.[63]

The Reveille matured right alongside the Journalism Department and in doing so, the paper underwent several minor changes during the 1920s. In 1925, it became the first college newspaper to publish semi-weekly editions. That lasted only a year before financial problems presumably forced *The Reveille*'s return to weekly status in 1926. Not until 1934 would the paper once more become a semi-weekly publication.[64]

Marvin Osborn assumed Hugh Blain's role as *Reveille* (and *Gumbo*) faculty adviser when he joined the faculty. He remained in his advisory position for both publications until 1941.[65] As adviser, Osborn had little authority to intervene in *Reveille* content matters, even those that could be problematical. He could advise, but he could not censor.

The Reveille's maturity was showing in other ways. For one, the barrier that Elmore Lawrence had broken when she became the paper's first female editor in 1920 had opened the floodgates for women. In the next ten years, nine more women would serve as *Reveille* editors, either during the academic year, the summer, or both. The list of women editors in addition to Lawrence included Ruth Harris, Beverly Latham, Marguerite Young, Margaret Richardson, Lillian Jacobs, Helen Gilkison, Georgia Wilson, Margaret Stephenson, and Bessie Hackett.[66]

The feminine touch at *The Reveille* came from positions other than the editor's chair. Beginning in 1924, members of Theta Sigma Sigma assumed *Reveille* publication responsibility for one entire issue.[67] The gesture probably was meant to allow women greater latitude with LSU student media. But in view of their editorial strength at the newspaper, it was obvious that women required no special treatment. They were doing just fine, and LSU enrollment figures showed that women were turning more and more to preparation for careers in journalism. According to comments by Marvin Osborn in a 1926 letter, "For a number of years women students have constituted from one-third to nearly one-half the total enrollment of journalism students in the department. For the current session [1926–1927] women students number 43 in a total enrollment of 107."[68]

Off-campus activities for LSU journalism students—gathering and reporting news for the Baton Rouge newspapers and annually touring the New Orleans newspaper facilities, for example—expanded in the late 1920s to include field trips to weekly newspaper plants in nearby towns. These trips were arranged especially for students enrolled in the "Country [later, Community] Newspaper" course. Students had a chance not only to see how small-town weekly newspapers worked, but in some cases they also actually gathered and edited news for these papers.[69]

The country newspaper was near and dear to Marvin Osborn. He said as much in a letter written to Conrad Lecoq, secretary of the Louisiana Press Association, in 1921. "Having been reared in the country," said Osborn, "I have a very clear conception of what the weekly paper means to the average country home, and my early convictions as to the value of the weekly to its community have been strongly confirmed since I have become intimately associated with the subject of journalism."[70]

Visiting country newspaper facilities had its rewards as well as its frustrations. For instance, Osborn arranged for his Country Newspaper class of "six wide-awake young would-be newspapermen and women" to visit the Hammond *Vindicator* in 1926.[71] Try as they might, the elements conspired against their visit. As Marvin Osborn explained in his letter of apology to *Vindicator* editor George B. Campbell, "We made a brave start yesterday [March 10, 1926] for Hammond, leaving here in the rain. However, by the time we had reached Denham Springs the down pour had reached the proportions of a cloud burst and despite storm curtains on our cars we were pretty well soaked and thoroughly chilled. So we turned around and came back."[72]

Marvin Osborn was well aware of the importance of outreach. In order for the LSU Journalism Department to have an impact and to make itself known around the state and around the country, the Department had to reach beyond the classroom and even beyond the campus. One audience in particular that Osborn was interested in reaching was that of high school students. And he decided the best way of doing that was by inviting high school journalists and journalism teachers to attend a high school newspaper conference at LSU in April 1925.[73] The idea for the conference likely had been bouncing around in Osborn's mind in response to letters from high school teachers received over the years requesting that he or someone from the Journalism Department faculty review and critique their high school newspapers.[74]

A newspaper writing competition also was planned to coincide with LSU's annual state high school rally. Newspapers entered in the contest would be judged according to a tough set of criteria, and those newspapers judged the best would receive certificates from the Department of Journalism.[75]

Two more publishing ventures connected the Department of Journalism with various LSU outreach efforts during the 1920s. The first occurred in 1920 when Marvin Osborn created the University Press Service that later would become LSU's Bureau of Public Relations. Osborn served as the organization's editor from 1920 to 1929. He also created and for a while edited the *LSU Alumni News*, whose inaugural issue appeared in February 1924.[76]

Things were happening at LSU that stretched beyond the Department of Journalism but that still impacted the Department's program. One of these was the coming of radio broadcasting—not just wireless communication as had existed previously, but actual broadcasting—to the LSU campus. Preliminary investigations for building a campus radio station began in 1923 when Physics professor D. V. Guthrie traveled to New Orleans to examine Tulane University's new station. Chances were good that LSU in time could have a similar station on the air.[77]

Sure enough, a station assigned call letters KFGC and operated by the LSU Physics Department was licensed to LSU on April 20, 1923. After nine months of construction, KFGC signed on the air on January 4, 1924. It had the distinction of being Baton Rouge's first radio station and for more than a year, the city's only station. The KFGC program schedule was confined to Friday evenings only, beginning at 8 p.m. central standard time but with special programming aired at other times. The station was assigned a frequency of 1180 (later changed to 1120 kilocycles in December 1924) and a power of 100 watts. D. V. Guthrie was named KFGC's director and H. W. Hendrix the station's operator.[78]

A musical program featuring Julia Morse, vocalist, and accompanied by Mrs. J. O. Perry, pianist, apparently was KFGC's inaugural broadcast. And even though the station operated at a very low power, its nighttime signal, judging from letters sent to LSU, stretched as far as Ohio, Illinois, and Missouri. The LSU band performed on KFGC's second night of broadcasting on January 11, 1924.[79]

By late January, KFGC was beginning to transition from more-or-less experimental broadcasts, arranged to test the station's efficiency, to regular broadcasts. The signal continued strong with reported listeners as far away as New York. Musical programs remained the primary program form aired on KFGC, although a debate between LSU and the University of Alabama was scheduled for the evening of February 8, 1924.[80]

One of the most memorable (and by far, most unique) KFGC broadcasts occurred on Thanksgiving day, 1924. The traditional LSU-Tulane football game was scheduled for what is now Tiger Stadium. This would be the first game played in the new stadium on the new campus, and D. V. Guthrie wanted to broadcast it. Problem was, no facilities existed at that time to air the game directly from the stadium. So, former football player Sterling "Buck" Gladden was recruited to phone play-by-play results from the field to the KFGC studio where Guthrie then relayed the information to station listeners.[81]

All was well with KFGC until time came following its final program in spring 1925 to dismantle the station for its move from the old campus to the Physics Building on the new campus. By then, many more high-powered stations had begun broadcasting, and KFGC's audience had dwindled significantly. Commercial radio stations could provide big-name entertainers and splashy shows that LSU simply could not match. So when the station apparatus arrived in its new location, Dr. Guthrie and his Physics Department colleagues saw little use in rebuilding KFGC. The final blow to chances that the station might resume operation came in January 1926, when the federal government refused to grant KFGC a broadcast license renewal due to management's inability to guarantee that the station could air at least one program per week on a regular basis.[82] Baton Rouge was without a radio station but not for long. LSU, on the other hand would have to wait for many years before the University once more would have its own station.

President Thomas Boyd, in his twenty-eighth year as LSU President, tendered his resignation to Governor John Parker, effective at the end of the 1924 spring semester. Boyd reportedly had spoken with the governor on several occasions about his desire to retire, but Governor Parker had talked him out of it each time.⁸³ Now the public announcement of Boyd's intentions seemed to make the decision more definite. But LSU alumni and members of the LSU Board of Supervisors joined in concert to plead with President Boyd to withdraw his resignation, at least until the University's move to its new campus was complete. Boyd agreed to their requests.⁸⁴

After two more years at the helm President Boyd once more submitted his resignation to the LSU Board of Supervisors in June 1926. This time it was irrevocable. Boyd asked to be relieved of his duties on August 1, 1926, exactly thirty years to the day since he had been named as LSU's President. The Board reluctantly accepted the resignation.

Thomas Boyd was named President Emeritus upon his retirement and continued to occupy his office in Alumni Hall on the old campus. He and his ailing wife also continued living in the only home they had known in Baton Rouge, on the corner of the old campus. Mrs. Boyd died in March 1931, and later that year construction of the new Louisiana State Capitol required that Thomas Boyd vacate his old home and move to a new house nearby. On November 2, 1932, Boyd himself passed away. His funeral service was an impressive one, attended by an honor guard of LSU cadets. The service ended with taps played by Frank T. Guilbeau, said to be LSU's first bugler.⁸⁵ Thomas Boyd's death marked the first time in LSU's history when a Boyd was not actively engaged—usually at the highest level—in University affairs.⁸⁶

A remarkable chapter in LSU history ended with Thomas Boyd's death, and a new phase began with the selection of President Boyd's successor. The person chosen would have to have administrative experience at the college level, be physically up to the task, and be able to deal with the kind of politics unique to Louisiana. A Board of Supervisors Selection Committee named Colonel Campbell B. Hodges as its choice. Hodges at the time was Commandant of Cadets at the U.S. Military Academy at West Point. He was interested in the LSU position but unwilling to leave his post at West Point immediately, since he needed only two more years to reach military retirement eligibility. The Board of Supervisors agreed to wait and in Hodges's place appointed Thomas W. Atkinson, Dean of the College of Engineering, as LSU Acting President in June 1927.⁸⁷

Another kind of life-changing event for many Louisianans of the 1920s resulted not from man-made forces but rather from the forces of nature. Rain that had begun falling throughout the Mississippi River Valley in August 1926 seemed never ending.⁸⁸ All through the winter tributaries continued to dump water into a dangerously rising Mississippi River. By spring 1927, the River began to overflow its banks and to break through its levees. The result was the "Great Mississippi River Flood of 1927."[89] The flood was described as "the greatest natural disaster the country had ever suffered, leaving nearly a million Americans homeless—with approximately two hundred thousand of them in Louisiana."[90] Much of eastern Louisiana, as far west as Monroe down through the Atchafalaya River Basin and east to St. Bernard and Plaquemines Parishes below New Orleans, was under water.[91] In fact, it was said that the Mississippi River "had grown to more than a hundred miles wide" in some places and that travel by boat was possible from Monroe to well past Vicksburg, to the east.[92]

Baton Rouge and LSU remained protected by levees, although LSU cadets were on the alert to move to any part of the levee within reach to assist with any breaks or potential breaks.[93] Rooms in the vacated Pentagon Barracks on the old campus also were prepared to shelter flood refugees if necessary.[94] LSU students from various campus organizations assisted the Red Cross and other relief agencies in numerous ways—"collecting magazines, mending clothes and making bandages" for flood victims. Sorority members were collecting and distributing toys and looking after children in makeshift play areas. Students from the Home Economics Department were busy making all kinds of garments for babies and adults as well.[95] All in all, it was a massive humanitarian relief effort to care for the many flood victims who sought help and shelter at LSU. The University's students, faculty, and staff once more would lend themselves to a similar relief effort some eighty years later in the aftermath of Hurricane Katrina.

College students often are not as aware of events happening off-campus as are nonstudents. To a degree, students remain isolated (often by their own design) from events of the world, the nation, or just outside their campus gates. The Great Mississippi River Flood of 1927 focused the attention of LSU students probably like nothing since the Civil War. Things might have been returning to normal as the flood waters receded had it not been for another force—this time, not of nature, but rather of politics and personality—that had arrived in the state. That force was Huey Long, elected Governor of Louisiana in 1928. As the next chapter shows, Governor Long would place an indelible stamp on LSU in the early 1930s that would remain in place for decades.

8

The J-School Settles In

The LSU Department of Journalism made its transition to School of Journalism in 1931 and entered a period of settling in. The academic program that had been so carefully crafted during the 1920s now was ready for fine-tuning by a School of Journalism faculty that itself was comfortably in place and at home. Personnel changes would be made, of course, but students were able to rely on a kind of continuity developing among both faculty and curriculum.

As evidence of the student isolation mentioned in chapter 7, the economic depression that engulfed most of the world during the 1930s and the darkening threats of war that accompanied the decade's end seemed to have little visible effect at LSU—if front-page stories appearing in *The Reveille* were good reflections of student attitudes. Nonetheless, LSU students, faculty, and administrators could not help but be drawn into a political morality play during the 1930s whose stage ranged back and forth between Louisiana and Washington, D.C.

Huey Long had been Governor of Louisiana for two years when the 1930s began. Love him or hate him—and for most Louisianans there seemed to be one or the other and absolutely nothing in between—Long caused a stir. He was a dominating and, according to contemporary accounts, a domineering person, and one thing he was determined to dominate was LSU. He treated the University as his own, and in doing so, Huey Long built LSU into an academic place of distinction. A depression may have gripped the rest of the country, but LSU was doing just fine, thank you!

LSU President James Monroe Smith, who had succeeded Thomas Atkinson in 1930 when Atkinson was forced to retire due to health problems,[1] performed one of his first official acts when he elevated three departments—journalism, music, and geology—to school status. Their elevation, according to Smith, "was based on the national recognition which they have achieved, the standing of their respective faculties, and the character of the work which they are doing as evidenced in the outstanding success which a large number of their graduates have achieved."[2]

The Department certainly had met these standards and bore the Class A ranking of its fellows as proof. But while the designation as *School* instead of *Department* would seem to have moved journalism education at LSU into some new administrative realm, it actually did nothing of the sort. Prestige may have been the only benefit to come from the new School of Journalism's nominal change. For the School was still a unit within the College of Arts and Sciences, just as it had been from the beginning. That kind of attachment held major disadvantages for LSU's journalism program. And so, among all else happening at the School of Journalism beginning in the 1930s, separation from Arts and Sciences and subsequent designation as an autonomous unit (e.g., an independent college, equal to but not part of another college), ascended quickly to the topmost position on the School's priority list. Such autonomy indeed would be in the School's future, but even at this early stage, plans were in the works to pursue that objective.

The School of Journalism faculty grew both in numbers and in quality during the 1930s. The faculty also began to take on the characteristics that would come to identify it from that point forward. That is, the core of the faculty—call it the "Old Regulars"—would be firmly in place for years. One or two of the Old Regulars occasionally would leave (or pass away) and one or two new faculty eventually might join the ranks of the Old Regulars if they were around long enough. But persons also would join the faculty, stay there for only a year or two, and then move on. Such are the ways of an academic family.

The Old Regulars of Osborn, Arbour, Wilkerson, and Ogden (from the *Morning Advocate* and *State-Times*), who were in place as the 1930s began, proved to be remarkably well entrenched throughout the 1930s. Marjorie Arbour was the single defection, leaving the faculty in 1939 to become LSU's first female agricultural extension editor.[3] Arbour later would distinguish herself and LSU in 1950 when she became the first woman elected to serve as president of the American Association of Agricultural College Editors.[4] At the *Morning Advocate/State-Times*, Maggie Dixon assumed Ida Ogden's duties in 1938 as the paper's advisor to LSU students working there.[5]

Joining the School of Journalism faculty as the 1930s progressed were four more persons whose longevity at the School eventually accorded them "Old Regular" status. Among the newcomers were C. R. F. Smith in 1932,[6] Ernest

Gueymard in 1934,[7] Richard Wiggins in 1935,[8] and Bruce McCoy in 1936. McCoy actually was hired to perform double duty as a member of the teaching staff as well as field manager for the Louisiana Press Association.[9]

Two other persons of note who joined the School of Journalism faculty during the 1930s included Thomas ("T. C.") Shields in 1938[10] and Siegfried ("Sig") Mickelson in 1939.[11] Shields shared something in common with three other School of Journalism faculty members that placed him in unique company. He, Marcus Wilkerson, and Richard Wiggins all had served as *Reveille* editors during their student days at LSU.[12] Mickelson arrived at the University fresh from graduate school at the University of Minnesota. He actually was only temporarily at LSU, taking over duties for C. R. F. Smith, who was on a one-year sabbatical leave.[13] Mickelson left LSU after his short stay only to return several years later (from 1991 to 1993) as a distinguished professor, following his long career with the Columbia Broadcasting System (CBS), where he rose through the ranks to become the first president of CBS News.[14]

On December 30, 1938, Hugh Blain passed away. Although he spent most of his life engaged in a variety of careers, it was in journalism education where he probably would be most remembered. Hugh Blain was credited not only with starting the journalism program at LSU but with starting journalism programs at both Tulane and Loyola universities as well.[15]

The School of Journalism curriculum changed in various ways during the 1930s, according to *LSU General Catalogs* of the period. Course additions and deletions reflected either developing journalism trends or styles that had lost their relevancy during the decade. For example, the popularity of radio news by the mid-1930s and what likely was student interest in the subject led to implementation of a "Radio Survey" course during the 1935–1936 academic year. The "Radio News Processing" course that later replaced "Radio Survey" was specifically designed for instruction in radio news preparation and presentation.[16]

Although the genesis of "Radio News Processing" is unknown, it might well have been that School of Journalism faculty added the course in response to what the LSU Speech Department was doing. In 1934, members of that department had added two "Elementary Radio Technique" courses to their curriculum in order to introduce students to the broadcasting industry in general and specifically, to teach students radio performance skills. The second course in particular concentrated on "dramatic composition and presentation."[17] By designing courses that focused on radio news, the School of Journalism was able to lay claim to a portion of classroom instruction in broadcast technique that was most appropriate for a journalism education curriculum.

In years to come this dichotomy of purpose would grow as the Speech Department developed more courses in broadcast (radio and television) production and performance, and the School of Journalism extended its curriculum in broadcast news. The rationale of both the Department of Speech and the School of Journalism going their separate ways began to erode in later years. Broadcast course content in the two units began to overlap and, more important, parceling out expensive broadcast production equipment to one unit or the other eventually proved unworkable, wasteful, and illogical. By the 1980s, instruction in all phases of broadcasting (or electronic media, as it came to be called) came under the expanding curriculum umbrella of the School of Journalism.

The School of Journalism took a major step with its curriculum during the 1930–1931 academic year by adding its first graduate-only course, "Special Problems in Journalism."[18] Graduate students already were free to earn graduate credit for completing undergraduate courses in a program that is examined in greater detail later in this chapter. With the arrival of "Special Problems in Journalism," graduate students could for the first time enroll in a School of Journalism course designed especially for them. The "Special Problems" course allowed instructors to explore journalism-related topics in more depth than was possible in other, more narrowly defined courses.[19]

Two more graduate-only courses, "Public Opinion" and "American Journalists," were added to the curriculum during the 1931–1932 academic year. The "Public Opinion" course was a seminar in which students examined the role played by the press in forming and affecting opinion. "American Journalists" was essentially a reading course where students were assigned to read books and articles about the careers and professional contributions of prominent journalists.[20]

A study of curriculum trends among AASDJ member colleges and universities in 1937 showed that the LSU School of Journalism was very much in the curriculum mainstream of its sister programs. The study's author, Norval Luxon, took all courses offered by AASDJ programs—numbering thirty-two by 1937—and grouped them into twenty broad subject categories. LSU's curriculum contained courses that covered all but three of the categories. Interestingly, of the four other southern universities that now were AASDJ members (Georgia, Kentucky, Texas, and Washington and Lee), LSU led the pack in the variety of journalism courses offered. The LSU School of Journalism also compared favorably with other AASDJ programs with respect to additional elements of its academic program, such as number of journalism courses offered, number of hours required to complete a degree in journalism, and number of faculty members.[21]

School of Journalism students continued the spring semester tradition of editing an issue of the Baton Rouge *State-Times* and *Morning Advocate* during the 1930s.[22] The tradition that Marvin Osborn began of arranging for students enrolled in his "Community Newspaper" course to visit local newspapers also continued into the 1930s. In 1934 C. R. F. Smith, as part of his junior-level "Newspaper Publishing" course, actually arranged for several of his students to travel throughout Louisiana, spending an entire week at various places editing community newspapers. Essentially, Smith was taking the concept that had proven so successful at the *State-Times* and *Morning Advocate* into the field. From four to five teams of roughly five students each were chosen to travel at various intervals during the spring to publish either weekly or daily editions of local newspapers. Students were in complete charge of gathering and editing the news, writing the editorials, and selling and preparing advertising for their particular newspapers. All work was under careful faculty supervision.

Evidence of just how successful this field trip project came to be after only its first year appeared in a letter received by Marvin Osborn from J. P. Wade, editor-publisher of the *Jena Times*. "If any of the North Louisiana weeklies are to be considered by the Louisiana State University students this year when the time comes to go out and publish them," Wade asked, "we would like very much to have the Jena Times and the Olla Signal included."[23] The School of Journalism did make its stop in Jena but not until April 1937. Dozens of other Louisiana communities were treated to a student visit to get out the local newspaper during the 1930s. Stops included Bunkie, Eunice, Rayville, Winnsboro, Oak Grove, Minden, Tullulah, Houma, and many others.[24] By the end of the decade, LSU Journalism School student teams had guest-edited forty-four country newspapers.[25]

The country newspaper editing project was new to the South and quick to catch the attention of other universities. The project also achieved what may have been its most practical goal from the students' perspective. Publishers for whom the students had worked began to employ a number of them following graduation.[26]

Another student project was also connected closely with the country press. In 1930, Marvin Osborn began assigning seniors in his "History of American

Journalism" course to write the history of a Louisiana newspaper—one newspaper per student. Students fanned out across the state, usually during their Christmas holiday break, to research library and newspaper files and court house records and to interview publishers, editors, reporters, and local residents. By the time the project came to its completion in 1938, some 140 newspaper histories had been written as term papers.[27] Besides learning invaluable research skills, the students who wrote these histories compiled a remarkable story of newspaper development in Louisiana. Unfortunately, none of the histories seem to have survived. However, this work became the basis for three master's degree theses written in 1939 and 1940, that traced the development of the Louisiana country press from its beginning in 1794 to 1940.[28]

Students were active in an assortment of journalism-related extracurricular activities during the 1930s. The major female journalism sorority, Theta Sigma Phi, was active enough that members in 1934 decided to form a local branch of the sorority that would admit only freshmen women. Membership was based on scholarship and interest in journalism as a career.[29] The men's Sigma Delta Chi counterpart to the women's sorority somehow fell on hard times after its promising beginning in the 1920s. The fraternity's local Chi Sigma chapter indeed became inactive enough that it had to petition the Sigma Delta Chi national office in 1933 for reinstatement. The petition was approved, and the new LSU chapter was installed on May 1, 1937.[30]

Formation of groups or communities of like-minded students, regardless of whether their connections were scholastic or purely social, was exactly what should have been happening in a professional school. Likewise, the School of Journalism faculty as a corporate body as well as individually was meeting its obligations by offering leadership and expertise to the academic community as well as the professional community. Bruce McCoy, for instance, edited the LPA's *Pelican Press Messenger*, and he and C. R. F. Smith jointly founded *Folks*, a "nationally circulated publication for newspaper correspondents," which Smith then edited. McCoy also propelled his prominence as LPA Field Manager into the presidency of the National Newspaper Association Managers in 1938. And he became director of the National Editorial Association that same year.[31]

Bruce McCoy provided an extremely important link between the Journalism School and professional journalists. His employment in 1936 had been part of a joint arrangement between the School and the LPA to bring to Louisiana an LPA Field Manager, "whose duties it will be," as stated by Marvin Osborn, "to serve the newspapers (particularly the weekly papers) of the State and also to do some teaching in the School of Journalism."³² McCoy's new position as a kind of school-to-professional community liaison helped the LSU Journalism School by having a representative traveling about the state, meeting with editors and publishers, and carrying news of the School throughout Louisiana via the LPA's *Pelican Press Messenger*. The other side of the liaison, though, was equally important. Bruce McCoy was a well-connected professional journalist who could impart the most current thinking and practices of the newspaper industry to LSU journalism students.³³

Aside from the person serving as field manager, the position itself was indicative of the LSU School of Journalism's leadership role in journalism education. The School was among the first in the nation to have such an arrangement with its state press association. Twelve more universities would follow LSU's example by 1938.³⁴

Bruce McCoy's position also was indicative of the School of Journalism's prominence among LPA members. The organization gave full credit to Marvin Osborn for helping its reactivation in 1928 following LPA's "hibernation of more than a decade."³⁵ The LPA had met last in 1917 and had remained dormant during most of the 1920s. Intentions of reactivating the organization in 1921 failed to materialize. A North Louisiana Press Association had organized in 1926, and a South Louisiana Press Association had organized in 1927. Both groups had met separately until reuniting in 1928. The new LPA formed a strong bond with LSU from that point. Within the year a "newspaper clinic" was created whereby LPA members would submit copies of their respective newspapers to the LSU School of Journalism for critiquing. The best papers received a blue ribbon at the following annual LPA meeting. And as a show of LSU's influence, the proposal to create the field manager's position that Marvin Osborn brought before the LPA in 1936 was put before the group as a resolution and approved by a 48-to-4 vote.³⁶

Besides securing the field manager position, one of the most important LPA-LSU School of Journalism associations came in what was intended to be an annual Editors' Short Course begun in 1937. Participants in the Short Course gathered for a workshop/troubleshooting session on November 12–13 that, in Marvin Osborn's words, was intended "to give the School of Journalism an opportunity to reciprocate in some measure for the many benefits" received by LSU student and faculty alike from "the editors of the State."³⁷ An article in the *Louisiana Leader* described the event this way: "Inauguration of the . . . Short Course is not made with the intention of giving Louisiana's publishers a complete course in journalism in two days. Most of the instruction will be give-and-take, with publishers contributing perhaps as much as they receive."[38]

The LSU School of Journalism gave unofficial birth to the LSU Press in 1935. The early press developed as an offshoot of the School of Journalism and was very different from the LSU Press that later would evolve into one of America's most successful university presses. Originally, the LSU Press served as a kind of business clearing house for all university publications such as catalogs, bulletins, pamphlets, and so on. Marcus Wilkerson was picked to serve as acting head of the LSU Press.[39] Within a few years, Wilkerson had advanced to the position of LSU Press Director, and the Press itself had expanded into a publishing role that moved it more in line with its present function.

One of the first notable books to come from the LSU Press was Marcus Wilkerson's own *Thomas Duckett Boyd: The Story of a Southern Educator*, published in 1935. Other authors whose books would carry the LSU Press imprint during Wilkerson's tenure there included C. Vann Woodward, Caroline Durieux, Robert M. Hutchins, Hodding Carter, and Kenneth Burke. Marcus Wilkerson continued as LSU Press Director until his death in 1953.[40]

LSU Journalism School enrollment climbed steadily during the early 1930s as more and more students pursued a career in some phase of journalism. From 70 majors during the 1930–1931 academic year, the enrollment jumped to 121 the next year and to 155 by the 1932–1933 academic year.[41] The School of Journalism enrollment increase corresponded with overall LSU growth during the same period. But whereas LSU total campus enrollment continued to climb throughout the remainder of the 1930s,[42] the number of journalism majors dropped to 92 during the 1933–1934 academic year. From that point to the end of the 1930s, School of Journalism enrollment fluctuated yearly from a low of 101 (1936–1937) to a high of 127 (1937–1938).[43] Reasons for the fluctuations may be attributed to the uncertain circumstances—economically, politically, and administratively—that affected LSU students during the period. Regardless of the enrollment ups and downs, a higher number of journalism majors at the end of the 1930s than at the beginning was a positive sign that LSU's journalism program was growing.

Growth created a need for more room. The School of Journalism was facing a space shortage during the early 1930s that was affecting the entire campus. Indeed, comparing campus maps from *LSU General Catalogs* of the early 1930s with those of the later 1930s shows how many buildings were constructed at LSU to accommodate the need for more classroom and faculty office space.

As a result, the decade was characterized by department displacement as units were moved from one building to another in order to acquire the extra space that everyone coveted.

The Journalism School was caught up in the campuswide musical chairs. At some point prior to 1937, the School was moved from Stubbs Hall, where it had been since arriving on the new campus, to the west basement of Allen Hall,[44] one of the buildings constructed during the 1930s. Exactly when the Journalism School moved there is uncertain. What *is* certain, though, is that the School's faculty and staff were packing up for another move in January 1938.[45]

The new home of the LSU Journalism School was the North Administration Building, previously occupied by the LSU Law School but vacated when the Law School moved into the recently completed Leche Hall. Both academic units gained much needed additional space.[46] Precise location of the new journalism complex, circa 1938, is today's Thomas Boyd Administration Building where the Office of Academic Affairs is now housed.

The two-story building allowed placement of the Journalism School office, three faculty offices (including the director's), library and reading room, darkrooms for the photography classes, copyediting and newsroom, typewriting room, typography and advertising laboratory, and one large classroom on the second floor. The first floor was occupied by one additional faculty office and classroom but with most of the space devoted to *The Reveille* staff—editor, sports editor, editorial staff, and advertising staff—along with the newspaper's photoengraving and printing facilities.[47]

Marvin Osborn saw the close proximity of the teaching facilities with the *Reveille's* production facilities as a major advantage. From a pedagogical perspective, the first floor location of the photoengraving and printing plants made it possible to provide "students instruction in all branches of newspaper-making, from a practical as well as from a theoretical viewpoint," according to Osborn.[48] The practical perspective that Osborn alluded to was the ease with which "last minute news can be inserted and last minute corrections made."[49]

The School of Journalism's occupancy of its new home was a satisfying accomplishment. Marvin Osborn noted in his Annual Report for 1939–1940 that the improved arrangement and additional space "gave a decided impetus to [the School's] activities. Close contact between instructors and students, made possible by contiguous office, classrooms, and laboratories, has had a wholesome and stimulating effect."[50] But conditions were by no means perfect, and Osborn took full advantage of his Annual Report to caution LSU administrators that the Journalism School really needed to be continually updating, upgrading, progressing, and, above all, expanding. It was especially in regard to the expansion need that Osborn made a strong plea for a "building more adequately adapted to the requirements of instruction in newspaper making."[51]

Looking ahead or planning for tomorrow was not confined just to space and equipment needs. The media industry itself was changing rapidly during the 1930s, and the LSU School of Journalism could not avoid preparing itself for the changes. The new medium of radio was growing rapidly, and there was every chance that it soon would incorporate news into the medium's programming schedule.

The extent of radio's growth during the 1930s is remarkable, and broadcast historians refer to the period as radio's "golden age."[52] The number of U.S. radio stations grew from 618 in 1930 to 765 in 1940. A majority of these stations (59 percent) also was affiliated with a national radio network by 1940.[53] But the most impressive numbers associated with radio's growth during its golden age were reflected in the growth of U.S. households with radio sets. In 1925, approximately 10 percent of U.S. households owned radio receivers. That percentage rose to nearly 46 percent in 1930, 67 percent in 1935, and 81 percent in 1940.[54]

Entertainment programming was radio's big draw, but newscasts were becoming commonplace by the mid-1930s. Actually, some of the earliest radio programs had been coverage of news events. Radio networks were quick to realize the powerful attraction of news, much of which came from the same newswire services that newspapers relied on. When newspaper publishers objected to what they perceived as competition from this new electronic medium and attempted to limit network reporting of newswire stories, the networks reacted by forming their own newsgathering departments. Thus the newspaper industry unwittingly fueled the emergence of its major competitor. And as the country moved closer and closer to war during the 1940s, the influence of radio news grew accordingly.[55]

Radio at LSU had been treated as a novelty during the 1920s. Listeners were entertained and slightly informed by programs they heard on the University's short-lived KFGC. But once the station left the air, its limited range of programming apparently was not missed. Radio's role began to change during the 1930s when the medium's popularity and importance became so apparent. The need for LSU to re-enter the radio field, and this time to treat radio more seriously, was obvious. Here was a medium around which a burgeoning industry was developing. Trained personnel were needed to produce programming as well as attend to the industry's new business and advertising needs.

The LSU Physics Department once more took the lead in moving LSU into radio. All would be done, though, without LSU actually operating an on-air broadcasting station. The arrangement that brought broadcasting to the campus (or, more precisely, that *took* the campus to broadcasting) was unusual, but it worked. And, as noted above, it was the LSU Speech Department that first understood the potential in utilizing LSU radio as a teaching laboratory. The School of Journalism was not far behind, though. Journalism School faculty members soon developed the courses described above that would train journalism students to produce and report radio news.

The arrangement that made campus broadcasting possible at LSU came via Baton Rouge radio station WJBO. WJBO was a property of the Baton Rouge Broadcasting Company, which was owned by the Manship family and administered by Charles P. Manship, Jr.[56] The station, completely independent of LSU, nonetheless had constructed a remote broadcasting facility in the Music and Dramatic Arts (M and DA) Building on campus. What's more, installation of microphone outlets and soundproofing in M and DA practice rooms, studios, and performance areas made the entire building a virtual radio studio. WJBO actually could pick up by remote telephone line transmission any programming originating in M and DA and broadcast it to station listeners from its downtown location.[57]

WJBO was exceptionally accommodating in clearing space in its broadcast schedule for LSU. After all, as noted above, radio programming in these days was live, and where better was WJBO to find a reliable pool of talent than just down the road at LSU? The absence of a campus radio station was a boon to WJBO. Likewise, the availability of WJBO to LSU relieved the University of having to operate its own radio station.

With everything in place, the first WJBO/LSU program aired on Monday, February 15, 1937. The program was a fifteen-minute newscast presented, ironically, not by anyone from the School of Journalism but rather by Walter Madden of the Speech Department as part of Professor Harley Smith's radio technique course.[58] The newscast soon became a regular feature called "Reveille of the Air." And before long Walter Madden and fellow speech student Ralph Steetle had formed a campus radio news service, providing LSU campus news to other radio stations around Louisiana.[59]

By the following fall (1937), Harley Smith had assumed the position as LSU's director of radio activity and had organized an extensive schedule of campus radio programs. Actual preparation and production of the programs would provide laboratory training for Smith's students, but program content, which included lectures, interviews, and dramatizations, were meant as educational fare for adults and high school–age listeners.[60]

Where were LSU journalism students during all of this campus radio activity? The School of Journalism was a bit slow to catch up with the Speech Department. The journalism faculty actually had created the "Radio Survey" course, first offered during fall 1936, but only as a lecture course.[61] Finally, in fall 1938, C. R. F. Smith taught for the first time the School of Journalism's new "Radio News Processing" course whose laboratory component would allow students to learn practical radio news production techniques.[62] Smith likely learned as much as he taught, since the "art and science" of radio news gathering, processing, and delivery were so new there probably was no textbook for his course. Listening to the newly emerging network newscasts actually was one of the few things that an instructor could do to understand anything about technique and protocol. Everything learned would have to be organized in some fashion and then transformed into a classroom lecture or laboratory demonstration. The whole effort was classic flying by the seat of your pants!

When fall 1938 arrived, Ralph Steetle, who now was LSU's general program director of radio, had placed production responsibility for a news program called "Campus Comment" in C. R. F. Smith's control. The program, scheduled for Monday evenings, combined two other programs from the previous year, "March of Education" and "Reveille on the Air." It was produced entirely by students from Smith's "Radio News Processing" course.[63] At last, LSU journalism students were on the air.

A weekly fifteen-minute LSU campus newscast, aired on WJBO on Monday evening (later, on Thursday evening) and sponsored by *The Daily Reveille* and Sigma Delta Chi, became a regular feature in November 1939. The fifteen-minute program was produced and delivered by students enrolled in the "Radio News Processing" course then being taught by Sig Mickelson.[64] His students did not realize at the time that they were learning the radio news business from someone who shortly would be considered an authority on the subject.

The LSU School of Journalism had nudged into radio; still, the School's orientation remained focused on the print media, particularly newspapers. *The Reveille,* much more so than LSU's WJBO-connected programming, attracted the most student attention. And for good reason. *The Reveille,* during the 1930s, made almost as much news as it reported.

Some of that self-generated news resulted from changes that accompanied the newspaper's move along with the School of Journalism to new quarters in the vacated law school building. As noted above, the move began in fall 1937 to completely relocate *The Reveille* to the first floor of the new Journalism Building. *The Reveille*'s new printing plant—a "flat-bed printing press, two type-setting machines, and other necessary machinery"—was installed in the space formerly occupied by the Law School library. The new press was said to be "large enough to print 16 Reveille-size pages at once, at the rate of 3,500 an hour."[65]

Such volume was necessary because *The Reveille*, having appeared as a semi-weekly beginning in 1934, became a daily on February 3, 1938.[66] *The Daily Reveille* joined the exclusive ranks of only two other college dailies in the South, the *Daily Tarheel* at the University of North Carolina and the *Daily Texan* at the University of Texas.[67] The five-day edition, tabloid size *Daily Reveille* was said now to be "a newspaper in every sense of the word. Its typography was modern and attractive. Its news coverage was complete and impartial. Sports, features, and society news were receiving the same careful attention as news and editorial columns. Its photographic coverage was extensive."[68]

All of this was a positive sign for *The Daily Reveille*'s future. It also was a good indication that the newspaper had recovered from one of its most notorious and perhaps darkest moments. That occurred in 1934 when several members of *The Reveille* staff—later known as the "Reveille Seven"—clashed with U.S. Senator Huey Long. Events surrounding the confrontation began as a prank, spiraled into a First Amendment standoff, and ended (or so it appeared) with the dismissal from LSU of several first-rate journalism students—the Reveille Seven. Depending on one's perspective, the whole episode might be regarded as a harsh example of how actions, even if principled, often result in unfortunate consequences.

Much has been written about Huey Long—his colorful personality, his style of governing, his controversial social programs, and more.[69] He was elected Louisiana governor in 1928 and then elected to the U.S. Senate in 1932.[70] Among the many state offices, facilities, and operations that he oversaw as governor, LSU was one institution in which he held a special interest. He eventually identified himself so closely with LSU that, according to biographer William Hair, "he customarily referred to it as 'my university.'"[71]

Huey Long's interest in LSU has led to speculation about his role in hiring James Monroe Smith to succeed LSU President Thomas Atkinson following Atkinson's resignation in 1930. Smith was serving as the education dean at Southwestern Louisiana Institute (now the University of Louisiana at Lafayette) when Governor Long is said to have arranged his appointment at LSU.

Once in office, President Smith reportedly met often with Long to discuss LSU matters. Biographer T. Harry Williams regarded Huey Long's oversight of LSU business and academic affairs as minimal. Williams also said that Long refrained from interfering with what was taught in the classroom. However, there was *one* unwritten rule that was well understood by LSU faculty members, and that was a prohibition on any public criticism of Huey Long.[72] Whether this rule applied as well to any criticism coming from students was unknown. In fall 1934, students at *The Reveille* were about to find out.

The basic bits and pieces of the Reveille Seven incident have been told in several places, especially in the nearly daily press accounts of events as they unfolded.[73] The story began on November 10, 1934, when Huey Long (by then a U.S. Senator) summoned all LSU students to a mass meeting to help "elect" fellow student and football star Abe Mickal to a recently vacated seat in the Louisiana Senate. The election was not intended actually to elect Mickal who was not present and not even aware of the whole charade.[74] The matter might have ended then had it not been for a letter written to *The Reveille* by LSU student Duyanne Norman in which he called the sham election "a mockery of Constitutional government and democracy."[75] *Reveille* editor Jesse Cutrer Jr. considered the letter a legitimate statement of student opinion and decided to publish it. Had the letter appeared in *The Reveille* and had it been accepted merely as a statement of opinion, its content might not have stirred much interest. But because of a sequence of oddly coincidental events that happened next, the letter was anything but forgotten.

Much of the Reveille Seven story from that point forward comes from affidavits signed by Jesse Cutrer Jr., Cal Abraham, Carl Corbin, David McGuire, and Stanley Shlosman, all of whom were associated with *The Reveille* and who, along with colleagues Rea Godbold and Sam Montague, would come to be called the Reveille Seven.

The Norman letter was set to appear in the Friday, November 16, 1934, edition of *The Reveille*. The paper at the time was published at the Ortlieb Press, an off-campus printing plant near the state capitol building. As the edition containing Norman's letter rolled off the press during the evening of November 15, an LSU student happened to carry a copy to the senate press box in the capitol. Newspaper reporter Helen Gilkison caught a glimpse of the Norman letter and began reading it. As she read, Senator Long, who had been meeting with several state senators nearby, passed Miss Gilkison and asked what she was reading. When his attention was directed to the letter that criticized his actions he reportedly became quite angry. Among other things, Long purportedly said at the time that *Reveille* editor Jesse Cutrer had been politically motivated to print the letter. Cutrer's uncle was a state senator and a well-known Long opponent. The uncle's opinions had rubbed off on the nephew, so reasoned Long, and in his view the Norman letter was nothing more than anti-Long propaganda that should not be allowed to appear in the next day's *Reveille*. "I'll make 'em tear it out and run the damn paper over," he reportedly declared, and then he ended his tirade saying, "Let me get [President] Jim Smith on the phone."[76]

President Smith in turn phoned issue editor Grace Williamson who at the time happened to be the only *Reveille* representative present at the Ortlieb Press. Smith ordered Williamson to have the 4,000 *Reveille* copies already run destroyed and then to run new copies with the offending Norman letter deleted. She did so. *Reveille* editor Cutrer soon arrived at the Ortlieb Press office, was told by Williamson of President Smith's call, and concurred with her decision to destroy the 4,000 papers. "My reason for doing so," according to Jesse Cutrer's subsequent affidavit, "was that I reasoned with myself saying that as the letter was the personal student expression, and as the article was not my expression nor that of any of the editorial board of the *Reveille*, I felt that on President Smith's demand I would be justified in deleting it." Cutrer ended his statement saying, "At this time I did not know why President Smith asked that the letter not be run."[77] Had matters ended here, there never would have been a "Reveille Seven." But, in a sense, only phase one of the saga had concluded.

Both Jesse Cutrer and Grace Williamson were summoned to President Smith's office on Friday morning, November 16. If Cutrer by now had not learned of Senator Long's role in the destruction of the 4,000 *Reveilles*, he was about to find out in a very harsh fashion. According to Cutrer's affidavit, Smith "stated definitely that he would not do anything that would offend [Senator Long] and jeopardize the 'good of the university.'"[78] President Smith then informed Cutrer that he had appointed reporter Helen Gilkison to the School of Journalism faculty where her specific duties would be to advise *The Reveille* staff. Cutrer asked if Gilkison was being appointed as a "censor," and Smith assured him that she was not.

On Monday, November 19, Miss Gilkison was set to begin her official advisory duties and asked Jesse Cutrer to see page proofs for the next *Reveille* edition. According to yet another affidavit containing Cal Abraham's recollections, Cutrer and other members of *The Reveille* staff protested and decided to insert the following statement in the paper's November 20 edition: "This issue of The

Reveille has been approved by Miss Helen Gilkison, who . . . has been authorized to examine the contents of The Reveille before publication."[79] Gilkison objected to the insert and only after agreeing not to examine the remaining page proofs did Cutrer also agree not to include the insert.[80] The paper presumably was published without further incident.

The next morning (November 20), Jesse Cutrer, Grace Williamson, and Cal Abraham were invited to meet with Dean of Administration (roughly equivalent to today's Vice Chancellor for Academic Affairs or Provost) James F. Broussard. Broussard told the three that they had no choice but to accept "faculty supervision" (refusing to use the word *censorship*) for what was published in *The Reveille*. Abraham, Cutrer, and Williamson collectively balked at the idea of submitting to the kind of supervision that Dean Broussard was suggesting. And at that point the entire situation seemed at an impasse.[81]

The whole *Reveille* matter simmered for a few days, but on Monday, November 26, Jesse Cutrer was asked to meet with Marvin Osborn. He did so, accompanied by Cal Abraham and Carl Corbin. Osborn informed all three that President Smith, after a meeting with all of LSU's deans and directors, was emphatic about faculty supervision of *The Reveille*. Osborn was then joined by Dean Broussard and College of Arts and Sciences Dean Fred C. Frey who, according to the Cutrer affidavit, "tried to impress upon us the fact that the university is 'legally, morally, and financially responsible' for the Reveille."[82] Cutrer counter-argued that "as students pay for printing the Reveille and as the advertising pays for the salaries of the students employed, the university could not be financially responsible. . . . As for legal responsibility, we claimed that as publishers of the Reveille we were responsible."[83] Marvin Osborn and Deans Broussard and Frey suggested that Cutrer, Abraham, and Corbin present their views to President Smith, which they did, along with Grace Williamson, later in the day.

The students made their argument to Smith, but he remained adamant about his intention to restrict *Reveille* content so as not to present LSU or those upon whom the University relied in an unflattering fashion. Then President Smith presented an ultimatum: Either play by the rules that he had implemented or resign from *The Reveille*. At that point, Jesse Cutrer, Cal Abraham, and Carl Corbin resigned. They were joined, somewhat reluctantly, by Grace Williamson who resigned, according to Cal Abraham, only as a show of solidarity with her fellow *Reveille* staff members.[84] With *The Reveille* staff obviously in disarray, the Tuesday, November 27, 1934, edition of the newspaper never appeared.[85]

Yet another phase—one of the most decisive—of the Reveille Seven incident occurred at noon on November 27. Fellow journalism students, acting to support Cutrer, Corbin, Abraham, and Williamson, met to draw up a petition asking President Smith to reinstate the four. Twenty-six of the students signed the petition and immediately released copies to an Associated Press reporter who was at the meeting. As it happened, the petition was published in local newspapers before it arrived on President Smith's desk. Regarding as "gross disrespect" the petition's release to the press before he had had an opportunity to see it, Smith suspended all twenty-six of the petitioners.

On Monday, December 3, President Smith informed the petitioners that they would be reinstated if each of them submitted an apology to him. Twenty-two of the twenty-six students indeed did sign what the Baton Rouge *Morning Advocate* called a "statement of regret at any injury done the president of the university or the university," and President Smith subsequently reinstated all twenty-two.[86] The four who were not reinstated for their refusal to submit an apology or "statement of regret" were Sam Montague, David McGuire, Rea Godbold, and Stanley Shlosman.

The same day that President Smith reinstated the twenty-two journalism students (Tuesday, December 4), Cutrer, Abraham, and Corbin (all of whom were former *Reveille* staff members) along with McGuire and Shlosman testified for the previously cited affidavits. By then, their colleague Grace Williamson, who had reluctantly resigned her *Reveille* position, had had second thoughts, withdrawn her resignation, and been named *The Reveille's* new editor. She had even managed to produce a December 4 edition of the newspaper with a volunteer staff. Oddly, no news report of all that had transpired in the last few days regarding the censorship confrontation appeared in *The Reveille*. There was only an "explanatory editorial" in which Williamson said the former editor and several staff members had resigned because of their refusal to accept "faculty supervision." What's more, Miss Williamson prepared her own affidavit the next day, December 5, in which she gave a very different account of her and Jesse Cutrer's meeting with President Smith.[87]

Grace Williamson ended her affidavit by challenging the "censorship" contention that her former *Reveille* colleagues cited as their reason for resigning. She noted that President Smith had not intended that *The Reveille* be censored but that the staff was "asked to work under a form of faculty supervision . . . which has always been exercised over The Reveille."[88]

At some point on the same December 5 day that President Smith received the Williamson affidavit, he instructed Major Troy H. Middleton, LSU's Dean of Men as well as Commandant of Cadets, to prepare statements for dismissing Cutrer and McGuire and for indefinitely suspending Abraham, Corbin, Godbold, Montague, and Shlosman from LSU. Jesse Cutrer was being dismissed primarily "for uttering as true, under oath, that which is false." David McGuire was being dismissed "for being guilty of attempting to incite insubordination of students, reporting to the Press the proceedings of a closed meeting, and for making of himself a general nuisance." Reasons given for indefinitely suspending the other five ranged from "issuing statements derogatory to the Louisiana State University and subjecting it to unjust and unwarranted criticism" to "attempting to incite insubordination of students and forcing freshmen to distribute circulars on the campus and in the barracks."[89] The charge regarding distribution of circulars apparently referred to copies of the petition prepared by the twenty-six journalism students on November 27 that had been distributed around campus.[90]

A meeting in President Smith's office held later in the day and attended by several journalism students, including Jesse Cutrer, addressed all of the issues relevant to the censorship controversy but failed to change Smith's mind. On the singular issue of whether Cutrer had lied in his affidavit, which he vehemently denied, President Smith defended his position by referring to language appearing in the Williamson affidavit that gave a very different interpretation of what had been said.[91]

Among the Reveille Seven, Jesse Cutrer, Carl Corbin, Cal Abraham, David McGuire, and Stanley Shlosman were all seniors and presumably would have graduated from LSU at the end of the 1935 spring semester. Sam Montague was a junior. Rea Godbold's classification is uncertain, since he had transferred to LSU from the University of Texas prior to the beginning of the 1934 fall semester. All seven were journalism majors and persons of achievement, having earned scholastic honors and in most cases having held a number of media positions both inside and outside of LSU.[92] The publicity that the seven had received around the state led one anonymous person in New Orleans to create a fund from which each of the seven might borrow interest-free money to pay for completion of their education elsewhere.[93] All seven transferred to the University of Missouri where each eventually earned a Bachelor of Journalism degree.[94]

The plight of the Reveille Seven and the circumstances surrounding their dismissal from LSU stimulated considerable commentary in university newspapers elsewhere. The papers "uniformly denounced LSU for restricting freedom of the press and charged that Senator Long was behind the restriction."[95] The Southern Association of Colleges and Secondary Schools (SACS) also took note of the incident in response to a number of complaints received from Louisiana citizens. A SACS executive committee was charged with investigating the matter, but nothing substantial came of the effort.[96]

T. Harry Williams theorized that Huey Long did not think that his role in the Reveille Seven incident amounted to interfering with LSU. "Rather," said Williams, Long "thought that he was preventing his enemies from interfering with it. A letter critical of him had appeared in the paper edited by a nephew of a political enemy of his. Therefore, his enemies were using the *Reveille* to smear him. So he had to place the editors under responsible supervision."[97] Williams also theorized that *The Reveille* staff under Jesse Cutrer's editorship indeed may have harbored anti-Long sentiments that were exposed and amplified by the affidavits for which he and his colleagues were deposed and that subsequently were provided to anti-Long newspapers in Baton Rouge and New Orleans.[98] The theory may be valid, but regardless of motivation, anything that Cutrer or his fellow Reveille Seven cohorts might have done after the appearance of the Norman letter criticizing Senator Long probably would have been viewed in a political context. In other words, they would not have been above suspicion. But the Reveille Seven story, as far as LSU was concerned, did not end with the group's exit from the campus. There would be a happier ending in the not too distant future—one that is told in the next chapter, and it shows how standing for principle triumphed after all.

Huey Long's assassination in 1935, combined with the apparent assurance by Grace Williamson, who remained as *The Reveille* editor through the summer of 1935,[99] not to engage the paper in any additional political conflict, returned matters to some degree of normalcy in the LSU School of Journalism. Fortunately, the Reveille Seven incident happened during a very brief time frame just before the Christmas holiday break. Both *The Reveille* staff and the School of Journalism had time to recover.

As the 1930s came to an end, the 27 seniors receiving degrees in June 1940 made up the largest single class of LSU School of Journalism graduates to date. These new graduates soon would join 233 other Journalism School alumni who were employed in the newspaper business or some related journalism field throughout Louisiana, 22 other states, and 4 foreign countries.[100] There also were LSU students receiving master's degrees in journalism by 1940 as well, although just who these students were and the nature of their graduate study is not altogether clear. Individual LSU departments during the early years apparently did not create specific graduate curricula for particular disciplines. Some units such as journalism in fact did not even offer courses specifically created for graduate students.

Graduate work at LSU, according to the *1914–1915 LSU General Catalog*, was supervised by a Committee on Graduate Courses, but each department determined the "scope, form, and methods of instruction" that best fit its own students.[101] Students pursuing a Master of Arts (M.A.) degree in the College of Arts and Sciences appeared perfectly free to enroll in whatever courses they felt were most appropriate. They also were free to choose which discipline they felt was the best fit for concentrating their studies. Often this resulted in a student choosing a combination of disciplines.

The crossdiscipline, free form of graduate study during this period allowed graduate students to be very creative in the courses of study they proposed. It also meant that many graduate courses were of the kind that later came to be called "independent study." In fact, *most* graduate courses completed in journalism at the time probably were of that type. LSU did not begin extending graduate credit for completing actual Journalism School courses until the 1928–1929 academic year. And those courses for which graduate credit could be earned actually were upper-level undergraduate courses. Not until the 1930–1931 academic year when the "Special Problems in Journalism" course (noted above) was added to the curriculum and a year later when the "Public Opinion" and "American Journalists" courses (also noted above) appeared[102] could the School of Journalism claim to have its first genuine graduate-only courses.

The question of who actually received LSU's first M.A. in Journalism remains unsettled. Records do not say for certain. One candidate was T. M. McLamore who received his M.A. degree in 1916. McLamore listed "Journalism" as one of his major areas of concentration, but crowded alongside "Journalism" were "Economics," "History," and "Political Science,"[103] and his thesis entitled "The Civil War Campaign in Louisiana" suggests that McLamore's interest leaned more toward history than journalism.

A second possible candidate was Annie Byrne Monget who received her master's degree one year after T. M. McLamore and who, like McLamore, chose to combine journalism with history and literature as her graduate study concentration.[104] But Monget's thesis entitled "The Good Roads Movement in Louisiana" did not include specific journalism content.

Two other students, Yola L. Cohn and Agnes T. Maguire, were listed in the *1919–1920 LSU General Catalog* as pursuing M.A. degrees in economics and journalism (for Cohn) and journalism by itself (for Maguire).[105] But neither of the two apparently ever completed work on their degrees.

Julian Bernard Honeycutt was the first graduate student to indicate journalism as his only study concentration.[106] He received his M.A. degree from LSU in 1920, but his master's thesis entitled "Edgar Allan Poe's Attitude Toward the Immortality of the Soul" would hardly pass as a journalism study.

Marjorie Arbour, already a School of Journalism faculty member when she completed her master's degree work in 1925, apparently wrote the first journalism-related thesis at LSU. Like so many graduate students before her, Arbour also combined journalism with English as her preferred graduate study concentration.[107] And she managed to write a thesis entitled "The Outstanding Writers of Louisiana" that could pass muster among both English Department and Journalism School faculty. The thesis contained brief biographical sketches of writers of every variety, including novelists, historians, poets, and *journalists,* who either were Louisiana natives or were somehow associated with the state.

A big step in the School of Journalism's graduate program occurred in the 1934–1935 academic year when the *LSU General Catalog* first made specific reference to the Master of Arts in Journalism (M.A.J.) degree in the *Catalog's* "Graduate School" section.[108] The M.A.J. degree finally was official.

In view of all that had happened during the 1930s that had brought so much change to the LSU School of Journalism, it should not have come as any great surprise when Marvin Osborn proposed in 1937 that the School be separated from the College of Arts and Sciences. Autonomy would mean equality with other LSU colleges, but it would mean also that the Journalism School director's position would be elevated to that of a dean who then would take a place among other deans on the LSU President's Council of Administration. Most important of all, though, autonomy would mean that the School of Journalism could set its own policies and communicate directly with the LSU President's office without first having to seek approval from an intermediary administrative level in the person of the College of Arts and Sciences dean.

Marvin Osborn described the gist of all this in a 1937 memo where he apparently first proposed autonomy. The memo appears in Osborn's papers and is not addressed to any specific person, although its intended recipient likely was either the Dean of the College of Arts and Sciences or the LSU President. The case that Osborn made and the rationale for what he was asking were fundamental to the quest for autonomy that would fashion much of the LSU Journalism School's history for years to come. Osborn began his memo with reference to 1937 as marking "the Twenty-fifth Anniversary of the beginning of instruction in Journalism at the Louisiana State University."

> In connection with this event, and to enable the School of Journalism the better to keep abreast of the leading Schools of other sections of the country, it is respectfully recommended that the School be elevated to the rank of an autonomous unit in the University. The leading regional Schools have such a status....
>
> We believe that the LSU School of Journalism can best attain, if it has not already done so, and *maintain* leadership in the South if it is placed on an equal basis with the other leading regional Schools....
>
> Informed, disinterested observers have told the director of the L.S.U. School that he has assembled one of the strongest corps of instructors in the entire country. Facilities, actual and potential, for Journalism instruction here rank with the best....
>
> While present administrative relationships are most pleasant, we believe that it would simplify and make more effective the administration of the School of Journalism, with its growing student body and faculty, if its head were in immediate authority. Problems peculiar to Journalism that require prompt action are constantly arising. As a professional school, we wish, among other things, to tighten up regulations having to do with class attendance and with the elimination of students who are obviously unsuited to journalistic careers. Necessity for such administrative autonomy will be even greater when the School of Journalism occupies its own separate building.[109]

This memo was step one in a quest for autonomy that would continue through the remainder of the 1930s, through the 1940s, and into the 1950s. It would involve several players along the way—Louisiana newspaper editors and publishers, the LPA, a variety of LSU administrators, and several LSU presidents, among others. Marvin Osborn's efforts toward autonomy were not immediately ignored. In fact they were taken very seriously. But the time was not yet ripe for achieving the result that Osborn was seeking.

As it happened, initial administrative steps necessary to set in motion any separation of the School of Journalism from the College of Arts and Sciences had just begun when an extraordinary event occurring in the LSU President's office brought all other University activity to a halt. LSU President James Monroe Smith was described, depending on the source, either as an able, well-liked leader, or an unrepentant scoundrel. Truth is, he probably was a little of both. T. Harry Williams said of Smith that "he was an excellent administrator, imaginative and bold in devising new educational policies."[110] William Ivy Hair, on the other hand, quoted Huey Long as saying, "there's not a straight bone in Jim's body, but he does what I tell him."[111]

On Sunday, June 25, 1939, President Smith together with his wife disappeared just hours after learning that an embezzlement scheme in which he had invested—and lost—LSU funds in the stock market came to light. Smith and spouse eventually were captured in Canada and returned to Louisiana on July 4, 1939. An investigation subsequently found that President Smith had systematically falsified documents—LSU Board of Supervisors' minutes, for instance—to illegally enrich himself and several other LSU officials. The corruption that investigators uncovered eventually sent the former LSU President to the Louisiana State Penitentiary.[112]

The three-day sequence of events set in motion by disclosure of President Smith's embezzlement probably was the most bizarre in LSU's history. First to occur was a call to Smith by Louisiana Governor Richard Leche asking that Smith appear at the governor's mansion to address evidence of wrongdoing uncovered by the state's attorney general. Smith appeared, admitted his guilt, and then resigned his LSU presidency. His flight from justice began a short time later. Ironically, Governor Leche himself was set to resign from office the following day, purportedly for health reasons but actually in response to a charge of improprieties of his own.[113]

In one of Governor Leche's last official acts, he called a special meeting of the LSU Board of Supervisors for the following day, Monday, June 26, to choose a new president for LSU. The results of that nearly three-hour meeting was the selection of E. S. Richardson, then head of Louisiana Polytechnic Institute (today's Louisiana Tech University) as LSU's interim president. The appointment was effective immediately, but President Richardson's tenure at LSU was breathtakingly short. In a stunning development described in a *Reveille* "Extra" June 27 edition, Richardson announced his resignation, and Louisiana's new governor Earl K. Long, who had just succeeded Richard Leche, announced that Paul M. Hebert, dean of the LSU Law School, had agreed to accept appointment to Richardson's vacated position. E. S. Richardson later explained that he had been appointed as LSU's interim president "so rapidly that

I did not have time to think the situation over.... The job was a big job, too big for me to handle in the capacity as acting president."[114]

Whether E. S. Richardson resigned as LSU's president of his own accord or whether he was asked to resign by Louisiana's new governor is uncertain—and, actually, irrelevant. Paul M. Hebert would take firm control of his new office in the short two years that he would serve there, and he would calm matters sufficiently to move the University into its next decade.

This chapter closes by returning to former LSU President James Monroe Smith for one more fascinating twist in the whole episode involving his flight from justice. When Smith was finally apprehended in Canada and flown back to Louisiana, his plane landed at what then was Shushan (now Lakefront) Airport in New Orleans. Among several reporters gathered there to question Smith as he walked to a waiting car was New Orleans *Times-Picayune* reporter Carl Corbin. After quickly responding to questions from Corbin, Smith said, "I don't know who you are, but you are very impertinent." Corbin was surprised that the former LSU president did not remember him; Smith had dismissed the reporter from the University some four years earlier.[115] Carl Corbin was one of the "Reveille Seven," now reunited with his nemesis in an oddly reversed set of circumstances.

Alumni Hall, ca. 1906
Courtesy of Manship School

Alumni Hall, reconstruction, ca. 1934
Courtesy of Manship School

Alumni Hall, late 1930s
Courtesy of LSU Special Collections, LSU Photograph Collection, RG# A5000, Louisiana State University Archives, LSU Libraries, Baton Rouge, LA

Journalism Building, James Carville speaks to students in Holliday Forum
Courtesy of Manship School

Journalism Building entrance
Courtesy of Manship School

Journalism Building entrance
Courtesy of Manship School

Hugh Mercer Blain, founder and first faculty member, 1912–1920
Courtesy of LSU Special Collections, LSU Photograph Collection, RG# A5000, Louisiana State University Archives, LSU Libraries, Baton Rouge, LA

Marvin Osborn, director, 1920–1955
Courtesy of Manship School

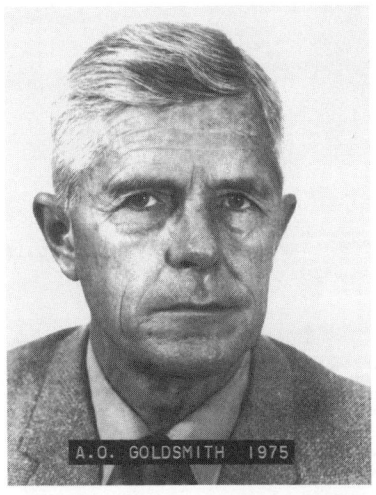

A. O. Goldsmith, director, 1955–1956, 1969–1975
Courtesy of Manship School

Jim Price, director, 1956–1969
Courtesy of Manship School

Ron Hicks, director, 1975–1980
Courtesy of LSU Office of Public Affairs

John Merrill, director, 1980–1983
Courtesy of Manship School

Bill Click, director, 1983–1987
Courtesy of LSU Office of Public Affairs

Bill Giles, director, 1987–1991
Courtesy of LSU Office of Public Affairs

Lou Day, interim director, 1991–1992
Courtesy of Manship School

Jack Hamilton, director, 1992–1994; dean, 1994–present
Courtesy of Manship School

Charles Manship, Jr.
Courtesy of LSU Office of Public Affairs

Douglas Manship
Courtesy of Manship School

Paula Manship
Courtesy of Manship School

1912–1913 *Reveille* staff and the first LSU journalism students
Gumbo, *courtesy of LSU Special Collections, LSU Libraries, Louisiana State University*

Marvin Osborn instructs students, Baton Rouge *State-Times* newsroom, 1934
Courtesy of Manship School

Six of the Reveille Seven during LSU reunion, December 1984. *Left to right,* Jesse Cutrer, Jr., L. Rea Godbold, Carl Corbin, Cal Abraham, Stan Shlosman, Sam Montague; David McGuire was deceased.
Courtesy of LSU Office of Public Affairs

Journalism faculty and staff, 1953. *Left to right,* Richard Wiggans; Ernest Gueymard, managing editor, Baton Rouge *State-Times;* Edythe Gelpi, city editor, Baton Rouge *Morning Advocate;* Marvin Osborn; Bruce McCoy; Jim Price; A. O. Goldsmith.
Courtesy of Manship School

Reveille's LSU centennial edition, Editor Smiley Anders and staff
Courtesy of Manship School

Manship School contemporary computer classroom
Courtesy of Manship School

Times-Picayune staff using Manship School computer facilities in the aftermath of Hurricane Katrina, September 2005
Courtesy of Manship School

WWL-TV staff using Manship School television production facilities in the aftermath of Hurricane Katrina, September 2005
Courtesy of Manship School

Marjorie Arbour, class of 1922, faculty member and noted agriculture journalist
Courtesy of Manship School

Marcus Wilkerson, class of 1924, faculty member and first director of LSU Press
Courtesy of Manship School

Margaret ("Maggie") Dixon, class of 1927, Baton Rouge *Morning Advocate* managing editor
Courtesy of Manship School

Wes Gallagher, class of 1936, Associated Press president
Courtesy of Manship School

Walter Hitesman, class of 1939, Reader's Digest president
Courtesy of Manship School

Carolyn Patterson, class of 1941, National Geographic senior editor
Courtesy of Manship School

Harry Middleton, class of 1947, special assistant to President Lyndon Johnson and LBJ Presidential Library director
Courtesy of Manship School

Bill Rivers, class of 1951, Washington correspondent, academician, and author
Courtesy of Manship School

Rex Reed, class of 1960, film critic
Courtesy of Manship School

Ray Strother, class of 1962, political campaign advisor
Courtesy of Ray Strother

Tom Ryder, class of 1966, magazine publisher and CBS Publications vice-president
Courtesy of Manship School

Kip Holden, class of 1974, legislator and Baton Rouge mayor
Courtesy of Manship School

Jay Dardenne, class of 1976, legislator
and Louisiana Secretary of State
Courtesy of Manship School

Cassandra Chandler, class of 1979, FBI
public affairs executive and special agent
Courtesy of LSU Office of Public Affairs

Sig Mickelson, Manship chair and
CBS Television News president
Courtesy of Manship School

Bill Ross, Manship School
distinguished professor
Courtesy of LSU Office of Public Affairs

9

World War II, Accreditation, and a Permanent Home

The LSU School of Journalism experienced very few academic or programmatic changes during the 1940s. All of the building blocks necessary to put journalism education firmly in place at LSU had been accomplished already. A little tweaking here and there would always be necessary, of course, in order to keep the program up to date.

The one big change during the 1940s came as a result of World War II. The number of journalism majors declined as many students, primarily males, left LSU to join the armed forces. Classes in the Journalism School and throughout LSU during the war took on a decidedly feminine tilt, although many women also left the University in order to participate in the war effort. Classes began filling once more following World War II as veterans returned to campus. Sadly, too many former students would never return.

The School of Journalism faculty also changed somewhat as various instructors left the classroom to serve the nation in a variety of ways. With faculty shedding their academic wardrobe for military uniforms, Journalism School Director Marvin Osborn had to cut corners as best he could.

There were some other major happenings during the 1940s that would move the Journalism School along and continue boosting the School's stature. Two of these were postwar: accreditation by the AASDJ and another move across campus into what would become the School's permanent home, the venerable and historic Alumni Hall. A third major happening was the School's quest for autonomy already begun by Marvin Osborn in the 1930s. Osborn was determined in his effort to raise the School of Journalism to college status.

The final major academic happening of the 1940s was in the realm of unfinished business. The specter of James Monroe Smith being led to prison and his coincidental meeting with Carl Corbin in New Orleans were reminders of an injustice that occurred in 1934 that at long last deserved correcting. The case of the Reveille Seven was making a return to LSU, and this time University officials at the highest level would make amends.

How it happened, why it happened, and at whose insistence it happened is uncertain, but at some point in late 1940, an official high in the LSU administration reopened the Reveille Seven case. Two persons most associated with the action were LSU Acting President Paul M. Hebert and LSU Board of Supervisors member John Y. Fauntleroy (former *Reveille* editor). Fauntleroy likely put in motion the process that led President Hebert, on November 12, 1940, to name a three-person fact-finding committee to investigate the basis for the Reveille Seven case. Committee members included Bruce R. McCoy of the School of Journalism, L. B. Lucky of the Social Science Department, and Dale E. Bennett of the Law School. The committee completed its investigation in December and submitted a report of its findings to President Hebert on December 20, 1940.[1]

What the committee found was very little evidence to support President Smith's decision to dismiss or to suspend the Reveille Seven students. No official record of President Smith's actions was available, nor had any files documenting the case been prepared by Smith or his staff. The investigating committee relied instead on the affidavits referred to in chapter 8 and interviews with LSU administrators who played prominent roles in the case. To a person, Dean of Administration James F. Broussard, former Dean of Men Troy H. Middleton, former College of Arts and Sciences Dean Fred Frey, and School of Journalism Director Marcus Osborn, each said that President Smith's final decision in the Reveille Seven case was done without their consultation or participation. The decision, in their words, had been made totally independent of any of their input. As a result of what evidence they uncovered and testimony they heard, the investigating committee concluded, among other things, that the "normal administrative and disciplinary machinery of the university did not function."[2]

Resulting from the investigating committee's findings, the LSU Board of Supervisors, acting on a motion by Board member J. Y. Fauntleroy, adopted a resolution by unanimous vote on March 10, 1941, that acknowledged the "grave injustice" done to the Reveille Seven students and applauded their "courageous stand in expressing their views" and their refusal "to sacrifice their principles to expediency." In order to make amends, the board moved that the official record of each of the seven be cleared of any mention of dismissal, that the LSU Board of Supervisors in the University's behalf extend full apologies to each student, and that all seven students be welcomed to re-enroll at LSU.[3]

President Hebert, as directed by the LSU Board, sent each of the Reveille Seven an official letter of apology, dated March 14, 1941.[4] To this, a responding letter, dated March 31, 1941, was sent to President Hebert and to the LSU Board of Supervisors over the signatures of each of the Reveille Seven. The letter, "written in expression of our appreciation" for the Board's recent action, was remarkably gracious. "There is no bitterness in our hearts for what has happened in the past," said the group. "We have never dis-owned L.S.U., nor have we allowed the circumstances of our enforced departure to affect our perspective toward the University and our friends on its staff."[5]

The news of the Board's action was carried in the Wednesday, March 12, 1941, edition of *The Daily Reveille* under the page one banner headline "Board Exonerates Ex-Students." A copy of the Board's resolution along with pictures of five of the Reveille Seven and the story of the Reveille Seven incident filled the newspaper's second page.[6] This was the first time that *The Daily Reveille* had told the story in full.[7]

Some forty-three years later, in December 1984, six of the Reveille Seven (David McGuire was deceased) returned to the LSU campus to meet with students and to be honored for their contributions to journalism.[8] In April 1996, the Reveille Seven: Carl Corbin, Stan Shlosman, and Sam Montague in person and Jesse Cutrer Jr., Rea Godbold, Cal Abraham, and David McGuire, posthumously, were honored once more by induction into the Manship School of Mass Communication Hall of Fame.[9]

The School of Journalism faculty remained little changed during the 1940s. While military leaves interrupted some of their regular campus duties, Marvin Osborn, Bruce McCoy, Richard Wiggins, and Marcus Wilkerson remained in place throughout the decade. The same was true for Maggie Dixon and Ernest Gueymard from the *State-Times* and *Morning Advocate* who were officially listed as assistants in the *LSU General Catalogs*. The School did lose C. R. F. Smith who had contributed much to improving LSU's journalism program and T. C. Shields who served on the faculty for only two years. Leonard Wall joined the faculty as a visiting professor during the war years and Jim Price started the decade as an assistant, rose to the instructor rank during the war, and ended the 1940s as an assistant professor. Allen Keplinger also joined the Journalism School faculty as an instructor during the late 1940s.

In the same way that the School of Journalism faculty remained intact, so did the School's curriculum. Three reasons possibly account for the decision to keep the curriculum developed during the 1930s essentially unchanged through most of the 1940s. First, the curriculum was solid. It had been developed with much thought as to what students needed to learn in the classroom as preparation for the journalism profession. And, as noted in chapter 8, the curriculum was as good, if not better, than most other university curricula in the country. So why tamper with success?

The second reason for keeping the curriculum intact was World War II itself. The war already was causing enough disruption and change of routine at LSU. There was no need to add to the confusion by making major changes (or any changes for that matter) to the Journalism School's curriculum. The School in particular owed those students whose education was disrupted by the war a curriculum that looked the same and that carried the same requirements once they returned to the classroom.

The third reason for not changing the curriculum was uncertainty as to how many faculty would be available to teach any of the courses and what size classes to prepare for. Official LSU course enrollment data from the war years are not readily available to indicate what courses actually were offered during a given semester. Chances are, however, that a number of them that continued to be listed in the Journalism School's official curriculum actually were not offered during World War II because of unusually low enrollment or because instructors were not available to teach. The only Journalism School course that was known for certain as a "war casualty" was "Radio News." The course was suspended during the war and was not offered again until the 1945–1946 academic year.[10]

Courses themselves remained in place, but course content underwent changes in response to addressing wartime needs and conditions. Things that might not have received such attention before World War II were viewed in a very different light as the war progressed. Marvin Osborn even outlined in 1943 ways by which journalism courses were "being administered with increasing emphasis upon phases most definitely related to wartime needs." He also took the opportunity to comment on the overall importance of journalism education in wartime and followed with examples of how classroom instruction could assist the war effort:

1. Skills in interviewing and concise writing of reports, which are of great value in the work of the various intelligence units (and in the FBI).

2. Public Relations and the armed services, communication agencies and public opinion, propaganda analysis and censorship. It is essential to the national morale that people should understand wartime communication—the reasons for censorship and its extent, and how to read the news intelligently.
3. News photography course that is of direct and immediate value both for aerial photography in the air force and for the Signal Corps and other units in the Army and Navy.
4. Advertising, which in addition to being a basic necessity in the publishing of newspapers, is proving to be a most effective medium in appealing for support of war saving bonds and stamps and for support of other war efforts.[11]

The AATJ had encouraged its members to revise course content as the LSU School of Journalism had done in order to accommodate wartime needs of the journalism community as well as the military and government. A committee on journalism education and the war was even created by the AATJ to assess how journalism programs might best prepare students for wartime service. One of the committee's recommendations was simply to keep journalism programs in operation. As college enrollment shrank nationwide, it would be easy to justify closing the doors to journalism classrooms where enrollment was unusually low. But newspaper and magazine publishers would be depending more and more on journalism school graduates to fill the places of employees who were or who soon would be headed for the armed forces.

While no major changes occurred in the Journalism School curriculum during the war, there was one significant quasicurricular change. Two distinct sequences or, as they later would be called, areas of concentration, were created. One sequence was designated "news-editorial" and the other "publishing-management."[12] Students now would be able to take sequence-specific courses that would better fit their particular career ambitions.

Annual enrollment statistics showed not only how LSU enrollment declined dramatically during World War II, but also how a pronounced gender shift during the period created a predominantly female student body, especially in the School of Journalism. Enrollment figures are somewhat difficult to interpret, given the criteria used by LSU officials in making their calculations, but what can be gathered from available numbers shows a total LSU-Baton Rouge campus enrollment of roughly 6,400 during the 1940–1941 academic year. That number declined steadily during the coming years to a low of just above 3,300 in 1944–1945. Enrollment began to climb as World War II ended, skyrocketing to roughly 9,800 in 1947–1948, before beginning a drop the next year. By the 1950–1951 academic year, LSU enrollment was a little under 6,800 and nearing what it had been the year prior to the beginning of World War II.[13]

Two reasons probably account for the enrollment bulge that began in 1946–1947. First, new students who had been unable to enter college during the war now were taking the postwar opportunity to earn a college degree, especially since the cost of attending college was covered by the *Servicemen's Readjustment Act of 1944*, better known as the G. I. Bill.[14] The comparable enrollment increase experienced by the LSU Junior Division (where all freshmen students were required to reside) proved the point. Enrollment there bounced from under 1,700 in 1944–1945 to approximately 4,500 during the 1946–1947 academic year.

The other reason for the 1946–1947 enrollment bulge likely was due to all the men and women whose education had been interrupted by their service in World War II now returning to LSU to complete their degrees. The enrollment decline during the rest of the 1940s suggested that these students were matriculating through the system, completing their coursework, earning their degrees, and moving on with their lives.

Enrollment in the LSU School of Journalism paralleled LSU's total enrollment in terms of losses and gains throughout the 1940s. Women journalism majors far outnumbered men during at least part of World War II. Enrollment had dropped to 52 during the 1942–1943 academic year when for the first time the number of women journalism majors surpassed the number of men by a 27-to-25 margin. Enrollment dropped to 39 the next year, when the number of male students plummeted to six. Enrollment was up to 52 in 1944–1945, but the female-to-male ratio was at its most pronounced: 50 women and only two men. The ratio became more balanced the following year (32 men and 35 women), and males returned to the majority in 1946–1947. Reflecting the overall LSU enrollment trend, School of Journalism enrollment for the 1940s peaked at 151 (109 men and 42 women) during the 1947–1948 academic year and moved steadily downward from there until 1950–1951, when enrollment stood at 77 (49 men and 28 women).[15]

Enrollment numbers provide a statistical story of LSU during the 1940s, but they hardly tell the personal stories of what became of all the LSU men and women whose lives were so affected by World War II. Many faculty and students alike left LSU to serve their country either at home or abroad. Quite a few performed journalism-related tasks for which they had been so well trained. Far too many more were assigned to combat duties at places around the globe where they probably never expected (or desired) to be. Most returned home after the war and resumed their lives. All who could re-entered LSU, but resumption of studies for other returning veterans who were faced with more pressing family responsibilities would have to wait. And then there were those whose lives were cut short by the war. The list of LSU students who died defending their country during World War II, just as in World War I, was long, and it carried the names of many from the School of Journalism.

Wartime contributions of Journalism School faculty included Marvin Osborn's assignment to coordinate LSU's public relations and publicity agencies[16] and Marcus Wilkerson's service on the War Production Board advisory committee on the Book Publishing and Manufacturing Industry.[17] C. R. F. Smith served as chief of the rural press section of the Office of War Information News Bureau as well as chief of the Program Activities Section of the War Production Board,[18] and Richard Wiggins was a U.S. Army infantry captain and served as a public relations officer and member of the Civil Affairs in the Far East research staff.[19]

T. C. Shields had been a member of the Journalism School faculty for only two years before enlisting in the U.S. Army in February 1941. He was killed in action during the Normandy invasion in June 1944.[20]

An unofficial list places the number of School of Journalism alumni who played a role in World War II at about 160.[21] That is only an estimate. Add to that list all the students who left the School before completing a degree. The names, ranks, duties, and locations of those who served are known only from what was reported at the time. *The Reveille* made a special effort to keep readers informed of what friends and colleagues from the LSU family were doing. The stories varied in length and depth—some bore the mark of brief, official notices, while others carried a more personal touch. The same was true for stories appearing in other newspapers, especially hometown newspapers.

From these reports came word that sixteen graduates of the class of 1941, who by unofficial records might have accounted for one-half or more of the entire class, were serving in the armed forces within one year of their LSU graduation. Among them, C. J. Alleman was teaching troops at Camp Walters, Texas; Robert Angers, Frederic King, James Green, Bruce Hunt, Teddy Roggen, Percy Rountree, James Stewart, and Robert Bruce Smith were serving in the U.S. Army; Dan Galouye was a member of the Naval Air Corps; E. K. Jesse was a yeoman in the U.S. Navy; William Koren was a U.S. Marine; and Joe Pennica was in the Army Air Corps.²²

The kinds of duties to which School of Journalism alumni were assigned were spread across the board. Some were serving in combat roles, while others were serving in a variety of public information positions or as military journalists. Walter F. Schubert, Louis Wortham, and Bennie Scarpero were in the public information group, and Glenn C. Rutledge, Edmund J. Land Jr., and William D. Laffler were either writing for or editing camp newspapers like *The Dixie* at Camp Blanding, Florida, or the official U.S. Army newspaper, *The Stars and Stripes*.²³ Roger Sheldon, a 1942 journalism graduate, joined the U.S. Navy in September 1942 and within a few months was editing the *Wing-ding* newspaper in New Guinea as well as performing photo reconnaissance missions.²⁴ Walter Hitesman, who joined the U.S. Marine Corps in 1940, was chosen because of his journalism background to become managing editor of *The Leatherneck*, the Marine Corps' official enlisted personnel newspaper.²⁵ Jerry T. Baulch's job as assistant press officer for General Douglas MacArthur in Australia gave him a ringside seat to critical wartime planning in the Pacific Theater.²⁶

Quite a few LSU journalism students joined the armed forces before completing their degrees. Bernard Reed was one of them; Lamar Simmons was another. Both left LSU to join the U.S. Marines shortly after the attack at Pearl Harbor.²⁷ School of Journalism sophomore Leslie Bennett departed the classroom in July 1943, to join the U.S. Army Air Corps.²⁸

Men were by far in the majority of those School of Journalism alumni or students who joined the military ranks, but quite a few women joined as well. One was Jeannette Hodson who had just completed her first year of graduate work when she joined the WACs on "D-Day" in 1944.²⁹ Hodson joined other LSU women who, by one 1943 estimate, put the total LSU female military enlistments at fifty-seven. "Auxiliaries, apprentice seamen, midshipmen by the score, comprise the list of women L.S.U. has sent into the armed forces," reported *The Reveille* in its pre politically correct language. Added to the list, continued *The Reveille* story, were "ten WAVE ensigns, one lieutenant (j.g.), two lieutenants in the Marine corps, one first lieutenant Army nurse, one WAC first lieutenant, and two second lieutenants."³⁰

LSU student journalists were moving into military ranks not just from the School of Journalism, but also from *The Reveille* newsroom. Several persons already mentioned held positions at the paper. What is remarkable, though, is that nine of the twelve male *Reveille* editors dating from 1933 until summer

1941 joined some branch of the armed forces. Richard Wiggins, Jerry Baulch, T. C. Shields, W. W. Hitesman, and William Laffler already have been mentioned. Joining the list were Karl Smith and Morton J. O'Brien, both in the U.S. Marine Corps, and Morrell Trimble and Robert Denley, both serving in the U.S. Navy.[31]

And then there were those whose lives ended in places far from LSU and far from their Louisiana homes. One estimate of the number of LSU alumni and students who either were killed in action or died while serving their country in some capacity during World War II was 405.[32] Among these were U.S. Army Major Thomas Walton Fort, School of Journalism class of 1937, and winner of the Bronze Star, who was killed in action in Luzon. U.S. Army Air Corps Lieutenant Stephen Borne, class of 1942, lost his life over Celebes Island. Another Army Air Corps Lieutenant, Harry Dugas, class of 1936, missing for over a year in Europe, was finally declared officially dead in 1943.[33]

The one death, however, that brought home to the School of Journalism so acutely and so personally the kinds of sacrifices made by student and faculty alike was that of T. C. Shields. He epitomized so much about the School. He was a journalism graduate, class of 1937, *Reveille* editor, and School of Journalism instructor who lost his life at Normandy. The circumstance of his death was described this way in the *LSU Alumni News*: "Killed in the invasion of Normandy, June 8, 1944. Sacrificed his life to enable his men to withdraw by directing screening American artillery fire from a suicidal position in front of them."[34] Between graduation from LSU and his return to accept his faculty position at the University, T. C. had worked as a reporter at the *Shreveport Times*. It was on the *Times* editorial page where a most fitting tribute was paid to Shields following his death. And while it spoke directly of only one person, the tribute really was an epitaph for all whose lives were cut short by war. Said the *Times*: "He was a gallant gentleman, possessing the highest attributes of American manhood. Had he lived, his contribution to the building of a better nation and better world would have been noble and enduring."[35]

While so many uniformed personnel were making wartime contributions in theaters of war across the globe or on military bases across America, others served the cause in civilian dress and in nonmilitary ways. Take, for instance, School of Journalism alumni who worked in one of the most important manufacturing plants in World War II America, Higgins Industries in New Orleans. Unofficial records show that at least four of the School's graduates, Alton Broussard, Marcella Kiefer, William Westbrook, and Mary Williams, worked at the

Higgins plant where landing craft that were so instrumental in beach landings such as those at Normandy on D-Day were designed and built.[36]

On the LSU campus, Jim Price, who served as *The Reveille's* faculty manager, worked hard to publish monthly editions of *Galley West* for distribution to some three hundred School of Journalism alumni worldwide. *Galley West*, named for the galley proofs or "narrow strips of newsprint used in newspaper composing rooms" originally had been intended only for Sigma Delta Chi members. But given the request for news about the School of Journalism and about former classmates in combination with receipt of news from so many persons, Price saw the need to expand *Galley West's* circulation area during World War II.[37]

One of the most significant noncombat contributions made during the war was that of J. Wes Gallagher, 1936 School of Journalism graduate turned Associated Press war correspondent. Gallagher's dispatches from European hot spots throughout World War II helped keep American newspaper readers informed of what was happening overseas. Much of his time was spent in occupied territory—Greece when the Germans occupied Athens, Yugoslavia when the Germans arrived there, Copenhagen when the Germans invaded Denmark, the Norwegian front, Budapest, Turkey, and more. All told, Gallagher covered the war in over sixteen European countries. He also was first to report the landing of U.S. Expeditionary forces in North Africa and later scored another first by reporting about President Franklin D. Roosevelt meeting with British Prime Minister Winston Churchill at Casablanca.

Following the D-Day invasion, Gallagher was appointed to head AP's western front field staff and in 1945, as the war neared its end in Europe, he was appointed as AP's bureau chief in Paris. Gallagher ended his war-related news reporting by covering the Nuremberg Nazi war criminal trials. For all of his World War II reporting accomplishments, Wes Gallagher was recognized by the U.S. Junior Chamber of Commerce as one of America's ten outstanding young men of 1945.[38] He eventually would climb through the AP's executive ranks, becoming the organization's general manager from 1962 to 1976, and then AP president from 1972 to 1976.[39]

Journalism School students and faculty attempted to continue extracurricular activities as normally as possible during the 1940s, but wartime disruptions obviously required some adapting. *The Reveille* continued publication, although it once more became a semi-weekly on August 11, 1942, due to a paper shortage. The shortage also forced the paper to limit its pages to four per issue. *The Reveille* returned to its daily status (excepting Sunday and Monday) in February 1947. And two years later, *The Daily Reveille* shifted from a morning to an afternoon paper.⁴⁰

With the absence of so many male students the wartime *Reveille* staff was nearly all female. In fact, during the 1943–1944 academic year the only *Reveille* positions not held by women were sports editor and cartoonist.⁴¹ From the 1941–1942 academic year through the 1945–1946 academic year, all of *The Reveille* editors were women. Included in the group were Jewel Claitor, Mary Carolyn Bennett, Dee Walker, Juanita Greene, Louise Schilling, Elayn Hunt, Eula Mae Smith, and Harriet Fox.⁴²

Reveille content changed somewhat during World War II as a reflection of world events and the need to provide as much information as possible about LSU alumni, faculty, and students participating in the war. One of the paper's few major content changes occurred after the war when *The Reveille* resumed a short-lived practice in 1947 that had originated in 1911 of reserving four inside pages of the paper each semester to carry LSU student literary pieces. The idea evolved the following year into a publication called *Delta* that was devoted exclusively to short stories, poems, and other literary works contributed by students.⁴³

Journalism News, published each summer since 1939 by the LSU School of Journalism, continued making its appearance during the war. The newspaper carried news about the School and its activities to alumni, LSU administrators, newspaper editors throughout Louisiana, and other journalism schools around the country.⁴⁴ And, of course, the relationship continued with the Baton Rouge *Morning Advocate* and *State-Times* whereby journalism students prepared campus stories for publication in one or both of the newspapers as part of advanced reporting course assignments.

The annual country press field trips also continued during World War II. Student editors led teams in April 1942 to edit the *Crowley Daily Signal*, the *Iberville South* in Plaquemine, the *Franklinton Era-Leader*, the *West Side Journal* of Port Allen, and the Kosciusko, Mississippi, *Star Herald*.⁴⁵ The practice of sending a team out of state was a new twist to this annual ritual.⁴⁶

There evidently was a field trip hiatus in 1945, but the practice continued in 1946 and presumably went through 1948.⁴⁷ The trips may have continued for a while longer, possibly into the 1950s,⁴⁸ but there is good evidence that the annual event that had proved so popular, that had provided such excellent professional real world experience, and that likely had helped launch a number of journalism careers definitely did not extend beyond the mid-1950s.

The field trip's demise as an important outreach tool was as much a loss to LSU in general as it was to the Journalism School in particular. Letters from appreciative publishers oftentimes appeared in Marvin Osborn's mailbox complimenting him and the School on a particular team's performance, and it was not uncommon for the writers also to send a similar note to the LSU President. Jules Fogel, editor/publisher of the *Vivian Caddo Citizen*, for example, following a field trip visit to his newspaper in 1941, wrote Osborn: "I was amazed at the vast knowledge this group showed in their understanding of the intricacies of publishing a newspaper and the solid foundation of knowledge that is required to make good newspaper people."[49]

Acknowledging receipt of his own letters very much like the above, LSU President Campbell Hodges wrote Marvin Osborn in 1943, "I am pleased to see the practical experience the students are acquiring and also to learn that they are conducting themselves so that they reflect credit upon your Journalism School and upon the University."[50]

Another of the School of Journalism's popular extracurricular activities, the "Editors' Short Course," was held in 1941,[51] but it was suspended in 1942 and 1943 because of the war.[52] The Short Course resumed in 1944[53] and continued on an annual basis at least through 1948[54] and possibly into the early 1950s.[55] But, like the student field trips, the Editors Short Course seemed destined to end at some point in the mid-1950s.

Another School of Journalism tradition began in 1950 and continues to the present day. That is the annual awarding of the Robert Ewing Scholarship to junior journalism majors. Money to fund the scholarship came from a permanent trust fund established by the children of the late Col. Robert Ewing, editor-publisher at the time of his death in 1931 of the Shreveport *Times*, Monroe *News-Star-World*, and New Orleans *States*.[56]

The School of Journalism continued its outreach within the academic community when Marcus Wilkerson was elected president of the American Association of Journalism Teachers during the AATJ's annual meeting in January 1947.[57] Wilkerson stepped into a position that many years earlier had been occupied by Marvin Osborn.

Several months after Wilkerson was honored with his new office, former School of Journalism instructor Marjorie Arbour also was honored. She had left her faculty position to become LSU's Agricultural Extension Editor, and in 1947, *Progressive Farmer* magazine named Arbour its "Woman of the Year in Service to Louisiana Rural Progress."[58]

Activity connected to radio at LSU continued to be more or less extracurricular for journalism majors during the 1940s. Radio broadcasting itself continued during World War II in the peculiar arrangement with WJBO that had been in place for several years. Radio's popularity during the War evidently convinced the LSU Board of Supervisors, in April 1945, to approve plans to move the University into actual broadcasting. The Board applied for a permit to operate an FM radio station on campus and allocated $56,000 for the station's construction and first-year operation.[59]

The Board's decision may have stemmed from two reasons. First, the Federal Communications Commission (FCC) had approved FM (frequency modulation) broadcasting in 1940, following several years of experimentation to perfect a transmission system whose sound quality was superior to the traditional AM (amplitude modulation) system.[60] Second, FM broadcasting seemed to hold great promise for educational radio; so much so that educational radio advocates successfully lobbied the FCC to set aside specific FM frequencies for the exclusive use of noncommercial stations.[61]

The LSU Board requested assignment of call letters "WLSU" and a transmitting power of 1,000 watts to the new LSU station. That much power would extend station coverage to a radius of about 75 miles. The FCC granted both requests. Prior to receiving the station license, a decision also was made to locate WLSU in a newly constructed studio/transmitter facility on Dalrymple Drive, facing the current Sigma Chi fraternity house. A 400-foot tower would be erected next to the building to hold the station's antenna.[62]

The variety of programming intended for WLSU was ambitious, to say the least. A series to supplement learning in subjects at the primary and secondary school and adult education levels was planned. Live coverage of public affairs events and important speeches was projected. The LSU School of Journalism, Speech Department, and School of Music also were invited to contribute programming elements to WLSU's overall schedule.[63]

Station construction began in May 1947. When completed, WLSU would be the first FM station in the Deep South[64] and would occupy one of the most modern radio station facilities in the country. On October 16, 1947, power was switched on, and WLSU was on the air.[65] Within the coming year, WLSU's programming would include broadcast of a full-length opera (Offenbach's *Tales of Hoffman*) from LSU's University Theater, a production of *The Merchant of Venice*, and on-the-spot coverage of the 1948 presidential election returns.[66]

Considerable activity centered on developing WLSU's programming and programming philosophy during the late 1940s. Absent from the LSU campus groups and committees that gathered to do this, though, was representation from the School of Journalism. Failure of the School's faculty to play any prominent role in WLSU's operation may be explained by the School's treatment of radio as a secondary medium. While the "Radio News" course was reactivated following World War II, the LSU Speech Department still took the initiative in adding courses to its curriculum that provided more and more avenues of opportunity for students wanting to develop radio-related skills.[67]

The School of Journalism's "Radio News" class still played an important role at WLSU, providing news copy for on-the-air reporting.[68] In addition, journalism majors were filling non-news roles at the station in such areas as script writing and announcing and spending many if not most of their elective course hours taking Speech Department radio courses.[69]

Whether the LSU School of Journalism's lukewarm embrace of radio would hamper its standing within the journalism education community would soon be tested. The School's "Class A" rating earned in 1927 had placed it among the elite journalism education programs in America. But much had changed in the nearly twenty years since then. If similar standards as those created in 1927 to judge the quality of journalism programs were once more applied to the LSU School of Journalism, would it rise to the same level of excellence as before?

Actually, the same questions about the quality of journalism education that had precipitated scrutiny of programs nationwide in the 1920s arose once more in the 1940s. Prominent journalism educators were especially concerned that the anticipated jump in postwar college enrollment not push colleges and universities to offer students second-rate preparation for a journalism career. In order to assure uniformity of quality, these educators decided that, as had occurred in the 1920s, careful studies of existing journalism education programs and any problems that existed within these programs would have to be undertaken. Based upon what these studies revealed, a set of "best practices" standards would be created by which all journalism education programs at colleges and universities across the country might be judged.

The first affirmative step toward this objective came in 1939 with creation of the National Council on Professional Education for Journalism. The Council, whose name later changed to the American Council on Education for Journalism (ACEJ), actually was an umbrella organization whose members included the American Association of Schools and Departments of Journalism (AASDJ), the American Society of Newspaper Editors, the National Editorial

Association, the American Newspaper Publishers Association, the Southern Newspaper Publishers Association, and the Inland Daily Press Association.[70]

Results of several studies along with other input relative to accreditation standards and procedures eventually led the AASDJ to adopt a resolution during its 1945 annual convention approving appointment of a Committee on Accreditation. The new committee would have "full authority to develop a body of approved standards, to examine the programs of schools and departments of journalism with respect to their compliance with its body of approved standards and to draw up a list of schools and departments of journalism which meet the requirements of these standards."[71]

The AASDJ resolution was distributed to all ACEJ member organizations for their consideration. All components of the accreditation plan embedded in the resolution subsequently were approved. Announcement of the ACEJ's action came during its April 27, 1945, meeting in New York. The ACEJ also assumed full responsibility for accrediting schools of journalism through an Accrediting Committee that mixed journalism educators with professional journalists. The Accrediting Committee was charged with establishing accreditation standards, submitting them to the ACEJ for approval, and once approved, beginning the process of corresponding with and inspecting journalism schools and departments seeking accreditation. Finally, accreditation recommendations were to be submitted to the ACEJ "for final action in all cases."[72]

Once decisions were made about financial arrangements to underwrite the ACEJ and its activities, machinery and procedures for accrediting college and university journalism programs in the United States were set in motion.[73]

The LSU School of Journalism was one of the first schools to request an ACEJ accreditation review. A four-person team chose February 13 and 14, 1948, as the dates of their campus site visit. The review process was quite similar (albeit nowhere near as extensive or exhaustive) as the current accreditation team review. LSU administrators were interviewed, as were School of Journalism faculty, students, alumni, and professional journalists who had had some connections with the School.[74] All were asked to comment on the quality of Journalism School courses and graduates and the School's reputation in the professional community.

The School of Journalism also asked that its two specialized sequences or concentration areas, "news-editorial" and "publishing-management," be reviewed for accreditation. Several special standards applied to sequence accreditation. For instance, there had to be evidence that "a substantial grouping of background courses . . . contribute to the specialization in the area." In addition, a sequence had to "have been in operation over a sufficiently long period to have graduated students who are working in the field and whose accomplishments can thus be appraised."[75]

The LSU School of Journalism's effort to win accreditation for the School at large and for its two sequences was a success. The June 11, 1948, announcement[76] surprised no one. Not surprising either was the leadership position that the School maintained. It was one of thirty-five journalism schools or departments to appear on the ACEJ's first list of accredited programs. And it was one of nine journalism schools or departments in the South to appear on the list. The LSU School of Journalism's news-editorial sequence was among thirty other news-editorial sequences—seven of them at southern universities—to be accredited. And the School's publishing-management (called newspaper management by the ACEJ) sequence was one of only four in the nation and the only one in the South to be accredited.[77] All in all, news from the accreditation front could not have been better!

News from the autonomy front was less encouraging. Marvin Osborn had written a memorandum in 1937 that eventually made its way to LSU President James Monroe Smith requesting that the School of Journalism be made an autonomous unit within the University. Osborn included in the memo his reasons for why autonomy would benefit the School, citing examples of successful autonomous journalism units elsewhere.[78] Indeed, a survey of the thirty-two AASDJ members at the time showed that ten of them were autonomous. Most prominent among these ten were the University of Missouri, Columbia University, and the only one in the South, the University of Georgia.[79]

Marvin Osborn's memo was referred to the LSU Committee on Organization for further review. The committee, chaired by Dean of Administration Paul M. Hebert, subsequently reported to President Smith on February 25, 1937, that Osborn had "made out an excellent case in support of his position" and that the Committee on Organization believed "that there are certain definite advantages which would flow to the University and to the School of Journalism if it were given autonomous rank." The letter concluded with a Committee recommendation "that this matter be discussed with the Dean of the College of Arts and Sciences in order that your [President Smith's] final decision may be made."[80]

Marvin Osborn was encouraged by the Committee on Organization's conclusion and what he perceived as its endorsement of the School of Journalism's autonomy request. And he had been led to understand that the Committee's decision would be final. But as Osborn later would disclose, President Smith "considered the Committee report to be favorable, but that the matter was being held in 'abeyance.'" Osborn then noted parenthetically that "subsequent developments at the University pushed this matter into the background."[81]

The "subsequent developments" that Osborn referred to likely were those that surrounded President Smith's resignation. Obviously, such time of administrative turmoil at LSU left little opportunity to pursue the School of Journalism's quest for autonomy. So the matter lay dormant for the next three years.

In November 1940, Marvin Osborn took the unusual, perhaps unprecedented, step of writing a letter to LSU Board of Supervisors member John Y. Fauntleroy[82] as well as Board member Homer L. Brinkley addressing the autonomy matter. Osborn reiterated his arguments for autonomy and noted that the LSU Committee on Organization had "virtually recommended" separating the School of Journalism from the College of Arts and Sciences some three years before.[83]

Marvin Osborn's letter, written directly to the Board of Supervisors and bypassing the College of Arts and Sciences Dean and LSU President, would be regarded as a violation of protocol today. It probably was a violation in 1940 as well. Nonetheless, Osborn's request made its way from the Board of Supervisors to Acting President Paul Hebert—the very same person who coincidentally had chaired the Committee on Organization in 1937. And it appears that President Hebert had not changed his mind about autonomy for the School of Journalism. To that end, Hebert requested that Marvin Osborn send him "a complete statement on the matter . . . to be signed by the entire journalism faculty."[84] A 5,500-word document was prepared and submitted to President Hebert in compliance with his request.

Next, Acting President Hebert appointed a Special Committee on the Granting of Autonomy to the School of Journalism in early January 1941.[85] The committee, composed of Frey, College of Engineering Dean Leo J. Lassalle, Dean James B. Trant of the College of Commerce, and Dean Jordan G. Lee Jr. of the College of Agriculture, submitted a set of questions to Marvin Osborn soliciting information from him and his colleagues about the Journalism School's current operation and anticipated changes that might result from autonomy.[86]

The Special Committee then met with the Journalism School faculty for a two-hour conference in advance of submitting its report to President Hebert on February 6, 1941. The report could not have been more favorable. The Special Committee stated unambiguously, "We recommend that the School of Journalism be granted autonomous status in the University, but that the time and method of putting this into operation be worked out by the President and the Dean of the University with the Director of the School of Journalism; of course, provided the Board of Supervisors approve of such a change."[87] The report was signed by all four members of the committee. A detailed plan for transitioning the School to an autonomous unit was quickly constructed and sent to Dean Fred Frey (Dean of the University). Dean Frey apparently gave his wholehearted approval.[88] And since it might be assumed that the LSU Board of Supervisors was responsible to some degree for pushing forward the autonomy issue, there was no reason to suspect opposition from any Board members to moving the matter along to what should have been its logical conclusion.

Unfortunately, the LSU School of Journalism once more fell victim to bad timing. For at the very moment that the Board of Supervisors' collective attention might have been focused on granting autonomy to the Journalism School, LSU was undergoing a change of leadership. Acting President Paul Hebert, one of the School's strongest supporters, was stepping aside for LSU's new President, General Campbell B. Hodges. Whenever a change of this magnitude occurs it is the usual practice to put on hold any major curriculum or academic unit alterations until the new president has had a chance to review them. So the School of Journalism's march to autonomy had come to either a lumbering detour or a screeching halt.

Now Marvin Osborn and his colleagues would have to become acquainted with the new LSU President, assess what he might think about Journalism School autonomy, and then educate him about the School's past efforts toward that end. By early July Osborn and the Journalism School faculty were ready to begin the education part in crash course fashion. All of the major steps that had occurred from the 1937 University Committee on Organization Report to the most recent Special Committee on Granting Autonomy Report of February 1941 were summarized in a four-page letter sent from the Journalism School faculty to President Hodges on July 9, 1941.[89]

The School received a boost from the professional community when H. A. Mangham, LPA President, wrote President Hodges on August 7, 1941, expressing the LPA's support for autonomy.[90] A special LPA committee also had been formed to prepare a resolution lending additional support to the Journalism School's autonomy effort.[91]

Having LPA's support reinforced by its proposed resolution probably would have provided the Journalism School some helpful leverage in its quest for autonomy. But, alas, providence once more sidetracked the whole effort. While World War II did not foreclose on any further discussion of autonomy, it nonetheless made the climb in that direction a lot steeper. After all, LSU's move to a wartime status together with the departure of so many students from campus and the decline in journalism student enrollment hardly would have provided much justification for pursuing autonomy.

Only briefly during the 1940s did the matter once more gain any attention. In May 1943, the LPA approved a resolution sanctioned two years earlier in which LPA members went on record in support of LSU School of Journalism autonomy.[92] Newly elected LPA President M. N. Lipp enclosed a copy of the resolution along with a letter he wrote to the LSU Board of Supervisors and President Hodges, dated May 24, 1943, personally endorsing the resolution's intent.[93]

The LPA support was a welcome gesture, but it held little sway at the time. With the exception of one brief return to the subject in 1951, the matter of LSU School of Journalism autonomy would lie dormant for the next forty years. Certainly, the matter was discussed informally, but nothing exists in the available record to suggest that any formal efforts were made to rekindle the Journalism School's quest for autonomy. One reason for the inactivity perhaps was the succession of LSU Presidents following Campbell Hodges' departure in 1944.[94] He was followed by William B. Hatcher from 1944 to 1947. Fred C. Frey was appointed to the position as an interim in 1947, following Hatcher's death. Then from 1947 to 1951, Harold W. Stoke served as LSU President.[95] It well could have been that Marvin Osborn realized enough about the inclinations of each of these presidents not to bother taking the autonomy issue to any of them.

The reason for raising the autonomy issue once more in 1951 came indirectly, as an opportunity that Marvin Osborn took advantage of in preparing a long memo written to new LSU President Troy H. Middleton who had just succeeded Harold W. Stoke in that office. The memo was typical of the kind submitted to a new chief executive in which the Journalism School's current operating condition and future needs were described and assessed. In providing all this information in summary form Osborn digressed to the autonomy matter, briefly reviewing much of what had occurred during the 1930s and 1940s, before concluding, "I was unable to get further action on the [autonomy] matter at that time, and respectfully renew the request that it be given serious consideration."⁹⁶ As far as can be determined, President Middleton gave no attention to the matter whatsoever. And once more, timing may have worked against such consideration. The Korean War (or "Police Action") was heating up and having its impact on the LSU student body. Readjustments of the kind called for by separating the School of Journalism from the College of Arts and Sciences would have to wait.

The School of Journalism did undergo separation of another sort in 1948, this one having to do with yet another move from Thomas D. Boyd Hall (the present name replacing the Journalism Building name in 1943 as a memorial to the late LSU President)⁹⁷ across campus to Alumni Hall. Switching places with the School would be the offices of the auditor, comptroller, purchasing agent, registrar, bursar, and student loan office. Fear that fire might destroy the records maintained by these various administrative offices prompted their move to the fireproof environs of Thomas Boyd Hall. In order to renovate Alumni Hall for Journalism School occupancy and to allow for construction of the new offices in Thomas Boyd Hall, the journalism faculty offices and classrooms along with the *Daily Reveille* offices and printing plant were located in temporary buildings on the south side of the campus.

The move to Alumni Hall began in late June 1948, and by mid-September the Journalism School was fully situated in its new home. No one knew at the time, of course, but Alumni Hall was to become the School's permanent home. Along with faculty offices, classrooms, darkrooms, and the journalism library, Alumni Hall space also accommodated new advertising layout and editing labs, the University Press, the LPA central office, and the *Reveille* editorial offices. The Alumni Federation offices that had occupied the building before the Journalism School arrived remained there as well. Not making the move to Alumni Hall were the *Reveille* business office, the *Reveille* printing facilities (presses, linotype machines, darkrooms, and photoengraving plant), the *Gumbo* editorial and business offices, and LSU's Office of Public Relations. All but the Office of Public Relations, which moved to David Boyd Hall, would remain for some time in their temporary "Naval Barracks" locations.⁹⁸

The reason for maintaining the *Reveille* facilities in a separate location was lack of Alumni Hall floor space to house the press machinery.⁹⁹ The separation did not set well with Marvin Osborn, who, as soon as he learned of the Journalism School's pending move in February 1948 and its certain consequence, wrote LSU President Harold Stoke to "register an emphatic protest against the proposal to break up and disperse component parts, which, together, make possible the effectiveness which now characterizes our program of education for journalism and the high standing enjoyed by the student publications under our supervision."[100] Osborn was just warming up. Driving home his reasons for maintaining the physical arrangement enjoyed for the past ten years, he noted that such arrangement had "made it possible to combine and co-ordinate resources and facilities and to begin publication of a daily student newspaper to implement and make more complete the practical phases of instruction and training."[101]

Marvin Osborn's arguments did not win the day, and his protest against the Journalism School's move to Alumni Hall went for naught. But he was not finished. Osborn simply waited until he could carry his protest to a new and perhaps more obliging president.

For all of Marvin Osborn's frustration over the Alumni Hall space limitations (frustrations, by the way, that would continue to needle one Journalism School director after another in years to come), his respect for history, especially for LSU's history, and the fact that he now resided in quite possibly the most revered building on campus must have given him at least some satisfaction. The building had a remarkable past, one that in time would blend well with Journalism School traditions. But how many students who have trod the hallways of what would come to be called the Journalism Building—home to the J-School for more than half a century—really knew its story or understood its role in LSU's history? And how many knew that the building where they stood actually had two lives, having been constructed originally on the old LSU campus and then later moved to the new campus? Here, in condensed form, is just a peek at the history of this fabled building.

The idea for what was called Alumni Memorial Hall before the name was shortened later to Alumni Hall began with a vision by New Orleans architect and LSU alumnus Charles A. Favrot in 1897 to construct such a building as "a tribute to alma mater that would be both useful and symbolical."[102] Funds to cover the estimated $15,000 construction cost were to be raised by a "subscription" or pledge program by which LSU Alumni Society members over time would contribute the full sum.[103]

The Alumni Society agreed in 1900 that Alumni Memorial Hall should "commemorate primarily the services of David F. Boyd, the true founder, first president and life-long friend" of LSU and that the building's official name should be David Boyd Memorial Hall.[104] Still, Alumni Hall in time would become the building's more common name.

By 1903, with subscription funds still trickling in and with cash on hand far below what had been anticipated, a decision nonetheless was made to proceed with drawing plans for the new building. Architects C. A. Favrot and A. F. Livaudais, of Favrot and Livaudais, were natural choices to take the job. The two already had agreed to drop their usual architectural fees by half but then decided to charge nothing for their work. Preliminary plans were submitted and approved by the LSU Board of Supervisors during the Board's June 1, 1903, meeting.[105]

Alumni Hall construction was slowed considerably by the failure of LSU alumni to contribute to the cause. Fundraising fell primarily to Alumni Society President Lewis S. Graham, who was relentless in his efforts to cajole his fellow alumni into fulfilling their commitments to pay for the building.[106] Sad to say that Graham would not live to see the completion of his work. He passed away on September 12, 1908, at his New Orleans home.[107]

A little over a year after Lewis Graham's death, on January 2, 1910, Alumni Hall was ready for use.[108] The building's total cost once it was ready for occupancy slightly exceeded $40,000. Arthur T. Prescott, LSU Professor of Political Science, remarked that Alumni Hall, from the moment it became operational, would be "more than an ornament to the campus; it will be the headquarters of organized efforts that must shape the destiny of the institution."[109] Alumni Memorial Hall fulfilled its mission for many years. Not only was it the "Controlling Center of the University," as *The Reveille* called it,[110] but Alumni Hall, situated as it was just beyond the entrance to LSU (roughly, where the Louisiana State Library now stands), greeted thousands of visitors to the campus.

Then came the move to LSU's new campus, or the "new plant," as it was called in 1925. Most of the functions that had been confined to Alumni Hall on the old campus now were transferred to newly constructed buildings on the new campus. Even the original intent of Alumni Hall as a memorial to David F. Boyd was transferred to a new Boyd Memorial Hall.[111]

In the next few years Alumni Hall would house an assortment of occupants. For a while, the LSU Agricultural and Home Economics Extension Divisions were located there. Then it became the Women's Administration Building with offices for the dean and assistant dean of women, an assembly room for LSU women students, and meeting rooms for other student organizations.[112] And as mentioned above, Alumni Hall also served as headquarters for the AASDJ-AATJ joint conventions hosted by the LSU School of Journalism in 1929. LSU President Thomas Boyd moved there when Alumni Hall opened and remained there as LSU's emeritus president until his death in 1932.[113] At about that time Alumni Hall also was occupied by the tax collector, then a cultural school for children moved in, and finally, except for special functions, the building was vacated altogether by 1933.[114]

At some point in 1933 a decision was made to disassemble Alumni Hall, transport salvageable portions of the building to the new campus, and then reassemble it. Who made the decision to move the building and for what reasons are not entirely clear. Most likely, the Alumni Federation (formerly, the Alumni Society) decided on the move as a way of maintaining LSU's link to its past and as a way of assuring that LSU alumni would continue to have a familiar home on the new campus. Part of this speculation is based on the role played by the Alumni Federation Executive Committee in choosing Alumni Hall's new location. The site chosen was a rise of land just to the east of Tiger Stadium and to the south of the gymnasium-armory, precisely where the LSU service station was sitting at the time.[115] This would become familiar territory to thousands of journalism and mass communication students in years to come.

The actual job of moving Alumni Hall fell to workers employed by the Civil Works Administration and Public Works Administration, two federal agencies created as part of President Franklin Roosevelt's economic recovery program.[116] One of those workers was Alton Broussard, who had driven his family's truck to LSU in hopes of using it to earn tuition money. Broussard's timing was perfect. He carried load after load of brick from the old campus to the new and in the process had a ringside seat to history as he watched Alumni Hall's rebirth. Broussard would go on to earn both a bachelor's and a master's degree in journalism at LSU but would complete both before the Journalism School made its move to Alumni Hall. Alton Broussard eventually joined the University of Southwestern Louisiana journalism faculty and retired as department chairman in 1975.[117]

The job of reconstructing Alumni Hall was given to the architecture firm of Weiss, Dreyfuss, and Seiferth, who, like their predecessors Favrot and Livaudais, worked for gratis. Their intentions were to use as much of the building material and to follow as closely the design and proportions of the original Alumni Hall as possible. They planned some slight architectural alterations in order to conform to the predominant Italian Renaissance style of the new campus. The Doric columns on the original structure's main (north) entrance and west entrance certainly would be part of the new building. Gone, however, would be some of Alumni Hall's interior features, including the large rotunda in the building's center. That space was converted to hallways, offices, and meeting rooms.[118]

Reconstruction evidently continued without a hitch through the 1934 spring semester. By May, the new Alumni Hall was ready for occupancy. First floor office space was assigned to the Alumni Federation secretary, commandant of cadets, treasurer, and bursar. Space also was reserved for an alumni reception room. Second floor office space was assigned to the athletic department, the news bureau, the official campus photographer, and the *Gumbo*. The biggest second floor space was reserved for the alumni auditorium.[119]

Alumni Hall's shared designation as a memorial to President David F. Boyd ended officially in 1943 when the two buildings of the South Administration Group just south of the Campanile were both renamed David F. Boyd Hall. The renaming occurred at the same time that the two buildings that made up the North Administration Group (one of which was then known as the Journalism Building) both were renamed Thomas D. Boyd Hall.[120] The story of Alumni Hall and the changes that would occur there once the School of Journalism moved in will continue in subsequent chapters.

The number of students graduating from the School during the 1940s obviously was affected by World War II. The total number of graduates no doubt was far below what it likely would have been had there been no war. And the number of male graduates nearly disappeared during the period. In all, 193 students received a B.A.J. degree from LSU during spring and summer commencements running from 1941 through 1950. Four M.A.J. degrees were awarded during the same period.

The number of students receiving journalism degrees during the 1940s paralleled LSU's enrollment shifts. For instance, twenty-two students received their B.A.J. degree in 1941, but only fifteen graduated in 1942, nine in 1943, and two in 1944. The number rose to fourteen in 1945, dropped back to four in 1946, and then began climbing to a high of fifty in 1949. The high number of graduates in the last years of the 1940s, of course, accounted for the number of World War II veterans who were returning to LSU and completing their degrees. The Journalism School's graduation numbers dropped to thirty-nine in 1950, possibly as a reflection of the end of the immediate influx of postwar students and also possibly as a reflection of the impact that the escalating conflict in Korea was having on LSU's enrollment.

What is most interesting about the graduation lists during the 1940s is that more women than men (six females to three males) received B.A.J. degrees in 1943 and that all School of Journalism graduates from 1944 through 1946 were women (two in 1944, fourteen in 1945, and four in 1946). Males once more dominated the list by 1949, with a lopsided 37-to-13 ratio. The number became more balanced in 1950, when twenty-three men and sixteen women received B.A.J. degrees.[121]

Keeping track of School of Journalism alumni has never been an easy task. Periodically, though, the School has conducted surveys that have yielded some interesting insights into where the alumni are and what they are doing. One such survey conducted in 1948 revealed that a very high percentage of the School of Journalism's roughly five hundred graduates and former students were "actively engaged in journalism and related positions." They occupied positions at newspapers, magazines, advertising departments and agencies, public relations departments, radio stations, and trade publications. Some were engaged in freelancing, some in photojournalism, and a few were in journalism education. Geographically, the alumni were spread throughout Louisiana, twenty-eight other states, and at least eleven foreign countries.[122]

The midcentury point was approaching and the LSU School of Journalism would celebrate nearly thirty years under the direction of Marvin Osborn. So much had happened during that span. The School had advanced academically to a point of preeminence among its peers in the South, and it had done so at a rapid pace. The School's faculty was educating a cadre of first-rate journalism professionals, many of whom in years to come would earn honors and recognition for their contributions. What was to happen in the School's next thirty years hardly would mirror its first. Changes were on the way that would push the School of Journalism to redefine its role within the University and within the journalism education community at large.

10

Changing Times

The LSU School of Journalism arrived at a plateau of sorts in the 1950s that would carry through until the end of the 1970s. The School began a leveling process where courses became more uniform—a few changes over time for updating purposes but no major overhaul of the curriculum—and faculty became more stable—a few new additions, but there was little turnover in personnel. The School's leadership changed five times over the period. That was certainly different. And even with a renovation of Alumni Hall in 1960, the building, renamed the Journalism Building by then, retained a character of datedness that too often also characterized the tools with which the faculty had to teach.

The School of Journalism and LSU in general were buffeted from outside and inside during the period. The 1950s began with the police action in Korea that carried through to mid-decade. Civil rights became a rallying cause when the U.S. Supreme Court's *Brown v. Board of Education* decision formally ended racial segregation later in the decade. The same decade and the next, the turbulent 1960s, saw the rise of McCarthyism, the beginning of the Cold War and the Vietnam War, the Cuban Missile Crisis, the literal launch of the Space Race, rioting in the streets and political assassinations, and finally, as the country moved into the 1970s, Watergate. All of these had profound effects on American society, and some—McCarthyism, the civil rights struggle, the Vietnam War, the assassination of John F. Kennedy, and Watergate, in particular—would affect just as profoundly the practice of how news was gathered and reported.

The impacts that all of these events or historical forces or shifts had on higher education were not always detectable or measurable. More measurable were forces closer to home and these were more decisive in terms of the quality of journalism education. Ebbs and flows of enrollment, for example, pushed the LSU School of Journalism student-to-faculty ratio to a near critical point. Budget cuts forced adjustments in the School's teaching staff and facilities that in turn affected the quality of education not only in the Journalism School but across the LSU campus. Added to budget woes was the incessant need for the School to keep pace with media technology that would match or nearly match the more and more sophisticated technology of the professional workplace.

In October 1951 Marvin Osborn submitted a statement to LSU's new president, Troy Middleton.[1] Middleton had assumed the position with the resignation of his predecessor Harold W. Stoke in late December 1950.[2] Osborn's statement likely was prepared in response to a request from the new LSU president that all department heads evaluate their unit's status, accomplishments, and needs. President Middleton had decided that LSU needed to reevaluate "its entire program of instruction, research and public service" as a means of setting the University's direction or redirection for the future.[3]

For all intents and purposes Marvin Osborn's "statement of (1) the capital needs for the established program and (2) the expansion of instructional and research programs of the School of Journalism"[4] was a wish list. Among the several needs he mentioned, a new building was the priority item. "If we are to improve—or even maintain—our position of leadership in the south-central region, expanded curricula, faculty, equipment and, soon, a new and adequate building are very much in order," said Osborn.[5]

Osborn was still chafing about the Journalism School's forced move of nearly three years earlier to Alumni Hall, and he stated very clearly to President Middleton why he considered the move such a mistake and what would be necessary to remedy the error.

> A School of Journalism building should again bring together under one roof the School and the Daily Reveille, student newspaper, with the many advantages accruing from such arrangement. Separation of the two in the moves made in the summer of 1948 was a crippling blow, and seriously impaired an instructional program that visiting journalists had spoken of as 'ideal.'
>
> As far as the quarters presently occupied by the School of Journalism in Alumni Hall is concerned, it is our opinion that it would be *difficult to justify expenditure in an effort to convert this 42-year-old, transplanted structure into a building suitable to the requirements of a modern school of journalism.*[6] (Emphasis added)

Marvin Osborn's wish list also included expanding the Journalism School's current faculty number by at least four over the next few years (at an estimated cost of some $20,000). The new faculty would enable the School to improve and enlarge its graduate program, to expand its curriculum, and to resume an outreach program that had begun to languish in recent years. Curriculum development was another key item. Osborn noted that the School of Journalism needed to expand its areas of study or concentration from the current news-editorial and publishing-management to other specialties. Expanding curriculum choices also meant adding a greater variety of courses to those already available to journalism majors.[7]

Marvin Osborn's wish list was impressive. Even so, there was no new building in sight. The LSU President and Board of Supervisors had other capitol projects in mind.[8] Nor was funding for new faculty readily available. As a result, the Journalism School's faculty size actually decreased and leveled off during the 1950s and 1960s and would not begin increasing until the mid-1970s.[9]

So, Marvin Osborn struck out on both big money items. He probably did not have much hope in their success, but he lost nothing in asking. What he and the Journalism School faculty did have some control over and even at its present size could exercise some change in was the School's curriculum. And curriculum was more important anyway. The range and content of the School's courses were one means of measuring the quality of its academic program. They also were a means of measuring how well the School of Journalism was keeping pace with journalism programs elsewhere.

Keeping up with what the folks at other universities were doing was not just important, it was vital. Colleges and universities did not then and do not today operate in a vacuum, setting an education agenda completely ignorant of what other colleges and universities were or are doing. Higher education is a competitive business. It is, for better or worse, a business built on part tradition and part trend. Ignoring some trends may in some cases prove wise but in others it could prove near fatal. The LSU School of Journalism was in a competitive field of study that was becoming more competitive by the day. For the School's faculty and director to ignore what the competition was doing, the kinds of curricula that other programs were offering, and the kinds of courses they were teaching would have been perilous. To suggest that the quality the School of Journalism was known for in the past would continue without the School's changing to compete with other programs was foolish. Complacence would maintain neither quality nor reputation, and Marvin Osborn knew it.

Part of what was motivating Osborn and his colleagues came from obvious trends that were pushing journalism education in certain directions at midcentury. Ralph Casey, director of the University of Minnesota School of Journalism, had spoken about what to expect as early as 1944. During a speech before the National Council on Professional Education for Journalism, he spoke of the postwar era of journalism education as a "period of challenge. It will require," said Casey, "intelligent and imaginative planning on the part of the [journalism] schools if they are to measure up to new opportunities and greater responsibilities."[10] And in a very prescient observation, Casey pointed to a reality that too few journalism educators of the old school were willing to accept—the recognition that "today's journalism is no longer the journalism of the press alone. The forward-looking teachers acknowledge that today's school of journalism is properly a *school of communications.*"[11]

Leaders in journalism education such as Ralph Casey were making important observations and pronouncements. They, essentially, were reporting on the state of the profession and suggesting markers for measuring where the profession needed to head. They were challenging their colleagues to prepare themselves as the next half-century began. The LSU School of Journalism would respond to that challenge incrementally, gradually changing the complexion of its faculty and its curriculum. How well these changes would accord with the standards established for journalism education in general would not be known for years to come.

Journalism School faculty during the three decades covered in this chapter fall into two major categories, long term and short term. Among those in the long-term group were faculty members whose LSU service extended for more than a decade. Faculty members in the short-term group served the School for less than a decade and in a number of instances were on the faculty for only one or two years.

Some of the Journalism School faculty could be accorded the "Old Regular" status, such as Marvin Osborn, Bruce McCoy, Marcus Wilkerson, Richard Wiggins, and Jim Price. All were definitely long-term faculty who were present to usher in the second half of the twentieth century. Wilkerson and Osborn would depart the faculty by the mid-1950s, McCoy would leave by the early 1960s, and Wiggins would be gone by the early 1970s. Jim Price would serve until 1976. His thirty-four years on the School of Journalism faculty (actually longer if his years as a graduate assistant are counted) nearly eclipsed Marcus Osborn's thirty-five years. Price also served as the School's director for thirteen years (1956–1969). Adolph ("A. O.") Goldsmith and Nicholas Plasterer were

Old Regulars of a later generation. Both served on the Journalism School faculty for nineteen years each, Goldsmith from 1955 through 1974, and Plasterer from 1957 through 1976. A. O. Goldsmith also served as the School's director twice, once as an interim from 1955 to 1956 (following Marvin Osborn's retirement) and then again from 1969 through 1974. A third set of Old Regulars from yet a later generation were Ronald ("Ron") Hicks, who joined the Journalism School faculty in 1963, and Elsie Hebert, who joined in 1969. Both were still there in the early 1980s, and, in fact, Hicks was the School's director in 1980, having succeeded A. O. Goldsmith in that position in 1974.

Several persons who joined the Journalism School faculty in the 1970s remained there into the 1980s. Among them were James ("Jim") Featherston, E. Joseph ("Joe") Broussard, Whitney Mundt, and Jon E. Fisher, all of whom arrived in the early 1970s. They were joined later by Jules d'Hemecourt, Robert Sheldon, Charles T. Jones, Douglas Wetherholt, and Jack Holgate.[12]

During this period, the average full-time faculty size numbered only about six in the 1950s, and about seven during the 1960s. The numbers rose during the 1970s for reasons that are more closely examined below. The number of full-time faculty moved from seven in 1971, to nine in 1972, ten in 1973, eleven in 1974, and twelve in 1975. The number ranged between eleven and twelve for the remainder of the 1970s.[13]

There were only two female faculty members occupying full-time positions at the School of Journalism during the entire thirty-year span covered in this chapter. And only one of these, Elsie Hebert, was a long-term employee.[14] Whether the abnormally unbalanced gender ratio could be blamed on the School's hiring practices or on the relatively low number of females available for journalism positions at the time, the situation would have to be corrected, quite decisively, during the 1980s.

In this period there were developments in the Journalism School's advertising program. Jim Price, whose expertise and interest were in news-editorial matters, nonetheless was responsible for teaching the School's only advertising courses during the 1960s. Price finally persuaded his former student Elsie Hebert to bring her professional advertising skills to the classroom. She joined the School of Journalism faculty in 1969, serving a dual role teaching advertising and advising the *Daily Reveille* staff. Advertising, at the time, occupied a secondary position to news-editorial. So it fell to Hebert, assisted occasionally by adjunct instructors from the Baton Rouge advertising community, to build the Journalism School's advertising program. Elsie Hebert remained the

School's only faculty member specializing in advertising until Alan Fletcher's arrival in 1985.[15]

LSU School of Journalism course offerings from the 1950s through the 1970s can be clustered as the School's faculty were clustered. That is, a number of courses that were offered at the end of the 1940s remained in place beyond the midcentury point. Some, in fact, remained a part of the curriculum unchanged through 1980. Others changed slightly, generally a cosmetic name change but in some cases a slight alteration of content or purpose. And there were several courses that became antiquated and were dropped from the curriculum, sometimes to be replaced by new courses whose content and purpose more closely tracked journalistic and mass media trends as well as student career interests.[16]

The Journalism School's advertising sequence saw the most growth in number and diversity of courses from 1950 through 1980.[17] The "Radio News" course was joined by a "Television News" course midway through the 1950s. These courses later spawned several other advanced radio-television courses as the School of Journalism made efforts to keep up with the need to train journalism students for careers in broadcasting.[18]

Interest among students for such training actually helped push the School of Journalism into a more cross-discipline (or interdisciplinary) arrangement in order to make its broadcast journalism sequence viable. Along with the journalism courses required of students pursuing work in the sequence were four required courses in the Speech Department. These courses represented a majority of the seven courses covering some phase of broadcasting—from acting, to writing, to announcing, to producing and directing—that had been developed and added to the Speech Department curriculum by 1972.[19]

Incorporating so much of one department's curriculum into another's, although both were part of the College of Arts and Sciences, demonstrated that such interdisciplinary cooperation was possible. Prior to the Journalism School and Speech Department finally agreeing to a workable arrangement, journalism students who wanted broadcast training were almost forced to earn a second degree in speech.[20] In years to come the example set by the cooperative venture between journalism and speech would prove even more beneficial.

Coordinating courses between two disciplines in order to accommodate students also was a major reason for the LSU Board of Supervisors' approval of the Journalism School's broadcast journalism sequence in 1971 (for implementation in 1972).[21] The new sequence proved so popular that by 1974, it had outdistanced the other two Journalism School sequences in the number of majors.[22]

School of Journalism faculty moved ahead in fall 1980 to create a fourth sequence, this one in public relations, for implementation by the following year. Framework for the sequence and the addition of one new faculty member with public relations expertise already had been approved by the College of Arts and Sciences. In addition, two new courses had been created for the sequence.[23] But approval of the sequence hit a roadblock at the upper levels of LSU administration, and it would be several years before what would become the Journalism School's most popular area of study was an officially sanctioned reality.

Meanwhile, LSU journalism majors began gravitating more and more to advertising as their preferred field of study. By 1978, in fact, advertising would become the School of Journalism's best enrolled sequence.[24] Advertising's impressive enrollment numbers were not unusual, either. Interest in studying advertising among students nationwide would push these numbers to higher and higher levels throughout the 1970s and 1980s.[25] The School of Journalism's graduate curriculum also grew considerably during the 1950–1980 span. Six graduate-only courses were available to master's degree students by the end of the 1970s.[26]

The direction that LSU and the School of Journalism took during the 1950s, 1960s, and 1970s was a product of circumstances and forces—some foreseen, some unforeseen, some from within the University, and some from beyond the LSU gates. Affecting much of that direction was the leadership that prevailed at both the departmental level and within the upper reaches of the University. At the top of the heap came not only new LSU presidents but new chief administrative officers, or chancellors, as LSU restructured in the mid-1960s.

Lt. General Troy Middleton was appointed as LSU's thirteenth president in 1951. He had achieved fame as one of the commanders of U.S. troops during World War II's Battle of the Bulge. Prior to his wartime service, Middleton had been LSU's Commandant of Cadets from 1930 to 1937. He then rose through LSU's administrative ranks as comptroller and dean of the administration both before and after his call to active duty during the war.[27] Middleton served as LSU president until 1962, when he was succeeded by John A. Hunter.[28]

A growing number of LSU branch campuses in New Orleans, Alexandria, Shreveport, and Eunice in addition to the LSU Medical Center necessitated raising President Hunter to a level that would give him administrative responsibility over all of these, including LSU at Baton Rouge, in 1965. A chancellor was appointed as chief executive officer at the LSU Baton Rouge campus. First in that position was Cecil Taylor, who served from 1965 to 1974. He was succeeded by Paul Murrill, LSU Chancellor from 1974 to 1981.[29]

The administrative office with which the School of Journalism director had the most immediate contact continued to be that of the dean of the College of Arts and Sciences. Serving as dean from 1950 until his appointment as chancellor was Cecil Taylor. Taylor was followed by Irwin A. Berg, who served as dean until replaced by Henry Snyder in December 1978.[30]

Marvin Osborn retired as director of the School of Journalism in 1955. His successors would face their own challenges and each would leave his own mark on the School. But none of them would have nearly the impact of Marvin Osborn, whose thirty-five years as director has yet to be surpassed. In fact, no one else has even come close. Beginning as a student, Osborn had spent over fifty years of his life at LSU. Hugh Blain may have given Marvin Osborn the blueprints to build LSU's journalism program so many years before, but it was Osborn's job to put it all together. And he did it in superb fashion. The editorial staff of *The Daily Reveille* dedicated its May 20, 1955, edition to the soon-to-be director emeritus "for the work he has done and the encouragement he has given in a field that is close to all our hearts."[31] And calling attention to the "nearly 1,000 graduates" who had received journalism degrees at LSU during Marvin Osborn's tenure, the Baton Rouge *Morning Advocate* said in an editorial tribute:

> When Prof. Osborn began his career as an editor and teacher at Louisiana State University, the journalism graduate with his new diploma sometimes was regarded with doubt and scorn by veteran newspapermen who had come up the hard way, learning their skills in the hard school of experience. Today the journalism graduate is welcomed in newspaper offices and has professional opportunities equal to the graduates of other schools.
>
> Much credit for this change must go to Prof. Osborn and others in his field at other colleges and universities who have given their graduates the scholastic background and the basic training in newspaper work that have made them better newspapermen.[32]

A. O. Goldsmith, like Marvin Osborn, was an LSU graduate, holding both a B.A.J. and an M.A.J. degree. He later would receive a doctorate in mass communication from the University of Iowa. Goldsmith had worked professionally at newspapers in Missouri and Arkansas before arriving at the LSU Press where he worked for several years in the early 1950s—one of those, 1953–1954, as its acting director. He moved to the School of Journalism as an instructor in 1953, and two years later was appointed by Dean Cecil Taylor for a one-year term as the School's acting director.[33]

Jim Price was elevated to the School of Journalism directorship in 1956. He had been a faculty member at the School for sixteen years and prior to his joining the faculty had been a reporter and editorial writer for the Baton Rouge *State-Times* and *Morning Advocate*. Price held a bachelor's degree from Louisiana Tech, an M.A.J. degree from LSU, and a Ph.D. in mass communication from the University of Iowa.[34]

When Jim Price decided to step down from the Journalism School director's position in 1969, Dean Berg and, by then, Chancellor Cecil Taylor did not hesitate about who they wanted to fill the position. According to Goldsmith, they "simply informed me that I was director. They knew that I would accept."[35] Asked about some of his plans for the School, Goldsmith mentioned the need for "an interdepartmental program in collaboration with the speech, English or history departments leading to a Ph.D. degree in mass communications."[36] The idea for an interdepartmental doctorate had little traction from the start, so the Ph.D. program would have to wait for more than a quarter century. But give A. O. Goldsmith credit for looking to the future.

Goldsmith's retirement in 1974 brought another LSU graduate to the director's position. Ron Hicks, who received his B.A.J. and M.A.J. degrees as well as his doctorate in sociology from LSU, was appointed director of the School of Journalism after serving on the School's faculty for twelve years. Hicks also served a concurrent twelve-year term as LPA manager.[37] His six-year term as Journalism School director would be a productive one, but accreditation issues in the late 1970s focused attention on serious weaknesses at the School that Hicks would have to deal with.

Directors and faculty alike in the School of Journalism would be confronted with a number of challenges during the 1950–1980 span. One of these was adjusting to the technological revolution that was permeating the media world. Funding was another challenge—funding to pay for increasing the faculty size in addition to paying for equipment upgrades. But the one challenge approaching a critical point was skyrocketing enrollment.

Trends showed that LSU's overall enrollment, after a questionable start, was headed upward during the 1950s, 1960s, and 1970s. The questionable start was caused by the impact the Korean conflict was having on college enrollment during the early 1950s. In July 1950, the U.S. Government began drafting young men, many of whom were college students, to bolster troop strength in defending South Korea against advancing North Korean troops. The armistice that formally ended the Korean conflict was signed on July 27, 1953.[38]

LSU enrollment began to reflect a loss of male students during the 1950–1951 academic year when enrollment dropped by roughly 13 percent, from 7,430 the year before to 6,359 in 1950–1951. Enrollment the following year was down another 10 percent but not as much as had been expected.[39] In 1952–1953, enrollment had inched above the 1950–1951 total, possibly resulting from educational benefits flowing to Korean War veterans following passage in July 1952 of a second G. I. Bill similar to the one passed by Congress for World War II veterans.[40]

Whatever was pushing enrollment at LSU, student numbers definitely were climbing as the 1950s wore on, reaching a record 9,601 during the 1956–1957 academic year.[41] And the numbers kept rising from there. A 1961 article in the *LSU Alumni News* magazine suggested that LSU's "enrollment boom" was similar to what was happening nationwide. The article quoted the LSU Registrar's Office prediction of nearly 18,000 students on the Baton Rouge campus by 1972. Noting that "the accuracy of previous forecasts by the Registrar has been phenomenal,"[42] the writer of the *Alumni News* article and the Registrar both must have been surprised when the actual enrollment in 1972 was a little over 22,000. By 1978, LSU enrollment was nearing 25,000, and by the 1980–1981 academic year, enrollment had topped 27,000.[43]

The LSU School of Journalism suffered significant enrollment declines in the early 1950s. The School's 1951–1952 fall undergraduate enrollment was down to 37 from the previous year's 71, a whopping 48 percent decline. Numbers were even more bleak the next year when fall enrollment was a mere 35 majors. Numbers began to slowly climb from that point, but not until the 1957–1958 academic year did they exceed the 1950–1951 figures—but only slightly. Unlike the dramatic loss of male students during World War II, at no time during the Korean conflict were there fewer male than female LSU journalism majors.[44]

By the 1960s, School of Journalism enrollment was tracking right in line with the zooming overall LSU enrollment. The rising enrollment also was in keeping with similar enrollment increases at other U.S. journalism schools.[45] Undergraduate enrollment in particular stood at 159 by fall 1967, had increased to 242 by fall 1972, and had jumped to 327 by fall 1974.[46] LSU Journalism School Director Ron Hicks also was reporting a significant increase in the number of nonmajor, undecided students as well as majors from other disciplines enrolling in journalism courses. Of interest, too, was the example of a gender revolution then underway in journalism education. Unlike in years past, with the exception of the World War II years, there now were more women than men enrolled in journalism courses at LSU.[47]

Journalism School enrollment numbers kept steadily increasing during the next few years and by fall 1980, enrollment data showed a combined undergraduate major and graduate student Journalism School enrollment of 535, a more than 100 percent enrollment increase from the School's 1971 combined undergraduate-graduate enrollment of a little over 200. And the gender ratio now stood at 369 women (357 undergraduates and 12 graduates) to 166 men (161 undergraduates and 5 graduates).[48]

As more and more students arrived on the LSU School of Journalism's doorstep, the natural question on the director's and faculty's minds must have been, what is motivating all these students to want to study journalism, and how are we going to accommodate them? The motivation question might have been answered in part by the math of proportionate growth. That is, with LSU's enrollment growth in general it was only natural that each of the University's units, such as the School of Journalism, would grow in proportion to that of the University at large.

Ron Hicks saw the School's attraction from a far different angle. He could not account for the burgeoning interest in advertising, but Hicks determined that enrollment in the news-editorial area was growing because students were genuinely excited about majoring in journalism. Speculating on why that was, Hicks suggested in a 1975 article in the *LSU Alumni Magazine* that newspaper reporting by Carl Bernstein and Bob Woodward, whose *Washington Post* stories had exposed the Watergate scandal, had helped create a "journalist-as-hero" image of the profession. The press's ability to exact change from within the system rather than from without as had been so prevalent during the 1960s was also seen as one of journalism's attractions. Ron Hicks saw the rise of what was called New Journalism, which incorporated literary writing styles to write about nonfiction subjects, as yet another attraction. Popular writers of the period such as Norman Mailer, Truman Capote, and Tom Wolfe were all practitioners of this new style of journalism.

Ron Hicks also cited a number of pragmatic reasons for students to be drawn to studying journalism. Journalism students were graduating with a solid background in the liberal arts as well as highly marketable communication skills. The job market had broadened by the 1970s to include employment opportunities in radio, television, public relations, film, and a host of other emerging media technologies and applications to add to what already existed in the newspaper, magazine, and advertising professions. And starting salaries across the board were better than ever before.[49]

As each of these areas and corresponding niches developed, employment opportunities grew exponentially. There is no accurate accounting for the number of new advertising agencies, public relations firms, or similar departments and other media units that came into existence from the 1950s into the early 1980s, but a good measurement of Louisiana radio and television station and newspaper (daily and weekly) growth during the period does exist. As of 1981, there were 24 daily newspapers and 87 weeklies serving the state.[50] In 1951, there were 59 radio stations (AM and FM) and only one television station in Louisiana.[51] By 1981, the number of radio stations had grown to 184 and the number of television stations to 22.[52]

But all the interest and the resulting enrollment increases had their down side. Ron Hicks and his immediate predecessor A. O. Goldsmith had little choice but to create additional class sections (to minimize the teacher-to-student ratio as much as possible) and to employ part-time or adjunct instructors to handle the crush of students. And they were forced to upgrade teaching facilities and technology as best they could. Worst of all, they were forced to do this with a budget that grew tighter every year.[53]

Still, the LSU Journalism School managed to do what was necessary to graduate students who were finding jobs in their chosen career field. Demand for journalism graduates, in fact, was far beyond supply, according to Journalism School Director Jim Price. He cited about three hundred job openings for only twenty B.A.J. and ten M.A.J. graduates in 1957.[54] "People who hire our graduates come back to hire others," A. O. Goldsmith said in 1972.[55]

As the Journalism School explored new directions for its academic program, faculty members began to rethink their mission and purpose. From almost the first days of its existence the School had stated the purpose of its curriculum as "based on the conception of journalism as a profession whose members are trained investigators of fact."[56] By the 1970s, though, that purpose had been modified and broadened to include other objectives. Journalism now was "conceived as a profession concerned with gathering and disseminating news, ideas and information of a timely nature, thereby serving the communication needs of a free society, in addition to creating an awareness of the ethical and legal responsibilities involved."[57]

Physical changes at the Journalism School accompanied intellectual changes. At the end of the 1960 spring semester, faculty members completely vacated the Journalism Building (still called Alumni Hall at the time) and moved to Prescott Hall in order to clear the way for a major renovation of the building's interior.[58] Marvin Osborn had complained from day one of the School's move to Alumni Hall; now the pending crush of students and the need to upgrade teaching, administrative, and *Daily Reveille* facilities left little choice but to give the building an interior makeover.

The Alumni Hall renovations were complete by the end of the summer, making the facilities "admirably suited to the needs of journalism education," in the opinion of Jim Price.[59] Construction along with some strategic moves— the LSU Press migrated to the Hill Memorial Building, for instance—opened much needed space. *The Daily Reveille* newsroom, editor and managing editor offices, reference and file room, and state-of-the-art photographic and darkroom facilities were relocated to the Alumni Hall first floor. Also occupying the first floor were several faculty offices, classrooms, and typing labs. On the second floor were the School of Journalism director's office and other administrative offices; an office for the LPA manager and director of the School's new Journalism Extension Service, both jointly headed at the time by Bruce McCoy; classrooms; a newspaper editing lab; and a reading room/library.[60]

One of the most significant changes to Alumni Hall accompanying the 1960 renovation was the building's name. The name change evolved from an interesting set of circumstances. To begin, the University in 1958 gave the LSU Alumni Federation the old president's house that stood (and continues to stand) on Highland Road across from the present LSU Union. President and Mrs. Middleton decided to ignore tradition in 1955 and moved back to their home just south of LSU.[61] The Federation renovated the building, turning it into the new home to LSU alumni, and renamed the building Alumni House.[62]

Since an Alumni Hall on one side of the campus and an Alumni House on the other was confusing, the Alumni Federation Council requested that the LSU Board of Supervisors change the name of Alumni Hall. There was little doubt that the Board would comply with the request, but what name would be chosen? The LSU Board's Committee on Naming University Facilities ordinarily would have renamed Alumni Hall in honor of someone closely connected to LSU. But no requests for adding new names were pending at the time and evidently none were proposed.

Since the building housed the School of Journalism, the Board of Supervisors decided by default that Alumni Hall should be renamed the Journalism Building.[63] This would mark the first time since its move from the renamed Thomas Boyd Hall that the LSU School of Journalism would occupy a building bearing a journalism designation. Nearly fifty years later, and after major changes both inside and outside, the Journalism Building is still called the Journalism Building.

Working space available to students in the Journalism Building of 1960 was supplemented by new and modern teaching tools such as tape recorders, opaque projectors, 16-mm film projectors, press cameras, and the like[64] that would seem quaint and even antique by later standards. But they were right in line with the state of the art at the time. Film cameras and editing facilities and a television production studio were added by 1975.[65]

Progress made in classroom technology from the 1950s to the 1960s and from there to the 1970s was enormous, but nothing could match the technology acceleration that was beginning by the mid-1970s. The computer age arrived in the LSU School of Journalism in fall 1975 when video display terminals (VDTs) were first used to instruct journalism students on video text compositions.[66] In only three years the VDTs had to be upgraded to a new generation system that was far ahead of the first.[67] Broadcast journalism students were becoming acquainted with new portable video cameras and video tape recorders (VTRs).[68] These and similar devices were costly (nearly $4,000 for each of the newest VDT models)[69] and stretched already meager Journalism School budgets. But they were necessary for instruction if students were to learn the tools of their trade.

A big change, indeed a revolutionary change, was announced for the School of Journalism in 1977. The LSU administration had decided to renovate Coates Hall, the former chemical laboratory building, and to remake it as a Communication Center. The idea was to bring the Journalism School, Speech Department, Computer Science Department, and Library School together under one roof so that "communications-related departments" could "cooperate and share equipment," said Ron Hicks.[70] All Student Media offices, which by then included *The Daily Reveille, Gumbo,* and WLSU radio, were to be located in the Coates basement. A new television studio was planned for the building along with several new laboratory facilities and classrooms. Renovation was scheduled for completion in fall 1978.

Opposition to the move began almost as soon as the Coates Hall renovation was announced. Most vocal were those who worried about the Journalism School's loss of identity.[71] The same Journalism Building that had been scorned less than twenty years earlier now was seen as the School's cherished home. As it happened, critics of the move got their wish. When the Coates Hall renovation was complete all but one of the units originally intended to occupy the building actually made the move. School of Journalism faculty chose not to go. In the long run, and more by accident than design, that turned out to be a very wise decision.

The Journalism School continued to mix its internal academic activities with its outreach programs throughout the 1950s, 1960s, and 1970s. One major outreach instrument was the School's Journalism Extension Service, created prior to the 1957–1958 academic year. The LPA Field Manager actually became director of the Extension Service, an arrangement that remained in place for the next twenty years. In 1974 the LPA Field Manager position was separated from the Journalism School, and the Field Manager's office was moved off campus. The LPA needed a full-time manager and bigger quarters, and the Journalism School needed the LPA space. The separation was mutually beneficial and on good terms, although a tradition that the School had started when Bruce McCoy arrived at LSU finally had come to an end. Ron Hicks, McCoy's successor, remained in the LPA manager's position until he was named the Journalism School Director.[72] His faculty colleague Joe Broussard was named to succeed Hicks as director of the Journalism Extension Service.

The Extension Service by the mid-1970s had grown to include a multitude of activities as part of its general function as liaison between the School of Journalism and the professional and high school media of Louisiana. Part of the Extension Service director's job included heading the Louisiana Scholastic Press Association (LSPA), an important organization about which more is said below. Broussard also was responsible for organizing workshops, conferences, and other activities. Finally, the Extension Service director was in charge of producing and distributing the School's occasional *Research Bulletins*.[73]

One of the Extension Service's more enduring legacies was the partnership it developed between the School of Journalism and the LSPA. The LSPA formed in 1952 when about two hundred high school students met at LSU to discuss their common interests in journalism.[74] Before long, the LSPA was meeting annually at LSU. School of Journalism faculty became heavily involved in the conferences, serving as session and workshop speakers and judges for the annual LSPA high school newspaper and yearbook contests.[75]

Student organizations within the Journalism School continued to function —some more actively than others—during the 1950s, 1960s, and 1970s. New groups appeared as older groups disbanded or simply withered away. Theta Sigma Phi and Sigma Delta Chi both showed they were here to stay. However, that did not prevent the near disappearance and the subsequent rebound of the latter group because of member disinterest in the late 1970s.[76] A local LSU chapter of the American Advertising Federation (AAF) was organized in 1972, joined later by the Federation's Alpha Delta Sigma (ADS) Honorary Society.[77] By 1975, the School of Journalism was home to an active chapter of Women in Communication (WICI), an honorary organization of college and professional women working in all phases of the media industry.[78] Finally, the national organization of Kappa Tau Alpha honorary society awarded the School of Journalism a local chapter in 1979.[79]

Journalism School alumni were right in step with the School's undergraduates when it came to organizing. Indeed, a group of graduates met in the School library during Homecoming 1955 to form the LSU School of Journalism Alumni Association. Alfred N. Delahaye was elected the group's first president and first representative to the LSU Alumni Council.[80]

LSU student media took some eventful twists and turns beginning in the 1950s and extending into the 1980s. One significant operational change happened at *The Daily Reveille* in April 1954, when the afternoon paper reversed course from a few years earlier and once more became a morning paper. The switch was meant only as an experiment, but *Reveille* staff felt the morning edition enabled them to publish fresher news. The A.M. edition proved preferable to readers as well.[81] So *The Daily Reveille* would remain a morning paper.

The Daily Reveille took a giant technological step in May 1957, when it began using a newly installed offset press. The new press, capable of producing roughly fifteen thousand newspaper copies per hour,[82] got a workout in October 1959, when *The Daily Reveille* staff, with editor Smiley Anders leading the way, produced a hundred-page LSU Centennial edition.[83] *The Daily Reveille's* structure and philosophy would change little from that point on. The paper's content continued to reflect the issues, major and minor, of the day. *Reveille* editorials and commentary during the 1950s, for instance, ranged from debate over whether to spend University funds to expand Tiger Stadium or build a new library to the perpetual complaint over LSU campus parking.[84] Editors gradually widened the paper's scope and began looking more seriously at major state and national issues. The issues of civil rights and the Vietnam War, in particular, found their way into *The Daily Reveille* more frequently. These ongoing subjects were controversial and stirred emotions; and discussions of each required the utmost care and solid judgment on the part of editors.

How *The Daily Reveille* covered efforts to integrate LSU during the 1950s and 1960s might best illustrate how committed the paper had become to reporting and commenting on difficult issues. Court-ordered admission of black students to LSU was the focus of many of the early stories. Interestingly, one of the first eight blacks to be admitted to the University was Leslie Barnum, who entered the School of Journalism's graduate program in September 1951.[85] Barnum thus became the School's first black student. There is no record that he completed his degree program, perhaps due to heavy work responsibilities after he became editor of *The Weekly Leader* in February 1952. The Baton Rouge paper was one of only a few in the state intended primarily for black readers.[86]

Integration of LSU classrooms was complicated when the U.S. Supreme Court issued its landmark *Brown vs. Board of Education* decision in 1954. The decision ended the "separate but equal" doctrine that had been in effect since the Court's 1896 *Plessy vs. Ferguson* decision,[87] but efforts to fully enforce the 1954 ruling, as chronicled in the pages of *The Daily Reveille*, were not entirely swift nor effective.[88] Attempting to clarify LSU's policy on integration, President Middleton issued a statement in April 1956, saying that blacks would be admitted whenever the courts so decreed. LSU would not put itself above the law, said Middleton, and blacks would be admitted to the University on the same basis as whites.[89]

The Louisiana legislature did not see court orders as the last word on segregation, however. Several legislators busied themselves writing and passing legislation that either directly or indirectly forced segregation to prevail at LSU, even if blacks were formally admitted. For example, a measure passed unanimously by the Louisiana Senate in July 1956 prohibited "dancing, social functions, entertainments, athletic games, sports or contests and other such activities involving personal and social contacts in which the participants are members of the white and Negro races."[90]

Darrell Eiland, editor of the 1956 *Summer Reveille* (the summer semester version of the *Reveille*) decided to engage the legislators by urging readers of his July 19 editorial not to "meekly [sit] back and let the advocates of segregation ram through idiotic pieces of legislation without even opening their mouths in protest."[91] State Senator W. M. Rainach responded to the Eiland editorial, calling it "an example of brainwashing of the worst sort" and decrying how "freedom of the press and academic freedom must be maintained, even though the enemies of our form of government and way of life use these freedoms to attack us."[92] Senator Rainach later suggested that the LSU School of Journalism be investigated and that *Reveille* editor Eiland be expelled.[93] Fortunately, neither happened.

Antisegregationist activity at LSU eventually did lead Senator Rainach to conduct a legislative hearing in June 1958, intended specifically to question whether a group of LSU faculty members who had signed an American Civil Liberties Union petition opposing several proposed segregationist bills had communist connections.[94] Once again, a *Summer Reveille* editorial, this one written by Jim Chubbuck, criticized Senator Rainach's reaction to the petition. "The act committed that caused the chain reaction that can very well destroy the higher educational system in Louisiana—and so angered Sen. Rainach and his colleagues," noted Chubbuck, "is one that the same Sen. Rainach and the rest of the Legislature are free to express everyday in their duties and private life: the right to express a dissenting opinion."[95] Other social issues in years to come would compel *Reveille* editors once more to take positions that were not always the most popular. But the paper was serving its purpose: informing on the one hand and stimulating discussion and debate on the other.

Things were not as promising with campus radio. Whatever progress WLSU might have made during the 1940s and 1950s, the station, in fact, was costing LSU considerable money to operate. And when the University suffered a major budget cut in 1957, President Middleton targeted WLSU as one expense that had to be eliminated. In June 1957, the station ceased operations. The WLSU antenna was disassembled and stored, and the station facilities were turned over to the LSU Bureau of Public Relations.[96]

WLSU returned as a radio station in November 1965, but rather than transmitting its signal over the air as a broadcast station, WLSU instead would transmit its signal via a carrier current or "wired-wireless" system. The station signal would be fed into the electrical power lines running through LSU dormitories and other selected buildings. The power lines then would act as weak transmitters whose output could be picked up by radio receivers either plugged into or located near the lines.[97]

Consideration was underway by late 1975 to convert WLSU back to an FM broadcast station. Not until 1979, though, would the FCC grant LSU a license for the station. Its assigned call letters would not be WLSU (which, by then, had been assigned to Wisconsin State University at LaCrosse) but rather WPRG. The existing carrier current station facilities, then located in the LSU Union, were moved to East Tiger Stadium, and on January 15, 1980, the new WPRG-FM signed on.[98] A special request to change WPRG's call letters to KLSU was granted by the FCC in 1983, when LSU successfully argued that the "K" prefix usually reserved for radio stations operating west of the Mississippi River could apply to an LSU station, since much of that station's signal actually reached listeners beyond the river's west bank.[99]

KLSU was staffed by a full-time news team whose key personnel—news director, public affairs director, sports director, and so on—usually were Manship School students. The station's Manship School faculty advisor also served as general manager.[100] The reason for KLSU's faculty advisor assuming a managerial role stemmed from station license requirements. As station licensee, the LSU Board of Supervisors was responsible for having a University employee in place who could exercise ultimate authority over station operation.

The kind of faculty oversight exercised at KLSU was not questioned. But questions did exist about the extent to which students were free to say what they pleased in the pages of *The Daily Reveille*. The paper never had been a laboratory for School of Journalism students, although it certainly gave that appearance during the days of Hugh Blain and Marvin Osborn. Since then, *The Daily Reveille* had become nearly independent of the School, save for the nominal role played by the faculty advisor. Little is known about what specific role the advisor served other than being on call to answer questions about how best to deal with difficult matters. LSU President Troy Middleton once had characterized the advisor's job as "counsel, critic, and father confessor to the editors."[101] The advising style of Jim Price, while he served as Journalism School director, was described by 1958 *Summer Reveille* editor Darrell Eiland as helpful but never censorial: "At my request he checked my work for lucidity, coherence, and other editorial bugaboos. He would sometimes advise me as to what results I could expect from various things I wrote and did, but he never attempted to get me to go against my conscience in anything I wrote."[102] A. O. Goldsmith, during the 1960s, was known to request monthly reports from *The Daily Reveille* managing editor on reporter job performance,[103] but even that kind of information might have been considered out of bounds by some *Reveille* personnel. There is no evidence that any subsequent advisors took an oversight route similar to Goldsmith's.

Advisors shared some of their oversight responsibilities with a body created in the 1940s called the Committee on Student Publications. This committee, comprised of LSU faculty and administrators, assumed the role once held by the LSU President of appointing student media editors and managers.[104] The Committee on Student Publications came under criticism in the late 1960s for having too few members familiar with the necessary qualifications of student media personnel. The criticism convinced LSU administrators by the early 1970s to replace the committee with the Student Communications Media Board, a new body that not only would appoint persons to various student media management positions, but also hear and attempt to resolve complaints of misconduct or unprofessional behavior lodged against student media personnel. The Media Board would make decisions using as its guide the American Society of Newspaper Editors' Code of Responsibility. The Code, in fact, would be included in the Media Board By-Laws along with a provision that expressly forbade censorship of student media expression by any Media Board member.[105]

LSU administrators, who more than any others at the University probably were most aware of what influence the student media could have, were very restrained in dealing with student reporters and editors. President Troy Middleton may have stated the most ideal working relationship with student media when he remarked that procedures were in place to safeguard against anyone abusing his or her role as a journalist. Otherwise, Middleton felt that students should have all the freedom necessary to practice the craft of journalism as long as that freedom remained tempered by responsibility.[106]

The School of Journalism received a major boost in its scholarship offerings in 1958 when fourteen Louisiana newspapers provided funds to support four-year scholarships for high school seniors living in the parishes where the newspapers were located and who chose to study journalism at LSU. Seven other newspapers contributed funds that were combined to create two Louisiana Press Association Scholarships. Sixteen four-year scholarships in all resulted from this show of generosity.[107]

A scholarship established by the *Minneapolis Star and Tribune* in 1965 was intended for one senior student in each of the forty-seven accredited schools and departments of journalism throughout the United States. As an accredited school, the LSU School of Journalism earned the privilege of awarding one of these scholarships annually.[108] Two other scholarships were established, one in 1966 and the other in 1968, to assist School of Journalism students with their studies. The first was the Charles P. Manship Memorial Scholarship given by Charles P. Manship Jr. to memorialize his father.[109] The second scholarship, the Hodding Carter Award for Responsible Journalism, was established by 1946 School of Journalism graduate Harriet Fox Deer to honor Hodding Carter's legacy as newspaper editor and publisher.[110] Two more scholarships, the Herbert S. and Lou Audrey Benjamin Memorial Scholarship and the Walter Hitesman Scholarship, were added in 1978 to the growing pool of financial assistance available to School of Journalism students.[111]

More than mere financial assistance, though, scholarships allowed the LSU School of Journalism to honor students for their hard work. They were awards for a job well done and in some cases for a student's potential. Recognition that scholarship recipients were among the best and the brightest placed these students in the company of some especially meritorious Journalism School alumni who not only had made names for themselves, but who also had brought honor to their alma mater. Consider, for instance, the contributions of just a few of these alumni.

William L. Rivers earned both his bachelor's (1951) and master's (1952) degrees in journalism from LSU and eventually became a member of the Stanford University communications faculty. It was during his time at Stanford that Rivers received the Sigma Delta Chi Distinguished Service Award in recognition of his influential book, *The Opinionmakers,* "an analysis of the interplay of politics and the press in Washington, D.C." Following his student days at LSU, William Rivers had worked as a congressional assistant in Washington, D.C., and later wrote for *Harper's, The Nation,* and the *New York Times Magazine.*[112]

In 1969, another School of Journalism alumnus, Wes Gallagher, whose many contributions to journalism are chronicled in chapter 9, was recognized as LSU's Alumnus of the Year.[113] Only a year before, Gallagher had been named the winner of the prestigious John Peter Zenger Freedom of the Press Award.[114] And an honor accorded to few came to Journalism School alumnus Harry Middleton (class of 1947) in 1969 when former President Lyndon Johnson tabbed him to become director of the Lyndon B. Johnson Library in Austin, Texas. Middleton had been an assistant in the Johnson White House, helping primarily to draft speeches. After the President returned to Texas, he asked Harry Middleton to help him with organizing his personal and presidential papers. That task led to a far greater one when he assumed the director's position at the Johnson Library.[115]

Five years after Wes Gallagher was honored as LSU's Alumnus of the Year, another Journalism School graduate, Walter Hitesman Jr. (class of 1939), was given the same honor. Neither their common background nor the importance of the two organizations they headed at the time went unnoticed by the *LSU Alumni News.*

> Numerically speaking, the graduates of LSU's School of Journalism represent only a drop in the huge bucket of War Skule alumnihood. Yet the splash they have made is disproportionately large: two LSU Alumni-of-the-Year in the nine years that the annual award has been in existence.

Although our J-School grads are not numerous enough to glut the job market, those two in particular have moved to commanding positions in their respective subdivisions of journalism:

Wes Gallagher . . . is president and chief executive officer of the Associated Press, the world's largest news service.

Walter Wood Hitesman Jr. . . . is president and chief operating officer of *Reader's Digest,* the world's most widely circulated monthly magazine.[116]

Walter Hitesman immersed himself in the newspaper business while an LSU student. He edited *The Reveille* and worked part-time at the Baton Rouge *Morning Advocate.* Mention was made in the previous chapter of his work with the U.S. Marine Corps' *Leatherneck* magazine during World War II. Following the war, Hitesman had joined the Reader's Digest organization, working his way up to the top job. He now commanded an international operation and one of the first multimedia companies, with divisions devoted not just to producing magazines, but also to publishing books and producing phonograph records, motion pictures, and television programs.

The occasion for honoring Walter Hitesman was nothing out of the ordinary —including meeting old friends, a banquet, the presentation of a plaque by the LSU Alumni Federation, a speech by the honored guest—until Hitesman made a surprise announcement near the end of the ceremony. The Reader's Digest Foundation, in Walter Hitesman's name, was awarding the LSU School of Journalism a $50,000 endowment, "provided only that the amount can be matched from local sources."[117] The quest to fully fund the Walter W. Hitesman Endowed Journalism Fund presented a challenge, but Journalism School Director Goldsmith and Journalism Alumni Association President William Bailey said they were up to the task. Hitesman himself got the fund drive off to a good start by donating $5,000. Once the endowment was fully funded the Journalism School director would be able to rely on annual interest earnings to help pay for scholarships, faculty research grants, faculty and student travel, and other needs as they arose.[118]

The uses to which the Hitesman funds could be put were many, and the needs obviously were great. There was, however, one catch in the endeavor to raise matching funds—a May 1, 1975, deadline. That gave Ron Hicks, who succeeded A. O. Goldsmith as Journalism School director on July 1, 1974,[119] and Joe Silverberg, who had succeeded William Bailey as Journalism Alumni Association president, little more than a year to raise the additional $45,000. Silverberg's first step in launching the fund drive was to appoint a steering committee of prominent Journalism School alumni to create mailings and to contact fellow alumni and media professionals to solicit donations. Ron Hicks reminded all contributors and potential contributors of the Hitesman Fund's importance to the School, saying, "It represents a unique opportunity for alumni and friends to give the school a real boost at a time when increasing enrollment and rising education costs are putting considerable pressure on existing facilities and resources."[120]

The LSU Journalism School's alumni and friends succeeded in meeting the deadline, actually topping the $50,000 goal by about $2,000. Contributions came from 223 individuals and organizations; even the LSU Student Government Association pitched in, to make the fund drive a success. The Hitesman Fund endowment would be managed by the LSU Foundation and would yield earnings as early as the 1976–1977 academic year.[121] One of the first benefits to flow from the endowment would be the additional undergraduate scholarships mentioned above.

Journalism School graduates like Walter Hitesman, Wes Gallagher, Harry Middleton, and William Rivers had achieved the kind of success that made their alma mater proud. But there were other graduates who had been equally successful, perhaps more at the local than at the national or international level, who deserved recognition similar to what Gallagher, Hitesman, and Rivers had received. The Journalism School, in other words, needed its own means of recognizing alumni achievements. The idea to create a Hall of Fame to do just that had set Ron Hicks to thinking and planning as soon as he became the School's director.[122]

Once the big push to raise matching funds for the Hitesman endowment was over, Ron Hicks turned his attention to organizing the School of Journalism Hall of Fame. The first group of inductees would be honored in a ceremony hosted by the Journalism Alumni Association during its October 1975 Homecoming dinner. The Journalism School faculty and director went to work to select the inductees. The selection criteria were simple: graduates of the School who had made significant contributions to the journalism profession, to an allied profession, or to journalism education; or a nongraduate who had made significant contributions to the School or had been associated with the School.

When the votes were tabulated, nine persons were selected to the Hall of Fame: Walter Hitesman, Wes Gallagher, William Rivers, Margaret "Maggie" Dixon, John Merrill, Marvin Osborn, Jim Price, A. O. Goldsmith, and Bruce McCoy. Three from the group—Dixon, Osborn, and McCoy—were deceased, and all but McCoy held either a bachelor's or a master's or both degrees in journalism from LSU.[123] Readers already should be aware of why seven of the nine merited selection. John Merrill, who may be unfamiliar at this point, is discussed more in chapter 11 as he assumed directorship of the LSU School of Journalism in 1980. His selection to the Hall of Fame in 1975 was based on Merrill's prominence as a journalism educator and scholar. He was a prolific writer whose books on journalism theory and criticism also had made him an internationally recognized and respected lecturer. Maggie Dixon had risen through the reporting ranks to become managing editor of the Baton Rouge *Morning Advocate*. She had served a number of years as a School of Journalism adjunct faculty member, and in 1951, Dixon became only the third woman to be appointed to the LSU Board of Supervisors.[124]

The School of Journalism Hall of Fame was a great success. The list of inductees would grow year by year, and by 2004 included the names of seventy-six alumni and friends of the School. Ron Hicks deserves much credit for bringing his idea for the Hall of Fame to reality. He also deserves more credit than he has received through the years for pulling the School through a near crisis in 1977 when it stood on the brink of losing its accreditation. For all that was accomplished at the School during the 1970s, particularly with regard to the quality of students who were choosing to major in journalism during the decade and the curriculum upgrades that went on, none of it would have mattered when compared with the loss of prestige that would have resulted from failure to be reaccredited. How the possible loss of accreditation happened, what it meant, and what changes came about once the matter was resolved—fortunately, in the School of Journalism's favor—are examined below. Before proceeding, though, some understanding is necessary regarding the debate that was taking place during the 1970s over the proper role of journalism education and the integral place of that debate in the entire philosophy of accreditation.

Competing points of view on journalism education's role were not new. Indeed, they were as old as journalism education itself. But at this point in history, debate on the issue was beginning to intensify. On the one side were the theorists; on the other were the practitioners. The position of the theorists and the direction they were charting for journalism educators was best presented in a *Journalism Quarterly* article written by Ted Peterson. Peterson described what he saw as a "dramatic change" or "transformation" that had "come over schools of journalism since the end of World War II." In brief, he said that schools of journalism have become less preoccupied with teaching students the tricks of the trade than with giving them a genuinely liberal education which puts the press, broadcasting and advertising into their proper social, economic, historical and philosophical contexts. They have begun to shift their allegiance from the newspapers of their states to the community at large. They have begun to replace the old pros on their faculties with serious scholars dedicated to a searching study of the mass media as an important social institution worthy of their concern. They have developed into centers of research, and in doing so they have looked to other fields of study for help in discovering what they can about the whole mysterious process of human communication. They are increasingly becoming centers of graduate study. Finally, they have started to become—hesitatingly, falteringly, to be sure—centers of informal criticism of the mass media generally.[125]

This hardly described the LSU School of Journalism. If this is what journalism education was supposed to be in the 1970s, then LSU was far behind the times. Ironically, Peterson's remarks came from an article written in 1960! He, in effect, was describing where journalism education programs had progressed during the 1950s. To persons who ascribed to Peterson's decidedly theory-based ideas for journalism training, the LSU School of Journalism not only was off track by the 1970s but had been off track for quite some time.

Persons who ascribed to a more pragmatic kind of journalism education did not see that the LSU School of Journalism had fallen behind times and was operating with a curriculum that was out of step with most other journalism schools. A. O. Goldsmith, for instance, said in 1972, "We at the LSU School of Journalism feel that the basic principles of journalism training must be for gathering and analyzing the news, and finally, writing it down."[126] Goldsmith deplored programs where students might earn a journalism degree "without ever taking a course in reporting or editing,"[127] in reference, it might be assumed, to Ted Peterson's theory-based ideas. But how might one know which approach would be the best? "The main way to assess the job a journalism school is doing is by the performance of its graduates," Goldsmith said, adding, "People who hire our [LSU's] graduates come back to hire others."[128]

These were the basics of the two competing philosophies. Question was, which approach was advocated by accreditors in charge of judging how well LSU's journalism program met the prevailing performance standards? If they agreed with the A. O. Goldsmith pragmatist approach to journalism education, then the LSU School of Journalism probably was in good shape. If they agreed with the theoretical approach espoused by Ted Peterson with all that it implied about faculty, curriculum, and research, then the School was in trouble.

All this talk of accreditation and the impact on a program of loss of accreditation suggests that the accreditation imprimatur of the accrediting agency, the ACEJ in this case, carried immense power. In the world of journalism education, the stamp of approval accreditation gives a program was extremely important, even in the early days when the ACEJ was just beginning the review process, and much more so today. A. O. Goldsmith condensed the importance of accreditation into very simple terms: "As a general rule, the employer is fairly safe in assuming that graduates of an accredited school or department of journalism will be competent. The unaccredited departments, however, are an unknown quantity."[129]

The School of Journalism's first reaccreditation effort occurred in 1957. Remember that the School was among the first in the country to be accredited by the ACEJ in 1948, and that the ACEJ accredited program *sequences* only and not the entire program. In LSU's case its news-editorial and publishing-management sequences were accredited. Both were reviewed for reaccreditation in 1957 by an ACEJ site team that inspected the Journalism School facilities, reviewed its curriculum and accomplishments, and interviewed faculty, students, administrators, and alumni with a battery of questions.[130] In actuality, there was little chance that the School's two sequences would not be reaccredited. Indeed, ACEJ reaccreditation occurred without a hitch in June 1957.[131]

The School of Journalism would undergo two more successful reaccreditations in 1964 and 1971 before problems set in. As time neared for reaccreditation in 1977, concern began building at LSU over the number of course credit hours that journalism majors were required to take. The number of hours, it so happened, exceeded the limit set by ACEJ standards. Ron Hicks argued that the extra hours were justified, since they allowed the School to expose majors to a set of common core courses as well as a set of required courses in their chosen sequence. Taking the extra courses, argued Hicks, improved a journalism graduate's chances for success in the job market.[132] But would the ACEJ site team accept Hicks's justification for the extra hours?

Hicks also worried about other potential problems. A 15 percent annual enrollment increase during the early years of the 1970s had pushed Journalism School facilities and resources to their limits; actually, past their limits. Between 1970 and 1977, according to Hicks, the School's enrollment had doubled.

The School's budget allotments also had failed to keep pace with needs. And escalating technology costs were especially troublesome.

There were a few bright spots, though. The School's faculty size had grown;[133] the broadcast journalism sequence was fully implemented; and the Hitesman Fund and Hall of Fame were realities. In small measures, a Senior Privilege Program that allowed qualified seniors to audit courses "to fill in some gaps" and a Journalism Student-Faculty Council used "to gain student input and improve communication between faculty and students" were both in place.[134] But, again, would the ACEJ site team be more impressed by the problems or by the improvements?

One problem that the site team had insisted needed correcting during the previous accreditation visit was the lack of faculty diversity.[135] Diversity issues would apply more to gender and race in years to come but for now the message in plain language was that too many faculty members had terminal degrees from LSU. The ACEJ regarded this as a kind of academic inbreeding that insulated students from exposure to new or different ideas brought to the classroom by faculty who were trained at a variety of other universities.

Of the seven full-time School of Journalism faculty in 1971, three of them, or 40 percent, had LSU degrees. What troubled Ron Hicks was that the percentage had steadily risen. Faculty arrivals and departures had moved the percentage having LSU degrees to 64 percent in 1974, 67 percent in 1975 and 1976, and 82 percent in 1977, the year of the ACEJ site team visit. The 1977 percentage rose sharply from the previous year due primarily to the retirement of Jim Price[136] and Nick Plasterer.[137] Price's departure also had another negative effect. Only three of the full-time faculty in 1976 held doctorates. With Price gone, that left two—Hicks and Whitney Mundt. Elsie Hebert brought the number back to three when she completed her doctorate at the University of Texas during summer 1977.[138] However, Hicks and Mundt had earned both of their doctorates at LSU (Mundt in English and Hicks in sociology). The academic inbreeding situation could not have been any worse than in 1977. And there was absolutely nothing at the moment that Ron Hicks could do about it.

His hands were tied even tighter when it came to budgetary matters. Budget woes were chronic at LSU. The University had struggled with the state legislature over budgetary slights from its earliest days. Nothing had changed since then. The level of revenue flowing into the state coffers reflected the health of the oil business from which so much of that revenue in recent years had come: gushers some years; dry holes in others! Postwar Louisiana revenues, and thus state appropriations to higher education, had been consistently inconsistent. It was hard to know from one year to the next what to expect. When money flowed, LSU, its academic programs, its faculty, and its students prospered; but when money was tight, the entire LSU community suffered.

LSU was in good financial shape during the 1950s. Most of the University's budgetary requests were granted by a very giving legislature. As a result, salaries grew and major building projects, such as the new library, were completed.[139] Dark financial clouds appeared in 1960, though. President Middleton, speaking to a group of LSU alumni in March, said, "We have difficult times ahead. You can rest assured that we're going to need everything we ask the legislature for this year, and if we don't get it, we're in trouble."[140]

The result of a lower-than-anticipated appropriation to fund higher education was a 1961–1962 fiscal year budget that was much the same as for 1960–1961. Without the increase in funds that LSU had built into the 1961–1962 budget there would be no salary increases, vacant positions would not be filled, and equipment purchases would be curtailed.[141] This litany of consequences would have a familiar ring in years to come. Holding appropriations at the same level as the year before while the cost of living continued to increase and inflation continued to push the price of practically everything to higher and higher levels resulted for all practical purposes in a budget cut. Absorbing cuts like this from a standstill budget was bad enough, but tacked onto the legislative appropriations for the 1970 fiscal year was the possibility of a 6.3 percent cut in the amount already appropriated.

When the budget cut became a reality, LSU once again was faced with freezing salaries, freezing all new hiring, and rejecting any requests for equipment purchases.[142] Arts and Sciences Dean Irwin Berg explained that faculty in his college would have to take on a heavier teaching load since colleagues who might be leaving for whatever reason (better pay elsewhere being one of the major reasons) could not be replaced. And, of course, hiring faculty to fill newly created positions was absolutely out of the question.[143] This was an especially tough result of budget cuts for the School of Journalism to have to deal with. Growing enrollment would require faculty to teach an overload of course sections. What's more, these sections would be populated by a higher than normal number of students.

Fortunately, LSU's budget woes did not impact the School of Journalism so severely that its 1971 ACEJ reaccreditation was threatened. The site team had some issues such as the academic inbreeding situation, but the School was judged well enough in compliance with ACEJ standards to merit reaccreditation. Unfortunately, a continued underfunding of higher education by the Louisiana Legislature during the 1970s would finally have its impact when time came for the next ACEJ accreditation site team visit.

The visit was scheduled for November 18 and 19, 1976. The team numbered only three, down from the seven of earlier years, and it consisted of two academicians and one media professional. Following their visit and deliberations on findings and impressions about what they had learned, the site team submitted a report to the ACEJ. Nearly six months passed before the LSU Journalism School received the bad news on May 12, 1977, that the ACEJ was withholding its accreditation of the School's news-editorial and advertising sequences. The major reasons cited for the ACEJ's actions were not surprises: lack of administrative support, abnormally high teaching loads, and a faculty overloaded with LSU graduates. There were other reasons—weakness in job placement, advising and counseling, and limited teaching effectiveness by some faculty, to name a few, but none had the impact of the major three reasons.

Response to the ACEJ decision came from Arts and Sciences Dean Berg. He made a plea that the School of Journalism be placed on probation and be allowed to correct its deficiencies before the ACEJ rendered its final verdict. And he noted that the journalism faculty already had begun working toward implementing needed improvements, even before receiving the ACEJ's May notification.[144] Indeed, the faculty, perhaps anticipating what might be coming, had met in March to review changes that could be made to streamline the curriculum by alleviating some course requirements and merging course content so that one course might now cover the same territory that two courses previously had covered. Besides content changes, the faculty agreed to make all journalism courses carry three hours of credit instead of the hodgepodge of two, three, and four hours of credit that had been in place for many years. And journalism majors now would be allowed a maximum of 33 credit hours as part of their 128 total hours required to graduate.[145]

The faculty inbreeding problem would be less easy to fix. Ron Hicks, after assuming the School's directorship, had been working with a standstill budget. On top of that three senior faculty members, A. O. Goldsmith, Nick Plasterer, and Jim Price, all had retired since 1974. LSU's policy was to hire junior faculty to replace senior faculty and to pay the new hires a minimal salary. Since LSU's tight budget ruled out inviting prospective faculty for a campus visit, Hicks had little choice but to hire persons who were available locally. As it turned out, this generally meant persons who had LSU degrees. This budget-induced dilemma would come back to haunt the School of Journalism when the ACEJ accreditation folks came calling!

Dean Berg had little choice but to loosen the budget purse strings in order to allow Ron Hicks to hire more faculty with non-LSU degrees. Once that was assured and with the course and curriculum changes in hand, Hicks traveled to Chicago in October 1977, to plead LSU's case that the ACEJ's decision to withhold accreditation be reconsidered. Ron Hicks would later recall that "that's how I came to spend the coldest, loneliest night of my life."[146]

Hicks was successful in persuading the ACEJ to change its mind and to move the School of Journalism's accreditation status to the probationary level. Another ACEJ team would make a site visit in February 1978, to determine whether all the changes that Ron Hicks promised had been or were in the process of being implemented.[147] What the ACEJ team learned during its February visit convinced team members that the School of Journalism's news-editorial sequence deserved reaccreditation and that the advertising sequence deserved a first-time accreditation. Announcement of the ACEJ decision came in May 1978. The School previously had decided not to seek accreditation of its broadcast journalism sequence until the next review period.[148]

The whole reaccreditation ordeal was stressful and brought plenty of unflattering attention to the School of Journalism. But when all was said and done, Ron Hicks insisted that the School's accreditation had never been lost, only delayed.[149] However Hicks chose to characterize it, the fact that the LSU School of Journalism once again was among the elite programs in the country gave its faculty and students some much needed and much deserved bragging rights. Only sixty-eight journalism programs in the nation and only one in Louisiana held that distinction.[150]

Changes that were promised the ACEJ began happening within the year. Curriculum revisions were ready for implementation and new faculty hires actually lowered the percentage of School of Journalism faculty holding terminal degrees from LSU down to 64 percent as the 1978–1979 academic year began. The number would drop to 50 percent the following year. During the 1980s, the percentage would continue dropping lower and lower.

The number of Journalism School graduates was unaffected by the School's accreditation problems. In fact, both official and unofficial graduation numbers through the 1950s, 1960s, and 1970s reflected LSU's overall enrollment growth to be sure, but more importantly, they reflected the growing interest in journalism. Annual graduation levels during the 1950s fluctuated as did the LSU enrollment. As few as eight graduated with B.A.J. degrees in 1953, but the number was up to 34 by 1960. The number of M.A.J. degrees awarded during the 1950s never rose above six for any given year. The average was three per year. The average for M.A.J. degrees awarded annually rose to four during the 1960s and to six during the 1970s. Undergraduate degrees, though, began a steady climb during the 1960s when B.A.J. degrees awarded annually hovered in the 30-to-40 range. Then into the 1970s the numbers hovered in the 70-to-80 range and eventually, in the 1978–1979 academic year, the School of Journalism awarded a total (combining summer, fall, and spring commencements) of 107 bachelor's degrees.[151]

Had students been disinclined to major in journalism at LSU, as a result of the Journalism School's accreditation woes, then graduation figures some four or five years after the School received probationary accreditation should have dropped noticeably. But just the opposite happened. The total number of B.A.J. degrees awarded in 1981–1982 numbered 95. The number reached a record high 143 the next year. By 1983–1984 the number of degrees awarded reached a whopping 190.[152] Clearly, students either were unaware of the significance of a possible loss of accreditation, or they simply were not concerned.

Another important trend was also observable in graduation statistics from the 1950s, 1960s, and 1970s. Males receiving B.A.J. degrees during the 1950s outnumbered females by a 2-to-1 margin annually. That began to change during the 1960s, as the number of females receiving journalism degrees was nearly equal to the number of males. A gradual shift happened during the mid-1970s when the School of Journalism began awarding more B.A.J. degrees to females than to males on a regular basis. Bachelor's degrees awarded females in 1980 were double the number awarded males by unofficial count. The trend toward a female-dominated discipline was underway and would become even more pronounced in years to come. The female-to-male ratio of M.A.J. degree recipients during the 1950s, 1960s, and 1970s remained fairly well balanced, with no sign of a similar kind of female dominance as was occurring at the bachelor's degree level.[153]

Ron Hicks decided to step down as Journalism School director at the end of June 1980.[154] The School was nearing the end of an era as the next decade approached. So much of the journalism program then in place from curriculum to faculty had clear links to the School's distant past. The recent accreditation imbroglio was an ironic reminder that fresh thinking was needed for the Journalism School's future. It also served to remind LSU in general that if University administrators so valued the stamp of approval that accreditation brought LSU's academic programs—indeed to the point of requiring that if a program *could* be accredited then it *should* be accredited—then those same administrators had better be prepared to pay for the privilege.

Ron Hicks's departure as Journalism School director was a significant break in the School's link with its past. He would be the last director who both held a degree from the School of Journalism *and* ascended to the School's top job after having served on the faculty for several years. Bill Giles would be the only future director who would be moved from a lower faculty position to assume the directorship, but his appointment was somewhat out of the ordinary.

When Ron Hicks announced his retirement from the directorship he took the opportunity to look toward what lay ahead for the School of Journalism. Enrollment would continue to grow, he said, and a new public relations sequence would become a reality. The School soon would be moving into its new Coates Hall quarters, so Hicks thought, and he was reasonably certain that a restructuring of academic units would lead to creation of a new "School or College of Mass Communication."[155] How accurate he was is discussed below. It was, however, in his closing remark where Ron Hicks made his most prescient projection. "There will be problems and pressures," he said, "but the 1980s should be good years for us all."[156] Problems and pressures there indeed would be in the School of Journalism, sometimes in multiples. How good the 1980s would be depended entirely on one's perspective. But however characterized, the 1980s for the School of Journalism most certainly would not be dull.

11

Uncertain Times

The years from 1980 to 1992 at the LSU School of Journalism were not years marked by major advances. More than anything, they were transition years that carried the School from near loss of accreditation to the achievement of autonomy. The Journalism School came under leadership changes four times during the period, ending with an acting director. That by itself caused uncertainty among faculty who also had to adjust to the ambitions and designs of new College of Arts and Sciences Dean Henry Snyder. Given all that was happening, the best that the faculty could do was to hunker down, concentrate on teaching and research, and struggle collectively to find the School's bearing.

Ron Hicks's announcement that he was stepping down as School of Journalism director set in motion a search to find his successor.[1] When the search ended, John Merrill, a University of Maryland professor with extensive teaching and lecturing experience, was the top choice. Merrill held an M.A.J. from LSU and a doctorate from the University of Iowa. He had plenty of professional experience, having worked in one capacity or another at several newspapers. And his scholarly credentials were impeccable. Once the LSU Board of Supervisors approved of the appointment, Merrill would step into his new position on July 1, 1980.[2]

Speaking to a *Reveille* reporter, John Merrill initially remained noncommittal about any changes planned for the journalism program. "I just want to slowly improve the School," he said, adding, "My first job is to learn the routine."[3] Merrill later revealed that he actually did have three objectives he hoped to accomplish. The first was to bring a more scholarly emphasis to the School of Journalism. The second was to separate the School from the College of Arts and Sciences. Merrill's third objective was the addition of more office and classroom space by expanding the existing Journalism Building.[4] To help transition to his new position, John Merrill appointed Jack Holgate as assistant director. This was a first for the School of Journalism, but given the new director's plans to travel the state for speaking and fundraising purposes, it seemed wise to have someone at the School who could assume administrative responsibilities when necessary.[5]

John Merrill's first formal remarks to his colleagues, students, and alumni appeared in the fall 1980 issue of *The LSU Journalist*. His words might have inspired a realist, but they would have unnerved an optimist. Merrill spoke his mind and in doing so it was plain to see that he had a low opinion of the Journalism School's current state. It was a program that needed fixing, and he was the fixer. He admitted to having "no revolutionary ideas, no cataclysmic programs, no startling changes in mind," but he hastened to add that the Journalism School, "like all such institutions, has its weak areas, its disappointing courses, its inadequacies of various types." Later, Merrill pointed to "self-respect and even pride" as among the School's "most pressing needs." And he observed, "Morale appears rather low."[6]

John Merrill's criticisms of LSU next turned to what students were learning. Basic language skills needed more emphasis, as did ethics. "I'm of the opinion that most of the weaknesses and problems of journalism, usually attributed to lack of skill or carelessness, are at the root nothing but ethical problems." And he vowed to do all that he could "to revitalize journalistic ethics in the School of Journalism."[7]

Did the new director see anything that seemed remotely encouraging? Well, yes. He felt that LSU administrators were sincere in wanting to see the School of Journalism improve and were willing to do what was necessary—and that included spending money—to see that happen. He was encouraged also by the interest at LSU in interdisciplinary education. Merrill was especially intrigued by the Journalism School's pending move in 1981 or 1982 to Coates Hall, where it would share space with the Department of Speech, an "allied field with which I hope we can work even more closely—especially in the field of broadcasting." Finally, the best that he could do to rally the troops was to tell his readers that "we have a good School; we have a competent faculty, and we have many good students. We will get better."[8]

John Merrill's personality and disposition were apparent both in what he said and the tone in which he said it. He probably was sincere in his desire to pull the School of Journalism up to what he considered a more respectable level. But if his assessment of the current state of affairs at the School was sobering, it also had the potential of antagonizing the existing faculty. Whether the School had fallen as far as he suggested was a matter of opinion, but there was one person who certainly seemed to share Merrill's sentiment: Dean Henry Snyder. Dean Snyder, who had taken the reins in the College of Arts and Sciences on New Year's Day 1979, was well traveled, well read, and brought extensive teaching and administrative experience to his LSU position. Snyder's expertise in the British publishing industry gave him at least a partial claim to being a journalist.[9] And it was perhaps owing to that claim that Dean Snyder seemed to take a greater interest in the Journalism School than any LSU dean before him. His interest in improving the School appeared at least equal to that of John Merrill's.

One indication of Dean Snyder's interest was his creation of a Journalism Advisory Council that was already in place when John Merrill arrived at LSU. The Council actually was Snyder's co-creation along with Baton Rouge broadcaster Doug Manship and was based on similar councils that operated quite successfully at other universities. The nine-member Council, whose members all were in media management positions, was meant to strengthen ties between the LSU School of Journalism and the state's professional media as well as assist the School with any new services or programs. In its brief lifespan the Council already had begun paying dividends. It had provided input on the selection of John Merrill, and it was working on ways to increase the number of student internships and to fund special projects at the School.[10]

Next on Dean Snyder's agenda was his determination to change the School of Journalism's orientation from the practical, where teaching the nuts and bolts was emphasized, to the more scholarly, where the theoretical approach advocated by Ted Peterson took equal billing with the pragmatic. But the current Journalism School faculty did not exactly fit the mold that the dean had in mind. Most had been recruited to the faculty because of their professional background, not because of their scholarly potential. Reorienting the Journalism School faculty, changing the mindset, and fashioning a program more in line with journalism programs at major research universities elsewhere was the task that fell to John Merrill. LSU was becoming a "publish-or-perish" kind of university, and Henry Snyder expected Merrill (who agreed entirely with the dean's scholarly emphasis) to deliver that message to his faculty. The message, to no one's surprise, would not be well received.

Also on Dean Snyder's repair list was the crossdiscipline situation that existed between the School of Journalism and the Speech Department's broadcasting courses. Rather than continue moving students between the two departments, Snyder decided to consolidate all broadcasting components, including courses, faculty, and equipment, under one of the two units. The consolidation plan, though, was only part of a much bigger plan. The dean was intending to create a School of Communication within the College of Arts and Sciences and to include in the new school four departments or areas: print journalism, public relations and advertising, broadcast journalism, and speech. "Each area would be semi-autonomous, with its own chairman," said Dean Snyder. Moreover, a graduate director would oversee the graduate program that would incorporate all four areas.[11]

Dean Snyder was determined to see this through and had informed the LSU Board of Supervisors of his intentions as early as April 30, 1980. Trouble was, very few faculty members from either the Journalism School or the Speech Department agreed with the plan.[12] In support of the School of Communication idea Dean Snyder argued that the "current structure of the departments has not adjusted itself to what is happening in communications. . . . In both areas, we have had two very traditional programs. It seems to me we need to reorganize our structure, while continuing our very fine traditions, to meet the present needs of the field."[13] John Merrill countered by reminding the dean that when he [Merrill] became director of the Journalism School "you stressed to me that journalism was an area in the university designated as a priority area for growth and development. . . . Under this new plan I feel that journalism would not get emphasis; rather a School of Journalism would disappear. Its areas would be scattered throughout the School of Communication where it would find itself with such incompatible areas as Speech. Journalism would, indeed, lose its identity."[14]

Debate over creation of the new school was not the only issue generating discussion during the 1981 spring semester. The Journalism School's pending move to Coates was an equally hot topic. The move was set for spring 1982 in order that the vacated Journalism Building could be renovated to create space for eighteen classrooms and be ready for use in fall 1982.[15] But the Journalism School faculty was having second thoughts, and most members had decided that remaining in the Journalism Building was preferable to moving to Coates.[16] Meanwhile, *The Daily Reveille* office personnel and newsroom staff vacated their Journalism Building location and joined with staff from the Student Media office and the *Gumbo* for a move to the Coates Hall basement that, by mid-October 1981, finally would bring all of them together in one place.[17]

The journalism faculty's decision to stay put was not unanimous. After all, there had been plenty of talk in the past of a major renovation for the Journalism Building and perhaps even a new state-of-the-art building to house the School. But nothing had come of it. Some faculty members had lost faith that it would happen. Because Coates at least offered something newer and bigger than what they had, one person advocated a move there because "it is, almost quite literally, a once-in-a-lifetime opportunity."[18] So why stay? Dean Snyder, perhaps after rethinking the whole matter, actually articulated the four best reasons:

1. Journalism schools have found that having their own buildings or units enhances morale among students and faculty and lends a professional atmosphere to the program.
2. Having a separate building makes it much easier to raise money from outside donors in the media—perhaps donors after whom the building(s) or the School itself might be named will respond favorably to discrete quarters.
3. The space in Coates Hall (set aside for the Journalism School) is quite limited and does not give ample opportunity for School growth.
4. Various publishers of Louisiana (as well as broadcast executives) believe that the School should have its own building and facilities, rather than being placed in what is essentially a general classroom building.[19]

Decisions affecting the Journalism School paralleled decisions coming from across campus at the same time that would affect LSU in general. Paul Murrill stepped down as chancellor in early 1981. For most of the spring Otis Wheeler had served as acting chancellor, and on June 1, James H. ("Jim") Wharton assumed the position full-time.[20] In less than a month, Carolyn Hargrave would be appointed as LSU's new Executive Vice Chancellor and Provost.[21] Chancellor Wharton had been in his new position only a short time when controversy erupted at *The Daily Reveille* over a condom advertisement appearing in the paper's August 24, 1981, edition. In order to distance the School of Journalism from the controversy, John Merrill insisted that the School was not responsible for what *The Daily Reveille* printed and lamented that the paper was a "constant cause of embarrassment." He added that journalism majors who worked at the paper were failing to apply all the good writing skills and ethical practices that they had learned in the classroom.[22]

John Merrill later lowered his criticism of *The Daily Reveille* and even praised the paper for its "courage, outspokenness and a kind of lively variety in its subject matter."[23] But his earlier remarks had struck a raw nerve among the *Reveille* staff. In days and weeks to come, pages of *The Daily Reveille* would carry student complaints about such things as the Journalism School's antiquated equipment, limited work space, and replacement of instructors who were well-liked and good teachers with faculty who only brought advanced degrees and scholarly credentials to the School.[24] The newspaper obviously had become the sounding board where any and all criticism, big or small, deserved or undeserved, about the School of Journalism and especially about its director could be aired.

Both Dean Snyder and Chancellor Wharton came to John Merrill's defense. Snyder admitted that insufficient state funding had prevented the School of Journalism from improving in areas most needing improvement—equipment upgrades and more faculty, to name just two. But he revealed that Chancellor Wharton had pledged at least $250,000 to be spent over the next four years to improve the School and that an effort was underway to find and secure funding from private sources that would help the School even more.[25] Part of what drove the chancellor's efforts was his determination that Louisiana's flagship university should house a first-rate journalism program.[26]

John Merrill had become the School of Journalism's lightning rod. His gruff and combative demeanor invited the adversarial relationships that he developed with many students and colleagues. Positions that he took were to the point, and he said what he meant. And as for his ideas about the kind of program he envisioned for the School of Journalism, there were no ambiguities. On the point of improving the School's intellectual environment by pushing scholarly research and publishing, he told one group, "Some of the faculty members don't like it. They'll just have to not like it." And on the point of pushing journalism students into that same intellectual environment by requiring them to take a greater range of "substantive academic courses" and fewer "basic journalism technique" courses, Merrill said the Journalism School "is not a trade school and I am not going to have anything to do with a trade school ever."[27]

The intramural conflict would run its course, and the John Merrill/School of Journalism detractors would make their points, not all of which were without merit. But by and by, the director was getting the job done. By 1982, more than forty new electric typewriters had replaced the roughly twenty manual typewriters in the Journalism School typing lab. A new advertising lab was in use. New photojournalism equipment was on the way, and eight new VDT units would be up and running by the 1983 spring semester. Further, radio and television equipment was being purchased for the new broadcasting area.[28]

The broadcasting area by itself was nearly an instant creation. With Dean Snyder's plan for a School of Communication going nowhere, he decided to go ahead with his idea to combine the broadcasting entities from the Speech Department into a formal broadcasting sequence housed in the School of Journalism. By fall 1982, four faculty members who specialized in broadcasting were moved to the School from the Speech Department along with the nine broadcasting courses they taught.

Efforts also continued under John Merrill's directorship to formalize public relations as a sequence.[29] To that end, John Butler, a widely respected public relations educator at the University of Iowa, was hired not only to oversee the anticipated implementation of the public relations sequence, but also to serve as the Journalism School's next assistant director.[30] But the Louisiana Board of Regents' failure to approve addition of the public relations sequence in May 1982[31] once more stalled efforts for Journalism School students to have access to a full-fledged public relations program. The Board's Academic Affairs Committee had determined that John Butler's addition still could not compensate for what committee members perceived as a weak public relations faculty combined with deficiencies in the proposed public relations program. The full Board of Regents confirmed its Academic Affairs Committee's recommendation to reject the program on May 27, 1982.[32]

Changes at the broadcasting and public relations level brought a new look to the School of Journalism both in terms of curriculum and faculty. In addition to John Butler's arrival in 1981, arrivals also included the four faculty members who were being moved from the LSU Speech Department—John Pennybacker, Ronald Garay, William ("Bill") Black, and Jerry Salvaggio—along with two new hires, Louis ("Lou") Day and Floyd McBride. Three more persons, John Windhauser, Douglas Birkhead, and Jay Perkins, were hired in the spring of 1982 and would join the faculty the following fall. Veteran faculty members—the Old Regulars—who would remain in place were Jim Featherston, Elsie Hebert, Whitney Mundt, Jules d'Hemecourt, and Jon Fisher.

The Journalism School faculty in 1983 was quite different from the faculty that existed when John Merrill arrived in 1980. For one thing it was more diverse in the media areas of expertise represented. The faculty also represented greater diversity as to professional and scholarly backgrounds. Each faculty member had worked in the media at some point in his or her career. Jay Perkins, whose LSU work assignment included advising *The Daily Reveille* staff, had worked as an Associated Press reporter for fourteen years.[33] Floyd McBride had served in public information positions in the armed forces for twenty years and was director of American Forces Radio and Television Service in Los Angeles prior to his retirement from the military and move to LSU.[34] Bill Black was a pioneer television personality in Baton Rouge, hosting a children's program as "Buckskin Bill" for many years.

Besides the wealth of professional experience, most of the new faculty had extensive publishing experience, with several books and dozens of scholarly articles to their credit. Eight of the fifteen full-time faculty members held doctorates, and only four (roughly 27 percent) of the total held his or her highest degree from LSU. The School of Journalism faculty was enhanced even more by outstanding part-time or adjunct faculty, all of whom were well-respected media professionals who agreed to take time from their busy schedules to teach at LSU.

If enrollment statistics are any indication, then word was beginning to spread that, regardless of what students might have been reading or hearing about its troubles, the School of Journalism was the place to be. The School's fall undergraduate enrollment from 1981 through 1983 grew from 596 to 738. Most of these students chose advertising as their preferred sequence, but broadcasting was coming on strong. Graduate enrollment also increased slightly, moving from twenty-eight in fall 1981, to thirty-four in fall 1983.[35]

John Merrill's years at the helm of the LSU School of Journalism were rough and tumble and in so many ways not the least bit pretty. But they were productive. In fact, the sharper the focus on all that was accomplished the better things looked, especially considering the odds that were not always in Merrill's favor. It was not a big surprise, then, when he announced in fall 1982, that he would be stepping down from the director's position at the end of the 1983 spring semester to resume teaching and writing as a regular full-time LSU faculty member.[36]

About a year before deciding to step down, John Merrill, working with Henry Snyder, set in motion the necessary procedures for securing a sizable financial gift to the School of Journalism. Merrill and the dean had alluded to their seeking funds from a private source, but they never said who the private source might be. That source, as it turned out, was the Manship family of Baton Rouge who for much of the city's history had owned newspapers and later radio and television stations both there and in other locations.

Douglas Manship Sr. once had remarked to LPA Board Chairman Steve Charton about "possible ways to challenge LSU into aggressively raising the standards of teaching at the Journalism School." After all, he continued, the School "is our source of future employees."[37] Manship's thoughts had turned to action a year later when he and other family members announced plans to contribute a multimillion dollar endowment whose income would be used by the School of Journalism. Among the major uses that John Merrill proposed for the Manship gift were provisions for funding distinguished visiting professors along with several undergraduate scholarships and graduate fellowships. Other portions of the gift could pay for such things as faculty and student travel and purchase of new equipment. And for the Manship family's generosity, John Merrill proposed that the School of Journalism be renamed the Manship School of Journalism.[38] Final arrangement for receipt of the Manship endowment and final decisions on how it would be used would await John Merrill's successor.

One more thing that John Merrill did before he left the Journalism School directorship was to write a kind of valedictory statement for publication in *The LSU Journalist*. His intentions were to address critics who had disagreed with the kinds of changes he had begun implementing at the School and to set the record straight for what he felt was a distorted interpretation of his philosophy about journalism education. Much of what he said is included here because in defending his own philosophy John Merrill actually created a remarkably lasting argument for what journalism education not only was becoming but what it continues to be at what is now the Manship School of Mass Communication. For anyone who questions why the School operates as it does, or who wants to know what the School intends to achieve, or what it is that its graduates should know and be able to do when they leave LSU, or who wonders what the School is all about, these words should prove illuminating.

> There has long been an argument in journalism circles about the best mix of "professionals" with academic types on faculties responsible for educating journalists. . . .
>
> I will admit that I am an "academic type." After all, this is supposedly an academic institution. So I make no apology for that. Perhaps I should say that when I came here just over two years ago, I suggested to the administration that all journalism faculty members should not be held to the "publish or perish" rule which held in the College of Arts and Sciences generally and that there be two tracks for faculty: one for scholarship and one for the non-researchers without doctorates. No realistic person in journalism education

can contend that only Ph.D.'s should be on a journalism faculty. Certainly I have never advocated this.

Nevertheless, let me hasten to say that I believe all faculty members—even in a School of Journalism—should be interested in scholarship, in the products of scholarship, in intellectual pursuits, in the overall purposes of the university, and certainly—in the case of journalism—in the contributions and contents of the liberal arts.

Every faculty member, to deserve his or her place in the university community, should recognize that a journalism school is not a trade school and that "journalism education" is not "journalism training." To deserve a place on a university campus, a school like the journalism school should be a part of the scholarly community and should win and keep the respect of faculty members in other university departments.

In my opinion, the School of Journalism at LSU must attempt to serve at least two masters—and this is not easy; it must have the respect of the academic community in which it exists. And, of course, it must have the respect of the practitioners in journalism. In addition, it must have the respect of the students which come to it; this last area of respect, however, will normally come with the respect from the other two areas.

Also, a journalism school must attempt to satisfy the demands of its accrediting association, its alumni who are all convinced that they know what is best for it, [and] various groups in the professional world.... The constituencies for a journalism school are many and complex. This is why a journalism school must strive to be academic, yet practical; professional, yet theoretical; down-to-earth, yet intellectual.[39]

A search committee went to work to find a new Journalism School director who could be in place by July 1, 1983.[40] The field of applicants soon narrowed to one person, John William ("Bill") Click, a professor at the E. W. Scripps School of Journalism at Ohio University. Click held a doctorate from Ohio State University, had worked professionally in a number of media organizations, and had held several university teaching positions before arriving at Ohio University. His views about journalism education, particularly with respect to the scholarly pursuits of faculty and the intellectual versus trade school environment for students, were remarkably similar to John Merrill's.[41]

Two of Bill Click's early objectives were to mend fences between the School of Journalism and *The Daily Reveille* and to strengthen relationships between the School and the state's professional media practitioners. Beyond that, accommodating the ever-increasing enrollment by expanding the faculty, further improving the curriculum, and continuing to upgrade equipment were high on the agenda. Sitting at the very top, though, was preparation for the next six-year accreditation review scheduled for fall 1984.[42] All of Bill Click's objectives were of his own making. He had not received the kind of mandates from Dean Henry Snyder that had awaited John Merrill when he became Journalism School director.[43]

No doubt, though, the new director had a full plate from day one of his arrival at LSU. Also staring him in the face were the lingering effects of an across-the-board 4.4 percent budget cut ordered by Governor David Treen the year before.[44] All LSU units were affected to some degree, and the threat of additional cuts was always in the background. Added to that was the state legislature's traditional practice of not fully funding LSU according to an existing formula for allocating money for higher education. The formula was based primarily on the number of student credit hours generated by each college or university in the state. Since LSU ordinarily required more operating funds as Louisiana's flagship research university, the formula severely undercut what the University received.[45] So, having to absorb a 4.4 percent cut tacked onto a less-than-full formula funding put LSU into a bind. And the School of Journalism's need for money, especially with an accreditation review just around the corner, made the new director's ability to secure funds as critical as ever.

The ACEJMC (the original ACEJ recently had been renamed the Accrediting Council on Education in Journalism and Mass Communications) site team visit was scheduled for November 1984, giving Bill Click little advance time to assess what required his most immediate attention. Programs undergoing accreditation review typically attempt to correct existing deficiencies or at the least put into motion some corrective measures prior to the site team's arrival. The more that can be done ahead of time, the better a program looks, and the more positive its evaluation.

The School of Journalism would have to contend with two major differences between the approaching accreditation process and those of the past. First, the School would be seeking accreditation for its broadcasting (or broadcast journalism) sequence and its graduate program for the first time. Second, the ACEJMC had changed its rules somewhat to require that a school or department could be considered accredited only if its accredited sequences were populated by at least 50 percent of its majors.[46] Regardless of the new rules, Bill Click was confident that the Journalism School would be reaccredited.[47]

Fall semester 1983 and spring semester 1984 were busy times for the School of Journalism. Faculty spent much of the time preparing the lengthy self-study report required by the ACEJMC in advance of its site team visit. In addition, faculty new to the School were becoming acclimated. Husband and wife team Peter and Judy VanSlyke Turk and Robert Picard had arrived at LSU at the same time as Bill Click. The Turks were hired especially to add some breadth in advertising (Peter) and public relations (Judy).

Apart from preparing for accreditation, School of Journalism faculty set to work developing a Five-Year Plan that would help frame and to some degree set in motion those things that the faculty hoped to accomplish in the coming years. The plan was ready by October 1984. It was, as most plans of this nature usually are, very ambitious. It was a combination to do list and wish list that was heavy on the latter. What's more, Bill Click regarded the plan as an instrument for leveraging additional resources for the School.[48]

Maintaining accreditation headed the Five-Year Plan's list of goals. Next came achievement in educating students, turning out valuable research, and stepping up participation in meetings of regional and national professional academic organizations. Strengthening the graduate program at the master's level and adding a doctoral program in the near future were high on the list. Also high were assessment of technology needs and acquisition of the necessary technological tools to adequately train students. Adding more faculty in all sequences was seen as a key to accomplishing everything on the list. And the one big item was a new building. Many of these goals required only effort and leadership to accomplish, whereas others—faculty, equipment, and especially the building—were big ticket items whose price tags were fairly hefty. The Five-Year Plan's projected personnel costs alone jumped from nearly $600,000 for the 1984–1985 academic year to approximately $1.3 million for the 1987–1988 academic year. Towering above all of this was the estimated eight million dollar cost of a new journalism building.

The importance of a new building stretched beyond the obvious. "A greater sense of professionalism, of a professional community, is needed. The best way to foster that sense is to unite the faculty, laboratories, classrooms and student media into a single building," said the Five-Year Plan. The cramped conditions of the Journalism Building and a faculty whose growing numbers now required that some of them be housed in other campus buildings made that kind of community difficult to achieve.[49] But a new building was at best a long shot. The LSU Board of Supervisors annually prepared a prioritized list of capital outlay needs to be submitted to the state legislature for funding. It so happened that the Board actually did include a new journalism building on its 1983 list—positioned at the list's number 37 spot. It obviously had little chance for funding.

Chances for renovating the Journalism Building also appeared remote. A better possibility was to not move faculty into the Building but as near to the Building as possible. Hodges Hall, a former men's dormitory just a few feet south of the Journalism Building, seemed the perfect place for converting former rooms into office, classroom, studio, and lab space that would fit the Journalism School's needs. In November 1985, Bill Click was informed that Hodges indeed would be renovated and that all Journalism School faculty then housed elsewhere should prepare to move there once renovation was complete.[50]

Bill Click requested that Chancellor Wharton also consider moving student media—*The Daily Reveille*, KLSU, and the *Gumbo*—into Hodges. He noted the importance to faculty and students alike of having student media in close proximity to the Journalism Building.[51] The request was approved, and plans were set in motion to convert a major portion of the Hodges Hall basement into a student media complex. Plans turned to actual renovation and by July 1987, student media personnel began their move to Hodges.[52]

Bringing the Journalism School faculty closer together was a promising development. Promising, too, were the opportunities in store for the School resulting from the Manship Endowment. A proposal for the endowment had been presented to Charles and Douglas Manship on February 7, 1984.[53] The list of enhancement expenditures planned for endowment funds had grown, but the basic outline first discussed between Dean Snyder and John Merrill remained essentially intact.[54]

Finally, on August 10, 1984, the official announcement came from the LSU Office of Public Relations: The Manship family—brothers Charles and Douglas Sr., and their children Douglas Jr., David, Dina, and Richard—had donated a million dollars to the School of Journalism to establish an undergraduate/graduate scholarship and fellowship endowment. An additional $600,000 gift would be used with $400,000 in state matching funds to create an endowed chair in journalism.[55] Dean Snyder said the gift was "of incalculable value." Bill Click noted that the Manship family's contribution would make it possible to "compete with any school for the nation's most promising students."[56] The Manship gift was put to work almost immediately. Bill Click announced that a search had begun for "either a prominent media person or a respected academician" as the first to occupy the Manship Chair, initially for a two-year appointment.[57]

Little more than a month after receipt of the Manship endowment, the School of Journalism faculty voted to rename the School the Manship School of Journalism. The new name did more than just honor the Manship family for its financial generosity; it recognized the Manships for their support and encouragement of the journalism program from its earliest days. That support had never wavered. Moreover, said Bill Click, the new name would recognize the Manships for their professionalism and for continually being "at the cutting edge of progress throughout the South in the field of journalism."[58]

The LSU Board of Supervisors gave its official approval in December both to the Manship School of Journalism name change and to the Manship Chair name for the School's endowed professorship.[59] Dean Snyder followed the Board's action by remarking that the Manship School joined a select group of universities that have, "through their names, identified with progressive and innovative individuals and families in the field of journalism." Douglas Manship Sr. said that he, his brother, "and all the Manships are pleased that our gifts to the School of Journalism caused such a tremendous reaction," and with respect to renaming the School, he said, "We accept the honor with great humility."[60]

Once the excitement over the Manship endowment and name change had subsided somewhat, the Manship School faculty had to turn to the business of accreditation. A five-person ACEJMC site team was scheduled to visit on November 8–9. The team's initial recommendation would be referred first to the ACEJMC Accrediting Committee and then on to the ACEJMC Accrediting Council whose members would make a final decision during the Council's April 1985 meeting.[61]

The site team's visit was a good one. The team's overall impression was positive—in fact, exceedingly positive and indicative of how far the Manship School had risen in the last few years. The team report's summary of strengths and weaknesses said as much: "After undergoing dramatic, almost traumatic, changes in faculty composition and administrative leadership over the past several years, the School is now on the upswing. The situation is generally positive and improving. . . . On the whole, the School is progressing, and its reputation on campus is much better than it was several years ago."[62]

The report also cited some troubling but not altogether unexpected deficiencies. In particular, read the report, "more faculty members are definitely called for—the need in advertising, especially, is crucial and simply must be remedied—and the necessity for a new building or an addition to the present one is evident."[63] The site team commended the School's Advisory Board but felt that stronger ties with professionals were needed along with a better job and internship placement system and a better means of keeping track of School alumni.[64]

In its final judgment the ACEJMC site team recommended full accreditation for the news-editorial and broadcast journalism sequences, and the same for the advertising sequence "but contingent upon the School's hiring two quality faculty members . . . before the ACEJMC Accrediting Committee meets in spring 1985."[65] The graduate program was given only a provisional accreditation due in great part to the School's heavy reliance on 4000-level courses (open to undergraduate seniors and graduate students alike) and not enough 7000-level graduate-only courses, the paucity of skills courses at the 7000-level, and the number of options such as nonthesis research projects that graduate students had to writing a thesis.

The contingency accreditation given the advertising sequence was a key element to the site team's overall evaluation. As noted above, the ACEJMC stipulated that a unit (the entire Manship School of Journalism in this case) could not be considered accredited unless a sequence or sequences comprising 50 percent or more of its students was accredited. Since the Manship School's advertising sequence held more than 50 percent of the School's majors (364 of the 725 total majors in fall 1984), the School could not consider itself accredited until the recommended faculty hires were made.[66]

Fortunately, this was an easy (and quick) fix. Searches already were underway to bring several new faculty members to LSU, chief among them Alan Fletcher and Donald ("Don") Jugenheimer. Fletcher was a well-respected advertising educator who currently served on the faculty at the University of Tennessee, and Don Jugenheimer, another nationally known and respected advertising educator, was teaching at the University of Kansas. Jugenheimer's prominence in his field was such that the faculty decided to jump one step beyond a typical appointment by naming him the School's first Manship Chair of Journalism.[67]

Arriving with Fletcher and Jugenheimer were two other new Manship School faculty members, Shirley Carter and Nick DeBonis, whose advertising area of expertise would add even greater strength to the advertising sequence. Several others, including Robert ("Bob") McMullen, were hired to help strengthen the broadcast journalism and news-editorial sequences.[68] The Manship School did what it promised, and the ACEJMC Accrediting Council lived up to its part by fully accrediting the advertising sequence in April 1985.[69] The graduate program remained on a one-year provisional accreditation pending implementation of those changes mentioned above. Promised improvements were accomplished quickly enough for the ACEJMC to remove provisional accreditation on May 9, 1986.[70] From that date not only was the graduate program fully accredited, but the entire Manship School, without qualification, was fully accredited.

Events at the Manship School during the mid-1980s helped to restore optimism at a time when optimism was in short supply elsewhere at LSU. A prevailing sentiment of gloom stoked by the ever present threat of lower-than-requested appropriations, budget cuts, or a combination of the two[71] seemed to have affected the psyche of everyone at the University. By early 1986, conditions were bleak and getting worse. Federal cuts in spending for higher education had pushed a heavier than normal financial responsibility onto the states. But for a state like Louisiana where education spending already was low, there was little chance of the state legislature picking up the slack resulting from federal cuts.

The cause of the problem was traced to one source: the dropping price of crude oil. The world's oil producers, particularly those countries in the Mideast, had flooded the marketplace with oil, forcing down the commodity's price worldwide. For Louisiana, a state that historically set its state appropriations on the anticipated income generated by oil production severance taxes, any decline in the price of oil meant a decline in revenue—and a subsequent cut in appropriations. Higher education usually was hardest hit by such cuts.

Already, Chancellor Wharton had placed a freeze on hiring and a moratorium on equipment purchases and maintenance. When word came in early 1986 that as much as 20 percent of LSU's appropriation for the next fiscal year might be cut, Wharton was forced to prepare contingency lists of what could be cut and what had to be protected. Entire departments and programs were on the cut list. The hiring freeze would continue, of course, as would the equipment purchase moratorium. And faculty and staff who had not had pay raises in several years would have to wait a little longer. Many faculty, fed up with LSU's financial instability and crisis stacked upon crisis, began searching for positions out of state.[72]

When the state legislature met in the spring it did what LSU administrators were anticipating; it cut the University's appropriation for the eighth time in four years. On top of that, administrators were told to prepare for the possibility of additional cuts during the 1986–1987 academic year. The cuts left Chancellor Wharton little choice but to eliminate nine undergraduate and seventeen graduate programs and to substantially scale back several others.[73]

The Manship School was not among the units undergoing cuts. Indeed, given the dire prospects for faculty in other parts of the LSU campus, the Manship School faculty might have considered themselves prosperous. After all, amid a hiring freeze, the Manship School actually was hiring new faculty. And amid an equipment purchasing moratorium, the School was buying new equipment. The reason for such good fortune came, first of all, from the private funding available to the School via the Manship endowment. The endowment by no means made the School self-sufficient, but it did serve notice that the School's director and Dean Snyder aggressively and successfully had explored means for the Manship School to help itself. The faith and support symbolized by the endowment also convinced Chancellor Wharton to provide the School with additional University funding.[74] Second, the attention given the School of late not only by the Manships but by the state's media leaders showed that it was an asset that professionals not only valued, but also one they were willing to actively support. That kind of attention probably insulated the School from any major cuts, although it would be forced like its departmental neighbors across campus to endure cuts at some level.

Finally, the accreditation process, coming when it did, probably was more help than hindrance. Acting on Chancellor Wharton's mandate to maintain its accreditation, Manship School faculty did what was asked of them to make that happen. When the program fell just short of full accreditation, Chancellor Wharton had little choice but to follow through on his previously stated objective of making the Manship School one of LSU's priority units. Acting on that assertion, the chancellor made certain the School got the money it needed.[75]

Budget cuts at LSU had taken their toll on faculty, but persons charged with administering the cuts were not immune from their impact. Dean Henry Snyder, citing Louisiana's seemingly perpetual financial crises, tendered his resignation to Chancellor Wharton in December 1985.[76] John Loos, chairman of the LSU History Department, was appointed as acting Arts and Sciences dean until a search committee could name a new full-time dean.[77]

The search was relatively short. Within four months David Harned, president of Allegheny College in Meadville, Pennsylvania, had been named as the new dean.[78] Dean Harned's teaching and scholarly background was rooted in religious philosophy and ethics. He seemed satisfied with the programmatic foundations established by his predecessor and unlike Henry Snyder, David Harned appeared content to leave the Manship School alone.[79] Little did he realize how his life soon would be complicated by matters at the School.

Another personnel change occurred at the Manship School itself when Don Jugenheimer's two-year stint as occupant of the Manship Chair ended in 1987. Selected to replace him was William ("Bill") Giles. Giles brought a varied background to the position. His thirty-five-year career in the newspaper business included several positions, from reporter to executive, at *The Wall Street Journal*, and editor of *The National Observer*, *The Detroit News*, and *The Sunday Monitor* in Singapore. Giles also served for several years as an executive with the Dow Jones publishing company. He had left the newsroom twice for academic positions at Baylor and Michigan State. LSU was Giles's third academic stop.[80]

Bill Giles had not yet settled into his new position before an event occurred that would significantly affect his near-term future in the Manship School. In June 1987, Bill Click unexpectedly announced his resignation as the School's director. The announcement, coming from Dean Harned's office, said only that the dean was honoring Click's wish to return to full-time teaching.[81] His departure created a vacancy that needed filling quickly.

Bill Giles was eyed immediately as a possible candidate to replace Bill Click, since Giles's executive experience provided the necessary administrative skills and his many years as a journalist gave him immediate credibility among Louisiana's media professionals. Dean Harned regarded these attributes alone as reason enough to appoint Giles as the Manship School's acting director. And when the dean officially offered Bill Giles the job full-time, Giles accepted. His official start date was August 1988.

Bill Giles had assumed the Manship School directorship at a particularly busy time. Once again, the School was preparing for its next ACEJMC accreditation, and once again, preparation of a self-study report was front and center. The pressure to succeed with the approaching accreditation review would be great, as always. But the Louisiana Board of Regents had raised the stakes for a successful reaccreditation to an even loftier height in spring 1989. The Board decreed that "all journalism/mass communications programs in Louisiana's public universities must gain national accreditation by the [ACEJMC] no later than June 1, 1994, or face automatic termination."[82] This was a tough ultimatum, but the Manship School seemed to have little to worry about.

There was yet another leadership change at LSU when Chancellor James Wharton announced his resignation, effective November 30, 1989. His tenure as chancellor had been rocked continuously by one budget cut after another; still, he had led LSU through it all. Lately, faculty criticism on nonbudget matters had persuaded Wharton that the time had come to step down.[83] Grady Bogue, chancellor of LSU-Shreveport, was appointed by the Board of Supervisors on December 9, to serve as interim chancellor on the Baton Rouge campus.[84]

The search for a new LSU chancellor began on February 1, 1989, and concluded on August 10, with the appointment of William E. ("Bud") Davis to the position. Davis previously had served as president of Idaho State University and the University of New Mexico, and just prior to his move to LSU was serving as chief executive of the Oregon State System of Higher Education.[85] Arrival of a new chancellor brought some excitement to campus. The big question on everyone's mind, of course, was how well Chancellor Davis would cope with the chronic money problems that would confront him almost immediately.

Meanwhile, Bill Giles and the Manship School faculty, in advance of the upcoming accreditation review, decided to enhance the School by hiring several young, newly minted or soon-to-be Ph.D.s, along with a few veterans. Most important among the new additions was Bill Ross, recently retired as chairman of the Department of Mass Communication at Texas Tech University. Not only did Ross bring a veteran's touch to the Manship School, but his advertising expertise was a big boost to that sequence. Most timely, though, was the knowledge that Bill Ross had about accreditation. He had gone through the process several times at Texas Tech, and he had served on several ACEJMC site teams. His contributions to preparation of the Manship School's own self-study and to the School's preparation for the site team visit would prove invaluable.[86]

The Manship School had helped itself immensely in recent months by securing funds to fully outfit new graphics labs with Macintosh computers and two new writing labs with IBM computers. Bill Giles was optimistic that money soon would be available to buy even more.[87] Another plus for the Manship School was the story it could tell the ACEJMC site team of what alumni and friends had done for the School during the 1980s as well as what Manship School students and faculty alike had accomplished during the decade. Gifts included the Manship endowment, of course. Added to that were sizable grants from Freeport McMoran, Inc., in 1985 and 1986, the latter grant helping to underwrite expenses incurred during various Louisiana Scholastic Press Association activities sponsored by the Manship School.[88] A 1987 grant from the Gannett Foundation enabled the Manship School to establish a multicultural journalism program that, according to Bill Click, was meant "to attract, recruit and retain ethnically and culturally diverse students in print journalism."[89]

In December 1989, the family of Baton Rouge businessman and civic leader Fred Greer Jr. presented the Manship School with a $125,000 gift as seed money for establishing an endowment that when fully funded would create the Fred Jones Greer Jr. Chair for the Humanities. The family committed to raising the additional $450,000 needed to reach the $600,000 level, at which point the Louisiana Board of Regents would provide the balance needed for the full one million dollar endowment.[90] The Greer Chair together with the Manship Chair would bring some of the most eminent media professionals to the Manship School.

One sidelight to the Fred Greer story was his decision to return to the classroom to earn his journalism degree. He had studied journalism at LSU from 1935 to 1939 but had left the University short of completing degree requirements. Now, in 1989, at age seventy-three, and following his retirement as a Union National Life Insurance Company executive, Fred Greer decided to return to the classroom on his way to earning the long-coveted B.A.J. degree.[91]

A decade of giving assisted the School and its students (and prospective students) in a number of ways. Paired with these were new scholarship funds and monetary awards for outstanding achievement that began flowing to the Manship School during the 1980s. A glance at the *LSU General Catalog*, in fact, shows that scholarships and awards administered exclusively by the Manship School (this excludes general LSU scholarships and awards available to students from all disciplines) and intended for incoming freshmen through seniors, rose from nineteen for the 1981–1982 academic year,[92] to thirty-six by the 1985–1986 academic year. Among the scholarships and awards available to students in 1985–1986 were the previously mentioned Robert Ewing Scholarship, the Walter Hitesman Scholarships, and the Manship Merit Scholarships, as well as the Benjamin F. Leeper Memorial Scholarship, the Jules L. Mayeux Scholarship, the Joseph M. Silverberg Memorial Scholarship, and the Margaret Dixon Journalism Award given annually to the Manship School's outstanding senior female.[93]

Proving that such gifts were having an impact on the quality of journalism students, the Hearst competition, which annually cites the top articles written by students attending ACEJMC accredited colleges and universities nationwide, recognized the Manship School as the "national champion in collegiate journalism" in 1985.[94] Manship School students repeated their performance in 1986, winning "their second consecutive national championship in collegiate journalism, only the third time such a feat [had] been accomplished in the 26-year history of the competition."[95]

Three new student organizations came to the Manship School in the 1980s. Campus chapters of the Radio and Television News Directors Association and

Public Relations Society of America were established.[96] And the graduate students decided in 1989 to reactivate the long dormant Journalism Association of Graduate Students (JAGS).[97]

A steady stream of professional journalists visited the Manship School during the 1980s. The School's Editor-in-Residence program brought nationally known newspaper executives to LSU to lecture in classes and to meet informally with students. Among the first program participants were Kuyk Logan, managing editor of the *Houston Post,* and E. B. Blackburn, managing editor of the *Rocky Mountain News* in Denver.[98] The Walter Wood Hitesman Lecturer in Journalism series began in 1981 when Leonard Sussman, executive director of Freedom House in New York and a member of the World Press Freedom Committee, visited campus.[99]

LSU student media expanded in the 1980s with the addition of television. The history of LSU campus television actually began in the early 1950s when the University considered plans for constructing an educational television station. Plans had progressed sufficiently enough that by 1955 a television studio had been constructed in Pleasant Hall and purchase of television cameras and other production equipment was underway. No actual broadcasting was intended at this point. The new TV and Film Center, as LSU called it, instead would be used to produce educational or instructional programming for statewide distribution. The Center also was used as a teaching laboratory for the Speech Department's "TV Workshop" course beginning in 1956.[100] The whole effort was cut short in 1957 due to the same budget cut noted above that closed down WLSU. Equipment intended for the TV and Film Center was transferred to the Speech Department[101] and moved to a new Himes Hall studio for use in teaching television production courses.

The first glimmer that LSU students might engage in actual on-air television programming came not as part of broadcasting but rather as cablecasting. As it happened, LSU students in 1984 began producing a Bulletin Board service for insertion into programs provided by LSU's on-campus cable television service. Two years later, owners of the cable service sold its facilities to LSU. The LSU-owned cable system provided a golden opportunity for students to produce and originate their own cable programming, and in 1987, the newly named LSU-TV began airing a student-produced/student-anchored newscast from its Himes Hall studio. Plans were eventually to produce other kinds of programs as well.[102] By 1989, Manship School faculty member and LSU-TV advisor Bob McMullen was overseeing construction of a new television studio and production facility in Hodges Hall. Program production had advanced considerably by then to several half-hour news and public affairs programs per week, produced by the Manship School's advanced reporting students.[103]

Manship School faculty members also were becoming more active in the 1980s. They were playing more prominent roles in national organizations and beginning to contribute more to the scholarly side of their profession. Several, for instance, held key positions in the AEJMC, journalism education's major academic association.[104] Others held editorial positions at major academic journals such as the *Journal of Advertising, Public Relations Review, Journalism Quarterly,* and the *Newspaper Research Journal.*[105] And faculty were contributing to all the significant scholarly journals in the mass communication field.

Several national honors came to Manship School faculty during the decade. Bill Ross was recognized in 1989 as the American Advertising Federation's Distinguished Advertising Educator of the Year. The Association of Newspaper Classified Ad Managers similarly named Elsie Hebert as its 1989 Advertising Educator of the Year.[106] And John Merrill was named a senior fellow at the Gannett Center for Media Studies at New York's Columbia University in 1987.[107]

All that was happening at the Manship School began attracting the attention of more and more students who were choosing to major in journalism. What otherwise might have been considered a welcome outcome was now regarded as a problem. The Manship School simply did not have the size faculty or facilities properly to accommodate an overflow of students. So, the School's admission standards that heretofore had been fairly lax were tightened in the mid-1980s to require that a student complete at least sixty semester hours and carry no less than a 2.50 grade point average or GPA (based on a 4.00 scale) in order to be admitted.[108] This would be the first of several hikes in admission standards that the Manship School would implement in coming years to better control the number of student majors.

The new admission requirements had a dramatic effect. The number of Manship School majors (including graduate students and Junior Division "pre-majors" not yet admitted to the School) numbered 1,294 in 1987. That number dropped to 817 in 1988, the year when the new admission requirements began taking effect. By 1991, the number was down to 614, a more than 50 percent decline from 1987.[109] The Manship School's proactive decision not to allow the quality of education to suffer because of an inundation of students had worked.

The number of Manship School graduate students, who were unaffected by any admission requirement changes, actually rose slightly (from fifty-two to fifty-four) between the 1987 and 1990 fall semesters before dropping to forty-three by the 1991 fall semester.[110] What is interesting to note at both the undergraduate and graduate level was the trend toward the feminine. Clearly, more and more women were entering the various journalism fields. Statistics to that effect were unmistakable. Roughly, 65 percent of Manship School majors during the 1980s, both at the B.A.J. and M.A.J. level, were female.

Graduation rates had continued climbing throughout the 1980s, commensurate with the Manship School's growing enrollment. The high mark came during the 1988–1989 academic year when 195 B.A.J. degrees were awarded.[111] The School's new admission standards that had cut enrollment so effectively would not affect graduation numbers until four years after the standards' 1988 implementation. Sure enough, the 123 B.A.J. degrees awarded in 1992–1993 were nearly 30 percent fewer than the 175 degrees awarded during the previous academic year.[112]

Official notice to prepare for reaccreditation review arrived at the Manship School in September 1989.[113] The ACEJMC site team visit was scheduled for about a year later, on October 21–24, 1990.[114] The School had accomplished much in the years since the last accreditation review, but there now were deficiencies in practically every nook and cranny of the School's program. Some were minor and only annoying, while others were major and potentially could damage chances for a positive review.

The exit report conveyed to Bill Giles on the site team's final day at LSU was as positive as could be. Passing over the scattered criticism which was totally expected and absolutely on the mark, the report on the whole found the Manship School in compliance with all twelve ACEJMC evaluation standards. The site team recommended an unqualified reaccreditation. Looking at some of the more important site team comments, the team found that Bill Giles's can-do attitude had been helpful in finding ways to upgrade equipment and support faculty travel and research. The team also acknowledged the "widespread faculty support for achieving autonomy." But rather than endorse that desire the team felt "that at present the school can make substantial progress while remaining in the current structure."[115] Whether site team members should have taken a position at all on what was a purely internal LSU matter was questionable, particularly in view of how their comments might (and eventually would) resonate with University administrators.

The curriculum in all sequences, including the graduate program, got passing marks. Nonetheless, the site team felt that more full-time faculty were needed in the broadcast journalism sequence and that the graduate program could be better focused. The team felt that the Manship School's computer labs and especially its broadcast equipment were adequate for instructional purposes. Even the Journalism Building was not regarded as that much of an impediment to the School's success, although the site team recommended that if the faculty could not all be housed in one building, then at the very least faculty offices should be in closer proximity to one another.

The most negative comments were reserved for the Manship School's female and minority faculty representation. The site team commended the School for its past efforts to hire minorities and women, but the team said emphatically that more faculty from each category had to be hired. The team pointed out in particular the Manship School's more than 60 percent female student population as an obvious reason why more women were needed on the faculty. Having pressed that point, though, the site team tempered its remarks by complimenting the School on its multicultural efforts among students.[116] All in all, the stated Manship School program deficiencies were few and manageable. The bottom line, once more, was that no reason existed, as far as the site team could determine, for awarding the School anything less than full reaccreditation.

Bill Giles was a happy and much relieved person when sharing the reaccreditation news with the Manship School faculty. He cautioned that final word on reaccreditation awaited approval by the ACEJMC Accrediting Council that would be meeting in May 1991. "However," he said, "it's clear we're in good shape."[117] Chancellor Davis added his congratulations in a letter to Giles.[118] But as it happened, the chancellor's sentiments were a bit premature, while Bill Giles's assumption that the School was "in good shape" was way off target.

One statement in the site team's report did not factor into its reaccreditation decision, but it did resonate with Bill Giles. The statement, noted above, referred to the Manship School's recently renewed effort to sever its ties with the College of Arts and Sciences. The autonomy issue, dormant for nearly forty years, revived in 1988 when the Manship School faculty once more voted in favor of independence. The reasons cited for converting the School to an independent, free-standing college had not changed appreciably from those cited earlier by Marvin Osborn.[119] Regardless of faculty advocacy, though, the ACEJMC site team did not think the time was right for autonomy.

Autonomy, though, remained on Bill Giles's mind and even figured prominently in his surprise announcement in March 1991, that he would be stepping down from the Manship School directorship and returning to full-time teaching. In making his announcement Giles added that Chancellor Davis had indicated a willingness to begin planning for the Manship School's independence once a new director was in place.[120]

Just how committed LSU administrators were to Manship School autonomy was not absolutely certain. Dean Harned seemed to think that Chancellor Davis now would begin investigating the possibility, but Davis himself said in a letter responding to the topic that the Manship School at present did "not have the critical mass in terms of students and faculty for autonomy."[121] Provost Hargrave shared the chancellor's reservations. It was, in fact, disagreement between Hargrave and Giles over several issues, chief among them his insistence that the Manship School be separated from the College of Arts and Sciences, that had precipitated Giles submitting his resignation and the provost accepting it.[122] Meanwhile, a search committee soon was making preparations to find a new director for the Manship School. The hope was to have someone in place by fall 1991.[123]

Bill Giles's announced resignation was followed shortly by Dean David Harned's announcement that he too would be resigning his position and returning to full-time teaching.[124] And less than a month later, another, more anticipated change occurred when Carolyn Hargrave ended her ten years as provost. She was succeeded by Roland Haden but would return as interim provost from December 1996 through August 1997.[125]

The ACEJMC met in Chicago on May 10–11. The organization's procedure was to hear reports from site team visits and subsequent recommendations of an Accrediting Committee on whether a program under review should be reaccredited. The Accrediting Council was the organization's ultimate decision-making component. When time came for consideration of the Manship School, both the site team's and the Accrediting Committee's recommendations for reaccreditation were read into the record. At that point all seemed well. That is, until discussion turned to information that had surfaced recently of more budget cuts at LSU, the Bill Giles resignation,[126] and a dispute among several Manship School faculty over the composition and procedure of the search committee formed to select the School's new director.[127] The dispute actually was only the latest example of a rift that had been brewing among the faculty for some time. The site team either had failed to observe or simply had overlooked the dissension.

The root of faculty discontent was a complex mix. To some extent, the professional versus academic conflict that had been so divisive when John Merrill had been the School's director continued to cause fissures. But philosophical differences also pushed faculty members into one camp or another. Every now and then these differences would bubble to the surface over key management, personnel, curriculum, or programmatic issues. As a result, personality conflicts arising from the uneasy mood among Manship School faculty were slowly eroding the collegiality that is so necessary for an academic unit's success. Added to this was the perception, regardless of any basis in fact, that Bill Giles's background as a professional journalist often led him to side with those faculty members with whom he had most in common. Besides the philosophical differences, Bill Giles's management style sometimes conflicted with administrative policies and procedures. Giles apparently had modeled his style after that found in the newsroom, but what worked in the professional media workplace did not always work so well in an academic setting. Try as he might, Bill Giles was never entirely able to reconcile the one style with the other.[128]

How these matters suddenly came before the Accrediting Council is uncertain. The fact remained, however, that they now were front and center in Council deliberations, and Council members would have to consider how the situation at the Manship School might potentially interfere with the School's effectiveness. The result of these deliberations was not good for the School.

A letter from ACEJMC President John Lavine to Chancellor Davis carried the bad news. The Manship School had been awarded only a provisional accreditation. Lavine said that several major problems at the School that had occurred following the site team's visit had to be addressed during the coming academic year. "Those problems," said Lavine, "centered on the need for additional resources to support the program, a replacement for the director, and a more collegial relationship among the faculty members."[129] Lavine further said that Kim Rotzoll, site team chair during the team's 1990 review, would be returning to LSU in 1991 to assess the Manship School's progress in resolving the above problems and that he then would make a follow-up recommendation to the ACEJMC on whether to grant reaccreditation.[130]

The sudden turn of events was a disappointment to the Manship School faculty. Among the several consequences of provisional accreditation was the chance, remote or not, that the Board of Regents could enforce its directive to terminate any nonaccredited journalism program. The Manship School certainly was not hovering at the brink of oblivion, but knowing of the Board of Regents' interest gave the School and LSU in general plenty of incentive to correct existing problems as quickly as possible.

Chancellor Davis was especially concerned about the School's situation. The LSU administration had "devoted considerable time and effort to strengthen the [Manship] School" in the last few years, only to have it become a "huge frustration," according to Carolyn Hargrave. The School's leadership during the period had failed to cope with the kinds of divisions that separated the faculty. Now, Chancellor Davis had to be wondering if the Manship School's lost luster ever could be restored.[131] Determined to understand how best to proceed, he formed a Chancellor's Fact-finding Committee on May 20 to investigate problems existing at the School and to report recommendations for action.[132]

While the Fact-finding Committee's work was proceeding, Bill Giles officially stepped down from the Manship School directorship on May 16, and Professor Lou Day was appointed by Chancellor Davis to serve as acting director.[133] Day was a perfect choice. He was a full professor, and, thus, a senior member of the faculty. He had maximum credibility among his colleagues. He was a teacher and scholar first and foremost and harbored no ambition whatsoever to become full-time director.[134] Most important, though, Day had the demeanor that fit the School's needs at the moment. All of this would benefit the Manship School faculty immensely, for unknown to any of them, Lou Day's tenure as acting director would stretch a good distance beyond the 1991 fall semester.

The Chancellor's Fact-finding Committee completed its work in late June and submitted its report to Chancellor Davis on June 26, 1991.[135] Among the Committee's several conclusions, the following was the most pointed: "Re-establishing a professional consensus is the critical issue which must be addressed if the Manship School of Journalism is to be stabilized, the faculty divisions healed, and the School restored to a position of respect both inside and outside the University community."[136] To help accomplish this the Fact-finding Committee recommended that one of its members, past LSU Faculty Senate President Ralph Kinney, be appointed as Chancellor's Liaison to the Manship School for an indefinite term to "work with the School's faculty, the Interim [Acting] Director, the administration of Arts and Sciences, and the Office of Academic Affairs to develop policies on mission, governance, hiring, promotion, tenure, etc."[137]

In the meantime, Lou Day busied himself during the summer months trying to "learn the job" of director and attempting to "keep a lid" on what he termed a "fractured faculty."[138] Ralph Kinney assisted Day by giving advice and serving as a "resource person." His role among the Manship School faculty was that of impartial mediator who could help resolve minor disputes. Bill Ross, whom Lou Day characterized as a "steadying influence," also provided much needed assistance, primarily with administrative matters.[139]

Lou Day had served as Manship School acting director for more than a semester when he was at last able to write Kim Rotzoll at the ACEJMC with details of some very positive and very encouraging steps the School had recently taken. Consensus building was happening, collegiality was being restored, and a new College of Arts and Sciences dean soon would be named. Most encouraging of all, John Maxwell ("Jack") Hamilton had accepted LSU's offer to become the Manship School's next director.[140] Things definitely were looking up, and the School's road to reaccreditation seemed almost certain.

Kim Rotzoll revisited LSU in February 1992. He met with the faculty, Bill Giles, Lou Day, and the director-designate Jack Hamilton. Outside the School, Rotzoll met with Chancellor Davis and the newly appointed Dean of the College of Arts and Sciences Karl Roider. Gathering what he could from conversations with all of these, Rotzoll was impressed by the kind of support shown for the Manship School and by the strides made by the School's faculty. Lou Day received high marks from Kim Rotzoll "as a stabilizing force." He had restored much of the collegiality that had appeared so lacking before. And he in so many ways had brought the Manship School "back from the brink."[141]

Kim Rotzoll's reexamination of the Manship School gave him every reason to recommend reaccreditation.[142] Next came a unanimous vote by the ACEJMC Accrediting Committee, based on the Rotzoll report, to recommend to the full Accrediting Council that the Manship School be reaccredited.[143] The same Accrediting Council that had stopped the School's reaccreditation bid the year before now had no such reservations during its May meeting in Chicago. The Council voted unanimously for unqualified reaccreditation.[144]

A major burden suddenly lifted from the Manship School faculty. But in a way, provisional accreditation may have been one of the best things that had happened to the School. The struggle over just where the Manship School was heading that began in the early 1980s had been boiling beneath the surface all this time. The faculty as a unit had managed to move the School forward, even under tremendous budgetary constraints, and to do the jobs expected of all of them. The School had accomplished much during the period, but what it had failed to do—what its leaders and faculty members themselves had failed to do—was to open unimpeded channels of communication among one another. For persons who supposedly were experts in the art of communication, they had been unable to practice what they preached.

So, now, the Manship School was at a turning point. It was destined in a short time to become a very different place. The faculty certainly was ready to make that happen. And so was the School's new leader. Kim Rotzoll noted in his report to the ACEJMC Accrediting Committee how impressed he had been with Jack Hamilton.[145] Don Schultz, Accrediting Committee chair, also mentioned a letter that Hamilton had written to ACEJMC President John M. Lavine regarding the Manship School as a key item leading to the Committee's unanimous vote for reaccreditation.[146]

The Hamilton letter, dated February 3, 1992, was a sobering assessment of what he saw as the Manship School's current condition and part manifesto of what changes he intended for setting the School in a new direction. The importance of Hamilton's letter, coming when it did and saying what needed to be said, cannot be overstated. It may have been the very document that swayed opinion among ACEJMC Committee and Council members to vote the way they did.

The Hamilton letter was remarkable as well because Jack Hamilton would not become the Manship School director officially until June 1, 1992. But in truth, Hamilton had begun planning the Manship School's future and preparing for his part in that future from the moment he had accepted the job in late 1991. He had stayed in almost daily contact by phone with both Lou Day and Bill Ross and had traveled to Baton Rouge as often as possible for even closer consultation. From Day and Ross, Jack Hamilton, who had no prior experience as a college administrator, began learning about his new role and about issues such as autonomy that he would face almost immediately. By the time the director-designate was ready to assume his official duties, he already was an expert on the Manship School, its faculty, LSU in general, and LSU's administrators.[147]

Once Jack Hamilton was firmly settled as the Manship School's new director, he was prepared to set in motion a practical, workable, and imminently achievable plan that not only would engage the Manship School faculty, but that also would set the School on a course far different from anything experienced in the recent past. Testing Hamilton's new model of inclusiveness and teamwork would challenge a faculty not known for either. But Hamilton the workaholic was determined to make everything happen. There would be some bumpy moments ahead, but by and by, faculty, students, administrators, alumni, and friends of the Manship School were set for quite a ride.

12

Return to Prominence

The 1980s were years of transition both in the practice of journalism and in journalism education. The very concept of journalism was transforming into mass communication. And mass communication as an industry and business was ever expanding and diversifying. Technology was becoming more sophisticated and more omnipresent in the workplace. Mass communication as a field of study was attracting more and more persons, while the mass communication job market was becoming more competitive.

Changing standards of academe were moving journalism education further away from a trade school orientation and closer to an intellectual, scholarly orientation. Economic realities were forcing the Manship School in particular to operate with reduced funding while at the same time mass communication industry realities were forcing the School to integrate expensive technology into the classroom and labs. Accreditation standards were becoming more rigorous. And faculty roles, expertise, and expectations were changing.

Meeting these conditions carried certain demands. Journalism education programs in general were forced either to adapt themselves to meet these demands or to stay unchanged. Those that met the demands remained relevant and emerged as leaders in both the academic and professional communities. Those that did not floundered and became irrelevant.

The Manship School chose to chart its new course in the most progressive manner possible. Its faculty vowed to refashion the School in such a way that it would emerge from the 1990s as a model for journalism education in the twenty-first century. Leading the way would be the School's new director, set to begin work on June 1, 1992.[1]

Jack Hamilton would be a very different kind of leader than any of his predecessors. In so many ways he was of a newer generation. He viewed journalism from the perspective of a successful scholar and media practitioner, but he also possessed organizational skills learned in the business world. Above all, Jack Hamilton loved the clarity of purpose that planning—practical, aggressive, and effective planning—provided. And his lead-by-example nature would fashion an effective consensus-building management style.

Jack Hamilton held a doctorate in American Studies from George Washington University. His academic experience was limited to teaching as an adjunct there and at American University, and for a period as a visiting professor at Northwestern University's Medill School of Journalism. Hamilton's professional experience began at the *Milwaukee Journal* while attending Marquette University. Following graduation, he worked as a freelance journalist in the United States and abroad, reporting for such news organizations as the *Christian Science Monitor* and ABC Radio. In addition he had held positions with the U.S. House Foreign Affairs Subcommittee on Economic Policy and Trade and the U.S. Agency for International Development. At the time he was hired for the Manship School directorship, Jack Hamilton was serving as the senior counselor for development education at the World Bank in Washington, D.C. Hamilton's biography of journalist Edgar Snow was cited by the Frank Luther Mott–Kappa Tau Alpha Research Award panelists as one of the best books of 1989.[2]

Besides Lou Day at the Manship School helm and the soon-to-arrive Jack Hamilton, there were four other persons at LSU who would play prominent roles in overhauling the School in 1991 and 1992. Two of these, Bill Ross and Sig Mickelson, were members of the Manship School faculty. The other two were LSU administrators Roland Haden and Karl Roider. Haden, Executive Vice Chancellor and Provost, played a key role along with Jack Hamilton in shepherding the School through the critical reaccreditation review in May 1992. He, in fact, had been present along with Jack Hamilton at the ACEJMC Accrediting Council meeting in Chicago. Hamilton insisted that such a show of support by LSU's chief academic officer impressed the Accrediting Council and no doubt was a major factor in helping improve the Council's attitude toward the Manship School.[3] Karl Roider, on the other hand, was new to the scene, appointed as dean of the College of Arts and Sciences in December 1991.[4] It would be Dean Roider who would work with Jack Hamilton to plan and at long last to carry through the necessary procedures for the Manship School's autonomy.[5]

Bill Ross was on the Manship School faculty when Jack Hamilton arrived. His advice on the mechanics of running the School, coming from seventeen years' experience managing the mass communication program at Texas Tech, would prove immensely important to the new director.[6] Ross, in fact, would become of such value to the Manship School that when he finally retired from LSU and returned to Texas in 1994, Hamilton appointed him as a distinguished visiting professor.[7] His job as advisor/consultant would keep Bill Ross attached to the Manship School long past his "final" retirement from full-time teaching. Ross even returned to LSU in 1997 to assume the position of interim director of public relations when longtime director Jackie Bartkiewicz retired.[8]

Sig Mickelson had briefly served on the LSU Journalism School faculty in 1939 and returned to LSU in fall 1991 as the newest Manship Chair professor,[9] replacing Bill Giles. As already noted, Mickelson had done quite well for himself during his absence from LSU, rising through the ranks to become president of CBS News in 1954. He left CBS in 1961 and eventually returned to the classroom, first as a professor at Northwestern University's Medill School of Journalism, later at San Diego State University, and finally back to LSU in July 1991.[10] Bill Ross and Lou Day would join with Sig Mickelson to serve Jack Hamilton and the Manship School as an invaluable resource team for years to come.[11] Together, their impact, contacts, energy, skills, collective wisdom, and, most important, their devotion to the Manship School would help raise the School to a new level.

Jack Hamilton's arrival at LSU brought him face to face with a problem with which every Journalism School and Manship School director before him had had to grapple: financial uncertainty. LSU, in fact, was about to suffer one of its most severe financial crises ever. The Louisiana Legislature, in September 1992, cut $45 million from the state budget. For LSU, that amounted to a $9.3 million cut or 7.3 percent of its 1992–1993 fiscal year budget. Chapter 11 noted the regularity of budget cuts through the 1980s—eleven midyear cuts in all. The state's financial strain became increasingly severe as oil revenues—Louisiana's primary income source—continued to diminish with no appreciable rise in taxes to offset the losses. Now, LSU was hit with what Chancellor Davis called "the largest one-time cut in the last decade."[12]

What to do in such dire straits? There was some talk of LSU implementing an exigency plan, described by Chancellor Davis as the academic equivalent of declaring a Chapter 7 bankruptcy, whereby anyone, including tenured professors, could be terminated. Davis would not resort to such a drastic step, but what he did intend to do was no less painful. Equipment and supply purchases as well as faculty travel and hiring would be frozen. Faculty teaching loads would increase, while class sections would decrease. Certain staff personnel would be furloughed, and faculty would be asked to take unpaid leave. With these and several other measures, Chancellor Davis determined that LSU could avert any declaration of financial exigency.[13]

Regardless of the University's plight, Jack Hamilton was determined to push ahead. He tackled the easy things first. The Manship School faculty had voted in 1990 to rename the School the Manship School of Mass Communication,[14] but additional steps to make the new name official became stalled for the next two years. In June 1992, Jack Hamilton reinstated the effort by requesting that Chancellor Davis approve the name change in order that it might "better represent the varied disciplines of the School." Hamilton also pointed to a general trend among similar academic units across the country that were dropping *Journalism* from their name in exchange for *Mass Communication*.[15] Davis approved the change, and the Board of Regents granted it administrative approval on July 29, 1992.[16] From that date, what had begun as the Department of Journalism nearly eighty years before would be known as the Manship School of Mass Communication.

Shortly after the name change approval, Jack Hamilton made an additional request that the degrees offered by the Manship School be changed to Bachelor of Arts in Mass Communication and Master of Mass Communication.[17] Official approval of both title changes was granted by the Board of Regents in September 1992.[18]

Jack Hamilton's next step was creation of an agenda for the future in what would become the Manship School's Five-Year Plan for Excellence. This was actually the School's second such plan, the first having appeared in 1984 under Bill Click's directorship. The newest one, however, bore little resemblance to the first. The new plan was more philosophical and more cognizant of the need to prepare students to work in a rapidly changing information industry. The plan's "Macro-Vision," in fact, described a mass communication world far removed from the one that Hugh Blain presented to his first class of journalism students in 1912.

> To be sure, mass media no longer course through narrow, easily defined channels. Newspapers still exist—and will for the foreseeable future but there are fewer of them. . . . Even more important, the line between print

and electronic information is blurring. . . . In this Information Age, every business executive and political leader must know something about gathering and using information, and they need staff skilled at information gathering and communications. As a result, the market for well-trained mass communications graduates will grow, especially in non-traditional areas.[19]

Within the context of this broad view of mass communication the Manship School would focus specifically on creating "renaissance communicators," strengthening both the undergraduate and graduate programs, developing selected specialties and a professional orientation, and improving the School's interdisciplinary relationship with its campus neighbors.[20]

How were these goals to be achieved? The Five-Year Plan gave specific steps. Renaissance communicators would complete a curriculum that would move from a rigid sequence-driven division where students in one sequence had little knowledge of what happened in other sequences to a core-driven division where all Manship School students would be required to complete a common core of six courses. The core would introduce students to media writing, research, law, and ethics, among other subjects, in which all mass communication students should be thoroughly grounded.

Developing strength in all modern facets of communication education meant broadening the School's three current sequences into five concentration areas—journalism, advertising, electronic media, and two new areas: public relations and political communication. The concentration area structure also would allow development of political communication as a specialty area.[21] Later to come would be a doctoral program, probably built around political communication but having a greater interdisciplinary focus than other mass communication graduate programs.

The Manship School's professional orientation would be emphasized by encouraging faculty to engage in applied research that would help track industry trends and examine issues relevant to the areas represented in the School's curriculum. Finally, a board of industry professionals would be formed to advise the Manship School faculty and director.[22]

The "Five-Year Plan Timetable" set up base line dates either for accomplishing specific objectives as noted above or for having structures in place for doing the same. Each step in the process would be thoroughly planned by faculty committees and approved by the entire faculty prior to implementation. Critical to everything else on the Manship School's five-year agenda was initiation of a "fund-raising program for a new or renovated building" and preparation of the School's self-study report in readiness for its next accreditation review.[23]

Sitting atop the Five-Year Plan was a blueprint for the Manship School's transition to an autonomous unit. Bill Ross had fashioned the blueprint by devising both a plan for autonomy and a timetable for its implementation. The plan included, first, the formation of committees—one to assess the School's relationship with alumni and the professional media community and several others (specifically, a Futures Committee, a Development Committee, and a Policies and Procedures Committee) to assess the School's internal operation. The committees helped encourage creative input on matters that were vitally necessary once autonomy became a reality.[24]

The planning process fulfilled another purpose as well—this one having nothing to do with organization, policy, or operational matters. The common goal of autonomy, as Jack Hamilton saw it, acted as a uniting force. The Manship School faculty now could refocus its collective energy from discord into something positive. In Hamilton's thinking, the discord actually proved beneficial by creating the perfect climate for change.[25]

Jack Hamilton had been assured by Chancellor Davis that if the Manship School's Five-Year Plan was a good one, it would be approved and the School would be headed toward independence. Hamilton, indeed, had passed along this assurance to the faculty. But when the chancellor received the plan in summer 1993, he delayed approving it immediately because of the autonomy issue. His reason was the potential cost that a new college might place on an already strained LSU budget. After not hearing anything from Chancellor Davis for several days, Jack Hamilton asked to meet with him. Hamilton later recalled his subsequent conversation with the chancellor going something like this: "Well, Chancellor," said Hamilton, "when you brought me here you said that if we got the School organized . . . that we'd become a separate unit. We've now done that. I'm not going to have much credibility with the faculty if we don't become separated." The chancellor "immediately saw that argument" and "understood that that was the deal," said Hamilton.[26] Before the meeting ended, Chancellor Davis called Provost Haden to his office with instructions to set in motion procedures for making the Manship School an autonomous unit.[27]

Official sanction for the Manship School's independence came from the LSU Board of Supervisors on October 28, 1993. The official date for the School's separation from the College of Arts and Sciences was set for July 1, 1994.[28] A quest for autonomy that Marvin Osborn had begun nearly fifty years before finally would be realized.

To make certain that activity associated with the School's organizing would not be hindered by financial worries, the Douglas Manship family made another gift of $100,000 to the Manship School. Richard Manship commented when presenting the money that he and his family believed the School "has the potential to become one of the best in the country."[29]

Part of the Five-Year Plan already in motion prior to its official approval was formation of an Advisory Committee of "key executives from New York, Washington, and Louisiana to assist the Manship School in making its program more relevant to the present day world of communications."[30] The Committee was similar in purpose to the advisory group that Dean Henry Snyder had formed prior to John Merrill's arrival in the early 1980s. The newest version of the Advisory Committee would be organized (and chaired) by Sig Mickelson and consist of "senior executives who could make decisions."[31] Board members in addition to Mickelson included Premier Bancorp CEO G. Lee Griffin; Louisiana Chemical Association President Dan Borne; Freedom Forum Media Studies Center Director Everette Dennis, and the Center's Deputy Director Duncan McDonald; CBS News President Eric Ober, and CBS Vice President of News Services John Frazee; Franklin Press President Jensen Holliday; Louisiana South Central Bell President Elton King; Baton Rouge *Advocate* editorial page editor Douglas Manship Jr.; *Baton Rouge Business Report* publisher Rolfe McCollister Jr.; American Express Executive Vice President Thomas O. Ryder; Powell Tate Vice President Len Sanderson; *Alexandria Daily Town Talk* Chairman Joe D. Smith; LSU Vice Chancellor and Provost Roland Haden; and Manship School Professor Bill Ross.[32]

The Advisory Committee was formalized in spring 1993 as the Manship School Board of Visitors. Board members chose Jensen Holliday as vice chair to assist chairperson Sig Mickelson.[33] Board of Visitors membership would change over the years as new members replaced old, but the Board would remain a vital link between the Manship School and the professional community both at the local and the national level.

A Student Advisory Council was also formed. Ron Hicks had created a similar group called the Journalism Student-Faculty Council in 1975.[34] Like its predecessor, the current Student Advisory Council was composed of student leaders from the various mass communication–related campus organizations (undergraduate and graduate) and student media and intended to meet with Jack Hamilton regularly to serve "as an information liaison between the school administration and the student body."[35]

Advisory groups would be helpful, but key to the Manship School's ultimate success was the faculty. The eighteen full-time faculty members in place when Jack Hamilton arrived would nearly double in number in the coming years. Veteran faculty soon would be joined by a group of talented new hires. One new hire in particular was longtime LSU administrator Laura Lindsay. Lindsay, in fact, would take leave of her faculty duties at one point to serve as the University's interim provost. Another new hire, Richard Nelson, was named the Manship School's Associate Director for Graduate Studies and Research. He joined Ronald Garay, appointed earlier by Jack Hamilton as the Manship School's Associate Director for Undergraduate Studies and Administration.

There were faculty additions at the endowed chair level, too. Peter Kohler, former CBS and Gannett Broadcasting executive, arrived in January 1994 to begin a two-year stint in the Manship Chair. He would be succeeded by former *U.S. News and World Report* editor Nathan Kingsley in January 1996. The first occupant of the new Fred Jones Greer Jr. Chair in Media Business and Ethics was George Lockwood, a former managing editor of the *Milwaukee Journal* and winner of a 1967 Pulitzer Prize.

Finally, there were staff personnel whose arrival at the Manship School now would comprise the necessary elements for turning a department into a college. Linda Rewerts, assistant to the director and later, assistant dean, was central to the School's smooth transition. Helen Taylor arrived as student counselor (and, eventually, assistant dean).[36] Mary Ann Sternberg, a longtime Baton Rouge community leader, author, and member of the Manship School Board of Visitors, joined the staff after volunteering to organize the School's intern program. She later accepted Jack Hamilton's invitation to become the School's internship coordinator, an essential job that she did gratis. Sternberg in time would become one of Hamilton's most trusted advisors, assisting him primarily in fundraising and in acquiring art for the soon-to-be-renovated Journalism Building.[37]

Changing the Manship School curriculum to conform to the new core course/concentration area structure required several revisions. First, existing courses were moved to their most appropriate concentration area. Second, major content changes were planned for several courses in the journalism concentration. Newsgathering courses, in particular, were revised to include instruction in techniques of researching, gathering, and reporting news that applied to all existing and emerging media. The revision was designed to teach the principles of "convergence." Convergence, the new buzzword in the media world during the 1990s, applied to the rapid transformations then occurring in the way reporters were performing their jobs. Reporters were likely to be preparing a print media story at one moment and then quickly having to convert that story to an electronic media version the next moment. This kind of operation was the essence of convergence. In order for reporters to feel comfortable in the new convergence environment, the Manship School determined to prepare them well in the techniques they would employ.

A third revision was the addition of public relations as a concentration area. The problem the Louisiana Board of Regents encountered during the 1980s when public relations was proposed as a Manship School sequence now would be circumvented administratively by making public relations a concentration area and not a sequence. Addition of concentration areas to the curriculum did not require the same Board of Regents approval as addition of a sequence.[38] More important, though, the current public relations program was better organized, more substantive, and included more faculty than its unsuccessful predecessor. The fourth and final major revision was the addition of a political communication concentration area. As Jack Hamilton later recalled, "This was initially thought to be a relatively insignificant program, in place primarily because media and politics were to play a large role in the graduate program. In time, however, this program became a magnet for outstanding undergraduates, several of whom became student body presidents."[39]

The number of Manship School majors had dropped steadily through the late 1980s and early 1990s, presumably in response to implementation of the School's 2.50 GPA admission requirement. The number of majors appeared to bottom out in fall 1992 and began rising in the following years.[40] One reason for the increase probably could be traced to LSU's more rigorous general admission standards. As the ability of students entering the University improved, so did their ability to meet the Manship School's own admission standards.

Graduation rates were affected as well. The number of Manship School undergraduates receiving baccalaureate degrees continued to drop annually after the 1992–1993 academic year. But the trend bottomed out in 1995–1996 when ninety-one degrees were awarded. The number would rise in successive years until the School awarded a record 251 B.M.C. degrees during the 2001–2002 academic year.[41]

Enrollment figures reflected both good news and bad news for the School. The good news came from what the growing numbers were saying about the popularity of studying mass communication at LSU. Revision of the curriculum seemed to be having an effect, particularly with regard to the addition of public relations as a concentration area. By 1995, students concentrating in journalism accounted for 40 percent of all mass communication majors. Students concentrating in advertising accounted for 30 percent, and those in public relations accounted for 21 percent. Percentages for all three areas would become more balanced in years to come.

Also on the positive side was the quality of students deciding to major in mass communication. The Manship School could count on recruiting a sizeable number of high school valedictorians each year, and it could count on having a student body whose collective GPAs were among the best at LSU. Clearly, many students were not turning to easier disciplines as the Manship School admission requirements became more rigorous but instead were accepting the challenge of the School's tougher standards.

The downside to all of this, of course, was a Manship School that was unprepared for the sudden onslaught of majors. The School had neither the faculty nor the facilities to handle such numbers. With resources stretched to their limit, the Manship School turned to adjunct instructors to handle some of the load, but these stopgap measures could not be used indefinitely. The only solution that might work with certainty was raising admission standards once more, developing a selective admissions procedure, and placing a cap on enrollment. This would allow the School not only to control the size of its student body, but also to balance enrollment levels to keep pace with changes in faculty size and teaching/laboratory facilities.

With these three steps in mind the Manship School faculty voted in 1997 to approve new admissions procedures for undergraduates requiring that they make formal application for admission to the School. Applicants would have to complete at least thirty semester hours and earn at least a "B" in "Media Writing" and a 3.00 GPA in all completed courses. Students with less than a 3.00 GPA might be admitted but only on a space-available basis. The new admission standards, if approved by the University, were set to go into effect in fall 1999.[42]

The new energy and enthusiasm levels that seemed to be affecting everyone at the Manship School were affecting alumni, too. Alumni had gathered informally—at homecoming, for instance, or for the rededication of the Journalism Building in spring 1993[43]—but nothing of a more formal, organized gathering had occurred among Manship School alumni in many years. An effort had been made several years earlier to form a Journalism School alumni group, but the group never officially got off the ground. Finally, in 1993, the Mass Communication Alumni Association was revived with Sam Hanna as its first president.[44]

In July 1994 the Manship School of Mass Communication became a free-standing unit. Commenting on the significance of the School's newfound independence, Jack Hamilton said, "We were part of a unit [College of Arts and Sciences] that had worthwhile goals and standards worth aspiring to but were not quite on the mark for a professional school like ours. It's a question of vision. . . . If you're going to live up to the vision, you have to have the freedom to take the necessary steps."[45] Although officially a college, the Manship School would retain the "school" designation "as befits our professional orientation," said Hamilton.[46] Several title designations did change in the process, however. Jack Hamilton was now Dean Hamilton, and his two associate directors now were associate deans.

The new college had organized and gotten on its feet without transferring any additional financial assets from the College of Arts and Sciences.[47] But organizing costs, in fact, had been considerable. Once more the Manship family, like the cavalry arriving just in time, came to the Manship School's assistance. This time it was Charles P. Manship Jr., president emeritus of Capital City Press, who came forward in spring 1994 with a $100,000 gift to assist the Manship School's transition to independence.[48] The financial squeeze that LSU continued grappling with made the latest Manship gift even more appreciated.[49]

Private funding, in fact, was an ever-increasing ingredient of the Manship School's well-being. Money provided by the state barely covered essentials, but private money helped to add muscle and texture to the School's academic program. Private contributions "permit extra investments in equipment and other teaching materials, and they allow the school to attract outstanding faculty," commented Jack Hamilton.[50] Private money did not just appear out of thin air, though. Hamilton remarked that the Manship School's "bare bones" financial situation when he arrived made him realize that he had little choice but to spend more and more time raising funds. "I had a choice," he said. "I could sit there and complain. . . . Or I could go out and raise the money. . . . So I worked like crazy to raise the money."[51]

And there is nothing like success to convince potential donors to consider contributing to the cause. As the newly independent Manship School began to establish a track record of accomplishments, that record would stimulate giving.[52] And the kind and number of gifts about to arrive at the Manship School were spread among an impressive group of benefactors.

First came the Excellence Fund created and sustained by the Mass Communication Alumni Association. Cash contributions to the Excellence Fund rose from approximately $45,000 in 1993–1994 to roughly $105,000 in 1997–1998.[53] Next came full funding of the Greer Chair. Jack Hamilton had convinced local business leaders John Davies of the Baton Rouge Area Foundation and Milton Womack to contribute to the cause.[54] Their generosity brought the Greer Chair endowment to the $600,000 level that qualified it for matching funds from the state's Eminent Scholar Fund (formally, a part of the Louisiana Education Quality Support Fund or "LEQSF"). The one million dollar total endowment would fund the Fred Jones Greer Jr. Chair in Media Business and Ethics that George Lockwood eventually would occupy.

Then came Premier Bank's contribution of $180,000 to fund creation of three endowed professorships of $60,000 each, to be matched by $120,000 ($40,000 per professorship) from the Eminent Scholar Fund. Added to Premier Bank's gift was a contribution by Mr. and Mrs. J. B. Swanson to fund creation of an endowed professorship in honor of their son Bart who had earned a master's degree from the Manship School in 1986.[55] All told, announcement of these gifts showed that "support came when a program had ambitious goals that it met."[56]

But there was more on the way—true affirmation of success breeding success. Two more endowed chairs were announced in 1997 and 1998. Heidel Brown, a Baton Rouge civic leader and owner of C. J. Brown Realtors, was honored by his wife Imo with an endowment gift to create a chair in his name.[57] The chair when fully funded would be known as the Lemuel Heidel Brown Chair in Journalism. Another chair, to be called the Kevin Reilly Sr. Chair in Political Communication, was underwritten by the Kevin and Dee Dee Reilly Fund and the Baton Rouge Area Foundation. Reilly had served in the Louisiana House of Representatives for sixteen years, was the former CEO of outdoor advertising giant Lamar Advertising Company, and was presently serving as the Secretary of the Louisiana Department of Economic Development.[58] Kevin Reilly, while a member of the Louisiana House, also coincidentally had written the legislation that created the matching funds program for endowed chairs. Jack Hamilton was especially enthusiastic about prospects for the Reilly Chair, calling it "the keystone in our plan to build the premier program dedicated to teaching, thinking about and bettering political discourse in this country. . . . Equally important to us in securing this chair," Hamilton added, "is the fact that Kevin Reilly exemplifies candid, principled political communication."[59]

The Manship School had no endowed professorships before 1993. Within five years of that date, the School was the recipient of thirteen endowed professorships, all but four of which were fully funded. The professorship donations came directly from persons for whom the professorships were named, or from relatives or friends to memorialize someone, or from a company in recognition of an employee.[60] Persons also contributed money to the Manship School in support of student scholarships. Some of the scholarships were endowed; others were not endowed but grew on a donation by donation basis. The unendowed scholarships were awarded to students based upon the amount the individual scholarship funds happened to hold.[61]

Contributions came to the Manship School to help build its program in other ways. The Paula G. and Charles P. Manship Jr. Advanced Video Facility was created by a $125,000 gift from Paula Garvey Manship, widow of Charles P. Manship Jr., to house the Manship School's advanced technology video production center.[62] And Elton King, head of Regulatory and External Affairs at Bell South and Manship School Board of Visitors member offered a challenge grant of $120,000 from his company to build an advanced media lab that would be used to teach layout and design. Bell South committed to paying half the $120,000 if others would contribute the remaining half. That challenge was shortly met by the combined contributions of the Baton Rouge Area Foundation, Entergy, the Lamar Corporation, John and Virginia Noland, and the Irene and C. B. Pennington Foundation.[63]

The range of subject matter covered during numerous conferences, seminars, and special events sponsored by the Manship School during the 1990s was truly extraordinary. Here was the smallest LSU college in terms of faculty size taking its public obligations very seriously. Every faculty member was expected to contribute in meeting these service obligations, and none failed to do his or her utmost in getting the job done. As a result, conferences were organized to assist reporters in covering international trade issues and nonprofit organizations, in utilizing technology to improve newspaper advertising design, and in researching and reporting health and environmental risk news.[64]

Part of the Manship School's effort to promote discussion of new ideas and techniques was to recognize the contributions of innovators in the media industry by annually awarding the Manship Prize for Exemplary Use of Media

Technology (later renamed the Manship Prize for Exemplary Use of the Internet and Political Communication). First recipient of the Manship Prize in 1998 was Michael Bloomberg, founder and CEO of Bloomberg Financial Markets and future Mayor of New York City.[65]

The Manship School also expanded its international outreach during the 1990s, dispatching faculty members to conduct workshops and assist journalists in such far-flung countries as Russia, Sierra Leone, and Brazil. At the same time, the presence of journalists and students from overseas became commonplace at the Manship School. Arriving on campus in 1995–1996, for example, were visitors and enrollees from Yugoslavia, Angola, Uganda, Albania, China, El Salvador, Germany, Great Britain, Holland, South Africa, and Venezuela.[66]

Manship School students were the beneficiaries of most of the flurry of activity that went on at the School in the 1990s. The organizations that had become integral parts of student life in the School picked up steam,[67] and student media continued growing and changing. LSU-TV became Tiger-TV. *The Daily Reveille* changed its name in 1998 when the January 20 issue appeared for the first time in many years without the word *Daily* in its title. From that point forward the paper would be known only as *The Reveille*.[68] Another major change occurred when *The Reveille* resumed publishing a Monday edition on August 26, 2002.[69] Financial problems in 1950 had forced reduction of the paper's Monday-Friday publication run to a Tuesday-Friday run.[70] Both *The Reveille* and KLSU also developed an Internet online presence by the turn of the century that extended their access to readers and listeners worldwide.

Honors and recognitions coming to students during the 1990s filled the pages of the Manship School's *Annual Report*. So, too, were honors and recognitions coming to a faculty whose accomplishments and service records were becoming more and more impressive. The transition that John Merrill and Henry Snyder had begun engineering in the 1980s was well underway in the 1990s. The Manship School faculty had blossomed. Its members were more visible, more active, and more integral in the service roles they now were playing on the LSU campus, in the community, and in the national and international academic arena. They not only were participating, they were leading—chairing faculty committees, pushing campus initiatives, and directing campus governance. The same was true at the national level where Manship School faculty were presenting more papers, organizing more panels, and chairing more committees in the leading academic organizations. More important, their research was finding its way into more journals and more books.

The Manship School's progress soon would be measured in the most rigorous fashion as time for ACEJMC accreditation approached. Once more the Manship School faculty busied itself in 1996 and early 1997 preparing the substantial self-study report that would be submitted to the ACEJMC site team prior to its LSU visit scheduled for October 1997.[71] Before that happened, another administrative shift occurred at LSU when Chancellor Davis resigned in November 1996. The LSU Board of Supervisors moved quickly to replace Davis with Executive Vice Chancellor and Provost William J. ("Bill") Jenkins.[72] Jenkins had replaced Roland Haden as interim and then as full-time provost in fall 1992, and before that he had been dean of the LSU School of Veterinary Medicine. Here was someone who was aware of conditions at LSU, budgetary conditions in particular, because he had experienced them from several unique perspectives. Stepping into Jenkins's former position as Executive Vice Chancellor and Provost would be Daniel M. ("Dan") Fogel, who, like Jenkins, had been at LSU for many years.[73]

The time Chancellor Jenkins had spent as dean of a professional school would prove beneficial to Jack Hamilton and the Manship School. Jenkins understood the purpose of a professional school, and he was determined as well to create better working conditions for faculty and closer ties between LSU and its alumni.[74] One year after assuming his new position, Chancellor Jenkins could report for the first time in many years that LSU was benefiting from a budget *increase* engineered by Governor Mike Foster and the state legislature. Money now would be available to allow the state finally to fund its 40 percent part of the many endowed professorships that had been sitting in an unused state of limbo awaiting the state to live up to its financial obligation. Money also now could be used to build a vital campuswide computer network and multimedia classrooms.[75]

Chancellor Jenkins's vision for LSU, and the University's improving finances, would be helpful when the ACEJMC site team came calling in October 1997. The team basically was pleased with what it found. Its attention was drawn especially to all the Manship School improvements since the previous accreditation review, ranging from greater budgetary support from both the state and private donors to better overall morale among faculty. The team was impressed with the new curriculum and in particular with the Management Committee and Budget Committee created by Jack Hamilton to help share administrative responsibilities. Faculty scholarly productivity and the good blend of academic credentials and professional workplace experience that was spread among the faculty also impressed the site team. The one area with which the team was least impressed was minority faculty representation. In fact, the "Standard 12" section of the site team's accreditation report was the only one for which the Manship School was considered "Out of Compliance." But the ACEJMC site team's overall impression of the Manship School remained very positive. The team's unanimous recommendation was for reaccreditation.[76]

That recommendation soon would be challenged. When the site team report reached the ACEJMC Accrediting Committee, committee members focused more fully on the Manship School's minority hiring situation. As a result, the committee recommended to the ACEJMC Accrediting Council that the School receive only a provisional accreditation. Jack Hamilton immediately called upon several of the School's African American alumni, requesting that they evaluate the School's minority hiring practices and then communicate their findings to the ACEJMC Accrediting Council. Based on these findings and the accompanying strong support given the Manship School by its alumni, the ACEJMC Council reversed its position and awarded the School full accreditation.[77]

When all was said and done, the ACEJMC recognized how far the Manship School had come and the efforts that so many persons, both inside and outside the School, had made to improve the School's quality. The School indeed had a few problems that had to be resolved. The diversity issue would be the toughest. Finding, hiring, and retaining qualified minority faculty had never been easy. The pool of minority applicants remained small, and the competition among other mass communication programs for their talents was intense. Nonetheless, Jack Hamilton and the Manship School faculty committed themselves to meet the diversity issue head-on.

The massive effort required for undergoing accreditation review now out of the way, the Manship School faculty and dean prepared to review how effectively the School had achieved all it had set out to do in the Five-Year Plan for Excellence that was concluding at the end of the 1997–1998 academic year. Assessing whether goals had been met was easy. Each goal, in fact, either had been met (in most cases exceeded) or was in the process of being met.[78] In fact, one of the major goals in process that was moving forward with all deliberate speed was implementation of a doctoral program. The Louisiana Board of Regents, in December 1997, had approved the Manship School's letter of intent for creating the new degree program, and the LSU Graduate Council, Courses and Curriculum Committee, and Board of Supervisors all had approved the full doctoral degree proposal in spring 1998. The last step would be a return to the Board of Regents, where the Board this time would be looking at the entire proposal.[79]

The progress made by the doctoral proposal was surprising. Chances for creating the new degree had seemed uncertain after LSU had declared a moratorium on all new doctoral programs shortly after the Manship School had begun planning for one. But the faculty would not be dissuaded. Planning continued, and when time came for the School to argue its case for approving the doctoral proposal, LSU administrators agreed to let it proceed to the Board of Regents.[80]

Before the Board acted on the proposal, though, the Manship School embarked on its next Five-Year Plan; this one formally entitled "Excellence in the Age of Information, A Strategic Plan: 1998–2003." The Plan, more commonly called the Strategic Plan, contained the blueprint that would propel the School into the twenty-first century. The Strategic Plan listed several broad goals that in many respects were similar to those in the first Five-Year Plan. Not until a listing of specific goals did the Strategic Plan reveal something of its true nature. Whereas the first Five-Year Plan had a basically programmatic intent, the new Plan's intent was more instrumental. The goals it laid out—implementation of undergraduate admission standards, approval of the doctoral program, inauguration of a Center for Media and Public Affairs, completion of a new television studio, and renovation of Hodges Hall and the Journalism Building[81]—were the physical and intellectual bricks and mortar for building excellence.

As the Manship School moved through the 1998–2003 years of the Strategic Plan, anyone newly arrived at the School might have thought that little was happening. But looks were deceptive. There was plenty happening. The faculty was continually reviewing what the School had done, deciding what to enhance, what to revise, what to add, what to delete. This had become a dynamic mass communication program whose dynamism was set to grow, once all that was planned for the coming years was in place.

Most of the veteran faculty—the Old Regulars—had settled in, and many of the new full-time persons who had arrived during Jack Hamilton's first years as director and then dean were settling in as well. As happens, a few from that group departed company with their Manship School colleagues over the years, but their replacements arrived with outstanding credentials, both academic and professional. Among the new faculty additions were David Kurpius, Anne Cunningham (later, Osborne), Renita Coleman, Emily Erickson, Craig Freeman, Larry Snipes, Kirby Goidel, Jinx Broussard, Andrea Miller, Lisa Lundy, and Lance Porter. Renee Pierce also joined the Manship School staff as its Information Technology Manager. Her role became critical as the School continued to incorporate more and more sophisticated technology into its computer facilities.

Several changes occurred among faculty who filled the term-limited endowed chairs. William ("Bill") Dickinson served a four-year term in the Manship Chair and was replaced by Bradley ("Brad") Martin. Mike Beardsley replaced George Lockwood in the Greer Chair. Once the Reilly Chair and Brown Chair endowments were fully funded, they were filled by Norman ("Norm") Sherman and then Timothy ("Tim") Cook, both in the Reilly Chair, and Eileen Meehan in the Brown Chair. George Lockwood and Bill Dickinson joined Bill Ross as distinguished professors following their Manship and Greer Chair tenures and returned to the Manship School occasionally for lectures and special events.

Bill Dickinson came to LSU after having served for eighteen years as director of the *Washington Post* Writers Group and editor and vice president of *Congressional Quarterly*. Norm Sherman's credentials included press secretary to Vice President Hubert Humphrey, prolific writer, and former director of public affairs at the Agency for International Development and vice-president of the Roosevelt Center for American Policy Studies. Mike Beardsley had previously served a two-year term as a Knight International Press Fellow, working at television stations in Hungary, the Czech Republic, and Romania. Brad Martin served for many years as a foreign correspondent and at various times had been Asia bureau chief and editor of *Newsweek*, *The Asian Wall Street Journal*, *The Baltimore Sun*, *Asia Times*, and *Asian Financial Intelligence*. Eileen Meehan was a much published media economist who had held the Garrey Carruthers Distinguished Chair in Honors at the University of New Mexico prior to her arrival at the Manship School. Tim Cook, recognized as one of America's outstanding political scientists, came to LSU from Harvard University's Kennedy School of Government where he had been the first occupant of the Laurence Lombard Chair at the Joan Shorenstein Center on the Press, Politics, and Public Policy.

Jack Hamilton's efforts to recruit first-rate leadership to help build the Manship School's doctoral program paid off when he persuaded Ralph Izard, former director of the E. W. Scripps School of Journalism at Ohio University and most recently Freedom Forum Fellow at Columbia University's Media Studies Center, to join the faculty in 2000 as its new Associate Dean for Graduate Studies and Research. Izard stepped down as Associate Dean in 2003, and was replaced by Margaret ("Peggy") DeFleur who moved to LSU from her position as director of the master's program in health communication at Boston University.[82]

Problems with growing enrollment seemed finally under control when LSU approved the Manship School's enrollment management policy. The School's new selective admissions process would allow admission of prospective majors on a more controlled basis. The selection process became effective during the 2002–2003 academic year, and by the following year, enrollment already had begun falling.[83] The School's new admissions policy was working. As a result, goal one of its Strategic Plan had been achieved.

Two interesting characteristics applied to the resulting Manship School student body in 2003–2004. First, roughly 74 percent of the majors were female. Far from being unusual, this percentage reflected a national trend. The second characteristic was that most mass communication majors were choosing public relations for their concentration. Journalism and advertising were about even in number of majors.[84]

The Manship School accomplished goal two of its Strategic Plan when the Board of Regents approved the School's doctorate in Mass Communication and Public Affairs. The focus on media and politics would require cooperative efforts between the Manship School and the LSU Department of Political Science. The Manship School would be home to the twenty-fourth mass communication doctoral program in the country and the only one built around politics. "This highly focused emphasis," said Jack Hamilton, "was designed to give the School a leadership role in a nascent but sure-to-grow academic discipline."[85]

Selection of the inaugural group of doctoral students began in 1999, and by fall 2000, the School's first six Ph.D. candidates were ready to begin their studies. The group of six—Cleo Allen, Mohamed El-Bendary, Craig Flournoy, Eric Jenner, Sonora Jha Nambiar, and Danielle Sarver—included persons from India (Nambiar), Egypt (El-Bendary), and Canada (Jenner). And one of them, Craig Flournoy, was the recipient of a Pulitzer Prize, won as an investigative reporter during his twenty-two years with the *Dallas Morning News*. Flournoy would hold the distinction of being the first student to earn a Ph.D. from the Manship School when he graduated in August 2003.

Intentions were to admit about five or six new students to the doctoral program each year until the balance between incoming students and those graduating would leave about twenty who were actively pursuing their degree. This also would bring the average number of all graduate students pursuing either an M.M.C. or doctoral degree to about fifty per year.[86]

The undergraduate curriculum was revised slightly during the 2000–2001 academic year when the Manship School faculty decided to eliminate the electronic media concentration area. There never had been a clearly defined objective for the area, so it was decided to distribute all electronic media courses among the four remaining areas. The Manship School faculty also decided that diversity and ethics issues should be introduced into every course when practical.[87]

The Manship School Board of Visitors continued assisting the School into the new century. Board leadership changed hands, though, when Sig Mickelson was forced by health problems to relinquish his chairmanship to Robert ("Bob") Mong, president and editor of the *Dallas Morning News*. The Board's rotating membership also continued to bring the highest caliber of media professionals to the group.

The Manship School finances kept improving through the 1998–2003 period. Jack Hamilton's fundraising efforts coupled with those of so many of the School's alumni and friends had raised the endowment level (including pledges) to over $14 million by the 2003–2004 academic year. They also had secured twenty-nine endowed professorships for the School, most of which were fully funded by 2003–2004. And the Excellence Fund Committee announced in fall 2003 that the $155,555 raised over the past year was a new record. Actually, it was the ninth consecutive "new" record.[88]

Financial improvement came from a different direction in fall 1999 when the Manship School was designated as one of LSU's twelve Foundations of Excellence. What's more, the Manship School was the only college-level unit to receive this priority program designation.[89] Each of the twelve programs "was selected because of its present strength and ability to advance to levels that will command national and international attention." What the designation meant in practical, economic terms, though, was the most important benefit for the twelve Foundations of Excellence designates. According to Dan Fogel, "These programs can expect priority in fundraising, resources to support areas of focus, coordinated efforts to hire distinguished faculty, enhanced support for doctoral students, and special attention to computing, libraries, facilities, and other resources."[90]

The Manship School's financial condition along with that of the entire LSU community continued improving, thanks to a generous legislature and governor. The generosity also was due in part to the ability of LSU's leaders to work with state lawmakers in convincing them of the University's needs. Chancellor

Jenkins certainly had been one of the most effective in that regard. Given the respect that Louisiana's higher education leaders in general had for Bill Jenkins, his elevation to the post of LSU System President in April 1999 came as no surprise. Replacing Jenkins as chancellor was Mark Emmert, former chancellor of the University of Connecticut.[91] Emmert and Jenkins made an outstanding team in pushing for LSU support, but Chancellor Emmert's appreciation for LSU's history, particularly its recent years of budget-cutting distress, made him an especially effective advocate for the University.[92]

Even better was Chancellor Emmert's fondness for the Manship School. He liked to use the School's success to show the effectiveness of the Foundations of Excellence program. And he often cited the School's excellent student-to-faculty ratio, its scholarly record, its appointment of what the chancellor called "impact players" to the faculty, and the caliber of students at both the undergraduate and graduate level who were attracted to the School.[93]

Mark Emmert's time as chancellor was successful but brief. He left LSU in 2004 to become president of his alma mater, the University of Washington.[94] Returning to his old position on an interim basis was Bill Jenkins, who served dual roles as LSU Chancellor and System President until succeeded as chancellor in 2005 by former NASA Administrator and Secretary of the Navy Sean O'Keefe.[95]

Chancellor O'Keefe, like his predecessor, would have just as much reason to be proud of the Manship School. Added to all the reasons noted above by Chancellor Emmert was another very special one that began taking shape in 1992 when Sig Mickelson suggested creating a "Center for 21st Century Communications" at the School. The Center would organize conferences, furnish research grants, and publish conference proceedings and papers or books resulting from its funded research.[96] Mickelson's idea soon evolved into the Center for Media and Public Affairs, doing much of what he had suggested but with a focus more aligned with the Manship School's doctoral program. Fundraising began during the 1997–1998 academic year to develop the new Center, and by mid-1999, more than one-quarter of the five million dollar endowment goal had been raised to fund the project. The Louisiana Board of Regents also gave its approval for the Center in fall 1999.[97]

The Center underwent one significant enhancement before becoming operational when the Manship School faculty voted to change the Center's name to the "Kevin P. Reilly, Sr. Center for Media and Public Affairs." The Reilly family had been generous with its financial contributions to the School over the years. In recognition of that support, the Center for Media and Public Affairs seemed a perfect vehicle to carry the Reilly name.[98] Jack Hamilton made the case quite eloquently in his letter to President Jenkins requesting the name change: "It would be an honor to have Kevin Reilly's name on the center. His name will give the center immediate credibility because all who know Kevin Reilly respect his integrity as a state leader, public servant, and political communicator—all the qualities we intend to promote in our center."[99] The LSU Board of Supervisors approved the name change in spring 2000.

The new Center, soon to be known informally as the Reilly Center, became operational in January 2000. That achievement meant that goal three of the Manship School's Strategic Plan had been met. The endowment drive to fund the Center ended the year with roughly $2,165,000 received or pledged. A search to find someone to direct the Center concluded successfully with the appointment of Adrienne Moore to the position. Moore was exceedingly well qualified with her many years of managing nonprofit organizations and working as a political consultant in Washington, D.C.[100]

Adrienne Moore was ready to put her considerable skills and political resourcefulness to work when the Reilly Center opened for business in 2000. Her first task was a big one: organize the inaugural Breaux Symposium, named in honor of U.S. Senator John Breaux. The Symposium would address the issue of "Press at the Turn of the Century" and would bring together three of America's most distinguished journalists—*Washington Post* columnist David Broder, *Time* magazine managing editor Walter Isaacson, and media commentator and former television network reporter Marvin Kalb—to contribute their views on the subject.

Building on the success of the Breaux Symposium, which would become an annual event at the Manship School, Adrienne Moore next organized an impressive array of symposia, conferences, workshops, discussions, and events in coming years. She worked with the LSU Press to launch a book series on media and public affairs. Moore also used Reilly Center resources to fund numerous research projects and to bring nationally and internationally known public policy fellows to the Manship School for extended stays. The Reilly Center helped as well to create in partnership with LSU's E. J. Ourso College of Business Administration, the Public Policy Research Lab whose purpose would be to collect data to assist LSU, state agencies, and nonprofit organizations in analyzing public opinion on various policy issues.[101]

One of the key ingredients of the Reilly Center's early success was the idea it fostered of partnerships across the LSU campus. Partnering with the Ourso

College in creating and operating the Public Policy Research Lab was one example. The Manship School extended itself in other ways, offering, for instance, endowed professorships to professors in political science and partnering with Student Media to create a $1,000,000 state-of-the-art digital television studio/control room complex that would be used by the Manship School for instruction and by Student Media for its Tiger TV cable system. Implementation of the new facility completed goal four of the Manship School Strategic Plan. Only one goal remained.

Years of working in a Journalism Building that had become totally inadequate for the needs of modern mass communication education were about to end for faculty and students. Moreover, the problem of housing Manship School faculty, if not in the same building then at least in close proximity to one another, was about to be solved. Solution to the latter problem came with LSU's decision to renovate Hodges Hall, next door to the Journalism Building, and to make office space, classrooms, and lab facilities available exclusively for use by the Manship School. The new digital television complex would be placed there as would all other Student Media facilities housed in the Hodges Hall basement. Renovation was well underway as the 1990s drew to a close.

First steps toward the long-anticipated Journalism Building renovation began during the 1998–1999 academic year. Architectural renderings by the Chenevert, Songy, Rodi, and Soderberg firm were prepared with the intentions of restoring several of the building's features that had been part of the original Alumni Hall.[102] Alumni Hall's evolution on the way to becoming the Journalism Building had left the building's interior in fairly deplorable shape. The architects' assessment said as much: "Overall there is not a consistent design theme or 'feel' within the building probably due to numerous disjointed renovations over the years."[103] Jack Hamilton characterized the advances made by the Manship School during the 1990s while in the confines of the Journalism Building as a "Rolls Royce engine trapped inside a Volkswagen chasis."[104]

The initial cost estimate for completing the Journalism Building renovation was three million dollars. Getting that money was no small matter. It was, as Jack Hamilton described it, "intensely political" and would require the help and intervention of a number of key players along the way.[105] What everyone would be aiming for was placement of the renovation project on the LSU Board of Supervisors' and the Louisiana Board of Regents' capitol outlay list. Governor Mike Foster's Chief of Staff Steve Perry assured Hamilton that he [Perry] would make certain that renovation funds would be approved *if* the project made it to the list. Carolyn Hargrave, LSU interim provost and later, Manship School Board of Visitor member, saw to it that, indeed, the project appeared on the list.[106] Nonetheless, according to Jack Hamilton, "the building did not make it to the list finally presented to the Board of Regents." Some effective "back channel lobbying," though, persuaded the Regents to reinsert the building on the capitol outlay list.[107]

From that point responsibility for finessing the project proposal through the next stages of the state's approval process fell to a Manship School alumni committee headed by Jackie Ducote.[108] The role now played by alumni in the building's most significant restoration would be a fitting one in view of the role alumni had played in the building's original construction. Jackie Ducote and her fellow committee members, Jim Harris, Renee Smith-Tadie, Jean Curet, Ann Singleton, and Ken Uffman, effectively used their collective influence to tout the renovation project. Considerable support also came from Chancellor Emmert and Provost Fogle, both of whom had taken a special interest in the Journalism Building project.

Their efforts bore fruit in 2000 when the state legislature and Governor Foster approved funds totaling about $225,000 to begin formal architectural planning for the renovation. The next step would be a legislative appropriation that would pay for interior demolition and subsequent construction. The appropriation came in 2001 when the legislature approved $2.9 million in construction funds. Hodges Hall renovation also moved along in 2001. The television production complex was completed on the first floor, and work began on the second floor to complete faculty and graduate student offices and classrooms.

The job of renovating the Journalism Building and restoring many of the original structure's lost (or covered) details was turned over to Jerry M. Campbell and Associates, an architectural firm that specialized in restoring historic buildings such as Louisiana's Old State Capitol. As plans were readied to begin work on the renovation, accommodations had to be made for moving all existing Journalism Building administrative and faculty offices, classrooms, and computer labs to another campus location. Space was provided in Johnston Hall, three buildings south of the Journalism Building.[109] The move to Johnston's somewhat cramped quarters occurred in summer 2002, under the supervision of Renee Pierce and Linda Rewerts. Pierce, in fact, would come to play a vital role in the renovation process. Her position as Manship School Information Technology Manager required that she closely monitor how well the architects and contractors incorporated computer technology into the Journalism

Building's design and construction. Jack Hamilton came to rely so heavily on Renee Pierce's input that he appointed her an unofficial liaison, responsible for reporting to him any construction problems she observed.[110]

Once the Journalism Building was cleared of all occupants, a demolition crew began dismantling the building's interior and a portion of its exterior. For the next two years work would continue in transforming the Journalism Building into an LSU showplace—appropriate for a structure that had played such a vital role in the University's history. The Manship School was operating out of temporary quarters, but School activities did not diminish. If anything, they picked up, both in quantity and intensity. The short time spent awaiting the Journalism Building renovation, in fact, capped the 1998–2003 period of what probably was the Manship School's most productive and most active time ever.

Because minority faculty and student representation had been the Manship School's one area that begged for more attention, Jack Hamilton made minority recruiting a priority. A diversity committee was formed and a plan devised for attracting minority applicants to faculty positions and for more effectively reaching out to prospective minority students. Collaborative efforts with Southern University were part of the School's diversity plan, as was a partnership with nearby McKinley High School in which Manship School faculty worked closely with minority students there who were interested in journalism. In addition, Ralph Izard traveled to several predominantly African American colleges to recruit minority students for the Manship School's graduate program. And the School created a Task Force on Diversity to discuss means of creating greater diversity in the classroom and the workplace. Much of the information that Manship School faculty were collecting on diversity issues eventually would be made available to all interested persons via the Manship School's "Race and Media" website.

Student, faculty, and alumni achievements were the finishing touches to the Manship School's second Five-Year Plan. The School had set itself some difficult goals to meet during the Plan's 1998–2003 time frame, but all had been achieved or were in the process of being achieved as 2003 neared its end. The doctoral program was up and running; new and tougher undergraduate admission standards were in place; the Reilly Center was in business and doing great things; and the new digital television complex became fully operational in June 2001. Hodges Hall renovation was completed in spring 2003. All new faculty and graduate student offices in the building were ready for occupancy, and two multimedia classrooms and two seminar rooms were ready for use during the following fall semester. Also ready for use was the Jean Harvey Curet Conference/Seminar Room in Hodges Hall. The Curet family had funded the room's furnishing in memory of Jean, a Manship School alumnus (class of 1951) and one of its most ardent supporters until her death in 2000.[111] The Five-Year Plan's only unmet goal was renovation of the Journalism Building itself, and that project was well on its way to completion.

All that had been accomplished in a five-year span was measurable not so much in quantity as in quality. Everything was of the highest order, undertaken with the best of intentions. If "Excellence in the Age of Information" was the broad objective of the Five-Year Plan, then success seemed obvious. The extent of the Manship School's collective success would be judged by the objective assessments of the ACEJMC site team, set to visit the School in fall 2003. Prior to their arrival, though, another measure of the School's success came with the Freedom Forum naming Jack Hamilton as the 2003 Administrator of the Year. The award for "leadership in the advancement of journalism education"[112] was more than a recognition of Hamilton's personal success; it was a fitting symbol of just how far the Manship School had advanced since his arrival.

Inviting the ACEJMC site team to campus with so much resting on its accreditation review probably would have been ill-advised for most units whose administrative team and facilities were in temporary quarters. But not so for the Manship School. The School's faculty were ready; they had worked hard to prepare the self-study report. The School's program was in fine shape for the review. And if necessary, the site team members could don hard hats and take a closer look at the soon-to-be-completed Journalism Building renovation if they needed additional proof of just how well the School was progressing.

The site team's visit ran from October 19 through 22.[113] After several days of interviewing faculty, administrators, students, alumni, and media practitioners, and poring over piles of documents, site team members were ready with their assessments. A copy of the team's final report was delivered to Jack Hamilton on October 22. The report clearly affirmed what the Manship School had been doing. It characterized the School as having emerged "as a major campus and national player." "Make no mistake," continued the report, "this is a strong program with a clear sense of what it is, what it is not and where it is headed."[114] The site team's comprehensive summary of conditions at the Manship School was long on strengths and very, very short on weaknesses. Most of the latter revolved around a need to continue tightening of course content, better integration of technology as a teaching tool, and a more focused integration of the public affairs theme with the undergraduate curriculum.

The School's strengths, though, crowded a lengthy list. Among the more notable were: "laudable, focused advancements in correcting deficiencies cited in the previous accrediting report"; "high-voltage leadership"; "collegial, consensual, collaborative and engaged faculty"; "student pride in and enthusiasm for the program"; "aggressive campus networking that has led to meaningful partnerships with other programs, generating new money and clearly leveraging resources in the process"; "superb intermediate and long-range planning"; "emerging recognition for its scholarly productivity, in no small measure a by product of a series of excellent junior faculty hires"; and "noticeable advances in faculty diversity since the last review—ethnic and gender—accompanied by a commitment to stay the course."[115]

Was there any doubt that the ACEJMC site team would recommend reaccreditation? Indeed the Manship School was found in compliance with all twelve accreditation standards—and this time the site team did not equivocate on anything.[116] Its final report was a solid endorsement of the School's total program—top to bottom, side to side. The team's recommendation for reaccreditation was affirmed by the full ACEJMC Accrediting Council in May 2004.[117]

May 2004 was time for celebration at the Manship School. Good things were happening, and none of them, save for one, were totally unexpected. The one out-of-the-ordinary happening actually was the final result of something that had begun early in the 2004 spring semester when Jack Hamilton received an unusual request from the relative of a former LSU journalism student named Lamar Simmons. It so happened that Simmons had left LSU one semester shy of graduation to join the U.S. Marine Corps at the outbreak of World War II. He saw action in several key South Pacific battles and was honorably discharged in 1945. Simmons did not return to LSU, but instead married, started a family, and went to work as a Baton Rouge radio executive. Now, in 2004—some sixty-six years after he first enrolled in the School of Journalism—his relative was asking if there was any chance for Lamar Simmons to receive his degree.

It was a question that persons from the Manship School, the LSU Registrar's Office, and the Academic Affairs Office, all of whom took the Simmons case to heart, were willing to pursue. Records had to be checked and procedures had to be followed, but the effort was rewarded on May 4, 2004, when Provost Risa Palm initialed her approval to award Lamar Simmons his long-delayed bachelor's degree in journalism.[118] He was handed his degree officially during the Manship School's commencement ceremony on May 21.

Shortly after spring commencement, news came that renovation of the Journalism Building would be complete in summer 2004. Finally, it was time for the Manship School staff and faculty who had not already vacated Johnston Hall for Hodges Hall to pack up for their move back to the "new" Journalism Building. The building was not new, strictly speaking, but there was very little of the old building's interior that remained from pre-renovation days. Some of what appeared in the renovated Journalism Building had been covered by earlier renovation projects. Plaster crown molding that now could be seen in the hallways had been covered by a dropped ceiling. The natural oak hardwood floors that now were restored had been covered by vinyl flooring. And the "elegantly carved doors and leaded windows" that now adorned the entrance to the dean's office originally had been part of the facade of the Journalism Building's exterior west entrance.[119]

The balcony overlooked what would become the Journalism Building's most distinctive feature, the Holliday Forum. The Forum, described as a "dynamic space in the center of the [Journalism Building] designed for symposia, debates, small study and research groups and university and community meetings,"[120] could accommodate up to 230 persons. The second floor balcony provided extra seating, and doors to the multimedia classrooms on either side of the Holliday Forum could be opened to expand seating even more. A three-television camera assembly and interconnection with the Hodges Hall television studio would allow for telecasting events from the Holliday Forum to any point on the globe. The rotunda-like Holliday Forum was centered under a dome that was added to the Journalism Building's renovated design and that actually was part of Alumni Hall's original plan. The forum was named in honor of the late Jensen Holliday who passed away in 2002. Besides serving as vice chairman of the School's Board of Visitors, Holliday was, in the words of Jennifer Eplett Reilly, "a creative catalyst for the school with his vision, leadership, and passion for excellence."[121] Jennifer and husband Sean took a leadership role in contributing to and helping to raise private funds to furnish the Holliday Forum and to equip it with state-of-the-art technology.

Original works of art, especially commissioned for the Holliday Forum and underwritten in memory of LSU Journalism School graduate (class of 1964) and LSU Law Center Professor Lee Hargrave, adorned the walls on either side of the Holliday Forum. A "cut-and-painted metal wall sculpture" by New Orleans-based African American artist John Scott was attached to the Forum's north wall. The sculpture was said to reflect "America's long-accepted tradition of free press and free expression, as well as the ongoing challenges faced within that tradition."[122] On the Holliday Forum's south wall hung a series of twelve paintings by Gia Bugadze, "muralist and visual philosopher" and rector of the Georgian Academy of Arts at Tbilisi, Republic of Georgia. Bugadzi traveled to LSU where he painted the canvases with symbolic scenes meant to convey his country's "struggle to build and nurture its free press."[123]

The Holliday Forum was the Journalism Building's centerpiece, but there was so much more to the place. Added to the two multimedia classrooms were four fully equipped computer labs, three faculty offices, a reading room, and the Information Technology Manager's office on the first floor. The Journalism Building's second floor offices housed the dean, associate and assistant deans, the Reilly Center and its staff, and the business manager, internship coordinator, and development director. The Holliday Forum and attached classrooms added 1,600 square feet of floor space to the Journalism Building, which required extending the exterior west wall by several feet.[124] Finally, a new terrace extended the Journalism Building about fifty feet toward Tiger Stadium and in the process created what would become a very popular gathering place for outdoor social events, particularly during football season. A final touch was the landscaping that now surrounded the Building. The new Journalism Building truly was a blend of the academic world with that of the artist—the architect, the painter, and the sculptor.

One of architect Jerry Campbell's special touches was the early-style *LSU* logo that he incorporated into the Holliday Forum carpet. The logo, about ten feet in diameter, was located in the center of the Forum. Having the *LSU* logo so prominently displayed would make an important statement about the LSU journalism program's evolution, from its early history of close connection to the campus, to a time when that connection was barely acknowledged, to a time in more recent years when the Manship School returned to its prominent role of earlier years to become an integral part of the University community.

All those persons—faculty, staff, students, and others—who have been associated with the Manship School throughout its nearly one hundred years have each helped to weave a portion of the School's legacy. This is the link that today's Manship School of Mass Communication has with yesterday's School of Journalism. In truth, though, the Manship School of the first decade of the twenty-first century has only a symbolic connection with the School of Journalism that preceded it—even as recently as a decade ago. The School has not just changed, or evolved, or improved. The School, in fact, has reinvented itself. It is a new School. Members of the Manship School faculty are quite unlike their predecessors—in training, in skills, in technological savvy, in educational philosophy, and in approach to journalism education altogether. And Manship School students are also unlike their predecessors. They bring to the classroom a different temperament, different aspirations, and different perspectives on the world, their country, their community, and their fellow citizens.

The Manship School of the twenty-first century had arrived, so it would seem, at a level of sophistication quite different from times past. The School's goal of excellence had been achieved, and its grand design had been set in motion. Where better to bring this story to an end? But readers who recall this book's introduction already know that this history can hardly end in such an ideal way. To the contrary, one cataclysmic event in the form of Hurricane Katrina would put all that the Manship School had become to the supreme test. It would be Katrina—unexpected and unwanted—that would force its presence into this book's final pages. The storm simply would not be ignored. And in the adrenaline-charged hours of Katrina and its aftermath, Manship School faculty, staff, and students would come face to face with human tragedy and triumph and journalistic heroics on a scale never imagined.

POSTSCRIPT

A Storm Like None Other

The big page one story in the Friday, August 26, issue of the Baton Rouge *Advocate* described a just concluded meeting in New Orleans where the importance of Louisiana's culture to the well-being of the state's economy was the major topic of discussion. Occupying a small portion of column six about midway down page one was a brief story about Hurricane Katrina, a category one hurricane at the time with maximum sustained winds of seventy-five miles per hour that had just brushed Florida's southeastern coast as it moved into the Gulf of Mexico. Hurricane Katrina's projected path would carry the storm northward where its next predicted landfall would be somewhere along the Florida Panhandle on Sunday evening, August 28.[1]

Things had changed considerably by the time Sunday arrived. Page one of *The Advocate* now looked more seriously at Hurricane Katrina in a story whose headline "Katrina Closer and Closer" streamed across the front page. Still, the story ran below the lead story about the slowed construction on the west upper deck of LSU's Tiger Stadium. Even so, an accompanying hurricane-related story said that Katrina could be a category five storm when it reached land. More ominous was the new map showing that Katrina's projected path had changed considerably in two days and now was aimed directly at New Orleans. The storm was currently a category three with maximum sustained winds of 115 miles per hour. Landfall was predicted for late Monday morning, August 29.[2]

The Tuesday, August 30, first page of *The Advocate* carried the two-word headline "Big Blow" that covered much of the page's top half above the fold. Just below these words was a horrifying picture of New Orleanians wading through waist-deep water that now covered much of the city.[3] The rest of the page and many of the inside pages carried the first of many stories to come documenting the long and torturous struggle by tens of thousands of citizens of New Orleans and other smaller towns along the Louisiana and Mississippi Gulf Coast to deal with the aftermath of what has been called the worst natural disaster in American history.

Everyone at LSU, like those in the rest of southeast Louisiana, had been watching the progress of slow-moving Hurricane Katrina as it churned through the Gulf of Mexico, bringing its point of landfall further and further west. On Saturday, August 27, LSU officials felt it was time to act. Chancellor Sean O'Keefe announced that for safety and security reasons, LSU would be closed on Monday, August 29. The next day, O'Keefe extended LSU's closure through Tuesday, August 30.[4]

What happened on the morning of August 29, 2005, in and around New Orleans was devastating. Any attempt here to add to the mass of articles, books, and news reports on the destruction wrought by Katrina and the plight of Katrina victims would be useless. But the story of what happened at LSU and the Manship School in particular during the days immediately following Hurricane Katrina's initial hit deserves retelling. It is the story of a remarkable community coming together under the most challenging circumstances.

Much of that retelling comes from a select few of the many e-mail messages sent to students, faculty, and staff by various LSU officials during the two-week post-Katrina period. For example, on September 1, 2005, LSU President Bill Jenkins and Chancellor Sean O'Keefe jointly described the campus activity then underway:

> LSU is rapidly becoming the central base for federal and state recovery efforts. The Louisiana Department of Health and Hospitals has set up a Special Needs Shelter in the Field House, converted the Pete Maravich Assembly Center into a treatment facility and hospital, and established a temporary 400-bed hospital next to the Assembly Center. Several federal agencies are setting up bases of operation around campus. Emergency vehicles and buses are shuttling refugees to the Assembly Center and there will be heavy traffic and restrictions to vehicular traffic along North Stadium.[5]

Provost Risa Palm dispatched an e-mail message the next day that spoke more directly to LSU's academic situation. Classes would resume on September 6, said the provost, but then she added that LSU had committed "to provide educational opportunities for many students in affected colleges and universities in New Orleans" by helping them enroll in classes on the LSU campus. How many "unanticipated enrollees" that might include was unknown, but the provost was predicting "several thousand."[6]

On September 14, after conditions had somewhat settled and the LSU campus was returning to some degree of normalcy, Chancellor O'Keefe spoke once more to the LSU community with his perspective on all that had happened in the past two weeks:

> I want to express to you all how proud I am of you and the efforts you have put forth to aid those who have been affected by Hurricane Katrina. During the darkest hours, I have seen the members of the LSU community shine brightly. From those who volunteered in shelters and collected supplies, to those who helped run the field hospitals set up on our campus, to those who helped LSU register approximately 3,000 students from universities in New Orleans, I have been amazed at how willingly and efficiently you have handled this situation. I know that many of you have worked long hours during the past two weeks, have sacrificed your personal time to aid in this effort, and have even opened your homes to evacuees. Your compassion and your unselfishness are a credit to LSU. I am honored to lead a university where the faculty, staff and student body have come together to help the citizens of our state in our hour of need.[7]

Journalists always look for the local angle to any big story, and, of course, that angle for the purposes of this book was the post-Katrina role played by the Manship School faculty, staff, and students. Assistant Dean Helen Taylor and Counselor Cathleen Jackson, for example, worked long hours meeting with students and visiting media professionals in need of help. Taylor and Jackson also spent day after day registering students from New Orleans area colleges and universities who now suddenly had been uprooted from their home campuses and were looking to LSU and the Manship School as their new but temporary home.

Associate deans Peggy DeFleur and David Kurpius worked to help New Orleans students make the adjustment to the Manship School. Other faculty, staff, and students helped at various locations around campus, caring for hurricane victims, providing shelter and clothing, organizing fundraising relief programs, and creating blogs as information sources for fellow students. Steve Procopio turned the Reilly Center Research Lab, whose thirty phones ordinarily would be used to collect survey data, into a "24-hour hot line to provide information, help locate families, direct people who needed shelter, medical treatment, food, counseling and just about everything else."[8] There was not a single person in the Manship School who did not rise to the occasion in one way or another to render assistance of some kind to one or more persons displaced as a result of Hurricane Katrina.

The Manship School also rose to the occasion in another way, somewhat unique to a university but absolutely in keeping with its service obligations to media professionals. Representatives from more than forty-six local, national, and international news organizations covered some aspect of the Katrina story from the LSU campus.[9] Manship School faculty and students assisted these organizations whenever and however needed. The biggest assists, though, were the ones given New Orleans television station WWL and the New Orleans *Times-Picayune*. The role played by the Manship School to keep these two news organizations in operation through the earliest post-Katrina days was extraordinary. Quite possibly, few, if any, academic units anywhere could have made the transition from teaching facility to professional news production center so seamlessly and so quickly as did the Manship School.

Ironically, executives from WWL-TV and the Manship School had met two years before Katrina to set up a plan for using the School's television production studio in the event that hurricane conditions might force evacuation from New Orleans. Who would have known that on August 28, 2005, David Kurpius would receive a call that would activate the two-year-old plan. WWL-TV satellite trucks were on their way to LSU to set up shop. Kurpius gathered together several students eager to assist in whatever ways needed, and when the folks from WWL-TV arrived, little time was lost in getting them on the air.[10]

WWL-TV's actual transmission was relayed back to the station's transmitter site in Gretna, across the Mississippi River from New Orleans. The site had been specially designed to withstand hurricane force winds and now, twenty station employees were there to keep the WWL signal moving. What had happened at the station as Hurricane Katrina neared and prior to commencement of broadcasting from LSU was described in *Broadcasting and Cable* magazine: "The WWL crew in New Orleans broadcasts until midnight [Sunday, August 28], then hands off all anchoring duties to the LSU team as the hurricane rages outside. They evacuate to the Hyatt Regency (which is connected to the soon-to-be notorious Superdome), where New Orleans Mayor Ray Nagin and other local officials are holed up."[11] WWL-TV remained on the air nonstop for the next several days—the only New Orleans television station able to do so.

By Thursday, September 1, nearly two hundred persons from WWL-TV and other television stations owned by WWL's parent company Belo had arrived in Baton Rouge, pushing the Manship School broadcasting facility to its limits. As a result, WWL-TV moved its base of operation across town to the studio of public broadcasting station WLPB.[12]

A call for help similar to the one from WWL-TV came from *Times-Picayune* editor Jim Amoss to Jack Hamilton. The newspaper staff had waited until Monday, August 29, to evacuate. About 240 of them had spent the night at the *Times-Picayune* plant but found that rising water was forcing their emergency departure "in the back of newspaper delivery trucks."

The Amoss call to Hamilton set off a quick chain of events at the Manship School. There was no predetermined plan of action like the one devised by WWL-TV, but no matter. Renee Pierce was ready to assist the *Times-Picayune* reporters and staff, making the entire first floor of the Journalism Building the paper's newsroom. "They needed a center of operation," said Pierce, "and we were able to provide space, computers, telephones, and Internet access so reporters could get to work."[13] *Times-Picayune* managing editor Peter Kovacs said of the Manship School experience, "We showed up with just the shirts on our backs, and they took us in. That's how we got back into operation."[14]

Times-Picayune reporters set up shop and quickly went to work publishing the paper's online edition. Not until September 2 did the first post-Katrina printed *Times-Picayune* appear.[15] The paper's management finally moved the *Times-Picayune* operation to a more spacious facility in another part of Baton Rouge. But for the week or more before the move and after classes had resumed at LSU, Manship School students were treated to the rare opportunity of sharing space with one of America's great newspapers.

For "distinguished achievement and meritorious service" in nonstop coverage of Hurricane Katrina news, WWL-TV received a 2005 Peabody Award, the most prestigious award in broadcast journalism.[16] Jim Amoss, New Orleans *Times-Picayune* editor, was named *Editor and Publisher* magazine's "Editor of the Year" in February 2006.[17] Two months later the *Times-Picayune* was awarded two Pulitzer Prizes, one for breaking news coverage and the other—this one shared with the Biloxi, Mississippi, *Sun-Herald*—for public service. The *Sun-Herald* had made a heroic effort of its own to serve its Mississippi Gulf Coast readers with post-Katrina news. There in the *Times-Picayune* newsroom to hear the announcement of Pulitzer Prize winners were several representatives from the Manship School.[18]

This was a joyful but nonetheless solemn occasion for the newspaper staff. For those from the Manship School, it was a moment of pride. They knew that the School had shown itself capable of applying in actual practice so many of the skills and techniques taught in its classrooms and labs. The Manship School also had shown itself to be a partner with the professional community. More than anything, though, the School had demonstrated that it was not just a leader but an incubator of leaders. The thirty-two Manship School alumni spread among the *Times-Picayune* and WWL-TV staffs[19] were a testament to the quality of the School's graduates. When time came to do the job, they were ready.

The story of what these men and women did will be one for the ages. The Manship School, its foundation still firmly anchored in the here and now, will continue to build on the legacy of its graduates, preparing leaders for the media industry and for the community at large. The Manship School—the "J-School"—born in 1912 to fulfill a need, quickly committed itself to a standard of excellence. Nearly one hundred years later, that dedication to excellence, so visible in what the School has achieved over the years, remains stronger than ever.

NOTES

FOREWORD

1. A. J. Liebling, *The Press* (New York: Ballantine, 1961), 34.
2. O. G. Villard, "Education and Journalism," *The Nation*, August 1903, 168.

1. VIRGINIA CONNECTIONS AND THE SEEDS OF JOURNALISM EDUCATION

1. Douglas Southall Freeman, *R. E. Lee: A Biography*, Vol. IV (New York: Charles Scribner's Sons, 1936), 423–25, 429–30.
2. Ibid., 232.
3. Ibid., 421.
4. Ibid., 422.
5. Ibid., 424.
6. Ibid., 423–25, 429–30.
7. Arthur Marvin Shaw, *William Preston Johnston: A Transitional Figure of the Confederacy* (Baton Rouge: LSU Press, 1943), 162–63, 185–86.
8. Freeman, *R. E. Lee: A Biography*, 425.
9. Brayton Harris, *Blue and Gray in Black and White* (Washington, D.C.: Batsford Brassey, Inc., 1999), 3.
10. Ibid., ix.
11. Ibid., 4–6.
12. George H. Douglas, *The Golden Age of the Newspaper* (Westport, CT: Greenwood Press, 1999), 11.
13. Harris, *Blue and Gray in Black and White*, 9.
14. Donald E. Reynolds, *Editors Make War: Southern Newspapers in the Secession Crisis* (Nashville: Vanderbilt University Press, 1970), 5.
15. Ibid., 4–5.
16. Harris, *Blue and Gray in Black and White*, 113, 115–16.

17. Douglas, *The Golden Age of the Newspaper*, 17–18.
18. Freeman, *R. E. Lee: A Biography*, 424–425.
19. Charles Bracelen Flood, *Lee: The Last Years* (Boston: Houghton Mifflin Co., 1998), 206.
20. DeForest O'Dell, *The History of Journalism Education in the United States*, Contributions to Education, No. 653 (New York: Teachers College, Columbia University, 1935), 19.

2. POST–CIVIL WAR CONDITIONS AND LSU JOURNALISM EDUCATION

1. Walter Fleming, *Louisiana State University, 1860–1896* (Baton Rouge: LSU Press, 1936), 36–38.
2. John Batty, "Board Okays Voluntary ROTC," *The Summer Reveille*, June 10, 1969.
3. Fleming, *Louisiana State University, 1860–1896*, 29.
4. Ibid., 23–26, 30–34, 45, 98–107, 112–16, 127–29, 184–87, 193, 431–44.
5. Ibid., 80–86, 229–31, 349, 448–50.
6. A. A. Gunby, "Life and Services of David French Boyd," *University Bulletin*, LSU, Baton Rouge, Series II, No. 2, June 1904, 9.
7. Harris, *Blue and Gray in Black and White*, x, 1; Douglas, *The Golden Age of the Newspaper*, 55, 63–64.
8. Douglas, *The Golden Age of the Newspaper*, 55, 65.
9. Harris, *Blue and Gray in Black and White*, 241.
10. John F. Marszalek, *Sherman's Other War: The General and the Civil War Press* (Kent, OH: Kent State University Press, 1999), 63–100; John Glen, "Journalistic Impedimenta: William Tecumseh Sherman and Free Expression," in *The Civil War and the Press*, ed. David B. Sachsman, S. Kittrell Rushing, and Debra Reddin van Tuyll (New Brunswick, NJ: Transaction Publishers, 2000), 407–17; Harris, *Blue and Gray in Black and White*, 239–51.
11. Fleming, *Louisiana State University, 1860–1896*, 210–11.
12. Ibid., 136–39, 207–10, 315–18.
13. Shaw, *William Preston Johnston*, 161–63, 166.
14. Fleming, *Louisiana State University, 1860–1896*, 379–401; Shaw, *William Preston Johnston*, 172–74.
15. Shaw, *William Preston Johnston*, 186–87.
16. Fleming, *Louisiana State University, 1860–1896*, 278–302, 405–09, 414–17, 443, 472–77.
17. Ibid., 400, 410; David Boyd, "Number of Cadets–By Sessions," February 26, 1898; "Enrollment of Students," n.d.; "Enrollment of Regular Students Since 1900, Graduates, and Admission Requirements," n.d.; "Louisiana State University, Growth in Two Years," n.d.; "Statistics–Student Enrollment, 1898–1927 [1888–1927]," Folder #971, Office of the President Records, RG# A0002, Louisiana State University Archives, LSU Libraries, Baton Rouge, LA (hereinafter cited as LSU Archives).
18. Joe Gray Taylor, "Louisiana: An Impossible Task," in *Reconstruction and Redemption in the South*, ed. Otto H. Olsen (Baton Rouge: LSU Press, 1980), 213.
19. Minns Sledge Robertson, *Public Education in Louisiana after 1898* (Baton Rouge: LSU College of Education, 1952), 27.
20. Ibid., 3–5.
21. Ibid., 12–13, 24–27, 55–63.

22. Taylor, "Louisiana," 211–12.

23. Ibid., 212.

24. Ibid.

25. Shaw, *William Preston Johnston*, 159.

26. Ibid., 159–60.

27. Ibid., 159–61, 162–63; Gunby, "Life and Services of David French Boyd," 19–21; Fleming, *Louisiana State University, 1860–1896*, 249–55.

28. Faculty listings appear in the *LSU General Catalog* issued for sessions or academic years beginning with 1866–1867. The *LSU General Catalog* exists as a generic title for a publication that has been re-titled several times since its first appearance. The titles and the sessions or academic years comprised by each are: *Official Register of the Officers and Cadets of the La. State Seminary of Learning and Military Academy, Near Alexandria, Louisiana* [1866–1867 through 1868–1869]; *Official Register of the Officers and Cadets of the Louisiana State University, Baton Rouge, Louisiana* [through 1876–1877]; *Official Register of the Louisiana State University and Agricultural and Mechanical College, Baton Rouge, La.* [through 1880–1881]; *Catalogue of the Louisiana State University and Agricultural and Mechanical College, Baton Rouge, La.* [1895–1896]; *Louisiana State University and Agricultural and Mechanical College, Baton Rouge, La., Catalogue* [through the remainder of the nineteenth century].

29. *LSU General Catalog, 1899–1900*, 34–37.

30. Joe H. Kirchberger, *The Civil War and Reconstruction: An Eyewitness History* (New York: Facts on File, 1991), 284.

31. Fleming, *Louisiana State University, 1860–1896*, 407–10.

3. JOURNALISM EDUCATION VERSUS PROFESSIONAL JOURNALISM

1. Richard Terrill Baker, *A History of the Graduate School of Journalism, Columbia University* (New York: Columbia University Press, 1954), 5.

2. Ibid., 6.

3. Charles F. Wingate, *Views and Interviews on Journalism* (New York: F. B. Patterson, 1875), 130.

4. Ibid., 151, 160.

5. Ibid., 11, 15, 102, 109–11, 208, 210–13.

6. Ibid., 183–85.

7. O'Dell, *The History of Journalism Education in the United States*, 40–41.

8. Ibid., 41–45.

9. Ibid., 21–22.

10. Albert Alton Sutton, *Education for Journalism in the United States from Its Beginning to 1940* (Evanston: Northwestern University, 1945), 10.

11. Willard Grosvenor Bleyer, *Main Currents in the History of American Journalism* (Boston: Houghton Mifflin, 1927), 427; O'Dell, *The History of Journalism Education in the United States*, 49–53.

12. O'Dell, *The History of Journalism Education in the United States*, 49–52; Sutton, *Education for Journalism in the United States from Its Beginning to 1940*, 39.

13. O'Dell, *The History of Journalism Education in the United States*, 46.

14. Ibid., 48.

15. Douglas, *The Golden Age of the Newspaper*, 17–18.

16. Harris, *Blue and Gray in Black and White*, x.

17. Ibid., 15–16.

18. Sara Lockwood Williams, *Twenty Years of Education for Journalism* (Columbia, MO: E. W. Stephens Publishing Co., 1929), 3; Sutton, *Education for Journalism in the United States from its Beginning to 1940*, 21.

19. Williams, *Twenty Years of Education for Journalism*, 3, 14–22.

20. James Melvin Lee, *Instruction in Journalism in Institutions of Higher Education*, Bureau of Education, Department of the Interior, Bulletin No. 21 (Washington, D.C.: Government Printing Office, 1918), 11–12.

21. Williams, *Twenty Years of Education for Journalism*, 28–29, 36–41.

22. Baker, *A History of the Graduate School of Journalism, Columbia University*, 16–17.

23. Ibid., 23–25.

24. O'Dell, *The History of Journalism Education in the United States*, 55–67.

25. Horace White, "The School of Journalism," *The North American Review*, 178 (January 1904), 25–32.

26. Joseph Pulitzer, "The College of Journalism," *The North American Review*, 178 (May 1904), 641–680.

27. Baker, *A History of the Graduate School of Journalism, Columbia University*, 68–70.

28. Bleyer, *Main Currents in the History of American Journalism*, 427.

29. Sutton, *Education for Journalism in the United States from Its Beginning to 1940*, 17, 21, 37–40, 58–59.

30. Lee, *Instruction in Journalism in Institutions of Higher Education*, 12.

4. THOMAS BOYD, THE *REVEILLE*, AND THE SEEDS OF LSU JOURNALISM EDUCATION

1. Marcus M. Wilkerson, *Thomas Duckett Boyd: The Story of a Southern Educator* (Baton Rouge: LSU Press, 1935), 3, 7–8, 11–12, 16, 20, 153, 346–49; Germaine M. Reed, *David French Boyd: Founder of Louisiana State University* (Baton Rouge: LSU Press 1977), 2.

2. *LSU General Catalog, 1871–1872*, 19, 32.

3. Wilkerson, *Thomas Duckett Boyd*, 75; Fleming, *Louisiana State University, 1860–1896*, 251, 309; *LSU General Catalog, 1877–1878*, 85; *LSU General Catalog, 1882–1883*, n.p.; *LSU General Catalog, 1886–1887*, n.p.

4. Wilkerson, *Thomas Duckett Boyd*, 8, 91.

5. Ibid., 3, 110–12, 130–57, 213.

6. Alfred Newton Delahaye, "A Critical Appraisal of Editorial Opinion and Policy in The Reveille, 1897–1950" (master's thesis, LSU, 1951), 5.

7. Fleming, *Louisiana State University, 1860–1896*, 229.

8. Marie Grover, "1897–1947: A Fifty-Year Span of Journalism at LSU," *The Reveille*, January 14, 1947; Ed Polnisch, "Reveille to Observe 53rd Anniversary; Daily Publication Started 12 Years Ago," *The Daily Reveille*, January 13, 1950.

9. Grover, "1897–1947: A Fifty-Year Span of Journalism at LSU."

10. *The Reveille*, January 30, 1897.

11. Delahaye, "A Critical Appraisal of Editorial Opinion and Policy in The Reveille, 1897–1950," 5–6, 107–11.

12. Rita Morrison, "Early History of Annual Reveals Why It Was Entitled 'The Gumbo,'" *The Reveille*, November 20, 1934.

13. "Student Publications," *The Reveille*, August 2, 1911.

14. Delahaye, "A Critical Appraisal of Editorial Opinion and Policy in The Reveille, 1897–1950," 108.

15. James Wilcombe, "Sherman's Post-War Visit to LSU Recalled By First Printer of Daily Reveille, Now 89," *The Daily Reveille*, October 15, 1948.

16. "Financial 1898," Box 4, Folder #94, Thomas D. Boyd and Family Papers, Mss. 808, 893, Louisiana and Lower Mississippi Valley Collections, LSU Libraries, Baton Rouge, LA (hereinafter cited as LLMVC).

17. "The Louisiana Tigers Again," *The Reveille*, January 10, 1908.

18. *The Reveille*, October 11, 1906.

19. Wilkerson, *Thomas Duckett Boyd*, 270–74.

20. Harris Jackson, "'Reveille' Looks Back on 40 Years of 'Earnest Ambitions of Founders,'" *The Daily Reveille*, February 24, 1938; Wilkerson, *Thomas Duckett Boyd*, 271–72; Delahaye, "A Critical Appraisal of Editorial Opinion and Policy in The Reveille, 1897–1950," 105–107.

21. "Reveille's Growth Striking Since Its Beginning in 1897," *The Reveille*, April 1, 1920; Delahaye, "A Critical Appraisal of Editorial Opinion and Policy in The Reveille, 1897–1950," 9.

22. Reed, *David French Boyd*, 293–94.

23. Jackson, "'Reveille' Looks Back on 40 Years of 'Earnest Ambitions of Founders.'"

24. Delahaye, "A Critical Appraisal of Editorial Opinion and Policy in The Reveille, 1897–1950," 135.

25. "Reveille of Today Result of Evolution Beginning '09," *The Reveille*, April 24, 1915.

26. "Student Publications," *The Reveille*, August 2, 1911. Other student publications alluded to in this passage included *The Demeter*, "a monthly magazine edited by the students in the Agricultural and Sugar Courses, and . . . designed to be the official journal for the scientific and agricultural work of the University"; *The Alumnus*, "issued quarterly" and "edited by the officers of the Society of the Alumni, and . . . devoted to alumni affairs as well as to the general interests of the University"; and *The Y. M. C. A. Handbook*, "issued near the close of the session" and containing "much valuable information, especially for new cadets." *LSU General Catalog, 1909–1910*, 54.

27. *LSU General Catalog, 1896–1897*, 79; *1903–1904*, 89; *1908–1909*, 228.

28. Wilkerson, *Thomas Duckett Boyd*, 198–207.

29. Ibid., 207–209.

30. *LSU General Catalog, 1896–1897*, 36–37; *1897–1898*, 37–41; *1900–1901*, 34–37; *1901–1902*, 35–38; *1907–1908*, 104–106.

5. HUGH MERCER BLAIN AND THE BIRTH OF THE LSU JOURNALISM DEPARTMENT

1. Thomas Boyd, letter to Hugh Mercer Blain, April 29, 1907, Letterbook, July 13, 1906–August 2, 1907, Reel 13, document #592, Office of the President Records, RG# A0002, LSU Archives; Hugh Mercer Blain, letter to Thomas Boyd, May 2, 1907, Box 15, Folder #237, Office of the Presi-

dent Records, RG# A0002, LSU Archives; Thomas Boyd, telegram to Hugh Mercer Blain, May 6, 1907, Box 15, Folder #237, Office of the President Records, RG# A0002, LSU Archives.

2. "Dr. Blain Reviews German Lectures," *The Reveille*, November 2, 1912; "Professor Blain Talks on Southern Writers to Mu Sigma Rho," *The Reveille*, December 5, 1914; "Dr. Blain Reads Fine Paper," *The Reveille*, April 24, 1915.

3. Magazine Section, *The Reveille*, October 1911; November 1911.

4. "Dr. Blain to Meet College Journalists," *The Reveille*, May 17, 1913.

5. "First Teacher of Journalism Here Talks to Class," *The Reveille*, February 17, 1933.

6. "L.S.U. Journalism Dept. Is Making Rapid Strides," *The Reveille*, May 15, 1915.

7. "First Teacher of Journalism Here Talks to Class."

8. *LSU General Catalog, 1911–1912*, 175.

9. "Journalism Class 'Guests of Item,'" *The Reveille*, April 5, 1913.

10. "Course in Journalism Offered," *The Reveille*, March 18, 1912.

11. "College Newspaper Distinctly American," *The Reveille*, December 12, 1912; "Dr. Blain Talks on Duties of Reporter," *The Reveille*, February 15, 1913.

12. "Enthusiasm Shown in Journalism Courses," *The Reveille*, September 27, 1913.

13. "Enthusiasm Shown in Journalism Courses," *The Reveille*, November 8, 1913.

14. *LSU General Catalog, 1913–1914*, 175–80, 189–91; Delahaye, "A Critical Appraisal of Editorial Opinion and Policy in The Reveille, 1897–1950," 132.

15. "Reveille of Today Result of Evolution Beginning '09."

16. "Journalistic Fraternity Established at La. State," *The Reveille*, March 6, 1915.

17. *LSU General Catalog, 1914–1915*, 164–65, 177–78.

18. *LSU General Catalog, 1915–1916*, 183–85, 199–200; *1916–1917*, 191–94, 206–208; *1917–1918*, 184–86, 199–201.

19. "Enthusiasm Shown in Journalism Courses"; *LSU General Catalog, 1914–1915*, 177.

20. "Journalism Class as Press Agency," *The Reveille*, October 11, 1913.

21. "Over 100 Papers to Receive Weekly News Letter," *The Reveille*, October 25, 1913; "Reveille of Today Result of Evolution Beginning '09."

22. "Journalism Class May Visit Item," *The Reveille*, February 15, 1913; "Journalism Class 'Guests of Item.'"

23. "College Journalists See How Big Newspaper Is Made," *The Reveille*, May 2, 1914.

24. "Publishers Co-Operating With Journalism Class," *The Reveille*, February 6, 1915; "Practical Journalism Is Provided By State-Times," *The Reveille*, March 23, 1916.

25. "Journalistic Fraternity Established at La. State."

26. "National Fraternity for Journalistic Students May Enter University," *The Reveille*, November 21, 1914; "Journalistic Fraternity Established at La. State."

27. "Dr. Blain to Meet College Journalists"; "Dr. Blain To Attend Journalistic Meeting," *The Reveille*, November 8, 1913.

28. "Dr. Blain To Attend Journalistic Meeting."

29. Ibid.

30. "Journalism Course Compares Favorably," *The Reveille*, December 6, 1913.

31. "Blain at Journalism Teachers' Conference," *The Reveille*, January 9, 1915.

32. "Dr. H. M. Blain Edits Monthly News Letter," *The Reveille*, February 20, 1915.

33. American Association of Teachers of Journalism, *Monthly News-Letter*, February 15, 1915; March 15, 1915.

34. Ibid., April 15, 1915.

35. Ibid., May 15, 1915.

36. Ibid., February 15, 1915, 3.

37. Ibid., March 15, 1915, 4.

38. "What We Think of the Monthly News Letter," editorial, *The Reveille*, February 20, 1915.

39. "Dr. Blain To Teach at N.Y. University," *The Reveille*, April 6, 1916.

40. "Dr. H. M. Blain," editorial, *The Reveille*, April 6, 1916.

41. "Prof. H. M Blain, Journalism, Annual Report, 1916," 3, Box 64, Folder #1203, Office of the President Records, RG# A0002, LSU Archives.

42. "Reveille Removed to New Quarters," *The Reveille*, September 20, 1916.

43. "Prof. H. M. Blain, Journalism, Annual Report, 1916," 3–4.

44. Ibid., 3–4.

45. Marion Tyus Butler, "History of the Louisiana Press Association" (master's thesis, LSU, 1939), Appendix, xxiv–xxv.

46. LSU Department of Journalism, letter to LPA, May 26, 1915, 1, Box 64, Folder #1202, Office of the President Records, RG# A0002, LSU Archives.

47. H. S. Johns, "Work Features 37th Press Association Meeting," *The Reveille*, May 4, 1916.

48. Editor's note, *The Reveille*, May 4, 1916.

49. Annie Walker, "Journalism Dept. Needs Printing Outfit," *The Reveille*, May 4, 1916.

50. T. P. Hale, "Trained Journalists Needed in Louisiana," *The Reveille*, May 4, 1916.

51. H. L. Johns, "Dr. Blain Gives Practical Suggestions for Improving Press," *The Reveille*, May 4, 1916.

52. "Expect 100 for First Editors' Short Courses," *The Louisiana Leader*, October, 1937.

53. "Wireless Station To Be Erected at L.S.U.," *The Reveille*, October 6, 1915; "Wireless Station Almost Complete," *The Reveille*, February 3, 1916; "Wireless Station Receives Messages from New Orleans," *The Reveille*, March 2, 1916; "Students Invited to Visit Wireless," *The Reveille*, April 6, 1916.

54. "Music Programs and Lectures to Be Broadcasted [sic]," *The Reveille*, February 16, 1923; "Radio Station KFGC," Box 53, Folder #909, Office of the President Records, RG# A0002, LSU Archives.

55. *LSU General Catalog, 1918–1919*, 72.

56. Ibid., 181–84.

57. "Journalism Dept. Gives New Course in Advertising," *The Reveille*, November 28, 1918.

58. *LSU General Catalog, 1919–1920*, 209–10.

59. "Blain Returns from Journalism Meeting," *The Reveille*, April 13, 1917; Sutton, *Education for Journalism in the United States from Its Beginning to 1940*, 26.

60. Sutton, *Education for Journalism in the United States from Its Beginning to 1940*, 26–27.

61. "Journalism Dep't Rated Class 'A' By National Body," *The Reveille*, January 6, 1928.

62. Wilkerson, *Thomas Duckett Boyd*, 298–303.

63. "LSU History Drafts, 1922–1925," Box 82, Folder #1603, Office of the President Records, RG# A0002, LSU Archives.

64. "Journalism Dept. Gives New Course in Advertising"; Delahaye, "A Critical Appraisal of Editorial Opinion and Policy in The Reveille, 1897–1950," 132.

65. "Lieut. H. Moyse Is Given French Croix De Guerre," *The Reveille*, March 6, 1919.
66. Ibid.; "Distinguished Service Cross for Lieut. Moyse," *The Reveille*, April 10, 1919.
67. Hugh Mercer Blain, "Woman and Journalism Are Greatest Factors in Progress of Today," *The Reveille*, March 22, 1917.
68. Wilkerson, *Thomas Duckett Boyd*, 301–303.
69. *Who's Who in the South* (Washington, D.C.: Mayflower Publishing Co., 1927), 83.
70. "Louisiana's Embryo Journalists," *The Reveille*, November 8, 1913.
71. "Exam for Staff Thursday, April 3," *The Reveille*, March 29, 1913.
72. "Press Association to Be Invited Here," *The Reveille*, May 15, 1915.
73. Butler, "History of the Louisiana Press Association," xix; H. L. Johns, "Work Features 37th Press Association Meeting."
74. Blain, "Woman and Journalism Are Greatest Factors in Progress of Today."
75. Ibid.
76. Ibid.
77. "Work on Giggler Nearly Completed," *The Reveille*, May 15, 1915.
78. *LSU General Catalog, 1919–1920*, 209.
79. Delahaye, "A Critical Appraisal of Editorial Opinion and Policy in The Reveille, 1897–1950," 13.
80. "Blain Leaves the University to Go to Rice Company," *The Reveille*, September 24, 1920.
81. Wilkerson, *Thomas Duckett Boyd*, 303.
82. "Dr. H. M. Blain," editorial, *The Reveille*, September 24, 1920.
83. "Under Management of Blain Rice Ass'n. Meeting Is Success," *The Reveille*, May 20, 1921.
84. John Smith Kendall, *History of New Orleans*, Vol. III (Chicago: Lewis Publishing Co., 1922), 1044.
85. "Under Management of Blain Rice Ass'n. Meeting Is Success."
86. *Who's Who in the South*, 83; John P. Dyer, *Tulane: The Biography of a University, 1834–1965* (New York: Harper and Row, 1966), 332; "Dr. Hugh M. Blain, Founder of Journalism School, Dies," *The Daily Reveille*, January 4, 1939.

6. LSU JOURNALISM PROGRAM AT A CROSSROAD

1. *LSU General Catalog, 1909–1910*, 267–79.
2. "18th Editor Reveille, J. Hubert Brown, Retires," *The Reveille*, May 16, 1914; "Former Reveille Editors Engaged in Many Fields," *The Reveille*, March 6, 1936; Delahaye, "A Critical Appraisal of Editorial Opinion and Policy in The Reveille, 1897–1950," 131–32.
3. *LSU General Catalog, 1914–1915*, 62.
4. Ibid., 62.
5. Ibid., 177.
6. "Press Association to Be Invited Here."
7. Hugh Mercer Blain, "Annual Report of the Secretary of the A. A. T. J.," *Monthly News-Letter*, April–May 1916, 2.
8. Lawrence W. Murphy, "Schools of Journalism, Past and Future," *Journalism Quarterly*, 15 (March 1938), 35–36.

9. "Dr. Blain To Meet College Journalists."

10. Advertising courses were taught in at least eleven colleges and universities by 1919 (LSU first offered an advertising course during the 1919–1920 academic year), but only six of these programs—led by the University of Missouri—actually awarded a degree in advertising. Billy Ross, "Education," in *The Advertising Age Encyclopedia of Advertising*, Vol. I, ed. John McDonough and Karen Egolf (New York: Fitzroy Dearborn, 2003), 517–18.

11. Frank James Price, "The Country Press of Louisiana, 1911–1940" (master's thesis, LSU, 1940), v, 2.

12. Ibid., 12–14.

13. Walter C. Johnson and Arthur T. Robb, *The South and Its Newspapers, 1903–1953* (Chattanooga, TN: Southern Newspaper Publishers Association, 1954), 23–24.

14. Ibid., 23–24, 33–34.

15. Ibid., 3–9, 25–26, 89–90, 97–99, 112.

16. Alfred McClung Lee, *The Daily Newspaper in America* (New York: The Macmillan Co., 1937), 66.

17. U.S. Department of Commerce, Bureau of the Census, *Fourteenth Census of the United States Taken in the Year 1920*, Vol. X, "Manufacturers, 1919" (Washington, D.C.: Government Printing Office, 1923), 583.

18. Ibid., 588.

19. Ibid., 584.

20. Ibid., 588.

21. Price, "The Country Press of Louisiana, 1911–1940," 61–100.

22. Ibid., 12–14.

23. U.S. Department of Commerce, Bureau of the Census, *Fourteenth Census of the United States, State Compendium, Louisiana* (Washington, D.C.: Government Printing Office, 1924), 8.

24. Ibid., 20, 22.

25. Lee, *Instruction in Journalism in Institutions of Higher Education*, 72.

26. Price, "The Country Press of Louisiana, 1911–1940," 10.

27. Anna Rothe, ed., *Current Biography: Who's News and Why, 1946* (New York: The H. W. Wilson Co., 1947), 95–97.

28. Hodding Carter, *Their Words Were Bullets*, Mercer University Lamar Memorial Lectures, No. 12 (Athens, GA: University of Georgia Press, 1969), 1.

29. Mary Alice Hebert, "Louisiana Journalism of the Civil War Period" (master's thesis, LSU, 1937), 12, 32, 46, 56–75.

30. Myrtle Buckley Harper, "The Country Press of Louisiana, 1794–1860" (master's thesis, LSU, 1939), 4–5.

31. Clarence S. Brigham, *History and Bibliography of American Newspapers, 1690–1820*, Vol. I (Worcester, MA: American Antiquarian Society, 1947), 182–94.

32. Harper, "The Country Press of Louisiana, 1794–1860," 5–6, 9.

33. Marcus Wilkerson, "The History and Development of Baton Rouge Newspapers" (master's thesis, LSU, 1926), 3, 5–6.

34. Donna L. Dickerson, *The Reconstruction Era: Primary Documents on Events from 1865 to 1877* (Westport, CT: Greenwood Press, 2003), xii.

35. Ibid., xiv; Richard H. Abbott, "Republican Newspapers and Freedom of the Press in the Reconstruction South, 1865–1877," in *The Civil War and the Press*, ed. David B. Sachsman et al. (New Brunswick, NJ: Transaction Publishers, 2000), 473–84.

36. Abbott, "Republican Newspapers and Freedom of the Press in the Reconstruction South, 1865–1877," 480.

37. Dickerson, *The Reconstruction Era*, xiii.

38. Clifton Edward Harper, "The Country Press of Louisiana, 1860–1910" (master's thesis, LSU, 1939), 38–136.

39. Fayette Copeland, "The New Orleans Press and the Reconstruction" (master's thesis, LSU, 1937), ii.

40. Historian Daniel Boorstin remarked, "By the time of World War I, people were asking for national brands in chewing gum, watches, hats, breakfast food, razor blades, and pianos. Advertising was becoming a technique, a science, and a profession." *The Americans: The Democratic Experience* (New York: Vintage Books, 1974), 146.

7. RAISING LSU JOURNALISM EDUCATION TO THE NEXT LEVEL

1. "Press Association to Be Invited Here."
2. "Baton Rouge Papers Boost University," *The Reveille*, September 22, 1915.
3. Hugh Blain, letter to Marvin Osborn, January 18, 1921, F-21q (#17), Marvin G. Osborn Scrapbooks, Mss. 1730, LLMVC.
4. Hugh Blain, letter to Marvin Osborn, June 28, 1921, F-21q (#17), Marvin G. Osborn Scrapbooks, Mss. 1730, LLMVC.
5. *LSU General Catalog*, 1909–1910, 276.
6. "Journalism Dept. Reorganized With M. G. Osborn Head," *The Reveille*, April 1, 1921.
7. "Osborn Begins 31st Year Here," *The Daily Reveille*, October 27, 1938; Wilkerson, *Thomas Duckett Boyd*, 5, 288.
8. "Journalism Dept. Reorganized With M. G. Osborn Head."
9. "Four-Year Course in Journalism to Be Offered Here," *The Reveille*, March 24, 1926; "Prerequisites Raised in L.S.U. Journalism School as College Announces Bachelor's Degree," Baton Rouge *Morning Advocate*, March 17, 1926.
10. "3 Departments Are Elevated to Schools," *The Reveille*, February 20, 1931.
11. Wilkerson, *Thomas Duckett Boyd*, 320–23.
12. Ibid., 305–36.
13. *LSU General Catalog, 1928–1929*, 45–46. A 1925–1926 journalism class schedule, in fact, notes that all but two classes would be offered on the new campus. The "News Writing and Reporting" course was divided into four sections, one of which was available on the old campus and taught by Marjorie Arbour. The "Reporting and Newspaper Practice" course was divided into three sections, one of which was taught by Marcus Wilkerson on the old campus. "Journalism Schedule, 1925–1926," F-21e (#5), Marvin G. Osborn Scrapbooks, Mss. 1730, LLMVC.
14. "New University to Open in the Fall," 1925, n.d., n.p., n.s., F-21a (#1), Marvin G. Osborn Scrapbooks, Mss. 1730, LLMVC.
15. "LSU Marks 87th Birthday on January 2," *The Reveille*, January 10, 1947.

16. "Department of Journalism," F-21e (#5), Marvin G. Osborn Scrapbooks, Mss. 1730, LLMVC.

17. "Journalism Dept. Reorganized with M. G. Osborn Head."

18. *LSU General Catalog, 1922–1923,* 236; *1923–1924,* 238; *1924–1925,* 250; Delahaye, "A Critical Appraisal of Editorial Opinion and Policy in The Reveille, 1897–1950," 133.

19. "University Press Will Be Founded," *The Reveille,* September 24, 1935.

20. *LSU General Catalog, 1929–1930,* 253.

21. *LSU General Catalog, 1925–1926,* 279–80; *1926–1927,* 235–37; *1927–1928,* 245–48; *1928–1929,* 260–63; *1929–1930,* 253–56; *1930–1931,* 201–03.

22. "Four-Year Course in Journalism to Be Offered Here"; "4-Year Course in Journalism for University," Baton Rouge *State-Times/Morning Advocate,* April 30, 1926.

23. *LSU General Catalog, 1925–1926,* 93, 277–80; *1928–1929,* 3.

24. *LSU General Catalog, 1930–1931,* 77–79.

25. "Journalism Dept. Reorganized with M. G. Osborn Head."

26. "Journalists Go To N. O. to Look Over Newspaper," *The Reveille,* May 12, 1922.

27. "State-Times Will Be Published One Day By Students," *The Reveille,* March 31, 1922.

28. Ibid., 1, 12.

29. "The Student Issue of the State-Times," editorial, *The Reveille,* March 31, 1922.

30. "A Job Well Done," Baton Rouge *State-Times,* April 12, 1922.

31. "Students to Edit Advocate, Times Monday, Tuesday," *The Reveille,* April 14, 1926.

32. "Journalism Students Anticipate Putting Out the Baton Rouge Dailies and Agree that Being 'Editor for a Day' Is One of the Finest Experiences in Four Years of College; History of Student Editions Is Reviewed," *The Reveille,* May 9, 1930.

33. "Provision for Journalism Students," *The Reveille,* June 30, 1922.

34. "Largest Number in History Enroll Journalism Dept.," *The Reveille,* September 28, 1923.

35. "Many Courses Are Added in School of Journalism," *The Reveille,* September 30, 1921.

36. "Notes of the Schools," *Journalism Bulletin,* 1 (March 1924), 34.

37. Philip Schuyler, "Close Contact With Local Dailies Aids Louisiana Journalism School," *Editor and Publisher,* January 16, 1926, 20; "Osborn and Work Given Prominent Magazine Space," *The Reveille,* January 22, 1926.

38. "Total of 144 in Journalism at the University," *The Reveille,* October 28, 1921.

39. "Journalism Dept. Has 168 Students Enrolled To Date," *The Reveille,* October 10, 1924.

40. One source refers to the Journalism Department's location in the "Drawing Room" building on the old campus and positions the building as the fourth one on the left of a street leading onto the campus from the main city street that paralleled the Mississippi River. The "Drawing Room" building was northeast of the current Pentagon Barracks and probably was situated precisely where the new state capitol now stands. Campus Map, F-21e (#5), Marvin G. Osborn Scrapbooks, Mss. 1730, LLMVC.

41. *LSU General Catalog, 1925–1926,* 43–44.

42. "Journalism School Shows Increase in Total Enrollment," *The Reveille,* October 7, 1927.

43. *LSU General Catalog, 1930–1931,* 77; *1931–1932,* 91.

44. Marvin G. Osborn, "Administrative Problems," *The Journalism Bulletin,* 2 (January 1926), 19.

45. *LSU General Catalog, 1930–1931,* 77.

46. *The Gumbo*, 1927, n.p.; *1928*, n.p.; *1929*, n.p.; *1930*, n.p.

47. "Osborn Elected Head Journalism Teachers' Assn." *The Reveille*, January 8, 1926; "Baton Rougean Honored," editorial, *The Reveille*, January 8, 1926.

48. "Journalism Dep't Rated Class 'A' By National Body."

49. "Editorials: Too Many Schools," *Journalism Bulletin*, 1 (June 1924), 61–62.

50. Sutton, *Education for Journalism in the United States from its Beginning to 1940*, 26–27; Bleyer, *Main Currents in the History of American Journalism*, 427.

51. "Official Notices: Principles and Standards of Education for Journalism," *Journalism Bulletin*, 1 (January 1925), 30.

52. Sutton, *Education for Journalism in the United States from its Beginning to 1940*, 36–37.

53. "Official Notices: Principles and Standards of Education for Journalism," 30–31.

54. *LSU General Catalog, 1930–1931*, 77.

55. "Journalistic Education in the United States," *The Journalism Bulletin*, 4 (November 1927), 12–13.

56. John Drewry, "Journalistic Instruction in the South," *The Journalism Quarterly*, 4 (January 1928), 32.

57. "Journalists to Meet First Time in South," *The Reveille*, December 20, 1929; "Large Group Attends Meet on Campuses," *The Reveille*, January 10, 1930; "Journalists To Begin Arriving Here Tomorrow," Baton Rouge *Morning Advocate*, December 28, 1929; "Convention Proceedings," *Journalism Quarterly*, 7 (March 1930), 55–69; "L.S.U. Entertains National Conventions of Journalists," *LSU Alumni News*, April 1930, 10–11.

58. "Department Is Now Member of Southwest Body," *The Reveille*, April 11, 1930.

59. "Osborn Named President of Press Group," *The Reveille*, April 27, 1934.

60. "Local Journalistic Sorority Will Not Petition National," *The Reveille*, December 3, 1920.

61. "Local Journalism Sorority Granted Charter by Nat'l," *The Reveille*, May 28, 1927.

62. "Alpha Kappa of Theta Sigma Phi, Chapter History, 1927–1928," Theta Sigma Phi Folder, Manship School of Mass Communication Archives (hereinafter cited as MSMCA).

63. "Install Local Organization in Journalism Honor Group," *The Reveille*, February 27, 1931.

64. Delahaye, "A Critical Appraisal of Editorial Opinion and Policy in The Reveille, 1897–1950," 13–14.

65. Marvin Osborn's Career, F-21a (#1), inside front cover, Marvin G. Osborn Scrapbooks, Mss. 1730, LLMVC.

66. Delahaye, "A Critical Appraisal of Editorial Opinion and Policy in The Reveille, 1897–1950," 132–33.

67. "Take a Look at Me; Journalistic Coeds Alone Edited Me!" *The Reveille*, January 16, 1925.

68. Marvin Osborn, letter to The National Council, Theta Sigma Phi, December 7, 1926, in A Petition to Theta Sigma Phi from Theta Sigma Sigma of Louisiana State University, Theta Sigma Phi Folder, MSMCA.

69. "Journalism Class Visits Plaquemine Newspaper Office," *The Reveille*, November 21, 1930.

70. Marvin Osborn, letter to Conrad Lecoq, August 15, 1921, F-21e (#5), Marvin G. Osborn Scrapbooks, Mss. 1730, LLMVC.

71. Marvin Osborn, letter to George B. Campbell, March 4, 1926, F-21e (#5), Marvin G. Osborn Scrapbooks, Mss. 1730, LLMVC.

72. Marvin Osborn, letter to George B. Campbell, March 11, 1926, F-21g (#7), Marvin G. Osborn Scrapbooks, Mss. 1730, LLMVC.

73. "Plans for First Annual Newspaper Meet Announced," *The Reveille*, March 6, 1925.

74. See, among others, Marvin Osborn, letter to Nancy Stumberg and Jo Stumberg, November 8, 1923, F-21m (#13), Marvin G. Osborn Scrapbooks, Mss. 1730, LLMVC.

75. "Plans for First Annual Newspaper Meet Announced."

76. Marvin Osborn Career Summary, F-21a (#1), Marvin G. Osborn Scrapbooks, Mss. 1730, LLMVC.

77. "Music Programs and Lectures to Be Broadcasted."

78. "Radio Station KFGC"; Boylston Lewis, "First Campus Radio Station Forgotten in Current Growth," *The Reveille*, March 31, 1938; "KFGC Loses Right to Broadcast; No Station Here Now," *The Reveille*, January 27, 1926.

79. "Band Concert To Be Broadcasted [sic] At Physics Bldg. Fri.," *The Reveille*, January 11, 1924.

80. "L.S.U. Glee Club To Render Radio Concert Fri. Night," *The Reveille*, January 25, 1924.

81. Lewis, "First Campus Radio Station Forgotten in Current Growth"; Thomas Ruffin, "The Greater University," *LSU Magazine*, Spring 1994, 27.

82. "KFGC Loses Right To Broadcast; No Station Here Now."

83. "Col. T. D. Boyd Resigns Presidency of L.S.U. After 28 Years Service," *The Reveille*, March 7, 1924.

84. Wilkerson, *Thomas Duckett Boyd*, 337–45.

85. Ibid., 346–57.

86. "Cadet Corps Joins Funeral Procession of President Emeritus of University; Thomas Boyd Rests in Magnolia Cemetery," *The Reveille*, November 4, 1932.

87. Wilkerson, *Thomas Duckett Boyd*, 353–54.

88. C. E. Richard, *Louisiana: An Illustrated History* (Baton Rouge: The Foundation for Excellence in Louisiana Public Broadcasting, 2003), 126.

89. John M. Barry, *Rising Tide: The Great Mississippi Flood of 1927 and How It Changed America* (New York: Simon and Schuster, 1997), 422.

90. Richard, *Louisiana*, 126.

91. Barry, *Rising Tide*, 170–71; Richard, *Louisiana*, 126–28.

92. Richard, *Louisiana*, 126.

93. "Men Students of L.S.U. May Help Fight Mississippi," *The Reveille*, April 23, 1927.

94. "Flood Refugees to Be Sheltered in Barracks," *The Reveille*, May 7, 1927.

95. "Campus Organizations Aiding in Flood Relief," *The Reveille*, May 28, 1927.

8. THE J-SCHOOL SETTLES IN

1. "A Gallery of Presidents," *LSU Almanac 1981*, n.p.

2. "One College, Three Schools Added to L.S.U. Organization," *LSU Alumni News*, April 1931, 2.

3. "Woman Ag Editor Plans 'Food for Defense' Program," *The Daily Reveille*, September 16, 1941.

4. "Miss Arbour Is First Woman to Head Ag Editors," Baton Rouge *Morning Advocate*, September 20, 1950.

5. *LSU General Catalog, 1940–1941*, 239.

6. "Smith To Take Givens' Place," *The Reveille*, May 13, 1932; *LSU General Catalog, 1932–1933*, 249.

7. *LSU General Catalog, 1934–1935*, 290.

8. *LSU General Catalog, 1935–1936*, 333.

9. "McCoy, Copeland Will Teach Here," *The Reveille*, September 25, 1936; *LSU General Catalog, 1936–1937*, 145, 349.

10. "Former Reveille Editor Returns As Instructor," *The Daily Reveille*, September 10, 1938; *LSU General Catalog, 1938–1939*, 236.

11. *LSU General Catalog, 1939–1940*, 239.

12. Delahaye, "A Critical Appraisal of Editorial Opinion and Policy in The Reveille, 1897–1950," 133–34.

13. "Journalism School Names Mickelson," *The Daily Reveille*, September 16, 1939.

14. Ronald Garay, "Sig Mickelson," in *Encyclopedia of Television News*, ed. Michael D. Murray (Phoenix, AZ: Oryx Press, 1999), 148–49.

15. "Dr. Hugh M. Blain, Founder of Journalism School, Dies."

16. *LSU General Catalog, 1935–1936*, 335; *1938–1939*, 237.

17. *LSU General Catalog, 1934–1935*, 328.

18. *LSU General Catalog, 1930–1931*, 203.

19. Ibid.

20. *LSU General Catalog, 1931–1932*, 249.

21. Norval Neil Luxon, "Trends in Curricula In A. A. S. D. J. Schools," *Journalism Quarterly*, 14 (December 1937), 353–60.

22. "Students to Edit Dailies Next Tuesday, *The Reveille*, April 8, 1932; "Student Staff Edits Dailies Monday, Tuesday," *The Reveille*, April 7, 1933; "Staffs Picked to Edit Local Daily Papers," *The Reveille*, April 20, 1934.

23. J. P. Wade, letter to Marvin Osborn, October 22, 1934, F-21g (#7), Marvin G. Osborn Scrapbooks, Mss. 1730, LLMVC.

24. "Students Editing Louisiana Papers," *The Reveille*, April 20, 1937; "Journalism Group Edits Eunice Paper," *The Daily Reveille*, May 10, 1938; "Student Editors Return From Trips," *The Daily Reveille*, April 29, 1939; "Five Journalism Teams To Make Field Trips," *Louisiana Leader*, April 7, 1940.

25. "Excerpts from Annual Report, 1939–'40," F-21f (#6), Marvin G. Osborn Scrapbooks, Mss. 1730, LLMVC.

26. C. R. F. Smith, "Field Trips in Journalism," *The Proceedings of the Louisiana Academy of Sciences*, 4 (15 November 1938), 78, 80.

27. "State Newspaper Histories Written by Senior Students," *The Daily Reveille*, February 4, 1938.

28. Myrtle Buckley Harper, "The Country Press of Louisiana, 1794–1860"; Clifton Edward Harper, "The Country Press of Louisiana, 1860–1910"; Frank James Price, "The Country Press of Louisiana, 1911–1940."

29. "Coed Journalism Group Is Formed," *The Reveille*, March 16, 1934; "Freshmen Club Plans to Honor Theta Sigma Phi," *The Reveille*, March 23, 1934.

30. "Journalism Group Form Fraternity," *The Reveille*, December 8, 1933; "Silverberg Heads SDX," *The Reveille*, May 4, 1937.

31. "Excerpts from Annual Report, 1939–'40."

32. Marvin Osborn, letter to Bruce McCoy, May 27, 1936, F-21i (#9), Marvin G. Osborn Scrapbooks, Mss. 1730, LLMVC; Marvin Osborn, letter to Edwin M. Roy, September 3, 1936, F-21b (#2), Marvin G. Osborn Scrapbooks, Mss. 1730, LLMVC.

33. "Journalism School Helps LPA," LPA Souvenir Booklet, March 1955, n.p., F-21b (#2), Marvin G. Osborn Scrapbooks, Mss. 1730, LLMVC.

34. Sutton, *Education for Journalism in the United States from its Beginning to 1940*, 40.

35. "Journalism School Helps LPA."

36. Butler, "History of the Louisiana Press Association," 123–24, 130–31 (Appendix) xx, xxv.

37. "Journalism School Head Welcomes State Editors," *Pelican Press Messenger*, 1937, LSU Journalism School, Microfilm Reel #81, LSU Archives.

38. "Louisiana Editors' Short Course," *The Louisiana Leader*, October 1937, F-21L (#12), Marvin G. Osborn Scrapbooks, Mss. 1730, LLMVC.

39. "University Press Will Be Founded."

40. Hilda Janet Simmons, "L.S.U. University Press Is One Publishing House With No Press, No Type," *The Daily Reveille*, March 24, 1938; "Marcus Wilkerson: Scholar, Teacher and Administrator," *LSU Alumni News*, May-June 1953, 22; Press Release, Bureau of Public Relations, LSU, April 15, 1953.

41. *LSU General Catalog, 1930–1931*, 284; *1931–1932*, 362; *1932–1933*, 384.

42. "Enrollment Over the Years," *LSU Almanac 1981*.

43. *LSU General Catalog, 1933–1934*, 311; *1934–1935*, 352; *1935–1936*, 403; *1936–1937*, 423; *1937–1938*, 260; *1938–1939*, 277; *1939–1940*, 280.

44. "Expect 100 for First Editors' Short Course," *The Louisiana Leader*, October 1937, F-21b (#2), Marvin G. Osborn Scrapbooks, Mss. 1730, LLMVC; Lewis A. Bernard, "School of Journalism Moves; Reveille Goes Daily Feb. 3," *The Reveille*, January 7, 1938.

45. Bernard, "School of Journalism Moves; Reveille Goes Daily Feb. 3."

46. "Leche Hall Is Boon to Journalism Group," *The Reveille*, April 5, 1938.

47. "Reveille in New L.S.U. Quarters In Former Law Building on Campus," *Baton Rouge State-Times*, February 2, 1938.

48. "Old Law Building Houses Journalism, Student Newspaper," *The Daily Reveille*, April 5, 1938.

49. Marvin Osborn, letter to Clifton E. Harper, July 20, 1944, F-21d (#4), Marvin G. Osborn Scrapbooks, Mss. 1730, LLMVC.

50. "Excerpts from Annual Report, 1939–'40."

51. Ibid.

52. Christopher H. Sterling and John M. Kittross, *Stay Tuned: A Concise History of American Broadcasting*, 2nd ed. (Belmont, CA: Wadsworth Publishing Co., 1990), 141.

53. Ibid., 632, 634.

54. Ibid., 656.

55. Ronald Garay, "News Reporting, Radio," *Encyclopedia of International Media and Communications*, Vol. 3 (San Diego, CA: Academic Press, 2003), 299–303.

56. "University Officials Inspect, Dedicate Radio Equipment," *The Daily Reveille*, December 16, 1938.

57. Lewis, "First Campus Radio Station Forgotten in Current Growth."

58. "Radio Class Gives News," *The Reveille*, February 19, 1937.
59. Lewis, "First Campus Radio Station Forgotten in Current Growth."
60. "Deserted WJBO Becomes Speech and Radio Lab," *The Reveille*, September 14, 1937.
61. *LSU General Catalog, 1936–1937*, 351.
62. *LSU General Catalog, 1938–1939*, 237.
63. "Radio Programs Start for Year," *The Daily Reveille*, September 22, 1938.
64. Betty Ray Boykin, "Deadlines That Won't Wait Face Students on Newscast," *The Daily Reveille*, November 3, 1939; "Student News Hour On Air at 9 P.M.," *The Daily Reveille*, February 29, 1940.
65. "Publication of Daily, New School Highlight Journalism Program," *The Reveille*, September 14, 1937.
66. Delahaye, "A Critical Appraisal of Editorial Opinion and Policy in The Reveille, 1897–1950," 14, 25–26.
67. "Reveille in New L.S.U. Quarters In Former Law Building on Campus."
68. Delahaye, "A Critical Appraisal of Editorial Opinion and Policy in The Reveille, 1897–1950," 14–15.
69. See, for instance, T. Harry Williams, *Huey Long* (New York: Bantam Books, 1970); Harnett T. Kane, *Louisiana Hayride: The American Rehearsal for Dictatorship, 1928–1940* (Gretna, LA: Pelican Publishing Co., 1971); William Ivy Hair, *The Kingfish and His Realm: The Life and Times of Huey P. Long* (Baton Rouge: LSU Press, 1991); and Richard D. White Jr., *Kingfish: The Reign of Huey P. Long* (NY: Random House, 2006).
70. Ronald Garay, "Huey Long" in Donald G. Godfrey and Frederic A. Leigh, eds., *Historical Dictionary of American Radio* (Westport, CT: Greenwood Press, 1998), 243–44.
71. Hair, *The Kingfish and His Realm*, 228.
72. Williams, *Huey Long*, 527–530, 548.
73. Ibid., 811–820; Delahaye, "A Critical Appraisal of Editorial Opinion and Policy in The Reveille, 1897–1950," 41–47; "L.S.U. Officials Quoted as Proof of Long Control," Baton Rouge *Morning Advocate*, December 5, 1934; "Dismissal of Two Students Is Announced," December 6, 1934, Baton Rouge *Morning Advocate*; "Declare Jobs Gag Council in L.S.U. Row," December 7, 1934, Baton Rouge *Morning Advocate*; Billy Laffler, "Board Exonerates Ex-Students," March 12, 1941, *The Daily Reveille*; Brett J. Blackledge, "Censorship a Ghost in Reveille's Past," *The Daily Reveille*, November 20, 1984.
74. Laffler, "Board Exonerates Ex-Students"; Blackledge, "Censorship a Ghost in Reveille's Past"; Delahaye, "A Critical Appraisal of Editorial Opinion and Policy in The Reveille, 1897–1950," 41–42.
75. Laffler, "Board Exonerates Ex-Students."
76. Special Committee Report, "Fact-finding Investigation of the Case of the Dismissal and Indefinite Suspension from Louisiana State University of Seven Journalism Students on December 5, 1934," submitted to LSU Acting President Paul Hebert, December 20, 1940, 6–7, MSMCA.
77. Ibid., 8.
78. Ibid., 8 9.
79. Ibid., 10.

80. Ibid., 10–11.
81. Ibid.
82. Ibid., 11.
83. "L.S.U. Officials Quoted as Proof of Long Control."
84. Special Committee Report, 12–13.
85. Delahaye, "A Critical Appraisal of Editorial Opinion and Policy in The Reveille, 1897–1950," 43–44.
86. "Dismissal of Two Students Is Announced."
87. Ibid.; Delahaye, "A Critical Appraisal of Editorial Opinion and Policy in The Reveille, 1897–1950," 44.
88. "Dismissal of Two Students Is Announced."
89. Special Committee Report, 13–14.
90. Ibid., 2–3; Delahaye, "A Critical Appraisal of Editorial Opinion and Policy in The Reveille, 1897–1950," 44.
91. Special Committee Report, 14–16.
92. *LSU General Catalog, 1932–1933*, 325, 328, 334, 336, 348; "Students Suspended or Dismissed from L.S.U. Have Good Records," Baton Rouge *Morning Advocate*, December 6, 1934.
93. Williams, *Huey Long*, 817.
94. Earl English, *Journalism Education at the University of Missouri—Columbia* (Marceline, MO: Walsworth Publishing Co., 1988), 53–54.
95. Williams, *Huey Long*, 817.
96. Ibid., 817–818; "4 Students Do Not Know Their Status," Baton Rouge *Morning Advocate*, December 4, 1934.
97. Williams, *Huey Long*, 819.
98. Ibid., 816–817.
99. Delahaye, "A Critical Appraisal of Editorial Opinion and Policy in The Reveille, 1897–1950," 134.
100. "Excerpts from Annual Report, 1939–'40."
101. *LSU General Catalog, 1914–1915*, 118.
102. *LSU General Catalog, 1930–1931*, 203; *1931–1932*, 249.
103. *LSU General Catalog, 1914–1915*, 235; *1915–1916*, 245.
104. *LSU General Catalog, 1916–1917*, 261.
105. *LSU General Catalog, 1919–1920*, 281.
106. Ibid.
107. *LSU General Catalog, 1923–1924*, 297; *1924–1925*, 315.
108. *LSU General Catalog, 1934–1935*, 204.
109. Marvin G. Osborn, "Memoranda Concerning the School of Journalism," 1937, F-21n (#14), Marvin G. Osborn Scrapbooks, Mss. 1730, LLMVC.
110. Williams, *Huey Long*, 527–529.
111. Hair, *The Kingfish and His Realm*, 229.
112. Kane, *Louisiana Hayride*, 226–385.
113. Ibid., 273–75, 283–84. Much of the effort to uncover wrongdoing in the state and practically all public disclosures of one after another sordid story of corruption was due to investigative

reporting by New Orleans newspapers. George E. Simmons, "Crusading Newspapers in Louisiana," *Journalism Quarterly*, 16 (December 1939), 325–33.

114. "Paul M. Hebert Is Named Acting President; E. S. Richardson Quits," *The Reveille*, "Extra" edition, June 27, 1934.

115. "Reporter Ousted at L.S.U. Interviews Old President, Now Charged in Funds Grab," New Orleans *Times-Picayune*, July 5, 1939.

9. WORLD WAR II, ACCREDITATION, AND A PERMANENT HOME

1. L. B. Lucky, Dale E. Bennett, and Bruce R. McCoy, letter and Fact-Finding Report submitted to LSU Acting President Paul M. Hebert, December 20, 1940. Reveille Seven Folder, MSMCA.

2. Ibid., 17–18.

3. "Excerpt from Proceedings of Board of Supervisors of Louisiana State University and A and M College," March 15, 1941, Reveille Seven Folder, MSMCA.

4. Paul Hebert, letters to Jesse Cutrer Jr. et al., March 14, 1941, Reveille Seven Folder, MSMCA.

5. Jesse H. Cutrer Jr. et al., letter to LSU Board of Supervisors and LSU Acting President Paul M. Hebert, March 31, 1941, Reveille Seven Folder, MSMCA.

6. Billy Laffler, "Board Exonerates Ex-Students."

7. Delahaye, "A Critical Appraisal of Editorial Opinion and Policy in The Reveille, 1897–1950," 44–45.

8. John Pope, "50 Years Later LSU Honors Six Who Defied Long," *The Times-Picayune/The States-Item*, December 6, 1984.

9. "'Reveille Seven,' Four Others Join LSU Hall of Fame," Baton Rouge *Saturday*, April 13, 1996.

10. "Journalism Course Is Resumed," *The Daily Reveille*, September 13, 1946.

11. "Excerpts from Progress Report for December [1943]," F-21b (#2), Marvin G. Osborn Scrapbooks, Mss. 1730, LLMVC.

12. *LSU General Catalog, 1946–1947*, 145–47.

13. *LSU General Catalog, 1940–1941*, 294; *1941–1942*, 300; *1942–1943*, 290; *1943–1944*, 296; *1944–1945*, 302; *1945–1946*, 313; *1946–1947*, 341; *1947–1948*, 310; *1948–1949*, 300; *1949–1950*, 308; *1950–1951*, 311.

14. 58 Stat. 284 (June 22, 1944).

15. *LSU General Catalog, 1940–1941*, 294; *1941–1942*, 300; *1942–1943*, 290; *1943–1944*, 296; *1944–1945*, 302; *1945–1946*, 313; *1946–1947*, 341; *1947–1948*, 310; *1948–1949*, 300; *1949–1950*, 308; *1950–1951*, 311.

16. C. G. Taylor, Assistant to the LSU President, Memo from Office of the President, July 29, 1942, F-21b (#2), Marvin G. Osborn Scrapbooks, Mss. 1730, LLMVC.

17. "Journalism Began in 1912; Director Here for 22 Years," *The Reveille*, October 30, 1942.

18. "C. R. F. Smith Accepts Appointment," *The Summer Reveille*, August 17, 1943; "Quarterly Progress Report, Louisiana State University," Vol. 4, No. 2, April 1945, 26, F-21p (#16), Marvin G. Osborn Scrapbooks, Mss. 1730, LLMVC.

19. Marie Grover, "Wiggins Takes Up Duties After 42 Months in Service," *The Reveille*, November 6, 1945.

20. "T. C. Shields Loses Life in Normandy," *The Summer Reveille*, July 7, 1944.

21. "Journalism Graduates in the Armed Services," 1944, MSMCA.

22. "Nation's Armed Forces Call 16 Graduates of 41," *Pelican Press Messenger*, February 1942.

23. "LSU Journalism Graduates Helping U.S. War Effort," *Journalism News*, August 1942, 1.

24. Elayn Hunt, "Sheldon Just Missed Pacific Crash Shot," *The Reveille*, January 19, 1945.

25. Jane Rod, "Marine or Newspaperman, Time Is Well Occupied," *The Summer Reveille*, June 13, 1944.

26. "Baulch Serves MacArthur As Assistant Press Officer," *The Daily Reveille*, April 25, 1942.

27. Juanita Greene, "Marines Land; Reporter Returns," *The Summer Reveille*, June 18, 1943; "L.S.U. Men—in the Service," *The Summer Reveille*, June 9, 1942.

28. "Sports Editor Bennett to Go In Air Corps," *The Reveille*, November 9, 1943.

29. "Joins WACs On D-Day," *The Summer Reveille*, June 13, 1944.

30. "57 Ex-Coeds Have Enlisted In Service," *The Reveille*, August 24, 1943.

31. "Former Reveille Editors Serve in Armed Forces," *The Reveille*, October 30, 1942; Delahaye, "A Critical Appraisal of Editorial Opinion and Policy in The Reveille, 1897–1950," 134.

32. "These We Honor," *LSU Alumni News*, May 1945, 5–29; "Memoriam," *LSU Alumni News*, September 1946, 10–11, 29–30.

33. "Obituary," *Editor and Publisher*, May 19, 1945, 63; "These We Honor," 7, 11, 12; unofficial obituary notices, n.d., n.p., MSMCA.

34. "These We Honor," 25.

35. "Editorial in Louisiana Daily Pays Tribute to T. C. Shields," LSU *Journalism News*, August 1944, 4, F-21h (#8), Marvin G. Osborn Scrapbooks, Mss. 1730, LLMVC.

36. "Journalism Graduates in the Armed Services."

37. "News Connects Journalists," *The Reveille*, December 14, 1943.

38. Harold Rubin, "AP War Reporter Visits Here Today," *The Daily Reveille*, March 13, 1942; "Journalism Grad Now in N. Africa," *The Reveille*, November 10, 1942; "Wes Gallagher, L.S.U. Grad., Lauded by Correspondent," *The Reveille*, June 8, 1943; "Journalism Grad Gets Job As Paris Bureau AP Chief," *The Reveille*, May 18, 1945; "'36 Graduate Covers Trials At Nurnberg," *The Reveille*, December 4, 1945; "Wes Gallagher 'Outstanding Young Man,'" *The Reveille*, March 12, 1946.

39. "James Wes Gallagher," in William H. Taft, *Encyclopedia of Twentieth Century Journalists* (NY: Garland Publishing, Inc., 1986), 123; John Butler, "James Wesley 'Wes' Gallagher," in Joseph P. McKerns, ed., *Biographical Dictionary of American Journalism* (Westport, CT: Greenwood Press, 1989), 254–55.

40. Delahaye, "A Critical Appraisal of Editorial Opinion and Policy in The Reveille, 1897–1950," 15; Lois Jones, "Reveille Survives, Grows With University 72 Years," *The Summer Reveille*, August 29, 1944; Grover, "1897–1947: A Fifty-Year Span of Journalism at LSU."

41. "Reveille Celebrates 71st Anniversary," *The Reveille*, November 5, 1943.

42. Delahaye, "A Critical Appraisal of Editorial Opinion and Policy in The Reveille, 1897–1950," 134–35.

43. Ibid., 115.

44. "Journalism News Printed by School," *The Summer Reveille*, July 27, 1945.

45. "Journalism Students Leave For Field Trips Next Week," *The Reveille*, April 9, 1942.

46. "24 Students Will Edit, Publish Five Papers on Field Trips," *The Reveille*, March 23, 1943.

47. "Journalism Students Edit Weekly Papers in Louisiana," *The Reveille*, April 9, 1946; Dan Hardesty, "LSU Journalism Students Find School Work Can Be Fun—When It Comes to Putting Out Paper," Baton Rouge *Morning Advocate*, April 21, 1946; "Teams To Publish 3 Papers On Journalism Field Trips," *The Daily Reveille*, April 15, 1947; "Journalism Students to Go In Five Teams on Field Trip," *The Daily Reveille*, April 23, 1948.

48. Marvin Osborn, letter to Troy H. Middleton, October 10, 1951, 4, F-21n (#14), Marvin G. Osborn Scrapbooks, Mss. 1730, LLMVC.

49. Jules Fogel, letter to Marvin Osborn, May 3, 1941, F-21g (#7), Marvin G. Osborn Scrapbooks, Mss. 1730, LLMVC.

50. C. B. Hodges, letter to Marvin Osborn, May 3, 1943, F-21i (#9), Marvin G. Osborn Scrapbooks, Mss. 1730, LLMVC.

51. "Editors' Short Course Begins on Campus Friday," *The Daily Reveille*, November 4, 1941.

52. "Editors to Meet at L.S.U. for a Short Course," *Publishers' Auxiliary*, September 30, 1944, n.p., F-21b (#2), Marvin G. Osborn Scrapbooks, Mss 1730, LLMVC.

53. "Siebert Is Speaker for Short Course," *The Reveille*, November 17, 1944.

54. "40 Journalists Attend Opening Sessions of Annual 2-Day Short Course for Editors," *The Daily Reveille*, November 6, 1948.

55. Marvin Osborn, letter to Troy H. Middleton.

56. "New Journalism Scholarship Established by Ewing Family," *The Daily Reveille*, March 6, 1950.

57. "Wilkerson Is AAJT Prexy," *The Reveille*, January 14, 1947.

58. Jimmie Terry, "Editor Arbour Chosen by Farm Magazine As 'Agricultural Woman of the Year,'" *The Reveille*, January 7, 1948.

59. "Board Plans Revised Housing and Radio Station," *The Reveille*, April 10, 1945.

60. Erik Barnouw, *The Golden Web: A History of Broadcasting in the United States*, Vol. II, 1933–1953 (New York: Oxford University Press, 1968), 40–41, 129–30.

61. Robert Blakely, *To Serve the Public Interest: Educational Broadcasting in the United States* (Syracuse NY: Syracuse University Press, 1979), 77.

62. "L.S.U. to Get FM Station in January," *The Summer Reveille*, July 26, 1946; "WLSU Frequency Modulation Station Will Beam School Programs Over State," *The Daily Reveille*, March 11, 1947.

63. "LSU's Radio Station Goes on the Air," *LSU Alumni News*, December 1947, 4, 6.

64. "Station WLSU Is Deep South's First FM Outlet," *The Daily Reveille*, September 16, 1947.

65. "LSU's Radio Station Goes on the Air."

66. "WLSU Is First College Station To Broadcast a Campus Opera," *The Daily Reveille*, March 12, 1948; Charles Fellers, "Progress Marks Station WLSU's First Anniversary; Membership in National Network Increases Air Time," *The Daily Reveille*, December 14, 1948.

67. *LSU General Catalog, 1941–1942*, 284, 287; *1942–1943*, 276, 278; *1943–1944*, 280, 283; *1944–1945*, 288, 290; *1945–1946*, 298, 300.

68. Robert Brouillette, "University Departments Work with WLSU to Plan Year's Programs," *The Daily Reveille*, October 21, 1949.

69. Beverly Laskey, "Programs Hit Air Waves With Help of 14 Students," *The Daily Reveille*, October 6, 1950; Robert Langhart, "WLSU, University's Radio Voice, Employs Seven Students as Announcers, Engineers," *The Daily Reveille*, February 24, 1950; Sammy Gennuso, "Future Kaltenborns Learn In Radio-Speech Classes," *The Daily Reveille*, March 28, 1950.

70. Sutton, *Education for Journalism in the United States from its Beginning to 1940*, 1, 33–35; "Association and Council Activities: Interim Report on Proposed Accrediting Plan For Education for Journalism," *Journalism Quarterly*, 22 (December 1945), 387–88.

71. "Association and Council Activities: Interim Report on Proposed Accrediting Plan For Education for Journalism," 387.

72. Ibid., 387–88.

73. Ibid., 388–90.

74. "Four Study Journalism School for ACEJ," *The Daily Reveille*, February 14, 1948.

75. "First List of Accredited Schools of Journalism Issued by ACEJ," *Journalism Quarterly*, 25 (September 1948), 317.

76. "'J School' Is Now ACEJ Accredited," *The Summer Reveille*, June 11, 1948.

77. "First List of Accredited Schools of Journalism Issued by ACEJ," 317–18.

78. Osborn, "Memoranda Concerning The School of Journalism," 1937.

79. Luxon, "Trends in Curricula in A. A. S. D. J. Schools," 353–54.

80. Paul M. Hebert, letter to LSU President James Monroe Smith, February 25, 1937, F-21n (#14), Marvin G. Osborn Scrapbooks, Mss. 1730, LLMVC.

81. School of Journalism Director and Faculty, "Education for Journalism at the Louisiana State University," 1940, F-21n (#14), Marvin G. Osborn Scrapbooks, Mss. 1730, LLMVC.

82. Marvin Osborn, letter to J. Y. Fauntleroy, November 6, 1940, F-21n (#14), Marvin G. Osborn Scrapbooks, Mss. 1730, LLMVC.

83. Marvin Osborn, letter to Homer L. Brinkley, November 6, 1940, F-21n (#14), Marvin G. Osborn Scrapbooks, Mss. 1730, LLMVC.

84. Faculty, School of Journalism, and Marvin Osborn, letter to LSU President General Campbell B. Hodges, January 9, 1942, F-21r (#18), Marvin G. Osborn Scrapbooks, Mss. 1730, LLMVC.

85. Ibid.

86. Marvin Osborn, letter to Dean Leo J. Lassalle, Dean Fred C. Frey, Dean Jordan G. Lee, Dean James B. Trant, Special Committee on Granting Autonomy to the School of Journalism, LSU, January 10, 1941, F-21n (#14), Marvin G. Osborn Scrapbooks, Mss. 1730, LLMVC.

87. Faculty, School of Journalism, and Marvin Osborn, letter to LSU President General Campbell B. Hodges, January 9, 1942.

88. Ibid.

89. Faculty of LSU School of Journalism and Marvin Osborn, letter to President Campbell B. Hodges, July 9, 1941, F-21n (#14), Marvin G. Osborn Scrapbooks, Mss. 1730, LLMVC.

90. H. A. Mangham, letter to LSU President C. B. Hodges, August 7, 1941, F-21n (#14), Marvin G. Osborn Scrapbooks, Mss. 1730, LLMVC.

91. "Journalism School Autonomy Asked," *The Daily Reveille*, November 8, 1941.

92. Louisiana Press Association, Resolution, May 8, 1943, F-21n (#14), Marvin G. Osborn Scrapbooks, Mss. 1730, LLMVC.

93. M. N. Lipp, letter to LSU Board of Supervisors and LSU President C. B. Hodges, May 24, 1943, F-21n (#14), Marvin G. Osborn Scrapbooks, Mss. 1730, LLMVC.

94. Had President Hodges not departed LSU in 1944, there might have been a very good chance that the School of Journalism would have been granted autonomy at the close of World War II. Tucked away in a folder in the LSU Archives is a handwritten note bearing Hodges' initials but undated on which is written these intriguing words: "Dean Fry. Should we make journalism autonomous? Frey *Yes* probably–but after the war–CBH." Note from "CBH" [Campbell B. Hodges, presumably] to self [presumably], undated, College of Arts and Sciences–Journalism, 1942–1943, Box 2, Folder #25, Office of the President Records, RG# A0002, LSU Archives. "Dean Fry" likely refers to Fred C. Frey who at the time was LSU Dean of the University and to whom President Hodges had posed the autonomy question. That the note survived among several letters and other documents related to the Journalism School autonomy issue suggests that Hodges was saving it for future reference. There is no indication that Marvin Osborn was aware that had Campbell Hodges still been LSU's president at war's end and had he [Osborn] made another request for Journalism School autonomy at the time, Hodges might have been more receptive to the idea.

95. "A Gallery of Presidents."

96. Marvin Osborn, statement to LSU President Troy H. Middleton, October 10, 1951, F-21n (#14), Marvin G. Osborn Scrapbooks, Mss. 1730, LLMVC.

97. "Minutes of Meeting of Board of Supervisors Held on May 29, 1943," *Minutes, Board of Supervisors, Louisiana State University,* Vol. 11, 173.

98. Bette Williams, "Alumni Hall Attic 'Haunt' of Old Records, Grades," *The Reveille,* March 23, 1943; Hubert Collins, "University Records Call for Fireproofing; Alumni Hall to Switch Tenancy with Boyd," *The Summer Reveille,* June 22, 1948; "Journalism School Movement Finished," *The Daily Reveille,* September 17, 1948; "Alumni Hall Houses School of Journalism," *Pelican Press Messenger,* September 19, 1948; "Reveille Celebrates 52nd Anniversary of Continuous LSU News Publication," *The Daily Reveille,* January 14, 1949.

99. "Journalism School Leaves Thomas Boyd Hall After 10 Years; Moves to Alumni Building," *LSU Journalism News,* September 1948, F-21h (#8), Marvin G. Osborn Scrapbooks, Mss. 1730, LLMVC.

100. Marvin Osborn, letter to LSU President Harold W. Stoke, February 9, 1948, F-21d (#4), Marvin G. Osborn Scrapbooks, Mss 1730, LLMVC.

101. Ibid.

102. Lewis S. Graham, "Historical Sketch of the David F. Boyd Memorial," *The Reveille,* February 1, 1905.

103. Ibid.

104. Ibid.

105. Lewis S. Graham, "Historical Sketch of the David F. Boyd Memorial," *The L.S.U. Alumnus,* April 1905, 7–10. It should be noted that this article appeared in the first volume of *The L.S.U. Alumnus* as a "distinctive periodical." Previously, all alumni news had appeared in special sections or issues of *The Reveille.*

106. See, for instance, Graham, "Historical Sketch of the David F. Boyd Memorial"; Lewis S. Graham, "Report of the President," November 11, 1905, in *The Alumnus,* December 1905, 34–47;

Lewis S. Graham, "Boyd Memorial Hall," *The Alumnus*, February 1907, 32–33; Lewis S. Graham, "Annual Report of President of the Society of the Alumni," May 28, 1907, in *The Alumnus*, August 1907, 77–78; Lewis S. Graham, "Annual Report of the President of the Society of the Alumni," May 23, 1908, in *The Alumnus*, July 1908, 250; Arthur T. Prescott, "Completion of Alumni Hall," *The Alumnus*, October 1909, 36.

107. "Lewis Spencer Graham," *The Alumnus*, October 1908, 1–3.
108. Carol Anne Blitzer, "Alumni Hall," Baton Rouge *Advocate*, May 24, 1999.
109. Arthur T. Prescott, "Completion of Alumni Hall," 36–37.
110. "The Controlling Center of the University," Alumni Memorial Hall picture caption, *The Reveille*, September 27, 1917.
111. *LSU General Catalog, 1925–1926*, 41–42.
112. *LSU General Catalog, 1928–1929*, 46; *1929–1930*, 46.
113. Wilkerson, *Thomas Duckett Boyd*, 354, 356.
114. "Alumni Hall Construction Is Going On," *The Reveille*, January 12, 1934.
115. Ibid.
116. Wilkerson, *Thomas Duckett Boyd*, 207, n. 15; "Alumni Hall First Planned To Be Regular Library," *The Daily Reveille*, April 5, 1938.
117. "Remember When," Baton Rouge *Morning Advocate*, n.d., n.p.
118. "Alumni Hall Construction Is Going On"; "Alumni Hall First Planned To Be Regular Library"; Blitzer, "Alumni Hall."
119. "Offices Assigned In Alumni Hall," *The Reveille*, March 2, 1934.
120. "Minutes of Meeting of Board of Supervisors Held on May 29, 1943."
121. Unofficial lists of LSU Journalism School graduates, from spring and summer commencement programs, MSMC Archives; "Graduation List Announced," *The Reveille*, May 16, 1944; "Candidates for Degrees Total 361," *The Reveille*, May 25, 1945.
122. "More Than 500 Alumni in Journalistic Positions," *LSU Journalism News*, September 1948, 1–10, F-21h (#8), Marvin G. Osborn Scrapbooks, Mss 1730, LLMVC.

10. CHANGING TIMES

1. Marvin Osborn, statement to LSU President Troy H. Middleton, October 10, 1951.
2. "Stoke Resigns Effective on February 1; Middleton Appointed New President," *The Daily Reveille*, January 5, 1951.
3. Frank James Price, *Troy H. Middleton: A Biography* (Baton Rouge: LSU Press, 1974), 326.
4. Marvin Osborn, statement to LSU President Troy H. Middleton, October 10, 1951.
5. Ibid.
6. Ibid.
7. Ibid.
8. "University's Needs Are Stated By Board," *LSU Alumni News*, November-December 1953, 3.
9. *LSU General Catalog*, variously from 1950s through 1970s.
10. Ralph D. Casey, "What Lies Ahead In Education for Journalism?" *Journalism Quarterly*, 21 (March 1944), 55.
11. Ibid., 56. Updating the definition of *journalism* so that it conforms to modern media and

contemporary uses of those media has been an ongoing exercise in creativity (some would say futility). Perhaps one of the best, most utilitarian, and most comprehensive definitions came from Bryant Kearl in the 1940s. He defined *journalism* as "the conveyance of timely information, ideas, counsel, guidance, emotional attitudes and advertising to a varying audience by means of organized media and written, oral or pictorial symbols." Bryant Kearl, "Journalism—What Is It? A Redefinition," *Journalism Quarterly*, 20 (March 1943), 44.

12. *LSU General Catalog*, April 24, 1951, 272; April 24, 1953, 223; April 24, 1955, 231; April 24, 1957, 246; March 1, 1959, 266; March 1961, 209; January 1963, 261; January 1965, 281; 1967–1968, 277; 1968–1969, 287; 1969–1970, 294; 1970–1971, 305; 1971–1972, 316; 1972–1973, 323; 1973–1974, 350; 1974–1975, 339; 1975–1976, 332; 1976–1977, 335; 1977–1978, 335; 1978–1979, 340; 1979–1980, 328.

13. Ibid.

14. Ibid.

15. Elsie Hebert, personal telephone communication with the author, June 20, 2007.

16. *LSU General Catalog*, April 24, 1951, 272–73; April 24, 1953, 223–24; April 24, 1955, 231–32; April 24, 1957, 246–47; March 1, 1959, 266–68; March 1961, 209–10; January 1963, 261–62; January 1965, 281–82; 1967–1968, 277–78; 1968–1969, 287–88; 1969–1970, 294–95; 1970–1971, 305–07; 1971–1972, 316–17; 1972–1973, 323–24; 1973–1974, 350–51; 1974–1975, 339–40; 1975–1976, 332–33; 1976–1977, 335–36; 1977–1978, 335–36; 1978–1979, 340–41; 1979–1980, 328–29.

17. Ibid.

18. Ibid.

19. *LSU General Catalog*, 1972–1973, 110, 374–77.

20. "Broadcast Journalism Is Now Being Offered," *The Daily Reveille*, September 23, 1971.

21. "Journalism Program Expanded," Baton Rouge *Morning Advocate*, July 31, 1971.

22. E. Joseph Broussard, "School of Journalism Enrollment Increases," *LSU Journalist*, Fall 1974, 1.

23. "Public Relations May Be Added As School's Fourth Sequence," *The LSU Journalist*, Fall 1980, 2.

24. "Enrollment Summary," LSU Office of Budget and Planning, Undergraduate and Graduate and Professional Enrollment, Baton Rouge Campus, By School, Division, Curriculum, Year Classification and Sex, Fall 1968–1969, through Fall 1978–1979.

25. Ibid., Fall 1979–1980, through Fall 1989–1990; Bill Ross and John Schweitzer, "Most Advertising Programs Find Home in Mass Communication," *Journalism Educator*, 45 (Spring 1990), 5–6.

26. *LSU General Catalog*, April 24, 1951, 272–73; April 24, 1953, 223–24; April 24, 1955, 231–32; April 24, 1957, 246–47; March 1, 1959, 266–68; March 1961, 209–10; January 1963, 261–62; January 1965, 281–82; 1967–1968, 277–78; 1968–1969, 287–88; 1969–1970, 294–95; 1970–1971, 305–07; 1971–1972, 316–17; 1972–1973, 323–24; 1973–1974, 350–51; 1974–1975, 339–40; 1975–1976, 332–33; 1976–1977, 335–36; 1977–1978, 335–36; 1978–1979, 340–41; 1979–1980, 328–29.

27. Jim Harroun, "Middleton, LSU's 13th President, Follows Long Tradition," *The Daily Reveille*, April 27, 1954.

28. "Hunter Appointed to Succeed Middleton Feb. 1," *The Daily Reveille*, September 19, 1961.

29. *LSU Almanac, 1981*.

30. "New A and S Dean," *LSU Alumni News*, December 1978, 18.

31. "Tribute; Farewell," *The Daily Reveille*, May 20, 1955.
32. "A New Chapter in a Valuable Career," editorial, Baton Rouge *Morning Advocate*, May 26, 1955.
33. A. O. Goldsmith, "Personal Data on Adolph Oliver Goldsmith," September 19, 1969, in MSMCA; "A. O. Goldsmith Appointed Head of Journalism School," *The Daily Reveille*, September 22, 1955.
34. "Dr. Price Named New Journalism School Director," Baton Rouge *State-Times*, August 6, 1956; "Four Professors Named to Administrative Jobs," *The Daily Reveille*, September 13, 1956.
35. A. O. Goldsmith, LSU Oral History Project Alumni Interviews, August 6, 1994, MSMCA.
36. "Goldsmith Named Journalism School Director at LSU," Baton Rouge *Morning Advocate*, January 19, 1969.
37. "Hicks Named Journalism School Head," Baton Rouge *State-Times*, April 6, 1974.
38. *America's Century* (New York: Dorling Kindersley, 2000), 228, 229, 230, 237, 243.
39. "Enrollments Over the Years," *LSU Almanac 1981*; Ray Maumus, "Enrollment Totals 5,507; Drop Less Than Predicted," *The Daily Reveille*, September 20, 1951.
40. "Enrollments Over the Years"; *Veterans' Readjustment Assistance Act of 1952*, 66 Stat. 663 (July 16, 1952).
41. "Enrollments Over the Years."
42. "Enrollment Explosion: The Forecast for LSU," *LSU Alumni News*, October 1961, 3.
43. "Enrollments Over the Years."
44. "Enrollment Summary," Fall 1950–1951, through Fall 1959–1960.
45. "15,820 Students in College Now in Journalism," Baton Rouge *State-Times*, January 14, 1965; Lee Becker, "Enrollment Growth Exceeds National University Averages," *Journalism Educator*, 44 (Autumn 1989), 3, 7–10.
46. "Enrollment Summary," Fall 1960–1961, through Fall 1974–1975.
47. Broussard, "School of Journalism Enrollment Increases," 1; "Enrollment Summary," Fall 1974–1975.
48. "Enrollment Summary," Fall 1975–1976, through Fall 1980–1981.
49. Ronald G. Hicks, "Wouldja Believe Journalism?" *LSU Alumni Magazine*, February 1975, 8–9.
50. *1981 Editor and Publisher International Yearbook* (New York: Editor & Publisher Co.), I-113–18, I-322.
51. *Broadcasting/Telecasting 1951 Yearbook* (Washington, D.C.: Broadcasting Publications), 154–60.
52. *Broadcasting/Cable Yearbook 1981* (Washington, D.C.: Broadcasting Publications), B-106–107, C-98–103.
53. Hicks, "Wouldja Believe Journalism?"
54. F. James Price, "What About A Career in Communications?" *LSU Alumni News*, January-February 1957, 20.
55. "Basics Said Foundation of Journalism at LSU," Baton Rouge *State-Times*, July 31, 1972.
56. *LSU General Catalog, 1951–1952*, 130.
57. *LSU General Catalog, 1975–1976*, 126.

58. Ed Cocke, "J-School Makes Way for Progress," *The Daily Reveille*, May 19, 1960.
59. "Journalism Building Renovation Completed," *The Daily Reveille*, September 20, 1960.
60. "LSU's School of Journalism In Newly-Renovated Building," Baton Rouge *State-Times*, September 15, 1960.
61. Price, *Troy H. Middleton*, 344.
62. "Now It Is *Our* Move," *LSU Alumni News*, September/October 1958, Special Section, 2.
63. Minutes of Regular Board Meeting, April 2, 1960, May 25, '59–Oct. 1, '60 Minutes, *Board of Supervisors, Louisiana State University*, Vol. 20, 178, LLMVC.
64. *LSU General Catalog, 1961–1962*, 78.
65. *LSU General Catalog, 1975–1976*, 127–28.
66. David McClellan, "New Ideas Taught Via VDT Lab," *The LSU Journalist*, Fall 1975, 6.
67. "New VDTs Arrive on Campus; Students Pleased With System," *The LSU Journalist*, May 1978, 1.
68. Rita Kranson, "Newswriting Lab To Utilize Tapes," *The LSU Journalist*, Spring 1976, 1.
69. "New VDTs Arrive on Campus: Students Pleased With System," 1.
70. Laura Myers, "Journalism School to Move to New 'Communication Center' in 1978," *The LSU Journalist*, May 1977, 2.
71. Ibid.
72. *LSU General Catalog, 1957–1958*, 110–11; *1975–1976*, 128; Ron Hicks, letter to Jules d'Hemecourt, n.d. MSMCA.
73. "Broussard Named LSU Journalism Extension Head," Baton Rouge *State-Times*, May 27, 1974.
74. "High School Students Meet to Start Press Association," *The Daily Reveille*, December 12, 1952.
75. "J-School Has Press Meet," *The Daily Reveille*, October 23, 1957; "LSPA to Hold Conference Monday," *The Daily Reveille*, February 18, 1966.
76. Kim G. Bagala, "Sigma Delta Chi Regroups, Inducts 18 New Members," *The LSU Journalist*, March 1979, 1, 6.
77. "18 Undergrads at LSU And 1 Faculty Member Join ADS Organization," Baton Rouge *Morning Advocate*, April 9, 1972; "10 Named to ADS Honor Society," *The LSU Journalist*, April 1980, 4.
78. *LSU General Catalog, 1975–1976*, 128; "Bombeck, ERA, Murphy Featured at WICI ANM," *The LSU Journalist*, Fall 1980, 3.
79. "KTA Grants Charter to Journalism School," *The LSU Journalist*, March 1979, 3.
80. "Journalism Alumni," *LSU Alumni News*, January-February 1956, 5.
81. Glynn Wood, "Morning Newspaper Proposed by Senate," *The Daily Reveille*, December 3, 1953; "Reveille Tries Five Issues as AM Paper," *The Daily Reveille*, April 23, 1954.
82. "LSU's Reveille Launches 88th Year," *The Daily Reveille*, September 13, 1960.
83. "Progress for the Reveille," editorial, *The Daily Reveille*, October 30, 1959; Smiley Anders, "Birthday Present," *The Daily Reveille*, October 31, 1959.
84. "The Stadium—Mandate or No Mandate?" editorial, *The Daily Reveille*, February 24, 1953; Jim Harroun, "Where to Park—A Major Campus Problem," *The Daily Reveille*, October 6, 1954.
85. "Roy Wilson Withdraws From School; Board Investigation Given as Reason," *The Daily Reveille*, January 18, 1951; "Negro Enters Grad School," *The Summer Reveille*, June 14, 1951; "Registration Figures Inconclusive; Classes to Start Friday Morning," *The Daily Reveille*, September 13, 1951.

86. Charles M. Magee, "A History of the Baton Rouge Newspapers" (master's thesis, LSU, 1957), 83; *Weekly Leader*, February 23, 1952.

87. "Supreme Court Rules Segregation Illegal," *The Daily Reveille*, May 18, 1954.

88. See, for instance, Dawn Caillouet, "Six Negroes Refused Entrance," *The Daily Reveille*, September 16, 1954; Graham LeStourgeon, "Board of Supervisors Discusses Segregation," *The Daily Reveille*, December 7, 1954; "Tureaud Ban Still in Court," *The Daily Reveille*, March 15, 1955; "Tureaud Admitted By Court Order," *The Daily Reveille*, September 15, 1955.

89. "President Middleton Issues Statement on Segregation," *The Daily Reveille*, April 10, 1956; Troy Middleton, "LSU and Segregation," *LSU Alumni News*, May-June 1956, 4–5, 33.

90. "Senate OK's Interracial Activities Bill," *The Summer Reveille*, July 10, 1956.

91. "The Rich, The Happy—And the Dumb!" *The Summer Reveille*, July 19, 1956.

92. "Reveille Editorial Called 'Brainwash,'" *The Summer Reveille*, July 31, 1956.

93. Price, *Troy H. Middleton*, 366.

94. Tom Harvey, "LSU Faculty Probe Underway; President Middleton Testifies," *The Summer Reveille*, June 12, 1958.

95. "The Horror of Silence and the Missing 32," *The Summer Reveille*, June 19, 1958.

96. "Middleton Warns Against Budget Cuts," *The Summer Reveille*, June 11, 1957; "WLSU Closed 3 Years, But News Work Continues," *The Summer Reveille*, July 26, 1960; Len Udes Jr., "Recording Services Housed at WLSU," *The Daily Reveille*, March 4, 1964.

97. "Student Radio Station Serving Dorms, Union; Located at 660," *The Daily Reveille*, January 5, 1966; Nora Norris, "From 'Ham Shack' to Wireless; History of WLSU Radio Related," *The Daily Reveille*, September 18, 1968.

98. Fritz McCameron, letter to Otis Wheeler, September 16, 1975, MSMCA; Ralph Gossard, letter to Oscar G. Richard, March 4, 1976, MSMCA; Paul Murrill, letter to Ralph Gossard et al., November 8, 1979, MSMCA; "WPRG-FM on Air," *LSU Alumni News*, February 1980, 20; "WPRG to Boost Power," *LSU Alumni News*, December 1980/January 1981, 14.

99. Leen Laricci, "WPRG Is Now KLSU," *The Summer Reveille*, June 7, 1983.

100. Jules d'Hemecourt, letter to Lynn Pesson, October 8, 1984, MSMCA; Jeff Duhe, "... And Then There Was KLSU," *The Daily Reveille*, January 21, 1986.

101. "Freedom of College Press Up to Editors—Middleton," *The Daily Reveille*, December 18, 1952.

102. Price, *Troy H. Middleton*, 366.

103. Lou Gehrig Burnett, "Reveille Follows Metropolitan Paper Routine," *The Daily Reveille*, October 17, 1961.

104. LSU President W. B. Hatcher, letter to Marvin Osborn, March 9, 1945, "College of Arts and Sciences–Journalism, 1944–1945," Box 2, Folder #27, Office of the President Records, RG# A0002, LSU Archives.

105. Barry Zander, "Reveille's Future Is In Hands of Those It Often Opposes," *The Daily Reveille*, December 6, 1968; Beverly Wells, "Journalism Society Recommends Criteria for Selection of Reveille Staff Positions," *The Daily Reveille*, December 11, 1968; Ede Day, "Reveille Status, Editor Selection Discussed," *The Daily Reveille*, May 2, 1969; "Complaint to Be Filed with Press Council," *The Daily Reveille*, April 27, 1971; Jim Whittum, "Publishers' Code Being Considered," *The Summer Reveille*, July 22, 1971; LSU Student Communications Media Board, "Code of Responsibility" and "By-Laws."

106. "Freedom of College Press Up to Editors—Middleton."
107. "Scholarships Established By Newspapers," *The Daily Reveille*, May 15, 1958.
108. "Journalism School Gets Scholarship," *The Daily Reveille*, September 22, 1965.
109. "News Editor Gets Award," *The Daily Reveille*, October 26, 1966.
110. "Journalism Award Set Up in LSU Fund," *The Daily Reveille*, October 23, 1968.
111. "Scholarship Changes, Additions Expand Financial Assistance," *The LSU Journalist*, January 1978, 3.
112. "Journalism Grad Given Top Award," *The Daily Reveille*, April 15, 1966.
113. "Newsman Honored at Alumni Banquet," *The Daily Reveille*, May 1, 1969.
114. George Cotton, "AP Journalist Stresses Fairness," *The Daily Reveille*, May 1, 1969.
115. "Harry Middleton: A Different Breed of Librarian," *LSU Alumni News*, October 1971, 6–9; "LBJ Library Directed by Journalism Graduate," *The Daily Reveille*, December 2, 1971.
116. "LSU's Alumnus-of-the-Year: Walter W. Hitesman Jr.," *LSU Alumni News*, June 1974, 2.
117. Ibid., 2–3.
118. "Readers Digest Grant Goes to LSU J School," Baton Rouge *State-Times*, April 22, 1974.
119. "Hicks to Head Journalism; Copping Named for Dentistry," Baton Rouge *State-Times*, April 7, 1974.
120. Ronald Hicks, "Journalism School Needs Money," *The LSU Journalist*, Fall 1974, 1.
121. "Endowment Fund a Reality," *LSU Journalist*, Fall 1975, 1.
122. Ronald Hicks, letter to Jules d'Hemecourt.
123. "Contemporary Journalism Issues To Be Discussed at Conference," *LSU Journalist*, Fall 1975, 1, 3; "The LSU Journalism Hall of Fame," *LSU Alumni News*, October 1975, 8–9; "LSU School of Journalism Inducts 9 Into Hall of Fame," Baton Rouge *State-Times*, October 6, 1975.
124. "Margaret Dixon Third Woman Named to Board of Supervisors," *The Daily Reveille*, June 26, 1951.
125. Theodore Peterson, "The Changing Role of Journalism Schools," *Journalism Quarterly*, 37 (Autumn 1960), 580.
126. "Basics Said Foundation of Journalism at LSU."
127. Ibid.
128. Ibid.
129. Ibid.
130. "Accreditors Tour Journalism School," *The Daily Reveille*, February 22, 1957.
131. "LSU J School Is Accredited," *The Summer Reveille*, June 13, 1957.
132. Ronald Hicks, "ACEJ to Review Accreditation in '76," *LSU Journalist*, Spring 1976, 2.
133. Ronald Hicks, "A Stewardship Report," *LSU Journalist*, Fall 1974, 4; George Cotton, "LSU Journalism School Accreditation Test Comes in February," Baton Rouge *State-Times*, October 30, 1977.
134. Ronald Hicks, "'State of School' Message," *LSU Journalist*, Fall 1975, 2.
135. Cotton, "LSU Journalism School Accreditation Test Comes in February."
136. Jim Featherston, "Price Retires, Plans to Travel," *LSU Journalist*, Spring 1976, 4.
137. Jim Featherston, "Plasterer Retires to Montana," *LSU Journalist*, Spring 1976, 3.
138. "J-School Faculty Members Writing, Obtain Degrees," *The LSU Journalist*, January 1978, 2.

139. Troy H. Middleton, "Report by the President to the Alumni: The State of the University," *LSU Alumni News*, September-October 1953, 1; Troy H. Middleton, "A Report to the Alumni," *LSU Alumni News*, September-October 1954, 2; Troy H. Middleton, "The State of the University," *LSU Alumni News*, September-October 1955, 3–4; Troy H. Middleton, "The Progress of LSU: Key to Louisiana's Future," *LSU Alumni News*, May-June 1956, 3, 35; Troy H. Middleton, "Report on the State of the University," *LSU Alumni News*, September-October 1956, inside cover.

140. Price, *Troy H. Middleton*, 361.

141. Ann McCoy, "Proposed LSU Budget Cut Explained by Middleton," *The Summer Reveille*, June 15, 1961; Ann McCoy, "Withholding Cut Makes Serious Financial Bind; Worst Since 2nd War," *The Summer Reveille*, June 27, 1961; Troy H. Middleton, "Fiscal Riddle," *The LSU Outlook*, July 1961, n.p.

142. Trudy Berger, "LSU's Problem of the '70s—Money," *The Daily Reveille*, January 8, 1970.

143. Kathleen McAdams, "Results of Budget Cut Told by A and S Dean," *The Daily Reveille*, January 9, 1970.

144. Edward Pratt, "LSU's School of Journalism Facing Loss of Accreditation," Baton Rouge *State-Times*, October 14, 1977.

145. Debbie Penny, "School Curricula Revamped With Major Course Changes," *The LSU Journalist*, May 1977, 2.

146. Ronald Hicks, letter to Jules d'Hemecourt.

147. "Journalism School to Get Accreditation," Baton Rouge *State-Times*, October 17, 1977.

148. George Cotton, "LSU Journalism School Gets Full Accreditation," Baton Rouge *Morning Advocate*, May 10, 1978.

149. "Reaccreditation Brings Changes In Faculty, Curricula, Support," *The LSU Journalist*, January 1978, 1.

150. Cotton, "LSU Journalism School Gets Full Accreditation."

151. Unofficial graduation lists, MSMCA; "Mass Comm Baccalaureate Graduates on GAF," LSU Office of Budget and Planning, Table of Graduates by College, Summer 1975 through Spring 1979.

152. "Mass Comm Baccalaureate Graduates on GAF," Summer 1981 through Spring 1984.

153. Unofficial graduation lists, MSMCA.

154. Ronald Hicks, "J-School Reflections—Past and Future," *The LSU Journalist*, April 1980, 2–3.

155. Ibid.

156. Ibid.

11. UNCERTAIN TIMES

1. "J-School Searches for New Director," *The LSU Journalist*, April 1980, 1.

2. Linda Daly, "John C. Merrill Takes Over Directorship of J-School," *The Summer Reveille*, July 8, 1980; "John Merrill to Head LSU Journalism," Baton Rouge *Morning Advocate*, May 8, 1980; "Merrill Becomes New J-School Director," *The LSU Journalist*, Fall 1980, 1; "Profile of a Journalism Director," *LSU Outlook*, September 1980, n.p.

3. Daly, "John C. Merrill Takes Over Directorship of J-School."

4. John Merrill, personal e-mail communication with the author, June 12, 2007.

5. "Holgate Appointed Assistant Director," *The Summer Reveille,* July 8, 1980.
6. John C. Merrill, "Areas for J-School Improvement Outlined," *The LSU Journalist,* Fall 1980, 2.
7. Ibid.
8. Ibid.
9. "Profile of a Dean—Henry L. Snyder," *LSU Outlook,* January 1979, n.p.; Roberta Green, "Eighteenth Century Research Goes High Tech," *LSU Magazine,* November 1984, 16–17, 48; "New A and S Dean," 18.
10. John Wright, "Advisory Council Formed for School of Journalism," *The Daily Reveille,* October 17, 1980; "Council Strengthens Ties Between J-School, Media," *The LSU Journalist,* Fall 1980, 2; "Advisory Council Formed," *LSU Alumni News,* December 1980/January 1981, 17.
11. Lisa Schelp, "Dean to Reorganize J-School," *The LSU Journalist,* Spring 1981, 1.
12. Fayette Tomkins, "LSU Journalism, Speech Faculties Opposed to Proposed Merger," Baton Rouge *State-Times,* May 19, 1981.
13. Schelp, "Dean to Reorganize J-School," 1
14. John Merrill, memo to Dean Henry Snyder, March 17, 1981, MSMCA.
15. L. L. Pesson, memo to Dean Henry Snyder, February 26, 1981, MSMCA.
16. John Merrill, memo to Dean Henry Snyder, March 2, 1981; Dean Henry Snyder, memo to Lynn L. Pesson, March 11, 1981; Lynn L. Pesson, memo to Quinn Coco, March 17, 1981, MSMCA.
17. Andrew McDonald, "Moving Day," *The Daily Reveille,* October 13, 1981.
18. John C. Merrill, memo to Dean Henry Snyder, March 2, 1981.
19. Dean Henry Snyder, memo, no recipient indicated, n.d., MSMCA.
20. "Leading Today With a Plan For Tomorrow," *LSU Alumni News,* August/September 1981, 3–5.
21. Carolyn Hargrave, personal communication with the author, October 18, 2007.
22. John Semien, "LSU Officials Order Paper To Pull Ad," Baton Rouge *Morning Advocate,* September 17, 1981; "LSU Reveille Ordered to Halt Condom Ad," Baton Rouge *State-Times,* September 17, 1981; John Hart, "Merrill Terms Reveille Adequate," *The Daily Reveille,* September 18, 1981.
23. John Semien, "Journalism Schools Criticized," Baton Rouge *Morning Advocate,* October 7, 1981.
24. James Freeman, "Students Say Journalism School Hurt by 'Antique' Equipment," *The Daily Reveille,* October 16, 1981; James Freeman, "Journalism Facilities Lack, Says Wharton," *The Daily Reveille,* October 15, 1981; James O'Byrne, "Decay in Academia," editorial, *The Daily Reveille,* December 8, 1981.
25. C. L. Parker, "Arts and Sciences Dean Defends J-School Changes," *The Daily Reveille,* December 4, 1981.
26. Hargrave, personal communication with the author.
27. Fayette Tomkins, "LSU Journalism Chief Eyes School's Future," Baton Rouge *State-Times,* October 7, 1981.
28. John Merrill, "Notes from the Director," *The LSU Journalist,* Winter 1982, 2.
29. Cathy Dressler, "Curriculum in P. R. to Begin This Spring," *The Daily Reveille,* September 24, 1981.
30. "Three to Join J-School Faculty," *The LSU Journalist,* Spring 1981, 2.
31. "Regents OK LSU Projects," Baton Rouge *State-Times,* May 28, 1982.

32. Gerard Killebrew, personal telephone communication with the author, October 15, 2007.

33. Jay Grelen, "New Reveille Adviser Plans No Changes," Baton Rouge *Morning Advocate*, July 31, 1982.

34. "Three to Join J-School Faculty," 2.

35. "Enrollment Summary," Fall 1981, 1982, and 1983.

36. "Merrill to Step Into Teaching Position," *The LSU Journalist*, Winter 1982, 1.

37. Douglas Manship, letter to Steve Charlton, November 11, 1980, MSMCA.

38. John C. Merrill, memo to Dean Henry Snyder, August 21, 1981, MSMCA.

39. Merrill, "Notes from the Director," 2.

40. "LSU Panel Seeking New Director of Journalism School," Baton Rouge *State-Times*, December 17, 1982; "Panel to Seek New LSU J-School Director," Baton Rouge *Morning Advocate*, January 6, 1983.

41. "Ohio U. Professor Click Chosen to Head LSU Journalism School," Baton Rouge *State-Times*, May 11, 1983.

42. "Director Lists Innovations of LSU Journalism School," Baton Rouge *State-Times*, March 27, 1984.

43. William Click, personal telephone communication with the author, June 13, 2007.

44. "The Budget Axe Falls," *LSU Alumni News*, December 1982/January 1983, 5–7.

45. Ibid.

46. J. William Click, memo to Carolyn Hargrave and William J. Cooper Jr., February 7, 1984, MSMCA.

47. Click, personal telephone communication with the author.

48. Ibid.

49. LSU School of Journalism, "Five-Year Plan," October 1984; "Five-Year Plan Update," October 1984; "Five-Year Plan Update," October 1985, MSMCA.

50. Bill Click, memo to Journalism Faculty, November 5, 1985, MSMCA; Click, personal telephone communication with the author.

51. J. William Click, memo to Patrick B. Cooper, November 6, 1985, MSMCA.

52. "Reveille Moves to Hodges, KLSU and Gumbo to Follow," *The Daily Reveille*, July 23, 1987.

53. "A Proposal to Endow the Manship School of Journalism at Louisiana State University," February 7, 1984, 1, MSMCA.

54. Ibid., 4–12.

55. "Manship Endowment to Aid LSU Journalism Program," LSU Office of Public Relations, News Release, August 10, 1984; "A Big Step Toward Excellence," *LSU Magazine*, November 1984, 49–50; Carl Redman, "Manships Give LSU $2.6 Million," Baton Rouge *Morning Advocate*, August 11, 1984. The Manship family coupled its Manship School gift with an additional one million dollar contribution to the LSU College of Arts and Sciences. The money was intended to stimulate matching funds donations for use by the departments of English, mathematics, foreign languages, and history. "A Big Step Toward Excellence," 49.

56. "Manship Endowment to Aid LSU Journalism Program."

57. "Funds Needed to Assure Quality," *LSU Journalist*, Winter 1985, 3. The Manship School indeed did intend to put the endowment to work immediately, but not until June 1987 did the

Board of Regents finally appropriate the state's portion of the endowment via the Louisiana Education Quality Support Fund. Stephen Ruiz, "LSU Gets $5.6 Million in Settlement," *The Daily Reveille*, June 30, 19

58. J. William Click, memo to Henry L. Snyder, October 8, 1984, MSMCA; "LSU Journalism School Renamed," *LSU Magazine*, February 1985, 6.

59. Carl Redman, "LSU Progressing Toward Consent Decree Fulfillment," *Baton Rouge Morning Advocate*, December 15, 1984; "Board Names School After Manship Family," *LSU Journalist*, Spring 1986, 1.

60. "New Name Suggested for Journalism School," *Baton Rouge Morning Advocate*, December 1, 1984.

61. "Accrediting Team Visits School," *LSU Journalist*, Winter 1985, 4.

62. "Summary By Visit Team," ACEJMC Accrediting Committee, *Journalism Accreditation Report*, November 9, 1984, MSMCA.

63. Ibid.

64. Ibid.

65. Ibid.

66. Ibid.; "Enrollment Summary," Fall 1984.

67. "Authority Named to Manship Chair," *LSU Magazine*, February 1986, 4; Yolanda Mitchell, "Manship School Adds New Faculty, *The Summer Reveille*, June 25, 1985.

68. Mitchell, "Manship School Adds New Faculty."

69. "Three Sequences Accredited, M.J. Program Nearing Same," *LSU Journalist*, Spring 1986, 1.

70. ACEJMC, *Report of On-Site Evaluation*, October 21–24, 1990, MSMCA.

71. Issues of *The Daily Reveille* were full of front-page stories about budget cuts, real or threatened, throughout the 1980s. Story headlines alone give the reader a good idea of what was happening budget-wise along with the severity of the situation. Here, listed in chronological sequence, are examples of some of the headlines: Angie Francalancia, "Wharton Gives LSU a Grim Look at Budget," *The Daily Reveille*, November 12, 1982; Joey Senat, "LSU Budget Cuts Coming, Sources Say," *The Daily Reveille*, October 15, 1983; "State Cuts May Top $200 Million," *The Daily Reveille*, March 30, 1984; "State Budget Cut by $51 Million," *The Daily Reveille*, February 13, 1985; Brett Blackledge, "Cuts Turn Dreams to Nightmare," *The Daily Reveille*, October 15, 1985; Clay Ward, "LSU to Cut Budget, Raise Tuition," *The Summer Reveille*, July 15, 1986; Leslie Zganjar, "Officials Plan Hiring Freeze," *The Daily Reveille*, October 29, 1986; H. Clay Ward, "EWE Bombards LSU Budget," *The Daily Reveille*, July 14, 1987; Bonna M. DeLaCruz, "Budget Cuts Loom," *The Daily Reveille*, May 2, 1989.

72. Bradley Keith, "University Prepares for Cuts," *The Daily Reveille*, March 18, 1986; Holly Snyder "Wharton Preparing for Cuts," *The Daily Reveille*, March 18, 1986; Leslie Zganjar, "Oil Industry: A Bleak Future," *The Daily Reveille*, March 18, 1986; Jennifer C. Kent, "Formula Funding Percentage Drops," *The Daily Reveille*, March 18, 1986; George Edmonston Jr., "The Wharton Interview," *LSU Magazine*, February 1986, 21–24, 40, 56.

73. Leslie Zganjar, "Welcome to LSU 86–87," *The Daily Reveille*, August 20, 1986.

74. Hargrave, personal communication with the author.

75. Click, personal telephone communication with the author.

76. Clay Ward, "Arts and Sciences Dean to Head West," *The Daily Reveille*, January 15, 1986.
77. T. Bradley Keith, "Search Committee to Find New Dean," *The Daily Reveille*, January 21, 1986.
78. Mary Beth Lewy, "Three Accept College Dean Posts," *The Summer Reveille*, June 10, 1986.
79. Mary Beth Lewy, "New A and S Dean Looks to Future," *The Daily Reveille*, October 7, 1986.
80. "'Can-Do' Spirit Motivates Director," *The Journalist*, Winter 1990, 1–4.
81. H. Clay Ward, "Journalism School's Director Steps Down," *The Daily Reveille*, June 11, 1987.
82. "The Louisiana Board of Regents Program Review and ACEJMC Accreditation"; Mary Cummings, "School of Journalism May Be Phased Out," *The Daily Reveille*, September 25, 1990.
83. Robert Pierre, "Committee Studies Wharton's Decision," *The Daily Reveille*, October 27, 1988; Robert Pierre, "Wharton Encouraged to Avoid Lawsuit," *The Daily Reveille*, December 8, 1988; Jim Crain, "Wharton Resigns as LSU's Chancellor," *LSU Magazine*, Winter 1989, 3.
84. "Grady Bogue Named Interim Chancellor, *LSU Magazine*, Spring 1989, 4; Bonna DeLaCruz, "Interim Chancellor Faces LSU's Future," *The Daily Reveille*, January 11, 1989.
85. Terry English, "Chancellor William E. Davis," *LSU Magazine*, Fall 1989, 30–31, 38; Deborah Day, "Search Ends: Davis Is Chancellor," *The Daily Reveille*, August 23, 1989.
86. "ACEJMC Team to Evaluate Program," *The Student Journalist*, Fall 1990, 1–2.
87. "New IBM Lab Opened for Students," *The Student Journalist*, Fall 1990, 4.
88. "LSU Gets Agriculture and Journalism Grants," *LSU Magazine*, February 1985, 54; "LSU Journalism Program Gets Boost," *LSU Magazine*, April 1986, 19.
89. "Diversifying Newsrooms," *LSU Magazine*, April/May/June 1987, 10.
90. "Greer Family Initiates $1 Million Chair," *The Journalist*, Summer 1990, 1; "Greer Family Donates $125,000 to Establish Fred Greer Chair," *LSU Magazine*, Spring 1990, 39.
91. "J-School Senior Is Back In Class After More Than 50-Year Hiatus," *Monday Memo*, 29 January 1990, 1; Johnelle LaMarque, "73-Year-Old Student Stresses Optimistic Viewpoint on Life," *The Daily Reveille*, February 22, 1990.
92. *LSU General Catalog, 1981–1982*, 44–45.
93. *LSU General Catalog, 1985–1986*, 45–46.
94. "LSU Wins National William Randolph Hearst Journalism Competition," *LSU Magazine*, June 1985, 7.
95. "LSU Wins Hearst Competition for Second Consecutive Year," *LSU Magazine*, June 1986, 4.
96. Manship School of Journalism Director's Report, 1988–1989, 2, MSMCA.
97. "New Journalism Association of Graduate Students Is Formed," *Monday Memo*, November 13, 1989, 1.
98. "Editors Participate in Residence Program," *The LSU Journalist*, Winter 1982, 2.
99. "Friedman Gives Hitesman Lectures," *The LSU Journalist*, Winter 1982, 2; "Freedom House Director Will Speak at LSU," Baton Rouge *State-Times*, April 20, 1982.
100. Delos Knight and Ansel Smith, "Television for LSU? Chances Slim Right Now," *The Daily Reveille*, April 24, 1952; "Middleton Appoints Group to Study TV Set-Up Here," *The Daily Reveille*, January 15, 1953; "TV and Education at LSU," *LSU Alumni News*, January-February 1955, 10–11; J. R. Carter, "New TV Equipment Now in Testing Stage," *The Summer Reveille*, August 2,

1955; Karl Feldner, "T. V. Workshop Is Now a Reality," *The Daily Reveille*, April 26, 1956; "Workshop to Give Actual Experience in TV Production," *The Summer Reveille*, June 14, 1956; Bill Biery, "University Radio Station Now Includes TV Center," *The Daily Reveille*, September 20, 1956.

101. R. A. Harold, "Practical Radio-TV Training Offered By Speech Classes," *The Daily Reveille*, May 18, 1962.

102. Michelle Perron, "LSU TV Channel May Be Expanded," *The Summer Reveille*, June 14, 1984; Dawn Laguens, "Campus Cable Buy Widens Possibilities," *The Daily Reveille*, February 5, 1986; Holly Ourso, "LSU Cable Airs Student-Anchored News Broadcast," *The Daily Reveille*, May 8, 1987; John W. Grubb, "Broadcast News," *LSU Magazine*, Summer 1988, 34.

103. Scott Kiker, "LSU-TV Plans for Upcoming Season," *The Daily Reveille*, August 31, 1989.

104. "Faculty Hold AEJMC Offices," *The Journalist*, Spring 1984, 1.

105. "New Faculty Bring Diversity to Program," *The Journalist*, Spring 1984, n.p.; "Faculty Updates," *The Journalist*, Winter 1990, 6.

106. "Faculty Updates," 5.

107. "Who's Doing What," *LSU Magazine*, June 1986, 11.

108. *LSU General Catalog, 1986–1987*, 144–45; *LSU General Catalog, 1987–1988*, 148–50.

109. Manship School of Journalism, *1991–1992 Annual Report*, 1. Counting majors only, fall undergraduate enrollment between 1987 and 1991 dropped, in successive years, from 745, to 590, to 415, to 349, to 337. "Enrollment Summary," Fall 1987, through Fall 1991.

110. "Enrollment Summary," Fall 1987, through Fall 1991.

111. "Mass Comm Baccalaureate Graduates on GAF," 1988–1989.

112. Ibid., 1991–1992, 1992–1993.

113. Susanne Shaw, letter to William E. Giles, September 15, 1989, MSMCA.

114. Susanne Shaw, letter to William Giles, September 3, 1990, MSMCA.

115. ACEJMC, *Report of On-Site Evaluation*, October 24, 1990, 7.

116. Ibid., 8–31.

117. Bill Giles, note to Journalism Faculty, October 24, 1990, MSMCA.

118. William E. Davis, letter to William Giles, October 30, 1990, MSMCA.

119. Joyce Tippy, "Journalism School Seeks Independence," *The Daily Reveille*, March 21, 1991.

120. Joyce Tippy, "Manship Director Resigns Position," *The Daily Reveille*, March 12, 1991.

121. Tippy, "Journalism School Seeks Independence."

122. Hargrave, personal communication with the author.

123. "Giles Announces Plans to Resign as Director," *Monday Memo*, March 18, 1991.

124. Daynel Hooker, "Arts and Sciences Dean Resigns to Teach," *The Daily Reveille*, April 4, 1991.

125. Hargrave, personal communication with the author.

126. ACEJMC Council Meeting Minutes, Chicago, May 10–11, 1991, 18–19, MSMCA.

127. Daynel Hooker and Lisa Roland, "J-School Search Committee Focus of Faculty Meeting," *The Daily Reveille*, May 3, 1991.

128. Louis Day, personal communication with the author, October 10, 2007.

129. John M. Lavine, letter to William E. Davis, May 14, 1991, MSMCA.

130. Ibid.

131. Hargrave, personal communication with the author.

132. Chancellor's Fact-finding Committee, memo to Chancellor Davis, June 26, 1991, MSMCA.

133. Robert Wolf, "Chancellor Names Acting Head for Manship Journalism School," *The Daily Reveille*, June 4, 1991.

134. Louis Day, personal communication with the author, June 21, 2007. LSU later recognized Day's teaching talents by naming him an alumni professor. In 2006, the Scripps Howard Foundation named Lou Day as its Journalism Professor of the Year.

135. Chancellor's Fact-finding Committee, memo to Chancellor Davis, June 26, 1991, MSMCA.

136. Ibid.

137. Ibid.

138. Day, personal communication with the author, June 21, 2007.

139. Ibid.

140. Louis A. Day, letter to Kim Rotzoll, December 6, 1991, MSMCA; Molly Thibodeaux, "Haden Steps into Provost Position," *The Daily Reveille*, June 13, 1991.

141. Kim Rotzoll, letter to Susanne Shaw, February 7, 1992, MSMCA.

142. Ibid.

143. Don Schultz, letter to Louis A. Day, April 13, 1992, MSMCA.

144. John M. Lavine, letter to William E. Davis, May 18, 1992, MSMCA.

145. Kim Rotzoll, letter to Susanne Shaw, February 7, 1992, MSMCA.

146. Don Schultz, letter to Louis A. Day, April 13, 1992, MSMCA.

147. Day, personal communication with the author, June 21, 2007.

12. RETURN TO PROMINENCE

1. Louis A. Day, memo to Journalism Faculty and Staff, November 20, 1991, MSMCA.

2. Sally Kuzenski, "Journalist and World Bank Executive Named New LSU Journalism Head," News Service Press Release, LSU Office of Public Relations, December 17, 1991; Brenda Murray, "International Executive Writer to Head J-School," *The Daily Reveille*, January 24; John Maxwell Hamilton, personal communication with the author, September 26, 2007.

3. John Maxwell Hamilton, personal communication with the author, June 14, 2007; Thad Slaton, "J-School Receives Full Accreditation," *The Daily Reveille*, May 6, 1992.

4. "Arts and Sciences Dean Named," Baton Rouge *Morning Advocate*, December 18, 1991.

5. Hamilton, personal communication with the author, June 14, 2007.

6. Bill Ross, personal e-mail communication with the author, June 12, 2007; Hamilton, personal communication with the author, June 14, 2007.

7. "Ross Named Interim Director of LSU PR," *LSU Magazine*, Winter 1997, 33.

8. Ibid.

9. "Of Note," *LSU Magazine*, November 1991, 7.

10. Ronald Garay, "Sig Mickelson," in *Encyclopedia of Television News* (Phoenix, AZ: Oryx Press, 1999), ed. Michael Murray, 148–49; Robert Wolf, "Journalism School Appoints Chair," *The Daily Reveille*, July 25, 1991.

11. Hamilton, personal communication with the author, June 14, 2007.

12. Jackie Bartkiewicz, "Under the Ax Again," *LSU Magazine*, Fall 1992, 28.

13. Chancellor William E. Davis, "We Need Your Help," *LSU Magazine*, Fall 1992, 30.

14. "Background Summary of Events," n.d., MSMCA.
15. John Maxwell Hamilton, memo to Chancellor William E. Davis, June 10, 1992, MSMCA.
16. Sammie W. Cosper, letter to Dr. H. Douglas Braymer, July 29, 1992, MSMCA.
17. John Maxwell Hamilton, memo to Chairman, Louisiana Board of Regents, August 14, 1992, MSMCA.
18. Sammie W. Cosper, letter to Dr. H. Douglas Braymer, September 14, 1992, MSMCA.
19. Manship School of Mass Communication Plan for Excellence, June 1993, 6–7, MSMCA.
20. Ibid., 7–8.
21. Ibid., 9.
22. Ibid., 10–11.
23. Ibid., 11–13.
24. Bill Ross, memo to Jack Hamilton, January 29, 1992, MSMCA; John Maxwell Hamilton, memo to Linda Rewerts, Bill Ross, Lou Day, March 4, 1992, MSMCA; Manship School of Journalism, *Annual Report 1991–1992*, 2; Ross, personal e-mail communication with the author; Hamilton, personal communication with author, June 14, 2007.
25. Hamilton, personal communication with the author, June 14, 2007; September 26, 2007.
26. Ibid.
27. Ibid.
28. "Independent Status Given to Mass Comm," *LSU Today*, November 5, 1993, 1, 3.
29. "Manships Launch New Plan with $100,000 Gift," *LSU Today*, October 1993, 1.
30. Manship School of Mass Communication, *Annual Report, 1992–1993*, 7.
31. Hamilton, personal communication with the author, June 14, 2007.
32. Ibid.
33. Manship School of Mass Communication, *Annual Report 1993–1994*, 7.
34. Ronald Hicks, "State of School Message."
35. Manship School of Mass Communication, *Annual Report, 1992–1993*, 12.
36. Manship School of Mass Communication, *Annual Report, 1992–1993*, 5; *1993–1994*, 5–6; *1994–1995*, 10; *1995–1996*, 28; *1996–1997*, frontispiece, 27; *1997–1998*, frontispiece, 17–18.
37. Hamilton, personal communication with the author, September 26, 2007.
38. Louis Day, personal communication with the author, October 10, 2007.
39. Jack Hamilton, personal communication with the author, September 26, 2007.
40. "Enrollment Summary," Fall 1989, through Fall 1998.
41. "Mass Comm Baccalaureate Graduates on GAF," Summer 1992, through Spring 2002.
42. Manship School of Mass Communication, *Annual Report, 1991–1992*, 1; *1992–1993*, 3; *1993–1994*, 2; *1994–1995*, 2; *1995–1996*, 3; *1996–1997*, 5, 6; *1997–1998*, 3.
43. "Journalism Building Rededicated," *LSU Magazine*, Fall 1993, 6.
44. Manship School of Mass Communication, *Annual Report, 1993–1994*, 6.
45. Amy Tidovsky-Wolfe, "The Manship School of Mass Communication Leads the Way into the Information Age," *LSU Magazine*, Winter 1995, 31.
46. John M. Hamilton, "From the Dean," Manship School of Mass Communication, *Annual Report, 1993–1994*, frontispiece.
47. Hamilton, personal communication with the author, June 14, 2007.
48. "Manship School Also Benefits from Gift," *LSU Magazine*, Spring 1994, 21.

49. William E. Davis, "LSU: A Flagship Or A Sinking Ship?" *LSU Magazine*, Summer 1994, 7.
50. Manship School of Mass Communication, *Annual Report, 1994–1995*, 3.
51. Hamilton, personal communication with the author, June 14, 2007.
52. Ibid.
53. Manship School of Mass Communication, *Annual Report, 1993–1994*, 3; *1994–1995*, 4; *1997–1998*, 4.
54. Hamilton, personal communication with the author, September 26, 2007.
55. "1913 Society Banquet Honors Benefactors, Celebrates School's College-Level Status," *Galley West*, Fall 1994, 1; "Fred Greer Chair Endowed," *LSU Magazine*, Winter 1995, 40; "Premier Bank Endows Professorships in Mass Communication," *LSU Magazine*, Winter 1995, 40.
56. Hamilton, personal communication with the author, September 26, 2007.
57. Manship School of Mass Communication, *Annual Report, 1997–1998*, 5.
58. Ibid.
59. "Reilly Chair Created in Political Communication," *LSU Magazine*, Spring 1998, 40.
60. Manship School of Mass Communication, *Annual Report, 1997–1998*, 8.
61. Manship School of Mass Communication, *Annual Report, 1991–1992*, 5; *1992–1993*, 10; *1993–1994*, 4–5; *1994–1995*, 5; *1995–1996*, 12–14.
62. "Paula Garvey Manship Continues Legacy of Support," *LSU Magazine*, Winter 1996, 44.
63. Manship School of Mass Communication, *Annual Report, 1995–1996*, 14; *1996–1997*, 8–9.
64. Manship School of Mass Communication, *Annual Report 1991–1992*, 6; *1992–1993*, 5–6; *1993–1994*, 7–8; *1994–1995*, 6–7; *1995–1996*, 17–21; *1996–1997*, 19–20; *1997–1998*, 11–12.
65. Manship School of Mass Communication, *Annual Report, 1997–1998*, 2, 15.
66. Manship School of Mass Communication, *Annual Report, 1992–1993*, 6–7; *1993–1994*, 8; *1995–1996*, 21–22; *1996–1997*, 22.
67. Manship School of Mass Communication, *Annual Report, 1991–1992*, 7; *1992–1993*, 11–12; *1995–1996*, 26–28; *1996–1997*, 21, 32–33; *1997–1998*, 22–23.
68. Linus Lee, "Newspaper Simplifies Name, Gets Facelift," *The Reveille*, January 20, 1998.
69. Kristen Meyer, "Reveille Invades Monday," *The Reveille*, July 22, 2002; Kristen Meyer, "New Outlook for New Semester," *The Reveille*, August 26, 2002.
70. "Reveille Suspends Monday Publications," *The Daily Reveille*, February 9, 1951.
71. Accrediting Council on Education in Journalism and Mass Communication, *Report of On-Site Evaluation, 1997–98*, 2, MSMCA.
72. Andy Crawford, "Preparing LSU for the 21st Century," *LSU Magazine*, Spring 1997, 31.
73. *LSU General Catalog, 1994–1995*, 265; *1997–1998*, 299; *1998–1999*, 305.
74. Andy Crawford, "Preparing LSU for the 21st Century," 32–33.
75. Andy Crawford, "Jenkins First Year In Review," *LSU Magazine*, Winter 1997, 29–30.
76. Accrediting Council on Education in Journalism and Mass Communication, *Report of On-Site Evaluation, 1997–98*, 2, MSMCA.
77. Jack Hamilton, personal communication with the author, September 26, 2007.
78. The Manship School of Mass Communication, "First Five-Year Plan in Review," attachment to *Excellence in the Age of Information, A Strategic Plan: 1998–2003*, 17–19, MSMCA.
79. Manship School of Mass Communication, *Annual Report, 1997–1998*, 4.
80. Hamilton, personal communication with the author, June 14, 2007.

81. The Manship School of Mass Communication, *Excellence in the Age of Information, A Strategic Plan: 1998–2003*, 3–7, 9, MSMCA.

82. Manship School of Mass Communication, *Annual Report, 1998–1999*, 23–24; *1999–2000*, 21; *2000–2001*, 34–35; *2001–2002*, 43; *2002–2003*, 44–45; *2003–2004*, 41.

83. Ibid., *1998–1999*, 3; *1999–2000*, 4; *2000–2001*, 4–5; *2001–2002*, 4–5; *2002–2003*, 5; *2003–2004*, 5.

84. Ibid., *2003–2004*, 5.

85. Hamilton, personal communication with the author, September 26, 2007.

86. Manship School of Mass Communication, *Annual Report, 1998–1999*, 3, 5; *1999–2000*, 4, 5; *2001–2002*, 6; *2002–2003*, 7; "Mass Comm. Offers Ph.D.," *LSU Magazine*, Spring 1999, 44; "750 Students Graduate at Summer Commencement," *LSU Magazine*, Winter 2003, 32.

87. Manship School of Mass Communication, *Annual Report, 2000–2001*, 5; *2001–2002*, 5–6; *2002–2003*, 6; *2003–2004*, 6.

88. Manship School of Mass Communication, *Annual Report, 1998–1999*, 6, 8; *1999–2000*, 6, 8; *2000–2001*, 6; *2001–2002*, 7–9; *2002–2003*, 8; *2003–2004*, 9.

89. Manship School of Mass Communication, *Annual Report, 1999–2000*, 3; *2000–2001*, 6.

90. Stacy Humphries, "Unfinished Business," *LSU Magazine*, Summer 2002, 27.

91. Sarah Sue Goldsmith, "Mark Emmert Named Chancellor," *LSU Magazine*, Summer 1999, 40.

92. David Funes, "A New Chancellor," *LSU Magazine*, Winter 1999, 19–20.

93. Humphries, "Unfinished Business," 27.

94. Mark A. Emmert, "Farewell and Best Wishes," *LSU Magazine*, Spring 2004, 1; Amanda McElfresh, "End of an Era," *The Reveille*, May 7, 2004, 1, 17.

95. William L. Jenkins, "A Message from the President and Interim Chancellor," *LSU Alumni Magazine*, Spring 2005, 1.

96. Sig Mickelson, letter to Jack Hamilton, March 31, 1992, MSMCA.

97. Manship School of Mass Communication, *Annual Report, 1997–1998*, 6; *1998–1999*, 3, 6.

98. Hamilton, personal communication with the author, June 14, 2007.

99. John Maxwell Hamilton, letter to Dr. William Jenkins, November 8, 1999, MSMCA.

100. Manship School of Mass Communication, *Annual Report, 1999–2000*, 6; *2000–2001*, 15–35.

101. Manship School of Mass Communication, *Annual Report, 1999–2000*, 12–13; *2000–2001*, 15–16; *2001–2002*, 21–28; *2002–2003*, Reilly Center insert; *2003–2004*, 8, 23–29.

102. Manship School of Mass Communication, *Annual Report, 1998–1999*, 12.

103. Blitzer, "Alumni Hall."

104. Linda Rewerts, "Creating the Future in the Oldest Building on Campus," *LSU Magazine*, Spring 2004, 38.

105. Manship School of Mass Communication, *Annual Report, 1998–1999*, 12; Hamilton, personal communication with the author, June 14, 2007.

106. Hamilton, personal communication with the author, June 14, 2007.

107. Hamilton, personal communication with the author, September 26, 2007.

108. Manship School of Mass Communication, *Annual Report, 1998–1999*, 12.

109. Manship School of Mass Communication, *Annual Report, 1999–2000*, 11; *2000–2001*, 8, 13; *2001–2002*, 7, 15; *2002–2003*, 14.

110. Renee Pierce, personal e-mail communication with the author, October 12, 2007.

111. Manship School of Mass Communication, *Annual Report, 1999–2000*, 6; *2000–2001*, 13; *2002–2003*, 14.
112. Manship School of Mass Communication, *Annual Report*, 2003–2004, 40, 43.
113. ACEJMC, *Report of On-Site Evaluation, 2003–2004*, 2, MSMCA.
114. Ibid., 5, 8, 15.
115. Ibid., 31–33.
116. Ibid., 2.
117. Manship School of Mass Communication, *Annual Report*, 2003–2004, 4.
118. Ronald Garay, letter to Risa Palm, May 4, 2004, MSMCA.
119. Hal Cohen, "What's Old Is New," *Baton Rouge Business Report*, November 23, 2004, 17; Erin Fink, "Journalism Building Evolves," *Galley West*, Spring 2003, 2.
120. Rewerts, "Creating the Future in the Oldest Building on Campus," 39.
121. Ibid., 39–40; Fink, "Journalism Building Evolves," 2; Manship School of Mass Communication, *Annual Report, 2001–2002*, 48.
122. Rewerts, "Creating the Future in the Oldest Building on Campus," 40; Manship School of Mass Communication, *Annual Report, 2003–2004*, 45.
123. Manship School of Mass Communication, *Annual Report, 2003–2004*, 45.
124. Cohen, "What's Old Is New," 17.

POSTSCRIPT: A STORM LIKE NONE OTHER

1. Ned Randolph, "Culture: Major La. Industry"; "Katrina Moves Ashore," *The Advocate*, August 26, 2005.
2. Mike Dunne and Mark F. Bonner, "Katrina Closer and Closer"; "Hurricane Katrina"; Scott Rabalais, "Tiger Stadium Project Close—But Not Quite," *The Advocate*, August 28, 2005.
3. Penny Brown Roberts, Michelle Millhollon, and Joe Gyan Jr., "Big Blow," *The Advocate*, August 30, 2005.
4. Office of the Chancellor, e-mail communication to LSU Community, August 27, 2005; Office of the Chancellor, e-mail communication to All Students, Faculty, and Staff, August 28, 2005.
5. President William Jenkins and Chancellor Sean O'Keefe, e-mail communication to LSU Faculty and Staff, September 1, 2005.
6. Provost Risa Palm, e-mail communication to LSU Faculty and Staff, September 2, 2005.
7. Chancellor Sean O'Keefe, e-mail communication to LSU Community, September 14, 2005.
8. "Katrina," Manship School of Mass Communication, *Annual Report 2005–2006*, 13.
9. Chancellor Sean O'Keefe, e-mail communication to LSU Community, September 14, 2005.
10. Rebecca Acosta, "Journalism Students Gain Invaluable Real-world Experience," *LSU Alumni Magazine*, Spring 2006, 14–15.
11. Allison Romano, "One Station Stayed On the Air," *Broadcasting and Cable*, September 19, 2005, 8–10.
12. Ibid.
13. Acosta, "Journalism Students Gain Invaluable Real-world Experience," 14; Deepti Hajela, "N. O. Paper's Katrina Work Wins Pulitzers," *The Advocate*, April 18, 2006.

14. Peter Johnson, "Public Service Pulitzers Honor Katrina Coverage," *USA Today*, April 18, 2006.
15. Hajela, "N. O. Paper's Katrina Work Wins Pulitzers."
16. "65th Annual Peabody Winners," www.peabody.uga.edu, April 5, 2006.
17. "'Times-Picayune' Editor, Publisher Respond to Pulitzer Wins," www.editorandpublisher.com, April 17, 2006.
18. Johnson, "Public Service Pulitzers Honor Katrina Coverage."
19. "Katrina," 14.

INDEX

Abraham, Cal, 94, 95, 96, 97, 98, 107
accreditation, 71–74, 105, 155–59, 160–61, 172–73, 175–77, 178, 179, 180, 184–90, 192, 205–6, 216–17; standards, 118–19
admission standards, 183, 199, 200, 209
Allen, Cleo, 209
Alumni Hall, 25, 33, 39, 74, 79, 105, 124–28, 131, 141, 142, 213, 218
American Association of Agricultural College Editors, 60–61, 71, 82
American Council on Education for Journalism (ACEJ), 118, 119, 120, 155–59, 172
American Association of Schools and Departments of Journalism (AASDJ), 40, 71, 72, 73, 74, 84–85, 105, 118, 119; Committee on Accreditation, 119
American Association of Teachers of Journalism (AATJ), 17, 33–35, 40, 71, 72, 74, 109, 116; *Monthly News-Letter*, 34–35, 49
American Society of Newspaper Editors, 118; Code of Responsibility, 149
Amoss, Jim, 225
Anders, Smiley, 145
Arbour, Marjorie, 63, 64, 82, 101, 116
Atkinson, Thomas, 39, 79, 81, 93
autonomy, 101–2, 105, 120–24, 185–86, 192–97, 201

Bailey, William, 151
Barnum, Leslie, 146

Bartkiewicz, Jackie, 193
Baton Rouge *Advocate*, 56, 221; *Daily Advocate*, 21; *Morning Advocate*, 32, 66, 67, 82, 85, 97, 107, 115, 137, 138, 151, 153
Baton Rouge *State-Times*, 32, 40, 47, 53, 64, 66, 67, 82, 85, 105, 115, 138
Baulch, Jerry T., 112, 113
Beardsley, Mike, 208
Benjamin, Herbert, 40, 66
Bennett, Carolyn, 115
Berg, Irwin A., 137, 138, 157, 158, 159
Birkhead, Douglas, 168
Black, William ("Bill"), 168, 169
Blain, Hugh Mercer, 19, 26, 27–44, 45, 46, 47, 48, 49–50, 58, 59, 60, 61, 63, 66, 71, 74, 75, 83, 137, 148, 194
Bleyer, Willard G., 17, 33, 72, 74
Bloomberg, Michael, 204
Board of Visitors, 197, 210
Boatner, Yandell, 29, 32, 47
Bogue, Grady, 179–80
Borne, Dan, 197
Boyd, David French, 7, 8–9, 11–12, 19–20, 21, 22, 23–24, 125
Boyd, Thomas Duckett, 9, 19–20, 21, 22, 25–26, 27, 37, 59, 60, 61, 78–79
Breaux, John, 212; Breaux Symposium, 212
Broussard, Alton, 127
Broussard, E. Joseph ("Joe"), 134, 144

267

Broussard, James F., 47, 96, 106
Broussard, Jinx, 207
Brown, Heidel, 202
budget, funding, 63, 131, 138, 147, 156–57, 167, 172, 177–78, 193–94, 201, 202, 205–6, 210–11, 213–14
Bugadze, Gia, 218–19
Butler, John, 168

campus radio, 77–78, 90–92, 117–18, 147–48; KFGC, 77–78, 90; KLSU, 147–48, 174, 204; WLSU, 117–18, 147; WPRG, 147
Carter, Hodding, 55, 88
Carter, Shirley, 176
Casey, Ralph, 74, 133
Charton, Steve, 170
Chenevert, Songy, Rodi, and Soderberg, 213
Chubbuck, Jim, 147
Civil Works Administration, 127
Claitor, Otto, 33, 37, 47
Click, John William ("Bill"), 171–72, 173
Coates Hall, 143–44, 161, 163, 165–66
Cohn, Yola L., 101
Coleman, Renita, 207
Committee on Student Publications, 148–49
community (country) newspapers, 50–51, 54, 76, 85, 115
"convergence," 199
Cook, Timothy ("Tim"), 208
Corbin, Carl, 94, 96, 97, 98, 104, 106, 107
Council on Education in Journalism (CEJ), 72–73
courses, 28, 30–31, 40, 47–48, 63–65, 76, 83–84, 108, 132, 135, 165, 198–99; cross-discipline (interdisciplinary), 135, 165
Curet, Jean, 214, 216
curriculum, 29–31, 40, 48, 63–65, 83–84, 108–9, 132, 133, 135, 141, 143, 153–54, 164, 184–85; concentration areas, 119–20, 198–99, 205, 210; graduate, 136; philosophies, 153–55, 170–71; sequences, 135–36, 195
Cutrer, Jesse, Jr., 94, 95, 96, 97, 98, 99, 107

Davies, John, 202
Davis, William E. ("Bud"), 180, 185, 186, 187, 188, 189, 193–94, 196, 205

Day, Louis ("Lou"), 168, 188, 189, 190
DeBonis, Nick, 176
DeFleur, Margaret ("Peggy"), 208–9, 223
degrees, 46, 70, 99, 128–29, 159–60, 184, 199; doctoral degree, 206–7, 209; graduate (master's), 99–101; renamed, 194; undergraduate (bachelor's), first recipient, 70
Delahaye, Alfred N., 145
Delta, 115
The Demeter, 30
Dennis, Everette, 197
d'Hemecourt, Jules, 134, 168
Dickinson, William ("Bill"), 208
diversity, 156, 185, 206, 215
Dixon, Margaret ("Maggie"), 67, 82, 107, 152–53
Ducote, Jackie, 214
Dugas, Benjamin, 63, 70

Editor-in-Residence program, 182
Editors' Short Course, 39, 87–88, 116
Eiland, Darrell, 146, 148
El-Bendary, Mohamed, 209
Emmert, Mark, 211, 214
endowments, 151–53, 169, 170, 174, 181, 201–3; endowed chairs, 174, 175, 179, 181, 198, 202, 203, 208; endowed professorships, 210
enrollment, 67, 68, 69–70, 88, 109–11, 139–40, 141, 155–56, 169, 200, 209; female, 109, 139; graduate, 183–84
Erickson, Emily, 207
Ewing, D. J., 24, 25, 28, 41, 46
Ewing, Robert, 116
Excellence in the Age of Information, A Strategic Plan: 1998–2003, 207, 209, 212, 215–16; Five-Year Plan, 173; Five-Year Plan for Excellence, 194–97, 206

facilities, 36, 88–90, 124–25, 131, 138, 141, 143, 165–66, 167–68, 173–74, 180, 185
faculty, 43, 63, 82–83, 132, 133–35, 138, 156, 158–59, 164, 168–69, 176, 180, 183, 187, 188, 189, 190, 192–93, 198, 204, 207–9
Fauntleroy, John Y., 46, 106, 121
Favrot, Charles A., 125, 126, 127
Featherston, James ("Jim"), 134, 168

Fisher, Jon E., 134, 168
Fleming, Walter, 7, 12
Fletcher, Alan, 176
Flournoy, Craig, 209
Fogel, Daniel M. ("Dan"), 205, 210, 214
Foster, Mike, 205, 213, 214
Foundations of Excellence, 210, 211
Frazee, John, 197
Freeman, Craig, 207
Frey, Fred C., 96, 106, 121, 122, 123

Gallagher, Wes, 114, 150, 152
Galley West, 114
Garay, Ronald, 168, 198
The Giggler, 43
Giles, William ("Bill"), 179, 180, 184, 185, 186, 187, 188, 189, 193
Gilkison, Helen, 67, 70, 75, 94–95, 96
Godbold, Rea, 94, 98, 107
Goidel, Kirby, 207
Goldsmith, Adolph ("A. O."), 133, 134, 137, 138, 141, 148, 151, 152, 154, 158
Graham, Lewis S., 126
Greer, Fred, Jr., 180–81
Griffen, G. Lee, 197
Gueymard, Ernest, 70, 82–83, 107
Gumbo, 21, 24, 60, 166, 174
Guthrie, D. V., 39, 77, 78

Haden, Roland, 186, 192, 197, 205
Hair, William Ivy, 103
Hall of Fame, 107, 152–53
Hamilton, John Maxwell ("Jack"), xvii, 189, 190, 192, 194, 196, 198, 199, 201, 202, 206, 207, 209, 210, 212, 213, 214, 215, 216, 225
Hanna, Sam, 201
Hargrave, Carolyn, 166, 186, 188, 214
Hargrave, Lee, 218
Harned, David, 178, 179, 186
Harris, Jim, 214
Hebert, Elsie, 134–35, 156, 168, 183
Hebert, Paul M., 103, 104, 106, 107, 120, 121, 122
Hicks, Ronald ("Ron"), 134, 138, 139, 140, 141, 144, 151, 152, 153, 155–56, 158, 159, 160–61, 197
Hitesman, Walter, Jr., 112, 113, 150, 151, 152

Hodges, Campbell B., 79, 116, 122, 123
Hodges Hall, 174, 183, 213, 215, 216
Holgate, Jack, 134, 163
Holliday, Jensen, 197, 218; Holliday Forum, xvii, 218–19
Hunter, John A., 136
Hurricane Katrina, xvii–xviii, 80, 220–25

Izard, Ralph, 208, 215

Jackson, Cathleen, 223
Jenkins, William J. ("Bill"), 205, 211, 212, 222
Jenner, Eric, 209
Jerry M. Campbell and Associates, 214, 219
Johnston, William Preston, 2–3, 5, 6, 9
Jones, Charles T., 134
Journalism Building, xvii, 93, 141, 142–43, 163, 165, 166, 173–74, 185, 213–15, 216, 217–19; renovation, 140–41, 166, 174, 213, 217–19
Journalism Bulletin, 35, 67
journalism education pioneers, 1, 17–18, 33; professional criticism, 13–16
Journalism Extension Service, 144
Journalism and Mass Communication Quarterly, 35; *Journalism Quarterly*, 35, 153
Journalism News, 115
"J-School," xviii, 226
Juggenheimer, Donald ("Don"), 176, 179

Kappa Tau Alpha, 75, 145
Kevin P. Reilly, Sr. Center for Media and Public Affairs, 211–13, 215
King, Elton, 197, 203
Kingsley, Nathan, 198
Kinney, Ralph, 188
Kohler, Peter, 198
Kovacs, Peter, 225
Kurpius, David, 207, 223, 224

Lasalle, Leo J., 121
Lavine, John, 187, 190
Lawrence, Elmore, 43, 44
Leche, Richard, 103
Lee, James Melvin, 17, 33, 36
Lee, Robert E., 1–3, 5, 6, 7, 8, 13, 14, 37
Lindsay, Laura, 198

Lipp, M. N., 123
Livaudais, A. F., 126, 127
Lockwood, George, 198, 202, 208
Long, Earl K., 103
Long, Huey, 80, 81, 93, 95, 99, 103
Louisiana Board of Regents, 168, 179, 187, 194, 199, 206, 209, 213, 214
Louisiana Leader, 87
Louisiana Press Association (LPA), 37, 39, 60, 76, 83, 86, 87, 102, 122–23, 170; Field Manager, 86–87, 138–44
Louisiana Scholastic Press Association, 144
Louisiana State Seminary of Learning and Military Academy, 1, 6–7, 19
LSU Alumni Federation, 127, 142; Alumni Society, 125, 127
LSU Alumni News, 77, 113, 139; *Alumni Magazine*, 140
LSU Board of Supervisors, 7, 25, 79, 103, 106–7, 117, 121, 122, 123, 126, 142, 153, 175, 196–97, 206–7, 212, 213
LSU College of Arts and Sciences, 39, 45, 47, 82, 100, 101, 102, 121, 135, 136, 137, 162–63, 164, 165, 185, 186, 201
LSU Committee on Organization, 120, 121, 122
LSU Department of English, 15, 18, 19, 21, 24–25, 26, 27, 31, 34, 39, 45
LSU Department of Physics, 39, 77, 78, 91
LSU Department of Speech, 83–84, 91, 117–18, 135, 163, 165, 168, 182; and broadcasting courses, 83–84, 91, 117–18
The LSU Journalist, 163, 170
LSU Press, 63, 88, 212
LSU School of Journalism Alumni Association, 145, 151–52
LSU-TV, 182–83; Tiger TV, 204
Lundy, Lisa, 207

Manship, Charles, 32, 66, 67
Manship, Charles, Jr., 91, 174, 201, 203
Manship, David, 174
Manship, Dina, 174
Manship, Douglas, 164, 170, 174, 175
Manship, Douglas, Jr., 174, 197
Manship, Paula G., 203

Manship Prize for Exemplary Use of the Internet and Political Communication, 203–4
Manship, Richard, 174, 197
Martin, Bradley ("Brad"), 208
Mass Communication Alumni Association, 201, 202
McBride, Floyd, 168, 169
McCollister, Rolfe, Jr., 197
McCoy, Bruce, 83, 86, 87, 106, 107, 133, 142, 144, 152–53
McDonald, Duncan, 197
McGuire, David, 94, 97, 98, 107
McLamore, T. M., 31, 33, 41, 100
McMullen, Robert ("Bob"), 176, 182–83
Meehan, Eileen, 208
Merrill, John, 152–53, 162–64, 165, 167, 168, 169, 170, 172, 174, 183, 186–87, 197, 204
Mickelson, Siegfried ("Sig"), 83, 92, 192, 193, 197, 210
Middleton, Harry, 150, 152
Middleton, Troy, 98, 106, 123–24, 131, 136, 147, 148, 149, 157
Miller, Andrea, 207
Mong, Robert ("Bob"), 210
Monget, Annie Byrne, 100
Montague, Sam, 94, 97, 98, 107
Moore, Adrienne, 212
Moyse, Herman, 24, 25, 28, 41, 46–47
Mundt, Whitney, 134, 156, 168
Murrill, Paul, 136, 166

Nambiar, Sonora Jha, 209
National Council on Professional Education for Journalism, 118, 133
Nelson, Richard, 198
New Orleans, xvii, 10, 32, 43, 44, 51, 53, 54, 55, 57, 66, 77, 80, 98, 104, 106, 113, 126, 221–25
New Orleans *Times-Picayune*, xvii-xviii, 32, 43, 53, 104, 224–26
Nicholson, J. W., 9
Norman, Duyanne, 94, 95

Ober, Eric, 197
O'Brien, Morton J., 113
O'Keefe, Sean, 211, 222, 223

Osborn, Marvin G., 59, 60–63, 65–66, 67, 68, 71, 74, 75, 76, 77, 82, 85, 89, 96, 101, 102, 105, 106, 107, 108, 111, 116, 120–21, 122, 123, 124, 129, 131, 132, 133, 137, 142, 148, 152, 185, 197
Osborne, Anne, 207
Ott, E. Stanley, 31, 41, 47

Palm, Risa, 222–23
Parker, John M., 61–62, 78–79
Pennybacker, John, 168
Perkins, Jay, 168, 169
Perry, Steve, 213
Peterson, Ted, 153–54, 155, 164
Picard, Robert, 173
Pierce, Renee, 208, 214–15, 225
Plaisance, Robert H., 20, 21
Plasterer, Nicholas, 133, 134, 156, 158
Porter, Lance, 208
Price, Frank James ("Jim"), 50–51, 52–53, 54, 107, 114, 133, 134, 138, 141, 142, 148, 152, 156, 158
Procopio, Steve, 223–24
Public Policy Research Lab, 212–13
Public Works Administration, 127
Pulitzer, Joseph, 14–15, 17; Pulitzer Prize, 55, 209, 225

Rainach, W. M., 146–47
Reilly, Dee Dee, 202
Reilly, Jennifer Eplett, 218
Reilly, Kevin, 202–3, 211–12
Reilly, Sean, 218
The Reveille, 19, 20–25, 26, 27–32, 36–38, 41–44, 46, 47, 58, 60, 64, 65, 66, 68, 75, 81, 89, 92–93, 94, 96, 97, 99, 107, 111, 112, 114–15, 121, 124, 131, 137, 142, 145–46, 148, 162, 165, 166, 167, 169, 171, 174; advisor, 28, 75, 169; censorship of, 97, 98; editors, 20, 21, 23, 24, 25, 28, 30, 31, 43, 44, 46–47, 63, 83, 95, 112–13, 115, 121, 146–47, 151; editorial issues, 23, 42–43, 145–47; magazine section, 27–28; name change, 204; *Summer Reveille*, 146–47; women editors and staff, 23, 75–76, 115
"Reveille Seven," 93–99, 106–7
Rewerts, Linda, 198, 214
Rivers, William L., 150, 152

Roberts, Robert, 20, 46
Robertson, Edward White, 24, 25, 28, 46, 47
Roider, Karl, 189, 192
Ross, Bill, 180, 183, 188–89, 190, 192, 193, 196, 197, 208
Rotzoll, Kim, 187, 189
Ryder, Thomas O., 197

Salvaggio, Jerry, 168
Sanderson, Len, 197
Sarver, Danielle, 209
Scott, John, 218
scholarships, 116, 149–50, 181
Scribblers Club, 43
Sheldon, Robert, 134
Sherman, Norman ("Norm"), 208
Sherman, William Tecumseh, 7, 8
Shields, Thomas ("T. C."), 83, 107, 111, 113
Shlosman, Stanley, 94, 97, 98, 107
Sigma Delta Chi (SDX), 33, 37, 74, 86, 92, 114, 144
Silverberg, Joe, 151
Simmons, Lamar, 112, 217
Singleton, Ann, 214
Smith, C. Alphonso, 21, 26
Smith, C. R. F., 82, 83, 85, 86, 92, 107, 111
Smith, James Monroe, 81, 93–98, 103, 104, 106, 120–21
Smith, Joe D., 197
Smith-Tadie, Renee, 214
Snipes, Larry, 207
Snyder, Henry, 137, 162, 164, 165, 166, 167, 169, 172, 174, 175, 178, 204
Southern Newspaper Publishers Association (SNPA), 51, 119
Southwestern Journalism Congress (SJC), 74
Steetle, Ralph, 91, 92
Sternberg, Mary Ann, 198
Stoke, Harold W., 123, 124, 131
Student Communications Media Board, 149

Tate, Powell, 197
Taylor, Cecil, 136, 137, 138
Taylor, Helen, 198, 223
Theta Sigma Phi, 74–75, 86, 144

Tulane University, 9, 44, 74, 77, 83
Turk, Judy VanSlyke, 173
Turk, Peter, 173

Uffman, Ken, 214
University of Missouri, 15, 16, 17, 40, 49, 71, 72, 98, 120
U.S. Civil War, 1, 4, 12, 13, 16, 55–57; and military/press relations, 8; and newspaper correspondents, 8

Washington College, 1–2, 4, 6, 7, 9, 13, 15, 17
Washington and Lee University, 1, 5, 27, 51, 74, 84

Weiss, Dreyfuss, and Seiferth, 127
Wetherholt, Douglas, 134
Wharton, James H. ("Jim"), 166, 167, 174, 177, 178, 179
Wiggins, Richard, 83, 107, 111, 113, 133
Wilkerson, Marcus M., 26, 63, 67, 82, 83, 88, 107, 111, 116, 133
Williams, T. Harry, 94, 99, 103
Windhauser, John, 168
Wing-ding, 112
WJBO, 91, 92, 117
Womack, Milton, 202
Wortham, Louis, 112
WWL-TV, xviii, 224–26